Little Minnesota in WORLD WAR II

THE STORIES BEHIND 140 FALLEN HEROES FROM MINNESOTA'S LITTLEST TOWNS

by Jill A. Johnson and Deane L. Johnson

Adventure Publications
Cambridge, Minnesota

How to Use This Book

This book tells the story of more than 140 soldiers from tiny Minnesota towns—places with a population around 100—who served in the armed forces, and died, during World War II. Despite their small size, these tiny places contributed an incredible amount to the war effort.

The individual accounts in this book are organized chronologically. The first service member in the book died at Pearl Harbor. Those occurring later in the book fell later in the war. By reading through the accounts chronologically, one can get a good handle on how—and where—the war progressed over time. In this respect, the book is not only a testament to Little Minnesota's heroes, it is also a personal, up-close look at the history of the entire war. The text also includes family interviews, letters home from the soldiers and medal citations, which provide a window into just how profound the sacrifice that these soldiers and their families made really was.

If you're looking for a specific person or want to find service members from a town or county near you, consult the index on page 191. There, you'll find the soldiers listed alphabetically by name and with page references, as well as each man's hometown and home county.

Maps

To further illustrate the chronology of the war, we've included maps (pages 8–9) showing where each soldier fell in the line of duty. Arranged chronologically, these maps provide a visual guide to where the war was being fought over time, and they illustrate just how global the Second World War was.

Photo Credits begin on page 183

Edited by Brett Ortler and Sandy Livoti

Cover and book design by Jonathan Norberg

10 9 8 7 6 5 4 3 2 1

Copyright 2017 by Jill A. Johnson and Deane L. Johnson
Published by Adventure Publications
An imprint of AdventureKEEN
820 Cleveland Street South
Cambridge, Minnesota 55008
(800) 678-7006
www.adventurepublications.net
Printed in China
ISBN: 978-1-59193-553-7; eISBN: 978-1-59193-757-9

Dedication

To the men who died in World War II from Little Minnesota and their families, and to our uncles who served with them:

Private First Class John Wayland Larsen. Headquarters and Base Services Squadron, 473rd Air Service Group: A military policeman in Italy and Berlin, John witnessed the public hanging of Benito Mussolini and his mistress, Claretta Petacci, on April 28, 1945, in Milan, Italy.

Private First Class Harold "Halle" Emery Melhus. 6th Armored Infantry Battalion, C Company, Rifleman: Halle fought across Europe and was the lone survivor when his transport truck blew up during the Battle of the Bulge.

Aviation Ordnanceman, Second Class Jack Robert Musburger. 109th Bomb Squadron, Fleet Air Wing 14, Crew 18. A waist gunner on the *Sugar Queen*, a Navy liberator B-24 Bomber with the famous "Reluctant Raiders" navy squadron. Jack flew 50 missions in the Pacific Theater and was awarded the Air Medal and a Presidential Unit Citation.

Lieutenant LeRoy "Roy" Wright. Office of Strategic Services, Detachment 101. Roy fought with the American-Kachin Rangers in Burma behind Japanese lines. Local Burmese villagers found Roy floating unconscious in the river with multiple bullet wounds and cared for him until evacuation by American forces. Chief of Staff Dwight D. Eisenhower awarded Detachment 101 the Presidential Unit Citation, as he believed they performed one of the most difficult and hazardous assignments ever given to a military unit. Roy also received the Purple Heart.

Seaman First Class Harold Thorson, U.S. Navy: Harold served on the destroyer/minesweeper USS *Tracy* (DD-214/DM-19) in the South Pacific. The *Tracy* provided escort and transport services throughout the Pacific and supported the invasion of Okinawa in April 1945 with anti-submarine and anti-small boat patrols. His ship narrowly missed a kamikaze air attack, and rescued survivors of *LCI (G)-82* after a suicide boat attack. Harold admitted that he was sick every day at sea.

Technician Fifth Grade Olaf Roisum, 84th Ordinance Battalion, D Company: Olaf worked as an ordnance truck driver and mechanic. He entered active service December 8, 1943, was stationed near the Palmolive plantation on New Guinea, and later moved to Luzon during the Allied drive to retake the Philippines.

Do not measure your grief by his worth, for then your sorrow has no end.
—Shakespeare, *Macbeth*, Act 5, Scene 8

Acknowledgments

Our heartfelt thanks to all contributors to *Little Minnesota in World War II*. So many were willing to help us with stories, letters, photos, and information, it is hard to know where to begin. Please forgive us if we left your name off this list, as everyone we talked to contributed in some way to our effort:

Military Organizations and Unit Histories

57th Bomb Wing Association, 401st Bomb Group Association, 83rd Infantry Association, 91st Bomb Group, 93rd Bomb Group, 351st Bomb Group, 384th Bomb Group, 485th Bomb Group, 12th Armored Division, 25th Infantry Division, 69th Infantry Division, 80th Infantry Division, 337th Infantry Regiment, 751st Tank Battalion, U.S. Army Signal Corps, Naval Air Station Fort Lauderdale, 390th Memorial Museum Foundation

Historical Societies, Museums and Libraries

Aitkin County Historical Society, Dwight D. Eisenhower Presidential Library, George G. Marshall Foundation, Grant County Historical Society, Iron Range Historical Society, Itasca County Historical Society, Lac qui Parle History Center, National Archives, Norman County Historical Society, University of Minnesota Archives, Wells Depot Museum

Local Newspapers and Other Publications

Albert Lea Tribune, All Hands Magazine, Brainerd Dispatch, The Brookings Register, Fergus Falls Daily Journal, The Forum, Glenwood Herald, Grand Rapids Herald-Review, Grant County Herald, Island X-quire CBMU 540, Kittson County Enterprise, The Monitor Review, Morrison County Record, Paynesville Press, Pope County Tribune, Red Lake Falls Gazette, Redwood Falls Gazette, Swift County Monitor-News, Thief River Falls Times, The Thirteen Towns, Tyler Tribute, Worthington Daily Globe

Individuals, Family Members and Researchers

Jarrett Emery Halverson, Carol Halvorson, Michael Pocock, John Johnson, Natalie Schmidt, Dana Charles, Nathan Swanson, Janice Tester Backus, Joe Stevens, Shane Olson, Jim Opolony, Joe Poor, Richard Poor, Boyd Rahier, Peter Dunn, Matthew David, Mark Flowers, Donna Novotny, Susan Kilianski, Craig Mackay, Richard Lynch, Merlin Peterson, Reed Anfinson, Rick Atkinson, Ryan Klemann, Ranier Kolbicz, Denise Chevalier, Vernice Cluett, Fern Head, Lieutenant Colonel Shirley Olgeirson, Cindy Risen, Amy Moe, Lori Fraley, Lisa Tichenor, Yuri Beckers, Rita Zepper, Errol Niemi, Jerry Dhennin, Patsy Terho, Hildy Bettin Dorn, Dale Victor Borgeson, Bob Cameron, Laurie Lewis, Donnie Anderson, Lorna Anderson, Jeane Buer, Joe Duran, Don Morrison, Carl Savich, Jerry Whiting, Renee Falk, Donald Hartmann, Paul Hartmann, Jim Hildebrand, Madeline Vaughan Michelson, Jennifer Morrison, Chief Rick Stone, Ailie Chernich Costello, Mary Satterwhite, Shirley Walli, Ryan McGaughey, Sena Santjer Knowles, Don Weigel, Barb Redpenning, Ted Trojahn, Gregory Glavan, Elizabeth Johnson, William Nicholas, Shelly Lammi, Carolyn O'Brien, Gayle Gilmore, Robert Neumiller, Nancy Probasco Zaske, Olga Harju Maki, Gay Jokela Aubin, Velma Newhouse, Lois Kanne, Terri Kanne, Mava Engholm, Leona Lendt, Robert Hildrup, Shirley Hoskins, Margaret Sehnert, Dianne Sundstad Carbine, Debra Jacobson, Robert Passanisi, Mary Beth Sundstad, Pat Braaten, Gary Kostrzewski, Walter Kostrzewski, Judy Sten, Mark Bando, Corienne Jacobson, Hans Houterman, Jeroen Koppes, Joan Kline, Gary Nellis, Sandra Nellis, Jim West, Tim Douglas, Roberta Pile, David Schroeder, Pat Curran, Barbara Bush Bellerichard, Linda Zieman, Teresa Dickelman, Gerald Forsberg, Susan Forsberg, Jacqueline Forsberg Phipps, Dee Millard, Anthony Urick, Karen Lound Cavalli, Steve Cole, Margaret Lound Norbeck, Ilane Shefveland Rue, Evon Pearson, Darlene Belsky, Cindy Wetterland, Carol Holmstrom Thompson, Judy Iverson Briski, Judy Iverson Skogerboe, Celeste Skogerboe, Josh Tharaldson, Marlyn Evanstad, Don Kaiser, Sandra Winjum Varner, Jim Pederson, Leon Carlson, Robert Bliven, Roseanne Bliven Barrett, Wandah Hegna Nielson, Renae and Joey Woods, Erling Anderson, Rodney Distad, Julie Gunderson, Helen Krajewski, Christine Carlson, Kathy Berger, Angela Hays, Deb Stadin, Ben Savelkoul, Muriel Nelson, June Richardson, Scott Hoff, Jim Childers, Dannie Nordsiden, Roman Susil, Jan Mahr, Loy Dickinson, Leo Hogetvedt, Henk Welting, Alan Soderstrom, Andrew Adkins, Jean Anderson, Vernon Maxa, Mark Bliss, Fred Preller, Richard Lohry, Lorie Kurth Kirtz, Donald Talberg, Marion Chard, Barbara Allen Moe, Sarah Stultz, Amos Cordova, Paul Struck, Eric Montgomery, John W. Anderson, Steve Bollum, Cindy Burger, Gary Burger, Myrtle Burger Houston, Frank R. Crow, Rebecca Crow, Ferdinand S. Kuznia, Stephen Messenger, Ralph Butkowski, Don Jones, Robert J. Cox, Tim Gordon, Chelsey Perkins, Don Byer, Andy Swinnen, Don Moore, Steven Peterson, Cheri Finley, Harriet Lindstrom, Bernice Johnson, Connie Fedick, Chris Harris, Gertrude Witschen, Leon King, DiAnn Zimmerman, Jim Hanson, Dawn Hanson, Evalee Janssen, Carol Dunn, Dodie McNew, Bonnie McNew Mattheson, Sam Pennartz,

Shawn Hennessey, Doug Eichten, Marlys Shelby, Larry Wayne, Gary Eichten, Pauline Eichten, Paul and Pam Struck, Irvin Kaufman, Dennis Wendland, Dale Cartee, William Lenches, Charles and Bill Ramm, Roberta Russo, Joseph Tisdell, Vince Connolly, Hal Anderson, Bob Barrett, John Tostrup, Gary Anderson, Ken Christensen, Haywood S. Anderson, Kathy Peterson, Bob Boe, Jon Lindstrand, Paul B. Barron, Violet Downer, Kay Powell, Phyllis Beckman, Jim Kiefer, Elodee Ranum, June Hodik Johnson, Lowell Ranum, Margaret Geertsema, John Wepplo, Everett Perry, Kathleen Loucks, Britta Arendt, Lilah Crowe, Ardis Fredrikson, Kay Nord, Joy Paulson, Wes Injerd, Karie Kirschbaum, Janice Knight Evensen, Gladys Ness Erickson, Dave Vangness, Joyce Rossow, Mary Jo Pauling, Steven Duerre, Richard Berg, Arnold Ringstad, Joan Maher, Jim Gowin, Russell Kastelle, Roseanne Nolan, Jessica Wilson, Larry and Lois Stoll, Mary Biederman, Leo Leitner, Joanne Schwan, Larry Elliot, Phyllis Broden, Sandy Mosher, Karen Paulson Syverson, Linda Uscola, Brenda Brusven, Stephen Lofgren, Jennifer Tongen, Rodney Ripley, Darold and Sharon Coulter, Gary Smith, Major Joseph Lipsius, Michael McKibbon, Dawn Hanson, Ed Lavelle, Florence Bashore, Joel Gilfert, Michael Jacobson, Joe and Arlene Reinart, Mark Behrens, Tracy White, Agustin Valvodinos, Linda White Fleck, Diane Schnell, Darlene Lange Haug, Nancy Tomhave, Marilyn Nugent, LaVonne Portner, Darrel Allen White, Richard Peterson, Matthew Von Pinnon, Minerva Bloom, Dennis and Janet Zierke, Carol Dunn, Kevin Anderson, Adam Hoogenakker, Ryan Welle, Lisa Crunk and Brent Schacherer.

Foreword

When researching our book, *Little Minnesota: 100 Towns Around 100*, we were astounded at the number of men who died in World War II from our state's tiniest towns. One hundred sixty-four men died from Little Minnesota in a heroic effort to defeat Adolf Hitler, Benito Mussolini and Emperor Hirohito. Several women from Little Minnesota served in the military but none died in war.

After the bombing of Pearl Harbor on December 7, 1941, thousands of young men and women answered President Franklin Delano Roosevelt's call to service. Little Minnesotans, the sons and daughters of farmers, loggers, shopkeepers, pastors and teachers, joined the Army, Navy, Air Force, Marines, National Guard and Merchant Marine. Two men joined the Royal Canadian Air Force after they were denied admittance to the U.S. Air Force due to their height. Little Minnesotans served as pilots, crewmembers on bombers, paratroopers, glidermen, sailors, medics, infantrymen, mariners and truck drivers. Most had never traveled outside their small towns and now fought in unknown places: Kasserine Pass, Monte Cassino, Utah Beach, Omaha Beach, and Sainte-Mère-Église; the Hürtgen Forest and the Ardennes; and on the other side of the world, Bataan, Guadalcanal, Saipan, Peleliu, Iwo Jima, Tarawa and Okinawa. One man died on the Alaskan island of Attu, the only battle in World War II fought on American soil. Four men were awarded the Bronze Star, nine men were awarded the Silver Star and two men received the Distinguished Service Cross. All received the award no one wanted—the Purple Heart.

Our editor, Brett Ortler, a World War II buff, provided the historical expertise and skills to shape the stories, help us pin down and work with sources, and sort through hundreds of photo options. He and the design and marketing teams at AdventureKEEN have worked hard to produce a book that best presents the stories of these men.

Little Minnesota in World War II would not be possible without the families of the men. They researched family history, dug through old trunks in attics, and reconnected with relatives and family historians. Along the way, they rediscovered a treasured family member who gave his life over 70 years ago in a war that changed the world. Their stories and photos are heartbreakingly beautiful and our thanks to them is unending. Along with the families, Jim Hanson, navy veteran from Grand Meadow, Minnesota, checked facts and provided encouragement. Military people cheerfully shared information, and if they didn't have what we needed, they found a colleague who did. Thank you to all the authors, museum stewards and others who found essential information and photos. Our gratitude extends to the hard-working archivists at the National Archives in St. Louis, Missouri, who patiently provided individual files on the men. Their exemplary service to families and veterans demonstrates government at its best.

Our deepest gratitude to the men who died in World War II from Little Minnesota—yours is truly the greatest generation.

Jill and Deane Johnson

Taps

Day is done,
gone the sun,
from the hills,
from the lake,
from the skies.
All is well,
safely rest,
God is nigh.
Go to sleep,
peaceful sleep,
May the soldier
or sailor,
God keep.
On the land
or the deep,
safe in sleep.
Love, good night,
Must thou go,
when the day,
and the night

need thee so?
All is well.
Speedeth all
to their rest.
Fades the light;
and afar
goeth day,
and the stars
shineth bright,
fare thee well;
day has gone,
night is on.
Thanks and praise,
for our days,
'neath the sun,
'neath the stars,
'neath the sky,
as we go,
this we know:
God is nigh.

Table of Contents

Soldiers from Little Minnesota Lost in the European Theater from November 1942 to September 1944
(soldiers with lower numbers died earlier in the war)

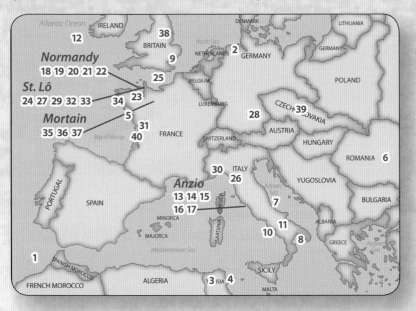

1. Ernest Haarstad
2. Cyril Curb
3. Herman Baumgart
4. Mathews Niemi
5. Einar Suomi
6. Arnold Holen
7. Harold Terho
8. Peter Chernich, Jr.
9. Leighton Zeiner
10. Ben Santjer
11. Harold Meyer
12. Morris Olson
13. Alvin Probasco
14. Robert Harju
15. Waldo Engholm
16. Robert Goudy
17. Rolland Rowe
18. Walter Kostrzewski
19. Ellsworth Onger
20. Arnold Wilsing
21. William Wendt
22. Carl Emery
23. Eugene Lusk
24. Fernly Bush
25. Rudolph Indihar
26. Ray Lound
27. Herman Holmstrom
28. Lloyd Iverson
29. Herman Hoffrogge
30. Harold Winjum
31. Paul Bliven
32. Verlyn Hegna
33. Leon Anderson
34. Jack Berger
35. Gerhard Petersen
36. LaVern Nelson
37. Vernon Hoff
38. James Graba
39. Leroy Johnson
40. LeRoy Veralrud

Soldiers from Little Minnesota Lost in the European Theater from September 1944 to Victory in Europe and Beyond

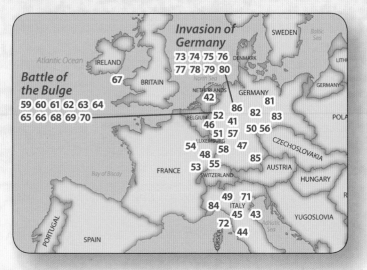

41. Gordon Maxa
42. John Sersha
43. Walter Kurth
44. William Talberg
45. Harland Mittag
46. Albert Longhenry
47. Donald Doyle
48. Donald Bollum
49. Alfred Bruns
50. John Reardon
51. Carl Horton
52. Otto Peterson
53. Rudolph Roner
54. Roy Lee
55. Arthur Gooselaw
56. Oscar Hanson
57. Robert Brady
58. Helmer Eichten
59. Victor Malmrose
60. Norbert Bruns
61. Vincent Dolan
62. Bertil Gustafson
63. Truman Meling
64. Andrew Brummer
65. George Boe
66. Wallace Skaar
67. Wallace Colson
68. Howard Hanson
69. Wilbur Wright
70. Emmet Loucks
71. Donald Swenson
72. James Knight
73. Myril Lundgren
74. Palmer Ringstad
75. Clarence Lehner
76. Frank Leitner
77. Cecil Stevenson
78. Robert Horne
79. Elmer Kittelson
80. Vernon Peterson
81. Glynn Daufney
82. Lawrence Storch
83. Clifford Thompson
84. Henry Kroll
85. Ira Bashore
86. Jerome Gorres

Soldiers from Little Minnesota Lost in the **Pacific Theater** *(soldiers with lower numbers died earlier in the war)*

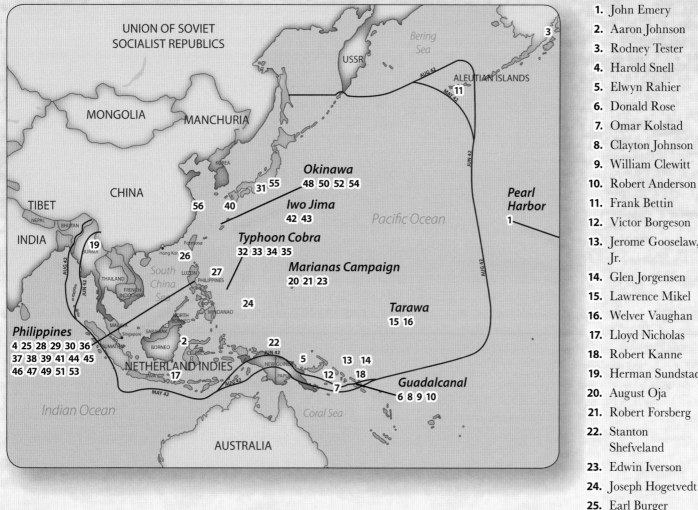

1. John Emery
2. Aaron Johnson
3. Rodney Tester
4. Harold Snell
5. Elwyn Rahier
6. Donald Rose
7. Omar Kolstad
8. Clayton Johnson
9. William Clewitt
10. Robert Anderson
11. Frank Bettin
12. Victor Borgeson
13. Jerome Gooselaw, Jr.
14. Glen Jorgensen
15. Lawrence Mikel
16. Welver Vaughan
17. Lloyd Nicholas
18. Robert Kanne
19. Herman Sundstad
20. August Oja
21. Robert Forsberg
22. Stanton Shefveland
23. Edwin Iverson
24. Joseph Hogetvedt
25. Earl Burger
26. Ferdinand Kuznia
27. Malcolm Gordon
28. Ernest King
29. Arthur Hackbarth
30. Larry McNew
31. Kenneth Swanson
32. Almon Armbrust
33. Warren Hakenson
34. Harold Kaufman
35. Lloyd Lundgren
36. Arthur Kolberg
37. Sylvester Beckman
38. Glenn Ranum
39. Edward Engblom
40. Archie Olson
41. Rubin Ness
42. John Parker
43. Glen Bixby
44. Henry Hunkins
45. Milton Stoll
46. Sigwald Anderson
47. Jerald Tongen
48. John Stevenson
49. Kenneth Nelson
50. Othmar Braun
51. Gerald Reinart
52. Howard White
53. Darvin Lange
54. Kenneth Davis
55. Gordon Nelson
56. Allen Nelson

John "Jack" Marvin Emery

U.S. Navy, USS Arizona, Gunner's Mate Third Class
APRIL 26, 1919–DECEMBER 7, 1941—The Bombing of Pearl Harbor

On December 8, 1941, Carl Emery answered the farmhouse telephone to hear what the family feared most: His 23-year-old son John Emery, known as Jack, was missing and presumed dead following the Japanese attack on Pearl Harbor the day before.

At 7:55 a.m., on a beautiful Sunday morning, December 7, 1941, 350 Japanese planes attacked Pearl Harbor and decimated the Pacific fleet. John "Jack" Emery was on board the USS *Arizona* when a bomb penetrated the deck, detonating aircraft fuel and powder magazines. An excerpt from the Battle Report by Commander Walter Karig and Lieutenant Welbourn Kelley described the sinking of the *Arizona*:

One bomb struck the forecastle. Another exploded on a faceplate on No. 4 turret aft. Still another ripped through the bridge and detonated on the boat deck. And then it was that one of the attacking Japanese pilots realized the dive-bomber's dream. His bomb dropped exactly into the Arizona's *stack, exploding in the boilers and setting off the vast amount of powder stored in the forward magazine.*

The ship's bow seemed to leap out of the water, and her weather decks cracked open as fire and debris shot skyward. Plumes of oil and water showered topside, and fires enveloped the forward part of the ship. The fate of the Arizona, *a 32,600-ton battleship within less than nine months of being declared over-age, was sealed in the first five minutes of the attack. The magazine blast broke the ship's back and she rapidly settled in the water. All told, the* Arizona *lost 47 officers and 1,057 men. Some hundred of the bodies were never removed from the sunken hulk of the ship.*[1,2]

Only 335 men survived the attack; some were lucky enough to be on shore for duty or liberty while others escaped the burning inferno. Among the 1,177 crewmen killed were all 21 members of the *Arizona* band. Historian Molly Kent wrote about the *Arizona's* musicians, who took their stations in the ammunition hold several decks below to pass ammunition to the deck and lost their lives when the ammunition magazine exploded. The United States lost a total of 2,344 men, 300 fighter planes and 14 warships damaged or destroyed. Congress declared war on Japan just 27 hours after the attack.[2,3,4]

Unlike most of the ships sunk or damaged that day, the *Arizona* could not be salvaged and still lies at the bottom of Pearl Harbor. To this day, oil rises from the wreckage to the surface of the water, "the tears of the *Arizona*."

John Marvin Emery is memorialized on the Courts of the Missing, Honolulu Memorial, Hawaii, the USS *Arizona* Memorial, and Nora Lutheran Church Cemetery, Gardner, North Dakota. Over the years, many men who survived the sinking of the *Arizona* choose to have their ashes interred within the wreck. In a military ceremony, U.S. Navy divers swim with the urn for placement inside gun turret No. 4, where they are reunited with their comrades who died at Pearl Harbor.[5]

Jack Emery was survived by his parents, Carl and Freda (Sandberg) Emery, and siblings: Esther (Oscar) Bjornson, Carl Robert Emery, Betty Ann Emery, Helen Emery and Jean Emery. Carl and Freda Emery lost a second son in World War II when Jack's brother, Private First Class Carl "Bob" Emery, died on June 7, 1944, while crossing the English Channel.

In a newspaper interview with the *Fargo Forum* in 1991, niece Carol Halvorson said their lives were changed forever: *It's something they never got over. You can't help but think how the family dynamics changed with those deaths, and how different things might have been had they not been killed. There were 2,403 people killed at Pearl Harbor, which means our family's story is the story of 2,402 other families.*[6]

Aaron Luverne Johnson

U.S. Navy, USS Houston CA-30, Shipfitter Fireman Third Class
JANUARY 18, 1917–FEBRUARY 4, 1942—Battle of the Flores Sea, Dutch East Indies

John Johnson recalls his uncle: *Everyone called him Luverne and he was a fun-loving guy who liked girls and cars. I remember the day I rode with him, my grandparents, and my father to the train station in St. Paul in my dad's 1940 Buick. I can still picture Uncle Luverne waving to us from the window as the train pulled away. My grandmother was beside herself with worry.*

Following his graduation from Dunwoody Institute, Minneapolis, Aaron Luverne Johnson worked on the family farm until his navy enlistment August 3, 1938. He was exactly what the navy wanted according to a Navy Department memo written in 1919: *The boy from the farm is considered by the naval recruiting service to be the most desirable material.* During basic training at the Great Lakes Naval Training Station in Illinois, Luverne qualified as a shipfitter who worked with sheet metal and plumbing, and he also sang in the Navy Choir. He later earned deep-sea diver certification in Bremerton, Washington, and Pearl Harbor before moving to the Philippines. After basic training, Luverne was assigned to the USS *Houston*, President Roosevelt's favorite warship. In a letter dated March 5, 1939, Luverne wrote of the President's friendliness to the sailors: *I can say I have been fishing with the Prez. He is a real guy. He can't walk but he is always happy.* [1, 2, 3, 9]

During a furlough at home, Luverne told his father, *"Dad, be sure you look me up a nice team of bay horses, for I'm all set to go farming when I get back."* His dream of returning home to farm ended during the Battle of the Flores Strait, also known as the Battle of Makassar Strait, in the Java Sea in the Dutch East Indies. Near midnight on February 3, 1942, the USS *Houston* joined an American-British-Dutch-Australian (ABDA) fleet to search for a Japanese fleet consisting of 20 troop transport ships, 3 cruisers and 18 destroyers. In a personal interview, Captain Arthur Maher, Gunnery Officer, reported: *The* Houston *was ordered to go up and accompany some Asiatic Fleet destroyers into a night attack. However, unfortunately, at the last minute* Marblehead *and the destroyers, both Dutch and American, were at anchor south of Madoere Island just outside of Soerabaja. There was no question but that they sighted our fleet but they made no attempt to attack. The conference broke up quickly and the fleet got underway and proceeded to sea with the units disbursing and orders to rendezvous the next morning. So, on the 4th of February,* we were all joined up again and headed in the direction of the Celebes when we were attacked by approximately 54 heavy Japanese bombers. The bombers singled out the Houston *and the* Marblehead *as their targets and for approximately an hour both ships were under severe attack. The* Marblehead *was hit by two bombs and badly damaged. The* Houston *was proceeding to the assistance of the* Marblehead *when she was struck by a large caliber bomb just forward of the after turret. This did considerable damage in that it disabled turret three, killed 48 men and wounded approximately 20 more.* [5] Shipfitter Fireman Third Class Aaron Luverne Johnson was one of those killed aboard the USS *Houston*.

With a disabled ship and many casualties, Rear Admiral Karel Doorman ordered the *Houston* and *Marblehead* to Tjilatjap, a port city on the island of Java, for repairs and burial in a Dutch cemetery. Following repairs, the *Houston* continued service with the ABDA fleet. Much of the fleet, including Doorman's flagship, was sunk soon thereafter. On February 28, the *Houston* and *Perth* entered Banten Bay where Japanese destroyers sank the *Perth*. The *Houston* fought on until midnight when she, too, was torpedoed and downed. From the original crew of 1,061 men, just 368 survived, only to be interned in Japanese prison camps. The Japanese victory strengthened their control of Makassar Strait and the Dutch East Indies. [6, 7, 8]

Following her son's death, Gunda Johnson made multiple button plates, treasured family keepsakes, to cope with her grief. On February 14, 1950, Aaron Luverne Johnson was reburied in Our Savior's Cemetery, Dovray, Minnesota.

On February 19, 1942, the *Murray County Herald* eloquently reported the death of Aaron Luverne Johnson, the second man to die from Dovray in World War II: *A second son of Murray County has given his life that freedom and the decent things of life may continue in the world. A message received by Mr. and Mrs. John Johnson, of Dovray, from the U.S. Navy department last Thursday brought the sad news that their son, Aaron Luverne, had been killed in action. And so, though separated from the war zone by vast open prairies, massive mountains and great spans of ocean, the seemingly peaceful and obscure little community and village of Dovray was called upon to spare another of her fine and noble sons.* [9]

Rodney Lee Tester

U.S. Army Air Forces, 11th Air Force, 28th Bomb Group, 77th Bomb Squadron, Private
JANUARY 5, 1918–APRIL 29, 1942—Aerial Photography Mission, Fort Richardson, Alaska

Janice Tester Backus remembers her brother: *We lived on a farm in Brookston, Minnesota, and survived the Great Depression with the help of my parents and their steadfastness during very hard times. My brother Rodney was 18 when he joined the Civilian Conservation Corps (CCC). He wanted to go to college but times were difficult, so he and many other young men joined the CCC. After leaving the CCC, he joined the Army Air Force and eventually was stationed in Alaska. He died in an air crash on a mission in April 29, 1942. In one of Rod's letters in February or March, he wrote about a funeral for one of his buddies who had died in an air accident. He was so impressed with the funeral, and just a short time later he died. He was buried in Fort Richardson, and in 1948, for some reason, the Air Force closed the cemetery and sent Rod home to be reburied in Oneota. I believe that my parents came to some closure at that time, but also they again relived the sadness of losing their firstborn. I was only 12 years old when he died, so I did not have a long relationship with him. I am fortunate that my mother saved Rod's letters from the CCC and the service. As I read the letters, I learned about Rod's personality and how much he cared for his family.*[1]

Rodney Tester enlisted in the service February 27, 1941, and graduated from radio technician's school at Scott Field, Belleville, Illinois, before his assignment with the 11th Air Force in Alaska. On April 28, 1942, Private Tester and his crew were ordered to Cold Bay via Kodiak Naval Station, and from there to Umnak for an aerial photography mission. The Aleutian Islands Campaign would begin only a few months later. The next day, the heavily loaded B-18 left Kodiak airfield with eight men on board, including Private Rodney Tester, who served as Radio Operator.

The Aircraft Accident Report states: *The pilot had made a previous takeoff and was forced to return due to the fact that he did not have a proper clearance. Before his next takeoff he had complained of how heavily his ship was loaded due to having an extra tank of gas, which he did not need, plus all the equipment aboard. The pilot showed an error in judgment in attempting to climb out the ridge without sufficient altitude for a safe clearance with a very heavy ship and in very turbulent air, when it would have been very easy to avoid the ridge by going around it. While passing over the ridge at about 150 feet the ship was caught in a severe downdraft, and in spite of all the pilot could do the ship struck the ridge at about*

150 feet below the summit. There was no engine failure. The weather conditions that existed on April 29 are peculiar to the region around Kodiak Island. The turbulence and drafts are exceedingly severe and are much more violent than a pilot not used to flying in this area could expect.

Incredibly, Sergeant Orville Blake, the bomber of the crew, survived the crash, which was nearly impossible due to the remote site, the severe damage to the plane, and the post-crash fire. Sergeant Blake's evacuation from the site is a story in itself. He gave this account of the accident: *After taking off from East to West we climbed steadily through the pass at almost 120 to 125 miles per hour. The air was very rough and turbulent. We got through the pass and turned left still climbing to get over the surrounding ridges. We were about 150 to 200 feet above the first ridge indicating about 120 when we hit a downdraft. There was no engine failure, and although Lieutenant Tuma did everything possible to prevent it, we hit the mountain.*

The wreckage of the B-18, including an engine with bent propellers, is still present on Sheraton Mountain, not far from the Kodiak Airfield.[2,3]

Private Rodney Tester, son of Earl and Mildred (Peterson) Tester, was reburied in Oneota Cemetery, Duluth, Minnesota. His father worked on the railroad in Brookston. Survivors included his parents; a brother, William, a paratrooper with the 101st Airborne "Screaming Eagles" Division; and a sister, Janice. Brookston American Legion Tester-Niemi Post 562 is named in honor of Private Rodney Tester and Private Mathews Niemi (page 23), who died on May 1, 1943, in North Africa.

Harold A. Snell

34th Tank Company, 194th Tank Battalion, A Company, Private
FEBRUARY 25, 1916–MAY 22, 1942—Battle of Bataan, Luzon Island, Philippines

On February 10, 1941, Private Harold Snell and the 194th Tank Battalion, originally the 34th Divisional Tank Company of the Minnesota National Guard from Brainerd, Minnesota, left for Fort Lewis, Washington. Private Harold Snell belonged to A Company with many of the men from Brainerd. Prior to the attack on Pearl Harbor on December 7, 1941, the 194th Tank Battalion trained near Clark Field on Luzon Island, Philippines. Just nine hours after the attack, the Japanese bombed Clark Field and Manila and on December 10, 1941, they invaded Luzon.[11] General MacArthur ordered his commanders to retreat to the Bataan Peninsula on January 7, 1942, where a lack of food and medicine resulted in widespread malaria, scurvy, beriberi and dysentery among the men. When General Ernest King, commander of the forces on Bataan, surrendered the starving and sick troops to the Japanese on April 9, 1942, the 194th Tank Battalion, along with 70,000 other American and Filipino prisoners, began the infamous Bataan Death March with their Japanese captors.

From April 10 to 13, the men marched 60-plus miles north from Mariveles on the southern tip of Bataan to San Fernando under brutal conditions without food or water. Here the Japanese packed 100 prisoners into small wooden boxcars and shipped them to Camp O'Donnell, a former Filipino base. Those who died in the boxcars remained standing and fell out upon arrival. The prisoners who survived walked without food the last ten miles to Camp O'Donnell. One survivor, Walter Straka, took ten days to complete the march from Mariveles to Camp O'Donnell. In Straka's own words, "All the food they gave us could have been put in a quart bucket."[1]

Over 10,000 American and Filipino troops died at the hands of their merciless captors. Private Harold Snell survived the death march but died of dysentery at Camp O' Donnell on May 22, 1942. Of the original 82 officers and men of the 34th Tank Company who left Brainerd, 64 accompanied the 194th to Luzon: 3 were killed in action, 29 died as Prisoners of War, and 32 returned to Brainerd at the end of World War II.[1, 2, 3]

Private Harold Snell, son of Hiram Snell and Maude (Whitted) Anderson was survived by his mother, stepfather Fred Anderson, and two half sisters, Opal and Mary Lee. His remains were returned to Island Zion Cemetery, Boy River, Minnesota, on October 22, 1948.[4]

Each year since 1998, soldiers and civilians gather at the Brainerd Armory for the Bataan Memorial March to remember the men who died and those who survived the fall of Bataan in World War II.[5] In 2002, a Bataan Memorial Plaque honoring the 194th Tank Battalion was installed on the Wall of Honor at the Minnesota State Capitol grounds. Former Minnesota Senate President Don Samuelson, who sponsored legislation for the plaque, wanted to honor the memory of his father, 1st Sergeant Walt Samuelson, who survived the Bataan Death March but died in a prison camp in Manchuria in 1942. Both Walt Samuelson and Harold Snell served together in A Company, 194th Tank Battalion. On November 11, 2013, Ken Porwoll from Harold Snell's 34th Tank Company died, leaving his grade-school friend Walt Straka as Brainerd's lone remaining survivor of the Bataan March.[6, 7, 8, 9, 10]

Private Snell's family did not receive confirmation of his death until two years later. On November 2, 1944, his mother, Maude Snell Anderson, wrote a poignant letter to the War Department for information on the burial site of her son:

Dear Sirs: I am writing about Private Harold Snell. I had a letter on the 6 September saying any information regards to Harold's remains. Could you tell me if he is buried at Camp O'Donnell or just where he is. Oh it seems as though I got to have some word of his grave. And when the time comes to bring the body home please send it to Remer, Minn. As I have a lot and one son there. And will you let me know when the time comes so I can have everything ready. Oh to have his body over here so I can visit his grave and over there I don't even think I could get to it. Any word you can give me I have many friends and kind women there that could visit his grave if it is marked. Thank you so very much. I Am Mrs. Fred Anderson, Boy River, Minn.[3]

Elwyn Owen Rahier

Effie (Itasca County)

U.S. Army Air Forces, 5th Air Force, 19th Bomb Group, 435th Bomb Squadron, Staff Sergeant
AUGUST 11, 1914–AUGUST 14, 1942, Reconnaissance Mission, New Guinea, Rabaul and Solomons

On December 5, 1941, Staff Sergeant Elwyn Rahier and his squadron arrived at Hickam Field, Hawaii, to prepare for a secret project to photograph Japanese military bases in the Marshall and Caroline Islands. Staff Sergeant Rahier, assistant flight engineer, and his bomb squadron were assigned to the 1st Photo Group and attached to the Ferry Command. The crew never made the trip. On the morning of December 7, as the crew prepared their plane for a flight check in hangar 15 before leaving on their journey, the Japanese attacked Pearl Harbor. A bomb hit the hangar, injuring Rahier and three other crewmembers and killing one.

Just three months later, after recovering from his injuries, Staff Sergeant Rahier flew on a flight of planes to the Philippines to evacuate General MacArthur and his staff to Australia. That same month, on March 5, 1942, the citizens of Seattle presented a B-17 to the Army Air Corps christened *Chief Seattle from the Pacific Northwest.* Boeing built the aircraft for $280,535 with funds raised by local citizens during a bond campaign sponsored by a local newspaper. The first B-17 named after a city, an artist painted *Chief Seattle* on both sides of the aircraft's nose, one of the first officially recognized examples of nose art used on a B-17.[1, 2, 5]

The *Chief Seattle* was assigned to the 19th Bomb Group, 435th Bomb Squadron, known as the "Kangaroo Squadron." On August 14, 1942, Staff Sergeant Rahier, flight engineer and upper turret gunner on *Chief Seattle*, left with a crew of ten from Port Moresby in Townsville, Australia, on a reconnaissance mission of New Guinea, Rabaul and the Solomon Islands to report enemy activity. Nothing was ever heard from the bomber again, and the military assumed that Japanese fighters downed the aircraft. Staff Sergeant Rahier and the crew were officially declared dead on December 7, 1945.[3] Although the disappearance happened over 70 years ago, the question is repeated every year at the 7th and 19th Bomb Group reunions *"Has* Chief Seattle *been found yet?"* Elwyn's nephew, Boyd Rahier, echoed those thoughts, *"The wreckage was never found, but I get the jumps every time they find one of those B-17s in the jungle or shallow water. I still think it will show up one of these days or years."*[4]

After the disappearance of *Chief Seattle* and her crew, 1st Lieutenant John T. Compton wrote a brief synopsis about the men from the 435th Bomb Squadron, including Elwyn Rahier: *S/Sgt. Elwyn Rahier, whose good gunnery had helped this crew out of many a close call, was the Aerial Engineer. He was an old hand and had a score to even, as he had been wounded in Pearl Harbor and returned to do his part. It was men like these that flew "Chief Seattle" out beyond friendly waters and far back of enemy lines, to bring back that ever-important information. Exactly what was the enemy doing at Rabaul Harbour, was what his crew went to find out. They were always ready for the toughest missions. How little did they know what awaited them this morning. How little did I think this ship, that the people of Seattle had given, carrying a crew that I knew well, fading out in the distance over the Owen Stanley Range would not again return that evening; and the crew would not be talking and everybody laughing about their troubles or luck that they would have that day. I waited that evening until long after there was no hope, long after I knew their gas would be gone. Then my hope was that they had landed somewhere on some other island and would be safe. Days, weeks, and now months have gone by. Nothing was ever heard. No radio contact was ever made. Where these brave boys may be or what their fates might be, whether their lives have been spared we do not know. But of the things we are sure, that there are no greater men than those who give their lives in war that we may live out in peace.*[5]

Staff Sergeant Elwyn Owen Rahier is memorialized on the Tablets of the Missing, Manila American Cemetery, Manila, Philippines. Elwyn was awarded the Distinguished Flying Cross and the Purple Heart. To this day, no trace of the *Chief Seattle* has ever been found.[8]

Donald Vincent Rose

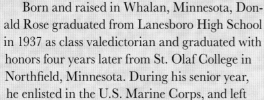

U.S. Marine Corps, 1st Marine "The Old Breed" Division, Marine Scout Bomb Squadron, Second Lieutenant

OCTOBER 28, 1918–SEPTEMBER 13, 1942—Battle for Guadalcanal, Solomon Islands

Born and raised in Whalan, Minnesota, Donald Rose graduated from Lanesboro High School in 1937 as class valedictorian and graduated with honors four years later from St. Olaf College in Northfield, Minnesota. During his senior year, he enlisted in the U.S. Marine Corps, and left for training shortly after graduation. On April 17, 1942, Donald was commissioned a 2nd Lieutenant and designated a naval aviator at Pensacola, Florida, 1st Marine Division. Following a furlough home in early summer, he reported for duty at the Marine Air Corps Station in San Diego.[9]

On August 7, 1942, the 1st Marine Division conducted the first invasion on a Japanese-occupied island, Guadalcanal. Commanded by Major General Alexander Vandegrift, the marines quickly secured the airfield under construction and named it Henderson Field after Marine Major Lofton Henderson, killed during the Battle of Midway two months earlier. Nicknamed the "Red Devils," 2nd Lieutenant Donald Rose from the 232nd Marine Bomb Squadron was among the first dive-bombers to see combat against the Japanese. On August 20, 19 Wildcat fighters from Marine Squadron 232 and 12 Red Devil Dauntless dive-bombers launched from the escort carrier USS *Long Island* and landed on Henderson Field's 3,000-foot dirt runway.[1, 2, 2, 4]

Just eight days later, 2nd Lieutenant Donald Rose flew in a successful air strike against four Japanese navy destroyers, which were transporting troops to Guadalcanal to reinforce Japanese ground forces for an attack on Henderson Field. As a result of the strikes, many of the Japanese troops did not make it to shore. For bravery and coolness under fire, 2nd Lieutenant Rose was awarded a Silver Star.[5, 7]

2nd Lieutenant Donald Rose wrote to his parents on September 8: *I'm out of ink so pencil will have to do. You don't mind, do you, especially when letters are so infrequent? Well, in case you've been wondering where I am, here it is— perhaps you've heard of the place? Guadalcanal in the Solomons. Grab your atlas and come and visit me sometime. This is quite a place as newspaper reports will bear me out. That is, at least I think so, haven't seen one for a month, nor have we any other contacts with civilization, so if you get around to write, don't forget those details. When I get back, if anyone even mentions camping, they will probably*

get hurt. You see the fact is I've had enough roughing it for awhile. The Japs have been very considerate to us—left us food, clothing and shelter and believe me, we are making good use of it all. Even eat their candy. You see, they moved out very quickly, leaving practically everything they owned for the new tenants, which was alright with us, of course. When I left San Diego I went to Honolulu in case you were wondering. Stayed there until August 1, just long enough to get one letter.

That is a very interesting place with very peculiar customs of dress, etc. All the police wear dark blue blouses and white knee length skirts with bottoms trimmed like this notches about eight inches deep. Very peculiar. Lots of things I could tell you about but I think I'll wait until I can tell you in person. I'm fine, by the way, and don't worry. You have all you can take care of combating the sugar, tire and gas shortages. (Joke.) P.S. Take this Jap bill and buy yourself a coke or something.[6]

What 2nd Lieutenant Donald Rose did not write was that the lack of fuel, food, water and ammunition forced the 1st Marine Division to survive on captured Japanese rations. They also endured heavy naval gunfire, air raids, and long-range enemy artillery fire nicknamed "Pistol Pete." Determined to regain the airfield, waves of Japanese soldiers descended on Henderson Airfield. Before the battle, Colonel Merritt "Red Mike" Edson told his marines, *"There it is. It is useless to ask ourselves why it is we who are here. We are here. There is only us between the airfield and the Japs. If we don't hold we will lose Guadalcanal."*[2] Marines on Lunga Ridge south of Henderson Field, later named Edson's Ridge, held their ground. During the assault, 2nd Lieutenant Rose was wounded on September 12 by shrapnel during Japanese naval bombing and died the next day.[7, 8]

Donald Rose was reinterred at Fort Snelling National Cemetery in 1948.[8, 9] Whalan American Legion Erickson-Rose Post 637 is named in honor of him and Ferdinand Erickson, a soldier who died in World War I.

Omar Julian Kolstad

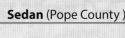

U.S. Navy, USS *Vincennes*, *Seaman Apprentice*
JULY 26, 1918–AUGUST 9, 1942—Battle of Savo Island, Solomon Islands

Omar Kolstad's father operated the blacksmith shop in Swift Falls, Minnesota, and Omar worked as his chief assistant at a young age. When he enlisted in the navy at age 24, Omar was a highly skilled mechanic and reportedly built an automobile out of tractor parts.

Following his navy enlistment in March 1942, Seaman Apprentice Omar Julian Kolstad was assigned to the cruiser *Vincennes* and immediately called to the war zone to protect and escort U.S. Marines landing on Guadalcanal, where Japanese forces were constructing an airfield. Determined to prevent the Japanese from consolidating control of the Pacific, the U.S. Navy sent men, warships and supply ships to Guadalcanal.

On August 7, 1942, 19,000 men of the 1st Marine Division landed at Lunga Point, Guadalcanal, and Tulagi, Florida Island, located directly across the Savo Sound from Guadalcanal. Three American heavy cruisers, *Vincennes*, *Quincy*, *Astoria*, and two destroyers, *Helm* and *Wilson*, blocked the strait between Savo and Florida Islands in defense of the landing zone. Another group guarded the area to the south. Japanese bombers from Rabaul attacked the marines on the beachhead, but failed initially, due to accurate anti-aircraft fire from the American ships. The *Vincennes* alone shot down nine "Betty" torpedo bombers in the first two days of combat.

Then the Japanese Eighth Fleet arrived unnoticed and torpedoed two ships in the southern group. When bad weather disrupted communications, the Japanese took the northern forces by surprise and hit the *Astoria*, *Quincy*, and *Vincennes* at 0137 on the 9th of August. The *Vincennes*, hit repeatedly by torpedoes, suffered a fatal list to port, rolled over and sank at 0250.

Milton A. Schneller aboard the *Vincennes* described the scene: *The first Jap hit smashed our sky aft to pieces. Then we took a torpedo right in our guts. We shuddered again, then came another direct hit and all lights went out. Shells and torpedoes meanwhile were coming fast. Number one fireroom was hit directly after us. The third torpedo hit the number four fireroom. The fifth hit the forward engine room and the sixth struck forward at the bow. Then the firing ceased almost as abruptly as it had started. We were still afloat but listing badly. On opening the hatch into the marine compartment, I found the place to be a raging inferno. When I came down the ladder into our control quarters, two and half decks below* topside, *I reported to Commander Hansen that in my opinion, it would be possible to escape if we went straight up and not through the officers' forward passage. There were 48 men in that area of the ship and Commander Hansen, upon receiving my report, said those who wished to go could do so, and that it was every man for himself. Nine of us got out. The discipline on the deck was wonderful. We had to throw some of the men into the water. They refused to leave the ship even after being ordered to do so. We floated for what seemed like hours. Hundreds of men were bobbing around in the sea. In my immediate vicinity some 75 men were floating in the neighborhood of a raft on which were 20 wounded soldiers. I was stationed about 100 feet out from one of the corners of the raft to act as a guard against sharks.*[3, 4]

During the one-hour Battle of Savo Island, a force of eight Japanese warships sank four heavy Allied cruisers, the *Quincy*, *Canberra*, *Astoria* and *Vincennes*. Total losses from the three ships amounted to 1,077 men killed and 709 wounded; the *Vincennes* alone lost 332 men with 258 wounded.[1, 2]

Seaman Apprentice Omar Kolstad, son of Simon and Eunice (Peterson) Kolstad was reported missing in action by the navy September 13, 1942, and declared officially dead August 10, 1943. A memorial service was held October 17, 1943, at Rolling Forks Lutheran Church in Sedan. He is memorialized at Manila American Cemetery, Philippines, and at Rolling Forks Lutheran Cemetery, Sedan, Minnesota.[5]

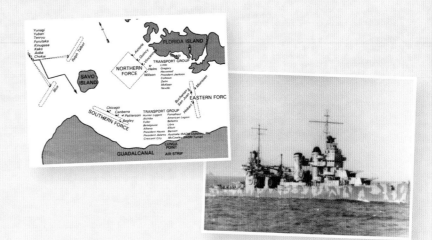

Ernest George Haarstad

U.S. Naval Reserve, USS Tasker H. Bliss, *Fireman Third Class*
JANUARY 27, 1912–NOVEMBER 12, 1942—Naval Battle of Casablanca, Moroccan Coast

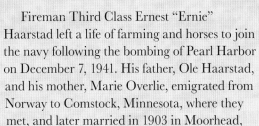

Fireman Third Class Ernest "Ernie" Haarstad left a life of farming and horses to join the navy following the bombing of Pearl Harbor on December 7, 1941. His father, Ole Haarstad, and his mother, Marie Overlie, emigrated from Norway to Comstock, Minnesota, where they met, and later married in 1903 in Moorhead, Minnesota. Ole Haarstad was the official Askegaard Farm "horse boss" and spent 35 years caring for the herd of 100 horses on the vast bonanza farm in Comstock. Ole's self-taught skills as a veterinarian were in hot demand, and he housed a good supply of medicines to treat horses. Described as a good worker, a lover of animals and a fine herdsman, Ole held an important position on the farm, as none of the hired hands could care properly for the horses like he could.[1]

Ernest graduated from Comstock High School and in 1935 joined the Civilian Conservation Corps in Cass Lake, Minnesota. He later worked for the Koester family in Comstock. In 1941, Ernest moved to Eatonville, Washington, to work for a lumber company, followed by work on a government project in the Aleutian Islands. He tried to enlist in the army but was denied acceptance due to medical problems with his legs. Determined to help his country, he applied for naval duty, was mustered into service on October 24, 1942, and trained at the Great Lakes Training Center in Chicago, Illinois.[1, 7]

In 1942, the German army was in control of much of Europe and a good swath of the U.S.S.R. Without sufficiently trained men or enough war equipment, U.S. military planners knew they didn't have strength or manpower to invade Europe yet. So Allied leaders decided to send American troops to French North Africa, where Axis defenses were weaker than in Europe. Plans were made for Operation Torch, the Allied invasion of French North Africa commanded by General Dwight D. Eisenhower, to begin on November 8, 1942. Ernest G. Haarstad set sail on the USS *Tasker H. Bliss*, a troop and cargo transport ship, on October 24, 1942, bound for the Moroccan coast. By the time the troopship *Tasker H. Bliss*, assigned to Task Group 34, arrived off Fedala, Morocco, on November 8th to unload supplies and troops, the Naval Battle of Casablanca was in full swing.

The battle delayed cargo unloading and the departure of Task Group 34 from the Moroccan coast. As dusk settled over Fedala on the evening of

November 12, the German submarine U-130, commanded by Ernst Kals, crept in and fired five torpedoes at three ships: *Edward Rutledge, High L. Scott* and *Tasker H. Bliss*. Both the *Edward Rutledge* and *High L. Scott* sank quickly, while *Tasker H. Bliss* burned for several hours before sinking. Of the 74 American servicemen who died on the transport ships anchored off Fedala, 31 of them, including Ernie Haarstad, lost their lives on the *Tasker H. Bliss*.[3, 4, 5, 7]

Ernest G. Haarstad is memorialized at the North Africa American Cemetery and Memorial, Tunisia, and Comstock Lutheran Cemetery, Comstock, Minnesota. Memorial services were conducted at the Comstock Norwegian Lutheran Church. Two of his brothers served in World War II: Walter, in the army, and Rudolph, in the marines.[1, 5, 7]

U.S. Navy, USS Barton (DD-599), *Machinist's Mate Second Class*
APRIL 26, 1918–NOVEMBER 13, 1942—Battle of Guadalcanal, Solomon Islands

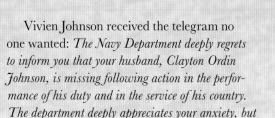

Vivien Johnson received the telegram no one wanted: *The Navy Department deeply regrets to inform you that your husband, Clayton Ordin Johnson, is missing following action in the performance of his duty and in the service of his country. The department deeply appreciates your anxiety, but details are not now available and delay in receipt thereof must necessarily be expected. To prevent possible aid to our enemies, please do not divulge the name of his ship or station—Rear Admiral Randall Jacobs, Chief of Naval Personnel, U.S. Navy*

After enlisting in the navy on December 7, 1938, Clayton Johnson was stationed on USS *Utah* at Pearl Harbor. Three years later, he miraculously survived the sinking of the *Utah* by swimming a considerable distance to shore through water covered with burning oil. His second ship fared no better than the first one.[1]

On May 29, 1942, Johnson boarded the *Barton*, a ship built by Bethlehem Steel Company in Quincy, Massachusetts. The USS *Barton* left the East Coast on August 23, 1942, and steamed to the Pacific, arriving at Tongatabu, Tonga Islands, on September 14, 1942. October proved to be a busy month for the ship. She participated in the Buin-Faisi-Tonolai raid on October 5, the Battle of Santa Cruz on October 26, and on October 29, she rescued 17 survivors of 2 downed air transports near Fabre Island.[4]

Two weeks later, the *Barton* joined Rear Admiral Daniel J. Callaghan's force of five cruisers and seven destroyers in Guadalcanal to stop Japanese warships heading toward Guadalcanal to bomb Henderson field. As the ship lined up in the eleventh position of the U.S. force, the crew prepared their battle stations for the Japanese.[2]

The Naval Battle of Guadalcanal began after midnight on November 13, during tropical rainstorms and squalls. In total darkness, *Barton* launched five torpedoes at the leading Japanese destroyer, while weaving violently to avoid collisions with friendly and enemy ships. Just seconds after shutting down completely to avoid a collision with another U.S. vessel, the Japanese destroyer *Amatsukaze* fired eight torpedoes, one of which struck the forward fire room, and another hitting the forward engine room. The ship broke in half and exploded, taking 164 men with her, including Clayton Johnson.

All who died were listed as missing in action for one year, until they were officially declared dead on November 13, 1943.

Heavy cruiser USS *Portland* picked up only 42 survivors while Higgins boats from Guadalcanal rescued others. In 1992, an expedition led by Dr. Robert Ballard discovered USS *Barton's* bow southeast of Savo Island. To date, the stern section of the *Barton* has not been found.[2, 3, 4, 5, 6, 7]

Clayton Ordin Johnson is memorialized at Manila American Cemetery and Memorial, Manila, Philippines. Survivors included his father, Carl, his wife, Vivien, and a brother, Lowell. Clayton's mother, Odine, died when he was seven years old, and his grandparents, Mr. and Mrs. Lars Fjelland, raised him in Clark, South Dakota. Clayton later lived with his father in Tintah, Minnesota, and in 1942, he married Vivien Vidger in Fergus Falls, Minnesota.[5, 7]

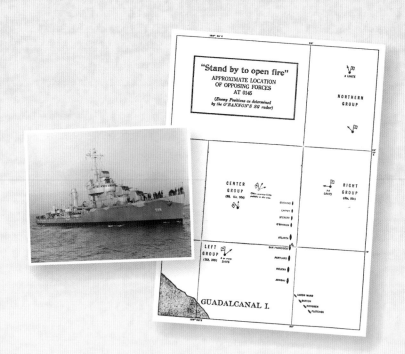

William Jackson Clewitt

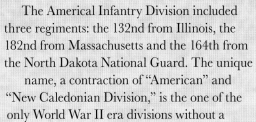

Americal Division, 164th Infantry Regiment, Third Battalion, I Company, Private First Class
AUGUST 3, 1918–NOVEMBER 23, 1942—The Battle of Guadalcanal, Solomon Islands

The Americal Infantry Division included three regiments: the 132nd from Illinois, the 182nd from Massachusetts and the 164th from the North Dakota National Guard. The unique name, a contraction of "American" and "New Caledonian Division," is the one of the only World War II era divisions without a number, and was activated on New Caledonia on May 27, 1942, where the division trained in jungle warfare. William Clewitt and the 164th were the first army unit to land on Guadalcanal; they did so on October 13, 1942, as reinforcement for the 1st Marine Division.

The marines were exhausted and depleted until the 164th Regiment arrived, a unit fresh and eager for jungle warfare. The North Dakotans had a strong leader and quickly proved their ability as soldiers—they fought so well that the marines tagged them "the best dogfaces in the world."[2, 6, 7] From October 24 to the 26, the Japanese battled furiously with the Americans to recapture Henderson Field. During these black, eerie nights, the heaviest fighting fell on the 7th Marines, who radioed William Clewitt's 3rd Battalion for reinforcements. As the marines fought to stop the Japanese, Lieutenant Colonel Robert K. Hall led the 3rd Battalion through dense jungle into position alongside the marines. For three days and nights, the 3rd Battalion fought in hand-to-hand combat and endured endless attacks by the enemy.[1, 2, 3]

The troops stuck to their positions with determination, and the 3rd Battalion earned a commendation from Marine Major General Vandegrift: *The commanding general commends the 3rd Battalion, 164th Infantry, U.S. Army, for the effectiveness of its operations against the enemy 24, 25, and 26 October, 1942. The First Marine Battalion, 7th Marines, occupying a defensive sector of a width of 2500 yards situated to south of the positions of the 1st Marine Division on Lunga Point, Guadalcanal, British Solomon Islands, having been attacked by a number superior enemy at about 1000, 23 October 1942, the 3rd Battalion, 164th Infantry, then in regimental reserve, was ordered to reinforce the line. Moving by a forced march at night by rain, over difficult and unfamiliar terrain, it arrived in time to prevent a serious penetration of the position, and by reinforcing the 1st Battalion, 7th Marines throughout its sector, made possible the repulse of continuous enemy attacks throughout the night.* The heroic fighting of the 164th Infantry earned them the nickname

"The 164th Marines," and the media dubbed them the "jungle fighters" because of the terrain on Guadalcanal.[4, 5, 6]

On November 19, all three battalions of the 164th advanced to Point Cruz near the Matanikau River and crossed the river the next day. Despite steep muddy hills, unbearable heat, and intense Japanese fire, the exhausted and malaria-ridden troops drove the enemy from two hilltop positions. Lieutenant Colonel Samuel Baglien wrote in his diary: *A slow advance toward objective further west is begun. The enemy is laying down heavy mortar and machine gun fire. They are well dug in and concealed. Coordinated mortar and artillery fire does not dislodge the enemy. They have dug in in the coral, and in draws and are quite secure. Any exposure of our troops draws accurate enemy fire. Casualties are fairly heavy. This situation continues on November 23 and 24. Advance is stopped and positions are consolidated. Men must live on "C" and "D" rations and coffee as movements draw heavy and accurate enemy mortar fire. Enemy light artillery appears to have been silenced by our air and artillery support. Snipers are active. Our planes continue to bomb and strafe enemy positions with unknown results. Our third battalion has suffered heavy casualties by artillery and mortar fire.*[4, 5, 6]

On November 23, Private First Class William Clewitt and 18 other men, survivors of the toughest fighting on Guadalcanal, died from artillery fire. Fellow soldier Harry Wiens watched eight men from I Company die: *Captain Panettiere, our Battalion surgeon, and Lieutenant Whitney killed; Macey Paul, our 1st Sergeant, wounded, and Corporal Kohnke also killed… Lieutenants Sloulin and Grytness had been killed that first afternoon on the hill, and both Dibbert and Clewitt were dead.* Wiens had been on furlough in the states with Clewitt who told him "stirring tales of adventure and amorous conquest." As he was dying, Clewitt asked Wiens to write his girlfriend and "tell her I thought of her anyway." Wiens admitted, "Even today when I think of him, my eyes still moisten."[7]

Private First Class William J. "Sonny" Clewitt was buried in Fort Snelling National Cemetery, Minneapolis, Minnesota. In 1911, his family moved from South Dakota to Kerrick, Minnesota, for life on a farm. In all, five men from Kerrick died in World War II, and all were redheads.[8, 9]

Robert "Bob" Garfield Anderson
Tamarack (Aitkin County)

2nd Marine "The Silent Second" Division, 6th Marine Regiment, 3rd Battalion, Headquarters Company, Private

JANUARY 20, 1920–JANUARY 15, 1943—Battle for Guadalcanal, Solomon Islands

Burton Anderson recalled a story of his brother during the Armistice Day Blizzard:

It was warm and a little foggy on the morning of November 11, 1940. Bob and neighbor Bernard Boyer decided to head up to a nearby lake to hunt for ducks. They were avid hunters and loved hunting ducks, not only for sport but also to feed their families. About 9:30 a.m. or so, it began to snow, and by noon the snow was getting very deep and Dad was getting very worried because Bob was not back from the lake. It was about a two-mile walk and the snow was not letting up. He asked Mom to pack him some supplies as he dressed to head out into the storm, concerned not only that he may not find the boys, but wondering that if he found them would they all be able to make it back home. Luckily, he had gone only a short distance when he saw Bob ahead pushing his way through what was now almost waist deep snow. Bob was covered with the ducks, using his bootlaces, his belt and whatever else he had as string to carry all the ducks. Dad was angry that Bob hadn't started for home when it began to snow and had waited until it was almost too late to make it, but all Bob could say was, "The ducks! The ducks!" There were just so many ducks they couldn't leave! The storm had grounded huge flocks at the lake and the hunting was by far the best he had ever seen. Not all hunters were that lucky, as many perished in the storm.

After Bob Anderson joined the marines in 1942, he wrote home from basic training in San Diego, California on June 26, 1942: *Dear Mom and all, We shot our rifles for record today, I made sharpshooter. Got 216 points out of 250. I needed 10 points for expert, only two boys made it. Both were from Minnesota. I'm back at the base now but I don't know for how long. I'll either get K.P. or sent out to Camp Elliot for more training. That's about 15 or 20 miles. It sure is good that my boot camp training is just about over. I got a package of cookies from Doris. I took a handful of them and set the rest on the table and in two seconds the box was empty. They were pretty good. Just signed the payroll. We get 50 dollars a month now. It will be the first time we have been paid. I've got to have my greens tailored, buy a leather belt, a pair of black shoes and a green cap. That stuff isn't issued to you. I hope this finds you feeling well as that's the way I feel. I guess I better close right away as the lights are going out pretty quick. Love, Bob*[1,2]

In November 1942, Private Robert Anderson and the 6th Marines arrived in New Zealand for combat training. There the regiment fell in love with the beautiful country and friendly people. Their idyllic tour ended when the 6th Marines landed on Guadalcanal on January 4, 1943, with orders to "attack and destroy the Japanese forces remaining on Guadalcanal."[3] On January 15, the 6th Marines, commanded by Colonel Gilder D. Jackson, moved to the front lines and replaced the beat-up 2nd Marines. During combat, Private Robert Anderson was killed in action and buried on Guadalcanal.

The 6th Marines fought on through deadly heat and jungle toward the beach where the 8th Marines joined them, proceeding through hills filled with Japanese machine gun nests. When the Japanese lost ground and over 600 men, they retreated and the marines reached the beach. By February 9, the island belonged to the Allies, but at great cost. During 6 weeks on Guadalcanal, the 6th Marines lost 53 men killed in action and 170 wounded.[3,4,5,6] The regiment battled on in Tarawa, Saipan, Tinian, and Okinawa before ending in Japan for occupation duty after the atomic bombs were dropped on Hiroshima and Nagasaki.

Robert Anderson was later reinterred in National Memorial Cemetery of the Pacific, Honolulu, Hawaii.

Cindy Risen recalls her uncle: *Bob was, from stories I heard, a very outgoing and friendly young man. He had lots of friends and was very well thought of. He didn't finish high school, only going through the 8th grade at the local one-room school. He stayed at home to help his parents on their small farm instead of moving away to go to school. Bob worked with the Civilian Conservation Corps in Oregon and Minnesota for a few years before joining the marines. My dad, his younger brother, said that when Pearl Harbor was attacked by the Japanese, all Bob could talk about was joining the fight and doing his part for the war effort. His family tried to talk him out of joining but there was no stopping him. He felt the need to do all he could for his country. He wanted to join the air force, but because he didn't finish high school, he couldn't, so joined the marines instead. He went to basic training and then straight into combat. When his family said goodbye to him at the bus station, little did they know that would be the last time they would see him.*[1]

Cyril Edward Curb

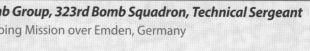

Mizpah (Koochiching County)

U.S. Army Air Forces, 8th Air Force, 91st Bomb Group, 323rd Bomb Squadron, Technical Sergeant

SEPTEMBER 18, 1917–FEBRUARY 4, 1943—Bombing Mission over Emden, Germany

The thundering ships took off one behind the other. At 5,000 feet they made their formation. The men sat quietly at their station, their eyes fixed. And the deep growl of the engines shook the air, shook the world, shook the future. —John Steinbeck[1]

Six weeks after the bombing of Pearl Harbor, in January 1942, the 8th Air Force was activated at the Chatham Armory in Savannah, Georgia. Young men, with an average age of 23, traveled from small towns, farms, the city and the Civilian Conservation Corps to join the Mighty 8th and crush the Nazi regime from the air. Just prior to America's entry into World War II, Cyril Curb enlisted in the Army Air Corps on October 31, 1941. He and his crew on the *Pennsylvania Polka*, one of the nine original B-17 crews in the 91st Bomb Group (H), 323rd Squadron, flew from Dow Field, Maine, in September 1942. The 8th Air Force moved to Royal Air Force Bassingbourn, southwest of Cambridge, England, in October 1942, where they began bombing German targets in Europe until June 1945. Approximately 200,000 men flew with the 8th, and of that number, 28,000 became prisoners of war, and another 26,000 lost their lives.[2, 3]

A typical morning for Technical Sergeant Cyril Curb and crew in England may have gone something like this: As they were awakened and given their mission for the day, the level of risk would determine their mood. When they took off, stress and airsickness would cause many to lose their breakfast before reaching the English Channel. "The lucky ones who returned at the end of the day were routinely offered a two-ounce slug of whiskey from the flight surgeon."[3]

On February 4, 1943, 65 B-17 bombers left from bases in England to attack the Hamm Marshaling Yards, but due to bad weather, they changed direction to bomb Emden, Germany, a western port. Five planes from the 323rd Squadron, including Technical Sergeant Cyril Curb, radio operator for the *Pennsylvania Polka*, participated in the mission. Technical Sergeant Curb flew with 1st Lieutenant Alan L. Bobrow's crew along with eight other men. As the plane flew to Germany over the Netherlands, eyewitness 1st Lieutenant William Toole reported the plane lagged behind formation when two enemy aircraft attacked and hit the No. 3 engine. The engine exploded

and the tail ripped off. The aircraft was last seen turning into the clouds followed by enemy aircraft. Only 39 bombers out of the original 86 attacked their targets that day, and 5 were lost.[4]

The daily report for the 323rd Bomb Squadron states: *4 Feb. 1943– Five ships of this squadron, piloted by Captain Bishop, Lieutenant's Birdsong, McCarty, Bobrow and Ellis took part in a mission against the Hamm Marshaling Yards. Due to weather conditions, an alternative target of Emden was bombed. Ships were loaded with ten five hundred pound general-purpose bombs. Results of bombing considered good. Heavy enemy flak encountered. Numerous enemy fighters engaged us. Two of our ships and their crews did not return. Believed missing as result of enemy fighter activity. Crews missing–ship 544, Pilot, Lieutenant Bobrow; Copilot, Lieutenant Saunders; Nav., Lieutenant Clinard; Bombardier, Lieutenant Andrews; Engineer T/Sgt. Bass; Asst. Engineer, T/Sgt. Wheeler; Radio Op., T/Sgt. Curb; Asst. Radio S/Sgt. Fredricks; Tail Gunner, Sgt. E.R. Campbell; Utility Gunner, Sgt. Blackburn.*[4, 5]

Technical Sergeant Cyril E. Curb is memorialized on the Tablets of the Missing at Cambridge American Cemetery, England, and at Evergreen Cemetery, Mizpah, Minnesota. The Mizpah American Legion and Auxiliary Curb-Lusk Post 541 was named in honor of Technical Sergeant Cyril Curb, and Staff Sergeant Eugene Lusk (page 51) who died June 14, 1944, in Normandy. Their names, along with other veterans are etched on stone in Memorial Park, Mizpah, Minnesota. During the war, Cyril's brother Orville piloted a B-24 in Italy, and his other brother Harold served with the 472nd Engineer Company in the South Pacific.

Herman William Baumgart

Wolf Lake (Becker County)

9th Infantry "The Old Reliables" Division, 47th Infantry Regiment, Anti-Tank Company,
Private First Class

FEBRUARY 12, 1917–APRIL 5, 1943—Battle of El Guettar, Tunisia

On November 8, 1942, Herman Baumgart and the 47th Infantry landed at Safi, 140 miles south of Casablanca, while Mathews Niemi (page 23) from Brookston, Minnesota, landed east of Algiers with the 39th Infantry Regiment. They were part of Operation Torch, the American and British invasion of North Africa. Their goal was to secure the northern coast of Africa, divide German forces at the Mediterranean Sea and drive out the Germans. The men entered combat immediately and secured both beachheads, which were essential to the eventual success of the North African invasion.[1, 2, 3, 4]

On February 17, 1943, the division's artillery proceeded on a 100-hour forced drive from Tlemcen, Algeria, through the Kasserine Pass to Thalal at the Tunisian front to stop General Rommel's advance. A column of 411 vehicles, 138 officers, and 2,032 enlisted men covered over 700 miles in 4 days on winding and slippery roads, through rain and snow.

When the Germans attacked through the Kasserine Pass on February 19, a lack of coordination among the inexperienced soldiers and poor leadership contributed to heavy losses among the Allied forces. However, the Allies regrouped with reinforcements and artillery, which halted the Germans, who were running low on gasoline and other supplies. Rommel withdrew his troops, ending their drive to push the Allies into Algeria, and retreated to defend the coast.

While Kassarine Pass was not an American victory, the military made changes in air power and desert warfare to improve their performance. Eventually, General Dwight D. Eisenhower took control and placed Major General George Patton in charge of the U.S. Second Corps.[3]

Under Commander Major General Manton S. Eddy, the 9th Infantry Division entered combat as a division for the first time in El Guettar, southern Tunisia, on March 28, 1943. The Germans possessed a superior air force, and their infantry hid in steep, rugged hills and gorges, where one veteran observed, "The Germans were looking down our throats all the time."[5] They also attacked at night for the first time, and three battalions got lost in the process. Later, from March 30 to April 1, the 1st Infantry Division and the 9th Infantry Division, supported by tanks, struggled against Italian-held positions at Hill 369, which the 1st finally captured on April 3. Herman Baumgart moved on with the 9th Infantry Division to attack Hill 772 where German tanks had arrived to reinforce the hill.[6, 7] During the attack Private First Class Baumgart died from a gunshot wound.[8]

After the battle, the 9th Division reported 1,508 battle casualties; the 47th Infantry Regiment lost 868 killed, wounded and missing in action, twice the number of casualties as the 39th Regiment. Allied forces used more than one million rifle and machine gun rounds to secure El Guettar in that week. As a whole, the division was credited with helping halt General Rommel's advances against Allied forces.[7]

Herman Baumgart is buried in Spruce Grove Union Cemetery, Menahga, Minnesota. Among his many survivors was his identical twin, Theodore. His niece, Rita Baumgart Zepper, recalls: *My dad and Herman were identical twins. During school, they would switch identities and fool everyone.* His brother died in 1993.[9]

Mathews J. Niemi

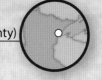

9th Infantry "The Old Reliables" Division, 39th Infantry Regiment, L Company, Private
OCTOBER 16, 1912–MAY 1, 1943—Tunisia Campaign, Second Battle for Sedjenane

On September 26, 1942, Private Mathews Niemi, 39th Infantry Regiment (the first of three infantry regiments in the 9th Division), left Camp Drum, New York, bound for England to prepare for the invasion of North Africa. In November 1942, American and British forces launched Operation Torch, the invasion of North Africa through French Morocco and Algiers. In the first campaign, the Americans fought against Germany under General Erwin Rommel, with the inexperienced soldiers facing off against a superb German army.

Mathews Niemi and the 39th Infantry landed east of Algiers on November 8, where the men guarded lines of communication between Algiers and Tunisia that stretched some 500 miles.

On February 17, 1943, the division's artillery began their 700-mile march on winding, treacherous roads from Tlemcen, Algeria, to the Kasserine Pass on the Tunisian front. At the pass, Private Mathews Niemi survived when his 3rd Battalion was among the American troops overrun by the German Panzers. The troops escaped, but lost their artillery.

After surviving the Battle of El Guettar in southern Tunisia on March 28, Mathews Niemi and the 9th Division moved to northern Tunisia. Berber tribesmen, dressed in traditional garb and part of the Corps Franc d'Afrique, fought alongside the Allies. On April 23, the 9th attacked the Sedjenane sector, which was a lead-up to the proposed capture of Bizerte, Tunisia, a major Allied objective.[1, 2, 3, 4, 5, 6] In the process, the 9th encircled two hills, the Green and Bald Hill positions, where Private Mathews Niemi died from machine gun wounds on May 1.[7]

The subsequent Battle at Sedjenane (named the "Pay-off Battle") on May 9 led to the capture of Bizerte, Tunisia, by the 9th U.S. Infantry Division. As Major Dean T. Vanderhoef played the *William Tell* Overture on his ocarina over the radiotelephone, troops rolled into Bizerte. The days of combat in North Africa were nearing the end.[4]

Errol Niemi recalls his Uncle Mathews Niemi: *My uncle was indeed a victim of General Rommel in Tunisia in 1943. My father used the word "ambushed" and apparently the first Americans in that first large-scale meeting consisted of "relatively untested and poorly led" troops. They suffered heavy casualties and were pushed back over 50 miles.*

Matt's parents were Matti Niemi (originally Kiviniemi) and Hilda (Jarvenpaa) Niemi. Their story is kind of interesting. Matti came to US from Rovaniemi, Finland. Hilda was a "mail order bride" from Finland. She was 16 when she left Finland, and the man who paid her passage was a drinker and was living in a railroad car with some cronies of his. Grandma was incensed and desperate. She went to a boarding house where lumberman came and slept and hired herself out as a cook and server. She worked there a few months and then asked the owner what kind of a guy this Matt was. She was told he was a very good worker and honest. They soon fell in love, and she and Matt had to pay off her passage to the man from the railroad car, and then they married.

It is told that their son, Matt, was a good-looking man and he liked to enjoy life. He had some friends of "questionable morals" that led to him getting in more than one incident. Still, Matt didn't change his ways and his father, for whatever reason, gave him $20 and told him it was time for him to find his way in the world. This happened about the year 1938. Matt went to Portland, Oregon and joined the Civilian Conservation Corps. As World War II was underway, the US was preparing for what might have been considered "inevitable." Men in the "CCC" were considered top candidates for the US Army. Matt joined the army and served for about 2 years before his discharge. He returned to Portland, Oregon, and worked in a hospital as an orderly. There he met a nurse who was also a nun. She left the convent, they dated and fell in love. They decided to get married. Then Pearl Harbor was attacked and all recently discharged service men were to report to the nearest military base immediately. Matt was sent to Fort Lewis near Tacoma, Washington…and that was the last time his family saw him.[8]

Private Mathews Niemi is buried in the North Africa American Cemetery, Carthage, Tunisia. All five of his brothers served in World War II.[9]

Einar Vernon Suomi

Squaw Lake (Itasca County)

U.S. Army Air Forces, 8th Air Force, 40th Combat Wing, 305th Heavy Bomb Group, 366th Bomb Squadron, 1st Lieutenant

MARCH 25, 1920–MAY 1, 1943—Bombing Mission over Saint-Nazaire, France

Jerry Dhennin, 81, recalls his cousin: *I hardly knew Einar. He was 14 years older than me and died when I was only 9, about the time my parents and I moved to Squaw Lake from Chicago. We bought the house that his parents, Gust and Katie, built and lived in.*[1]

Einar Suomi enlisted on November 7, 1941, and less than a year later, in August 1942, he and the rest of the 305th "Can Do" Bomb Group moved to Grafton Underwood air base in England for assignment to the 8th Air Force. He and his fellow airmen were trained to fly B-17s. By December 7, the Mighty 8th moved to their permanent base at the airfield near the village of Chelveston, England. From November 1942 until mid-1943, the Bomb Group attacked German defenses in France and Germany, including bombing navy yards at Wilhelmshaven and bombing an industrial target in Paris. Colonel Curtis Emerson LeMay, who commanded the group for nearly a year beginning in 1942 and personally led several dangerous missions, developed the "Bomber Combat Box Formation" for bombers attacking from different altitudes. He was promoted to General, and later oversaw the strategic bombing campaign in the Pacific.[2, 3, 4, 5]

On May 1, 1943, 1st Lieutenant Einar Suomi, pilot on a B-17 Flying Fortress, and nine crewmembers left the airfield near Chelveston to bomb a Nazi submarine base in Saint-Nazaire, France. While on their flight, fire from enemy aircraft hit their plane over the English Channel south of Belle Isle off the coast of central France. The Missing Aircraft Crew Report states: *Einar Suomi's crew was shot down over the Channel and it is believed their attempt to ditch in the water below was not successful resulting in the deaths of all ten crew members. Every plane on this mission sustained flak damage. One plane from the 366th Bomb Squadron was shot down by enemy fighters. This was Lieutenant Einar Suomi's crew."*[6]

Roger Freeman expands on the mission: *On May Day, 1943, heavy cloud frustrated a mission to Saint-Nazaire. Turning for home, the bombers were supposed to take a northwesterly course to ensure they skirted the Brest peninsula by 60 miles. The leading 306th Group somehow miscalculated and made a turn to the north and England too early. Losing altitude the group was suddenly made aware this due to flak from the Brest area, an error that cost three B-17s. The trailing*

91st Group saw what was happening and made a sharp turn left. This maneuver dispersed the formation and enemy fighters then arrived to take advantage of the situation.[3]

During World War II, the 305th Bomb Group flew 480 missions and lost 769 men. Over 154 of the 305th's B-17 Flying Fortresses were shot down or destroyed. When the war ended in Europe, the 305th converted into a photomapping unit and mapped many areas, including parts of North Africa, Iceland and Greenland.[2, 3]

1st Lieutenant Einar Suomi, son of Gust Suomi and Katherine (Niska) Kallroos, is memorialized at the American Cemetery, Cambridge, England. Survivors included his parents, his stepfather, Airo Kallroos, and two sisters, Erma and Verna. His cousin, Staff Sergeant Harold Terho (page 32), died seven months later on a bombing mission over Italy. The men grew up together in Squaw Lake, Minnesota.[1]

Frank Michael Bettin

7th Infantry Division, 32nd Infantry Regiment, 2nd Battalion, F Company, Private

OCTOBER 22, 1912–MAY 29, 1943—Aleutian Islands Campaign, Alaska

Hildy Bettin Dorn recalls her brother Frank: *Most of our ancestors crossed the Atlantic Ocean from Germany and Poland to settle in Urbank, Minnesota. No one was prepared for the terrible drought, contagious illnesses and the Depression years of the 30s. When our Dad had a stroke while down in the well looking for water, dying in 1939, Frank left to find work in the Dakotas on a ranch. Everyone knew more trouble was coming, and each evening after supper, the family gathered around the battery radio to keep us informed. Frank was drafted into the army. Everyone missed him; he was a likeable man, quiet, soft-spoken and never married. He never wanted to be in the spotlight and never wanted his picture taken. We were told that Frank and some other soldiers were in the barracks, when a Japanese man wearing an American Army uniform came in and stabbed him with a bayonet. Many years later, when my mother was dying from cancer, I was sitting by her bedside and suddenly she opened her sparkling blue eyes, smiled, and said, "Oh Frankie, it's so good to see you." Her youngest son had finally come home.*[1]

When Bettin left Urbank for the army in March 1942, he fought in the only World War II battle on American soil, the Battle of Attu in the Aleutian Islands, Alaska. On June 3, 1942, Japan invaded Attu and Kiska, the westernmost islands in Alaska's Aleutian Islands chain. Described in the *New York Times* as the loneliest spot on earth, Attu, roughly 35 by 15 miles, was extremely cold and composed of brown tundra, narrow beaches and snow-topped peaks. The Japanese believed that occupation of Attu would prevent a United States attack on Japan via the Aleutians and also disrupt Allied transportation routes. When Japanese pilots bombed the harbor, they flew so low that soldiers on the ground could clearly see their faces. The Aleutian Islands fell to the Japanese but were retaken a year later during the Battle of Attu.

Around 2,400 Japanese troops had occupied the island for just under a year when Frank Bettin arrived with the 7th Infantry Division on May 11, 1943, to reclaim Attu. Army leaders expected Attu to fall in just three days but did not anticipate Japan's organized resistance or the brutal climate. Previously trained in Nevada for desert warfare in North Africa, Private Bettin and the 7th Division abruptly moved to Fort Ord, California, for retraining in amphibious tactics for Attu. However, training on Monterey beaches did not prepare them for soft tundra, icy winds, constant wet feet and thick fog on Attu beaches where men lost sight of each other. When Bettin's F Company planned to land south at Casco Bay, they ended up north on Massacre Beach in dense fog and had to backtrack south to the beach. The three-day campaign expanded to two weeks of fighting to capture the island from the determined Japanese.[2, 3, 4, 5, 6]

By May 28, Colonel Yasuyo Yamasaki, commander of the Japanese forces, had only 700 men left, a loss of 70 percent of his force. Far superior in numbers, American forces pushed the enemy back to their base at Chichagof Harbor, a small flat space bordering the sea. Colonel Yamasaki knew that his only hope would be a brutal surprise banzai attack at night on May 29, a desperate move to capture American artillery, fade back into the hills and wait for reinforcements or rescue. The banzai charges failed in large part due to the 50th Army Engineers who fought as infantry in hand-to-hand combat. During the banzai attack, a Japanese soldier posing as an American soldier killed Private Frank Bettin. On May 30, 1943, the battle for Attu ended, but at great cost. The 7th Division lost over 1,000 men, while only 29 Japanese prisoners were taken, as most chose suicide rather than surrender.[6, 7]

During the campaign, two cemeteries were established on Attu to bury those killed in action: Holtz Bay Cemetery and Little Falls Cemetery, where Frank Bettin was buried. After the war, the frozen tundra began to take back the cemeteries, and in 1946, all American men were relocated as directed by soldier's families. Private Bettin was reinterred in Sacred Heart Catholic Church Cemetery, Urbank, Minnesota, the church where he was baptized and confirmed.[8]

Victor "Vicky" Nathaniel Borgeson

Norcross (Grant County)

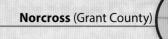

U.S. Naval Reserve, USS **Helena,** *Fireman First Class*
JUNE 23, 1921–JULY 6, 1943—Battle of Kula Gulf, Solomon Islands

The son of Swedish immigrants, Victor Borgeson grew up in a musically gifted family on the family farm in rural Norcross. In the 1930s, the family formed the Borgeson Orchestra and played often at dances at the Norcross Hall and surrounding town halls. Vicky and his brother, Reuben, were inducted in the navy together on April 17, 1942. After training at Treasure Island in San Francisco Bay, Fireman First Class Victor Borgeson was assigned to the USS *Chicago,* a cruiser sent to defend the marines on Guadalcanal.[1,3] On November 13, 1942, the U.S. and Australian Navy solidly defeated the Japanese, but Borgeson's ship, the USS *Chicago,* went down that night. Borgeson and his good friend Joseph Dougherty abandoned ship together and survived in spite of severe burns. Victor's parents received a letter from their son dated February 25, 1943: *Dear Folks, The hospital turned me loose a week ago so I'm ready for duty again. They sure done a good job on my face, I won't even have a scar. My right arm was burned bad, but will soon be OK. Oh, yes, I really got a close haircut and have only one eyebrow, and it wasn't a barber that did it either. You know that nice wristwatch I had? I still have it but it will never run again. It stopped when I hit the water. Yes, just 14 minutes after I jumped overboard my ship sank. It was a good ship and it took some of my good shipmates down with it. The crew that relieved my crew down in the fire room never came out. One of the boys had been with me since I entered boot training. We were only in the water an hour and then were rescued. Oh boy, I got three letters today, maybe I'll soon get my mail. Hope I get a whole seabag full of it and by gosh, I'll memorize every bit of it. Don't worry about me. I'm OK. The weather is fine and I sure have a good tan. I weigh 185 pounds so the food is good. Your son, Vicky[2]*

Following his recuperation, Borgeson boarded the 9,000-ton cruiser USS *Helena* on March 2, 1943 and immediately returned to action in the South Pacific. One of three cruisers and four destroyers, the USS *Helena* fired her guns ashore at New Georgia in the Solomon Islands, to defend troops landing at Rice Anchorage, in the battle of Kula Gulf.[2,3,4]

On July 3, 1944, Vicky wrote a final letter, very different from the letter he wrote to his parents four months earlier: *Dear Amanda, I hope to stay aboard this ship and not have to leave this one like I did the last one. That was a terrible experience, which I will never forget. We have been in a few more engagements since I came aboard but have been fortunate enough to come through it okay. A fellow just has to be lucky at a time like that, I know. Oh yes, I had a very pleasant surprise sometime ago when my brother Reuben came out to my ship. He is stationed over on the beach, just a few miles over, so we have gotten together quite often. He is just fine, although he hasn't much for living quarters. I have cleaner quarters and better food, he says, but at least he doesn't have those large guns going off overhead, and torpedoes exploding below. Yes, I know now why a fellow has to be physically fit to be in the service. It's an awful strain on a fellow, but guess a guy can take it if he's lucky like I was. I am to be awarded the Purple Heart, but I am just one of the many men who have been wounded in action with the enemy out here, but am none the worst for it all. The war news sounds real good at the present and I'm just waiting for the day when this all blows over and I can go back to Norcross and forget all about it. Must close, it's chow time. Bye, Vicky[1]*

Just before midnight July 4, 1943, the USS *Helena* moved into Kula Gulf where early on July 6, the *Helena* opened fire on ten Japanese destroyers. Just seven minutes later, the Japanese destroyers *Suzukaze* and *Tanikaze* torpedoed and sank the *Helena,* killing 168 out of 900 crewmen, including Victor Borgeson. Joseph Dougherty, who survived the sinking of the USS *Helena,* hitchhiked from Litchfield to Norcross to tell Vicky's parents the details of the battle.[1,4,5]

Dale Borgeson recalls his Uncle Victor: *My dad Reuben tells me that Vicky died July 5, 1943, after spending the July 4 holiday with Reuben and brother-in-law Albert (Tuffy) Reckner on Guadalcanal. His ship, USS* Helena, *was hit the next day in an attack on a Japanese convoy at Kula Gulf. Vicky was lost at sea. My grandpa and grandma took the news very heavily—Vicky was their youngest and very handsome with a winning smile. Growing up I remember the framed letter above the dining room table with condolences from the President of the United States. I also remember the miniature barn, complete in every detail that Vickie built as a teenager. My mom, Margaret Johnson Borgeson, was the best friend of Vicky's beautiful girlfriend Joan Niemackl. I have often thought what a lovely family Vicky and Joan would have made if he had survived the war.[1]*

Victor Borgeson is memorialized at the Manila American Cemetery Memorial, Philippines. The Hillestad-Borgeson American Legion Post 410 in Norcross, Minnesota, is named in honor of Victor Borgeson and a World War I-era soldier.[6]

AVENGE MONTANA'S GLORIOUS "HELENA" · buy WAR BONDS to replace *her!* 3rd War Loan

Jerome Gooselaw, Jr.

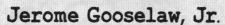

St. Vincent (Kittson County)

43rd Infantry "Winged Victory" Division, 172nd Infantry Regiment, 1st Battalion, B Company, Private
OCTOBER 20, 1919–JULY 17, 1943—New Georgia Campaign, Solomon Islands

Bob Cameron remembers the day that the aluminum coffins of brothers Private Jerome Gooselaw and Private Arthur Gooselaw were laid side by side in the former bank building in St. Vincent, Minnesota. Bob was only 13 years old but he vividly recalls the memories of the family: *The Gooselaw family had enough kids for their own baseball team with one extra thrown in for good measure. Besides being excellent athletes, the Gooselaws were terrific dancers and just good people. The Gooselaws had a dugout by the river covered with popple trees where the family stored their potatoes and the kids used the dugout as a fort where the soldiers always won.*[1]

A descendent of Cree and French Voyageur, Jerome Gooselaw grew up in St. Vincent, located in the northwest corner of Minnesota, bordering both Canada and North Dakota. His grandmother, Angelica Gooselaw, born to Cree parents in 1829 in Winnipeg, Manitoba, migrated south to settle in St. Vincent and nearby Pembina, North Dakota. Many of her descendants served in the military during war, including her grandson, Jerome Gooselaw, who entered the service October 7, 1942.[2]

On February 17, 1943, Jerome Gooselaw and the 43rd Infantry Division moved to Guadalcanal in the Solomon Islands, and after winning the Guadalcanal Campaign, the American forces continued their advance up the island chain to the Japanese supply base at Rabaul, on New Britain. On the way to Rabaul, the Americans planned to capture the Japanese air base at Munda Point on New Georgia, a mission named Operation Toenails. On June 30, the western landing force composed of the 169th and 172nd Infantry Regiments, 43rd Division, landed at Rendova Harbor on the New Georgia coast without resistance, but difficult terrain and a determined Japanese defense slowed their five-mile advance to Munda Airfield.

The 169th and 172nd marched from Zanana to the Barike River via the only trail to Munda Airfield, a jungle footpath called the Munda Trail. Japanese forces resisted their passage with deadly fire and ambushes from high ground that flanked the trail on either side, and dense jungle and knee-deep mud in the swamps of the Barike River slowed their progress. Delivering supplies of food and ammunition and evacuating the wounded became a struggle, which further weakened the exhausted troops. When troops evacuating casualties from the 169th Infantry were ambushed on the Munda Trail, they could not reach the medical station at Rendova, and were forced to establish a makeshift medical field station right in the middle of the swamp.[3, 4, 5]

On July 17, during the approach to Munda Airfield, Jerome Gooselaw died of wounds to his left arm and leg.[6] On August 4, 1943, Father McAleer of St. Patrick's Catholic Church informed the *Kittson County Enterprise* that Jerome Gooselaw had been killed in action. The newspaper reported that Jerome *was exceptionally well known, especially throughout the northern half of the county.*[7]

Jerome was buried in New Georgia Cemetery and six years later reinterred at St. Vincent Cemetery, St. Vincent, Minnesota. He had 11 siblings, and his mother, Adele Gooselaw, and the rest of family bore much sorrow during the war. Her husband died in 1942, just a year before Jerome died in New Georgia. A second son, Arthur Gooselaw (page 93), was killed in action November 15, 1944, during the battle for Metz, France. The brothers are buried side by side in St. Vincent. Another soldier from Arco, Minnesota, Glen Jorgensen (page 28), served with Jerome Gooselaw in the 172nd regiment and died ten days later.[7, 8]

Glen Lloyd Jorgensen

Arco (Lincoln County)

43rd Infantry "Winged Victory" Division, 169th Infantry Regiment, 3rd Battalion, I Company, Private

JUNE 14, 1922–JULY 27, 1943—Battle of Munda Point, New Georgia

Born and raised in Arco, Minnesota, Glen Jorgensen graduated from Arco High School in 1940. Prior to entering the service with the quota of men from Lincoln County on November 10, 1942, Glen farmed with his brother, Carl. He also worked for the Fredricksen-Jorgensen contracting firm.[1]

By February 1943, Guadalcanal, part of the Solomon Islands, rested in the hands of the Allies. Determined to capture the remaining islands in the chain, Glen Jorgensen and the 43rd Infantry Division advanced to another of its islands, New Georgia, with the goal of conquering Bougainville. An Allied airfield on Bougainville would allow the Americans to attack Rabaul, a major Japanese base on New Britain, which blocked American advance to the Philippines and Japan. The first step in the advance to Rabaul involved securing Munda Airfield in New Georgia.

After the Marine Raiders seized the islands of Rendova and Vanguru to protect the men and supplies coming into New Georgia, Private Jorgensen and the 169th Regiment, along with others, were called in to secure the beach in Rendova Harbor. As the exhausted men advanced on the five-mile march in knee-deep mud over the Munda Trail to Munda Airfield, they faced constant attack from the Japanese along the trail. Men sick with jungle diseases and the wounded were evacuated by hand over the treacherous jungle trail. Many casualties resulted from friendly fire, with men shooting at imagined Japanese soldiers.[2, 3]

On July 25, the attack on Munda Airfield began with the 43rd Infantry Division stationed near the coast, while the 37th Infantry Division advanced to the airfield from the north. The Army Operations Report gives details of the attack: *By July 26, our front line pressed against the defenses of the enemy main line of resistance, producing a long irregular front. Our left had not been successful against the Ilangana strongpoint. Our right was obliged to maintain contact with the 37th Division at the forward position secured earlier in the campaign by the 169th Infantry. The combat strength of the infantry elements at this time was low. On the morning of July 26, strong patrols searched the left flank, fixing the main pillbox positions. A tank reconnaissance was conducted in close contact with the patrols. Seventy-four pillboxes were found in depth on a 600-yard front. During the period 27 July–1 August, our advances were slow but gained ground steadily.*[3]

As the Americans fought in close combat to unearth concealed Japanese, Private Glen Jorgensen died from a gunshot wound on July 27 during the battle to capture the airfield.[4] The American forces cleared out the Japanese and claimed the airfield on August 5, 1943.

Private Glen Jorgensen is buried in Manila American Cemetery, Manila, Philippines, and memorialized in Arco City Cemetery, Arco, Minnesota. His father, Hans Jorgensen, and two brothers, Elmer and Oscar, all died in 1937. Glen was never granted a furlough; he went into combat within a few months after induction.[1]

Arnold "Arny" Manfred Holen

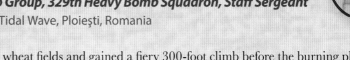

Louisburg (Lac qui Parle County)

U.S. Army Air Forces, 8th Air Force, 93rd Bomb Group, 329th Heavy Bomb Squadron, Staff Sergeant
OCTOBER 21, 1922–AUGUST 1, 1943—Operation Tidal Wave, Ploieşti, Romania

Donnie Anderson wrote about his great-uncle and the Ploieşti Raid: *I can't imagine what went through Arny's mind on 31 July 1943, as he prepared to undertake what historians still consider the most daring raid ever attempted. The planners of the Ploieşti Raids had told these men that this would be a very dangerous mission. In fact, General Ent had told them that if all of the men were lost, but the refineries destroyed, the mission would still be considered a success. It was thought that the destruction of the oil refineries at Ploieşti would hamper the Nazi war effort and help bring an earlier conclusion to the war. There can be little comfort when one commander tells his men that at the end of the day on Sunday, 1 August 1943, the lucky ones would be "prisoners of war.*[1]

On August 1, 1943, 177 B-24 Liberators took off from airfields around Benghazi, Libya. Their mission, Operation Tidal Wave, ordered an attack on nine oil refineries around Ploieşti, Romania, a city occupied by Germany and a major oil supplier to German forces. Staff Sergeant Arnold Holen was a gunner on *Hells Angels*, one of 37 planes from the 93rd Bomb Group ordered to destroy the refineries and shorten the duration of the war. Unfortunately, nothing went as planned, as the groups became separated in heavily overcast weather.[4, 5]

As the formation approached the refineries, Tidal Wave leader Colonel Compton turned right short of the planned approach point and headed for Bucharest. Colonel Baker, leader of the 93rd, saw the error and turned his plane, *Hell's Wench*, left toward Ploieşti, leading the 93rd into a path over a city heavily defended by German anti-aircraft guns, barrage balloons and fighters. Flying over the treetops, plane after plane was hit by ground fire, killing crewmembers and downing several planes, including Colonel Baker's. Although flak shattered the nose and blasted the waist area of *Hell's Angels*, Pilot 1st Lieutenant Roy Harms did everything he could to reach his target. When the navigator reported to the pilot that they were approaching the turn toward the target, Pilot Harms reported, "It looks rough…but here goes." As they approached the refinery, the radio operator reported that top turret gunner, Staff Sergeant Arnold Holen, had been hit. A blast of flak in the rear of the aircraft killed three other crewmembers and ignited leaking fuel. In a desperate attempt to save his crew, Pilot Harms turned east toward wheat fields and gained a fiery 300-foot climb before the burning plane crashed just east of the Concordia-Vega refineries.[4, 5, 6, 7, 8]

Out of nine crewmen, only one, Jack Reed, survived. He jumped from the plane at 300 feet and remained a POW of the Romanians until his release in 1944. As was the case with many survivors, Reed stated, "I don't know how I made it. I wish I had rode her to the ground and died with the fine men who didn't have the guts to jump." The event never left him and he suffered from nightmares the rest of his life.[9]

Only 88 planes returned to Libya, and of the 1,765 young men, most in their teens and twenties, who flew the "Black Sunday" mission, 446 were killed or missing in action.

Staff Sergeant Arnold Holen is memorialized on the Tablets of the Missing, Florence American Cemetery, Via Cassia, Italy; National Memorial Cemetery of Arizona, Phoenix, Arizona; and Louisburg Lutheran Cemetery, Louisburg, Minnesota. He enlisted in the service December 3, 1941.[11]

Arnold's wife enlisted in the Women's Army Corps on June 29, 1944. In letters dated in 1990, Mary wrote about life after her husband's death and her remarriage to Arthur Holden: *Arny wanted to be an airplane mechanic. I was an airplane mechanic at Travis AFB and rebuilt and installed engines and loved it. I never got over Arny's death, nor could accept it. I joined the WACS, but it didn't help. I went from a bride to a widow in eleven months and because we were 28 days short of our first anniversary, I wasn't able to get a widow's pension. I met Arthur Holden in 1944, and then the war ended. I had no widow's pension, no money, no job, no home, and no family to go to. I respected Arthur a lot, but love was out of the picture. He knew I could never love anyone but Arny. He still wanted to marry, so we did on September 1, 1945. I am a proud mother and I am sure Arny would be proud of me, too. I have worked hard and managed well. It has been a long, hard, lonely life but I have never loved anyone but him.*[1]

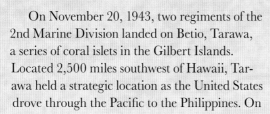

Lawrence Nicklos Mikel

Hillman (Morrison County)

2nd Marine "The Silent Second" Division, 8th Marine Regiment, 3rd Battalion, I Company,
Private First Class

APRIL 25, 1916–NOVEMBER 20, 1943—Battle of Tarawa Atoll, Gilbert Islands

On November 20, 1943, two regiments of the 2nd Marine Division landed on Betio, Tarawa, a series of coral islets in the Gilbert Islands. Located 2,500 miles southwest of Hawaii, Tarawa held a strategic location as the United States drove through the Pacific to the Philippines. On the largest islet, Betio, the Japanese defended their airstrip with 4,700 troops and mines. The 2nd Marine Division was ordered to rout the Japanese off Betio, one of the worst battles in U.S. Marine Corps history.

Many military historians consider the battle for Tarawa as the first amphibious assault where soldiers arrived on shore by Higgins boats and amphibious tractors. Trouble began immediately on November 20, when the assault boats arrived at an unexpectedly low tide, forcing the men to wade in far from shore, and subjecting them to razor-sharp coral and fierce enemy gunfire. Survivors hid in the sand, surrounded by the sea and the Japanese.[1, 2]

Lawrence Mikel's commanding officer, Major Robert H. Ruud, 2nd Battalion, 8th Marines, wrote in his headquarters report: *We were ordered to land on Beach Red 3 to protect the left flank of LT 2-8 and to assist in an attack, which was then under way. Our waves were dispatched by the control vessel at about 1200, and we drew no fire from the beach even when we got to within 400 yards. When we first hit the coral, however, we drew heavy fire, but I believe our casualties were light.*

Reinforcements with tanks and artillery arrived the next morning, and by the end of the day, the marines moved from the beach to inland. After fierce combat for two days, the marines secured Betio. The marine victory came with a high cost: 3,381 dead and wounded, including Lawrence Mikel. Out of 4,836 Japanese defenders, only 17 survived, proving their willingness to fight to the last man.[3, 4]

In his memoir, E.B. Sledge wrote: *There was loud and severe criticism of the Marine Corps by the American public and some military leaders because of the number of casualties. Tarawa became a household word in the United States. It took its rightful place with Valley Forge, the Alamo, Belleau Wood, and Guadalcanal as a symbol of American courage and sacrifice.*[1]

The bodies of 514 marines were never recovered during the Battle of Tarawa, including Private First Class Mikel, and they are officially listed as missing in action. Records show that both men were buried in temporary cemeteries on Tarawa Atoll, only to be lost during later cemetery reorganizations. The men are memorialized on Courts of the Missing, National Memorial Cemetery of the Pacific, Honolulu, Hawaii.[8, 9]

Renee Falk recalled her great uncle Lawrence: *Both of his parents were deceased when World War II occurred. His oldest brother, John Mikel, farmed the "family farm" in Hillman township, Morrison County, Minnesota. After Tarawa was bombed, two military officers visited the family farm and notified John Mikel that his brother was missing in action and presumed drowned in the Pacific Ocean.*[5]

Welver Charles Vaughan

Walters (Faribault County)

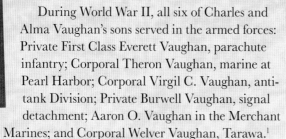

2nd Marine "The Silent Second" Division, 2nd Marine Regiment, 3rd Battalion, L Company, Corporal

FEBRUARY 18, 1918–NOVEMBER 20, 1943—Battle of Tarawa Atoll, Gilbert Islands

During World War II, all six of Charles and Alma Vaughan's sons served in the armed forces: Private First Class Everett Vaughan, parachute infantry; Corporal Theron Vaughan, marine at Pearl Harbor; Corporal Virgil C. Vaughan, anti-tank Division; Private Burwell Vaughan, signal detachment; Aaron O. Vaughan in the Merchant Marines; and Corporal Welver Vaughan, Tarawa.[1]

Welver's only sister, Madeline, now 90 years old, recalls her brother: *I was treated royally by all my brothers. Welver was tall, good-looking and very responsible. He was well liked, had lots of friends and loved to play baseball. He worked on farms in the area before he went into the service. service. We grew up in a big house on a corner lot in Walters with a big garden, an apple orchard and chickens. My dad worked at a filling station and my mother kept house. Sadly, his family disowned my dad, who grew up in a devout Catholic family, when he married my mother, a Lutheran. He carried this grief along with Welver's death throughout his life. Several of Welver's buddies who survived Tarawa wrote to my mother and she derived great comfort from the letters. They wrote that Welver died moving from the boat to the beach. Now, I am asked to submit DNA samples as they try to recover my brother's ashes.* Madeline Vaughan died July 15, 2015, just four months after this interview.[2]

Like Private First Class Mikel, Corporal Vaughan was part of the marine assault on tiny Betio, the largest island in Tarawa Atoll. The Japanese had fortified the two-mile-long and half-mile-wide island with concrete bunkers, barbed wire and mines, the heaviest defenses that America would face in the Pacific. Anti-aircraft guns, machine guns and tanks circled their airstrip, assuring Japanese Admiral Keiji Shibasaki that "the U.S. couldn't take Tarawa with a million men in 100 years."[3]

On November 20, Corporal Vaughan and the 3rd Battalion assaulted Red Beach after the naval bombardment lifted at dawn. An unexpectedly low "neap" tide grounded L Company's Higgins boats on coral reefs that were exposed or too shallow to clear with landing craft. This left men and equipment stranded well offshore, forcing the men to wade in through heavy and accurate enemy fire.[4] Those who made it ashore crawled across a beach littered with broken equipment and bodies. At the end of the first day,

1,500 of the 5,000 marines in the initial assault died, including Corporal Welver Vaughan.[3,4]

Corporal Welver Vaughan's commanding officer, Major Michael P. Ryan, wrote: *We landed on the coral to the left of the small ship on the reef, disembarked, and headed in. I was in Battalion Reserve, Company "L", which came in slowly and very disorganized. As soon as my company came in, we moved in behind Company "I." Men were still coming in in driblets. Two medium tanks got in over the reef, and the Engineers blasted a hole in the sea wall for them to come through. We put two companies abreast, took two medium tanks, but the two tanks were knocked out. It was then about 1630. We could not find a radio in communication with Division and later found the Second Battalion's.*[5]

On November 22, while the Marines advanced toward the airport and destroyed many fortifications, the Japanese launched a hopeless banzai charge. By the next morning, 17 Japanese soldiers remained alive. In 76 hours of battle on Tarawa, the Marines lost almost as many men as U.S. troops lost in 6 months in Guadalcanal.[3,4]

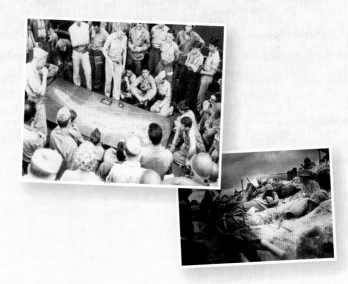

Harold Victor Terho

U.S. Army Air Forces, 12th Air Force, 57th Bomb Wing, 321st Medium Bomb Group, 448th Bomb Squadron, Staff Sergeant

AUGUST 31, 1921–DECEMBER 2, 1943—Bombing Mission over Chieti, Italy

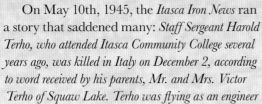

On May 10th, 1945, the *Itasca Iron News* ran a story that saddened many: *Staff Sergeant Harold Terho, who attended Itasca Community College several years ago, was killed in Italy on December 2, according to word received by his parents, Mr. and Mrs. Victor Terho of Squaw Lake. Terho was flying as an engineer gunner on the lead plane of a squadron over a bombing target in central Italy when his plane received a direct hit from enemy anti-aircraft, which set it afire. He had flown 16 missions and had been awarded the Air Medal with one Oak Leaf Cluster. He was posthumously awarded the Purple Heart.*[1,2]

Activated on June 29, 1942, and assigned to the 12th Air Force, the 321st Bomb Group trained on B-25s for duty in the Mediterranean theater. Strategic operations they carried out included bombing rail lines, highways, bridges, viaducts, and shipping harbors in North Africa, France, Sicily, Italy, Bulgaria, Yugoslavia and Greece.[3]

Harold Terho enlisted on July 18, 1942, and was shipped overseas to Africa on May 30, 1943, along with the 321st Bomb Group. In October, he transferred to Grottaglie, in southern Italy. His last mission was on December 2, 1943, when 23 B-25s left from Grottaglie to bomb a road bridge northwest of Chieti, Italy. Harold Terho was the mission's engineer/gunner when heavy flak hit their plane and the plane exploded.[3,4,5]

An eyewitness account by Pilot William Joli recalled the crash: *On the 2nd of December, 1943, during a combat mission in which our objective was a road bridge at Chieti, I observed the following—my position in the formation was 1st flight, 1st Element, number 3 ship, placing me on the left wing of ship #41-30326 (Terho's plane). At approximately 930, just before our point of release, ship # 41-30326 suddenly burst into a great sheet of flames. It held its position momentarily and then veered off towards me. In order to avoid a collision it was necessary for me to pull my ship up sharply. The ship then passed underneath me, and the heat from it was felt in my ship. The stricken ship was last seen in a steep diving turn enveloped in flames. Evidently the ship received a direct hit in its left wing gas tanks, spreading ignited gas over the entire ship and surrounding air. There was a small concussion from the exploding gasoline, but no parts were seen to disintegrate from the ship. From what I observed, it is my opinion that it was impossible for any of the members to escape because of the intense heat, and the attitude of the ship when last seen.*[5]

Pilot Joli was wrong. Both Pilot Paul Clark and Co-pilot James Bates escaped through the top hatch, parachuted to safety, and were captured by the Germans. Major Bates later wrote in the casualty report: *The plane was wildly spinning to earth and we each experienced difficulty leaving through the top hatch.* The navigator, 2nd Lieutenant Richard Abbe, also jumped from the plane but died when his parachute caught fire. During interrogation in a German hospital, German officials told Clark and Bates that Lieutenant Abbe's body was found with a burned parachute near the plane, and that the rest of the crew died in the crash.[3,5]

On December 2, 1943, the 321st Bomb Group War Diary states: *The first mission of the month was flown today, our planes taking off to bomb the road bridge northwest Chieti about 25 miles north of the front lines. The formation was scattered due to the lead ship being hit by flak just before the target. The east approach was believed to have been hit. Two of our planes failed to return from this mission; both were shot down by flak at the target. Major Bates was pilot of the lead ship, which was shot down and Lieutenant Clark was his co-pilot with Captain Brown, group bombardier, as bombardier. The loss of these men is deeply felt throughout the Group. It will be difficult to replace them. A second mission was flown today against the road bridge at Chieti with better results. The east approach was hit and direct hits were made on the road to the west of the bridge. Numerous near misses were made on the bridge itself.*[3]

Italian peasants buried Staff Sergeant Harold Terho in a field in Chieti. Later, he was moved to the U.S. National Cemetery at Bari, Italy. In 1944, Harold Terho was reinterred in Squaw Lake Cemetery where his final reburial service was held.

Just seven months earlier, Staff Sergeant Terho's cousin, Einar Suomi (page 24), was shot down on a bombing mission over the English Channel off the central coast of France.

Peter Anthony Chernich, Jr.

U.S. Coast Guard, USS *Samuel Tilden, Merchant Marine, 3rd Engineer*
MAY 27, 1912–DECEMBER 2, 1943—Air Raid at Bari, Italy

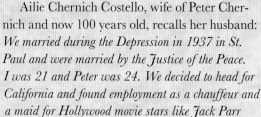

Ailie Chernich Costello, wife of Peter Chernich and now 100 years old, recalls her husband: *We married during the Depression in 1937 in St. Paul and were married by the Justice of the Peace. I was 21 and Peter was 24. We decided to head for California and found employment as a chauffeur and a maid for Hollywood movie stars like Jack Parr and Edward G. Robinson. We lived in San Francisco when Peter joined the Merchant Marine in 1943. Peter was colorblind, so other branches of the military wouldn't take him. After Peter died, I wrote to the War Department to find out if there were any survivors on the ship and they sent me five names. The closest man, Severn Koscal, lived in Chicago, so I traveled to see him. He was just out of the hospital recovering from severe burns from swimming in burning oil-covered water. He drew me a picture of the ship and told me what happened that night. He said all men below never came out alive, and that's how I knew Peter was never coming back. I thought he would come back someday. The letters were censored, and I didn't know if he would be home for Christmas, so I put up a big Christmas tree. Peter wanted a case of Scotch as a gift, but I could only buy a quart in wartime. I wrapped it in pink tissue paper and have it to this day. I wanted to join the American Legion Auxiliary in Cromwell/Wright, but they wouldn't accept me because the Merchant Marine was not considered part of the military. I did not receive a widow's pension.*[1]

After a long delay, Ailie Chernich learned that one of the worst bombing attacks against Allied ships during World War II occurred at Bari, Italy, on December 2, 1943. On that day, called the Pearl Harbor of the Atlantic, the Adriatic Sea port at Bari harbored 30 Allied ships unloading aviation fuel and other supplies for the Allied drive to Rome.

Merchant Marine Peter Chernich, 3rd Engineer, assigned to the Liberty steamship, *Samuel Tilden*, which bore essential medical supplies, beds, and X-ray equipment for the 26th General Hospital, which was set to open in an older Italian hospital building in Bari.[2] Along with other ships, the men unloaded cargo along the brightly lit harbor, unaware that German reconnaissance had spotted the operations earlier in the day, and that the supplies would never make it to the hospital.

The harbor had not been subject to air raids, so when 105 Ju-88 German bombers flew in under the radar, it took everyone by complete surprise.

The raid took out 17 ships from 7 different countries, most cargo and Liberty ships like the *Samuel Tilden*. The *Samuel Tilden* remained illuminated by a shore crane nine minutes into the attack, and a bomb scored a direct hit on her engine room and cargo of fuel drums on deck. Ten of her crew, including Chernich, died in the inferno. A burning oil slick spread over the harbor, incinerating some ships that had escaped the bombing, and further complicating rescue of the sailors blown into the water.

The SS *John Harvey* carried a secret load of 100 one-ton mustard gas bombs, which the Americans brought over in fear that the Germans, in desperation over their losses on the battlefields, might resort to chemical warfare. When the ship exploded, it sent a cloud of mustard gas all over the harbor. The hour-long attack killed more than 2,000 people, half of them civilians, and destroyed 35,000 tons of cargo.[3,4,5,6,7,8] The 26th General Hospital, scrounging up beds and a meager store of medical supplies from Italians and other sources, opened on an emergency basis December 4.[2]

Mary Satterwhite recalls her Uncle Peter: *Aunt Ailie, Peter's wife, was in contact with families who were involved with the attacks in Bari, Italy. She discovered that on the night Peter died, he was due to have shore leave but stayed on the ship. When the British turned the lights on, the ships were sitting ducks for the bombing. One of the sailors saw Peter go below deck during the attack but he was never seen again after that. My father told me that Peter's eyesight prevented him from joining the army or navy and he ended up in the Merchant Marine.*[9]

Merchant Mariner Peter Chernich is memorialized on the Tablets of the Missing at East Coast Memorial at Battery Park, New York. The East Coast Memorial, which faces the Statue of Liberty across the New York Harbor, honors the 4,601 missing American servicemen who lost their lives in the Atlantic Ocean during combat in World War II. Men of the Merchant Marine suffered the highest casualty rate of any branch of the armed services but were denied veterans benefits until 1988.[3]

Leighton Keith Zeiner

U.S. Army Air Forces, 8th Air Force, 94th Combat Wing, 351st Bomb Group, 510th Bomb Squadron, 2nd Lieutenant

MAY 1, 1917–DECEMBER 30, 1943—Crash Landing at Hawkinge, England

After graduation from Brewster High School in 1934 and two years at Hibbing Community College, Leighton Zeiner joined the coast artillery in January 1940, a year before the Selective Service Act authorized the draft. He trained at Camp Haan, California, and in August, transferred to Kodiak, Alaska. In December 1942, Leighton returned to California and entered the Army Air Corps for training in aerial navigation at Santa Ana Army Air Base and Mather Field.[1]

On April 15, 1943, 2nd Lieutenant Zeiner and the 351st Bomb Group arrived at Royal Air Force Station Polebrook in England to begin service with the 8th Air Force. Only one month later on May 14, their first combat mission with 18 B-17s successfully targeted a German Luftwaffe airfield at Kortrijk, Belgium. As the war progressed, the 351st Bomb Group struck other strategic sites in Germany, including tank factories, oil refineries, armaments factories and ball bearing plants. The unit received a Distinguished Unit Citation for October 1943, for accurately bombing an aircraft factory in Germany despite heavy flak and enemy fighters.

From November 29 to December 30, 2nd Lieutenant Leighton Zeiner and his crew flew five bombing missions to Bremen, one to Solingen and two to Emden, Germany. Zeiner's final mission took place on December 30, 1943, during a bomb run against the I.G. Farben Chemical and Explosive Factory at Ludwigshafen, Germany. The aircraft, hit by flak, lost its #3 engine, and then took a second hit over Frankfurt. They left the formation, and the Royal Air Force escorted the aircraft to its base at Hawkinge, where the plane crashed on landing.[2,3,6]

The *Worthington Globe* published this report: *Lieutenant Leighton K. Zeiner, son of E.C. Zeiner, Kinbrae, was one of five crew men of the Fortress Little Twink who were killed when the big bomber crashed near a U.S. base in England while returning from a New Year's Eve raid against southern Germany.*

The windmilling propeller on a shot-out motor set the ship afire at 3,000 feet. Pilot Joseph Adamiak, Holyoke, Mass., told the crew to bail out as the plane went into a dive. Seven men went out. But as the last five jumped, the ship was so close to the ground that their chutes did not have time to open. They were killed, among them the Kinbrae officer, navigator on the ill-fated flight.

Had these five remained with the falling ship, they would probably be alive today. The Associated Press *report today from England said the last three left aboard got out all right after the plane crashed through the treetops, ripped out telephone wires and skidded to a stop in a field.*[4,6]

Lieutenant Zeiner visited his father at Kinbrae last September, just after completing his course at the base at Ephrata, Wash.

Survivors included his parents, Emil and Irene (Parslow) Zeiner, and a sister, Marjorie Jean (Alfred) Block. His mother, Private Irene Zeiner, joined the Army Air Corps at age 49 and was stationed at Drew Field. 2nd Lieutenant Leighton Zeiner is buried in Cambridge American Cemetery, England. A member of the Brewster Presbyterian Church, he wrote in a letter: *"I haven't missed church yet."*[1,4,5]

More than 7,000 U.S. Army Air Forces personnel served at Polebrook during the war. One of the servicemen, famous Hollywood actor Captain Clark Gable, spent most of the war in England at Polebrook with the 351st Bomb Group. He flew five combat missions while filming footage for the movie *Combat America,* a recruiting film for aircraft gunners.

Ben Santjer

Fifth Army, 6th Armored Infantry, 1108th Combat Regiment, 48th Engineer Combat Battalion, C Company, Technician Fifth Grade
DECEMBER 15, 1919–JANUARY 7, 1944—Attack on Mount Porchia, Italy

Sena Santjer Knowles, 91 years old, recalls the memory of her brother: *Ben was a farmer's son. Our dad had a 320-acre farm. He was a caring and loving brother, and did his chores just like the rest of us. We had ten horses, cattle, sheep and chickens. We went to Bejou Christian Reformed Church (Calvinist), which was 5 ½ miles from our farm home. When he was small, Ben walked a mile to school. In 1932 Ben and his sister went by bus to the Bejou Consolidated School District. He graduated from the 8th grade but did not go to high school. He worked on the farm at home until he was called to serve his country. Ben left for the Army September 24, 1942, on a cold snowy afternoon. I remember we were filling our 45-foot silo at that time. He was five years older than me. My brother had a bayonet medal and a rifle medal, too. He also got a Purple Heart. Ben was with the 48th Engineers. Blessed be his memory. I loved him.*[1]

Following his enlistment in the army, Ben Santjer trained at Camp Wolters, Texas. In December, he transferred to Camp Gruber, Oklahoma, and made his last visit home in June 1943 before heading overseas. The Allies secured the North African Campaign on May 13, 1943, and invaded Sicily on July 10. By the time Ben Santjer and the 48th Engineer Combat Battalion arrived at Bagnoli, Italy, in the Bay of Naples on October 10, 1943, the Allies had captured Sicily and were heading for Rome. Assigned to the Fifth Army with Lieutenant Colonel Andrew J. Goodpaster in command, each battalion of the 1108th Combat Regiment held 32 officers and 640 enlisted men. Their dangerous work involved maintaining roads, clearing enemy mines, and repairing and building bridges.[2,3]

In December 1943, Ben Santjer and the 48th Engineers were assigned their most difficult task: to convert the railroad bed from Mignano to Mount Lungo, Italy, into a two-lane highway to allow two-way military vehicle traffic. They had just six days to complete the road. The Germans controlled this stretch of railroad, running into Cassino along a high embankment parallel to Highway 6, and they had completely plowed up and destroyed the existing rails, sprinkling mines everywhere. As the 48th worked with heavy equipment, the enemy subjected the men to constant shelling and strafing, and lurking German patrols in the area. Despite everything, they completed the new "Highway 48" in time.

On January 6, 1944, Lieutenant Colonel Andrew Goodpaster, Commander of the 48th Engineers, received orders that his battalion be attached to the 6th Armored Infantry to assist in securing Mt. Porchia. The Commander replied that he was *sorry he must commit the 48th engineers as infantry because they are the best damned engineers he has seen.* Halfway between Mignano and Cassino, Mt. Porcia overlooks Highway 6 and the railroad, the highest terrain in the valley except for Mt. Trocchio. The Germans used this natural fortress to rain down artillery fire on the Allies, and the attack on Mt. Porchia bogged down as infantry casualties climbed.

Called on as reinforcements, the engineers ended up in the heart of a bloody infantry advance against German machine guns and mortars. As they neared German positions they encountered small arms and machine gun fire, and Germans hurled potato mashers (stick grenades) at them. Lieutenant Thomas said, "They threw at least 25 of them at us and then let loose with machine pistols. The bullets came over like a flame of fire."[2,3,4]

The regimental history stated: *Technician Santjer dodged through the rocks in a flurry of bullets that twice wounded him. He crouched behind shelter, got a good shot at a German, saw him fall, and then dodged away." As they neared the crest, the fighting became confused as both sides fought desperately to hold on. Santjer bayoneted another German, shot two more, then as he rose, a German with a burp gun stood up and hit him point blank with automatic fire.*[2,5]

Ben Santjer and four other men were honored for their heroism on Porchia; Santjer received the Distinguished Service Cross, the second-highest award given by the U.S. Army for extreme gallantry and risk of life in combat with the enemy. The citation read in part, *Technician Fifth Grade Santjer's intrepid actions, personal bravery and zealous devotion to duty at the cost of his life, exemplify the highest traditions of the military forces of the United States and reflect great credit upon himself, his unit, and the United States Army.*[6]

Following services in the Bejou Christian Reformed Church, Ben Santjer was buried in Bejou Cemetery, Bejou, Minnesota.[7,8]

Harold Mittelstadt Meyer

Nassau (Lac Qui Parle County)

Fifth Army, 34th Infantry "Red Bull" Division, 135th Infantry Regiment, 3rd Battalion, I Company, Sergeant

JUNE 8, 1920–FEBRUARY 4, 1944—Battle of Monte Cassino, Italy

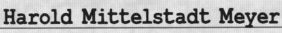

The 34th Infantry "Red Bull" Division, composed of men from Iowa, Minnesota, North Dakota and South Dakota, was the first American division to deploy overseas in World War II. In 1941, Harold Meyer joined I Company at the induction center in Madison, Minnesota, and trained at Camp Claiborne, Louisiana. The Minnesota Military Museum reports that just five weeks after Pearl Harbor, the division secretly shipped out for Belfast, Ireland, aboard HMTS *Straithard*. Meanwhile in Great Britain, newspapers announced the arrival of the first American, Private Milburn Henke from Hutchinson, Minnesota.

In Belfast, the 34th Division prepared for the invasion of North Africa, the first major Allied offensive in the war. The 135th boarded the HMS *Sheffield* for the port of Algiers and landed on November 8 to face German artillery and machine gun fire. Over the next six months the Allies seized the port of Algiers, secured Tunisia and finished Germany in North Africa. Now the 34th Division began to prepare for the invasion of Italy.

After an Allied victory in Sicily in August 1943, Sergeant Harold Meyer and the 34th Infantry landed at Solerno on September 21 and began the push north to Cassino and Rome. Rugged mountain ranges, heavy rains and determined German resistance combined for slow Allied progress. In late 1943, the Allies broke through the Volturno Line, a German defensive line on the Volturno River, and now faced the Gustav Line, another chain of German defenses, which spanned the Italian peninsula above Naples.[1, 2, 3]

After a rest to recover from trench foot and fighting, the 34th Division prepared to attack the Gustav Line on a bitterly cold New Year's Day. On January 4, during a night of house-to-house fighting, Sergeant Meyer and the 3rd Battalion cleared St. Vittore on their advance to Rome. At the center of the line, blocking the road to Rome, lay the town of Cassino, towered over by Monte Cassino, a mountain with a 1,400-year-old Benedictine abbey. Both the Germans and Allies promised the Vatican that the abbey would be spared as a military position. In preparation for the attack on Cassino on January 26, the 135th Regiment placed an anti-tank gun in the second story of a house to contain the enemy while the 168th Infantry crossed the Rapido River. A week later, the 135th, concealed by heavy fog, surprised the enemy and cut off

Highway 6, the main road running from Cassino to Rome.[2]

As Allied troops advanced toward Cassino, they endured constant fire from artillery, mortar and Nebelwerfer (artillery used to fire high-explosives). By now, the men were convinced that the Germans used the abbey on Monte Cassino to watch their every move. On the day Harold Meyer died, the 135th Regiment, less than 1,000 meters from the monastery, could not take control from the Germans.[2, 3, 4, 5] Don Weigel recalls: *Harold Meyer was my mother's cousin. I remember my mom telling me when he was killed in World War II. He and his squad were in a foxhole and were out of water. He volunteered to try and get water for the men. That was when he was killed.* The 3rd Battalion alone lost 165 men in 4 days, including Sergeant Harold Meyer.[6]

In the end, the Benedictine abbey was a casualty of war, too. On February 15, 1944, despite misgivings about its military necessity, General Mark Clark ordered Allied bombers to bomb the abbey. This completely destroyed the abbey, though its library and artwork were saved prior to its destruction.

The Battle for Monte Cassino continued until May 16, when General Albert Kesselring ordered his troops to withdraw. The price was high: the 34th Infantry Division lost 2,200 men, 80 percent of their division. Allied casualties totaled 55,000 and German casualties topped 20,000. But the battle for Monte Cassino opened the road to Rome and marked the beginning of the end for Germany in Italy.[2, 3, 8]

Sergeant Harold Meyer, the only child of Ernest and Mathilda (Mittelstadt) Meyer, is buried in Fort Snelling. The Nassau American Legion Meyer-Thompson Post 536 is named in honor of Sergeant Harold Meyer and Sergeant Clifford Thompson (page 140), who died on April 16, 1945, in Germany.[7]

The monks rebuilt Monte Cassino Abbey after the war ended and two cemeteries surround the abbey—the Monte Cassino Polish cemetery to the north, and the Cassino War Cemetery to the south. Many of soldiers buried there died fighting for control of the Abbey.[3, 8]

Lloyd K. Nicholas

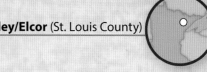

U.S. Navy Air Force, USS Enterprise, Torpedo Squadron 10, Lieutenant
JANUARY 18, 1917–FEBRUARY 4, 1942—Battle of the Flores Sea, Indonesia

After graduating from Gilbert High School and Eveleth Junior College, Lloyd Nicholas completed one year at the Minneapolis School of Art (now the College of Art and Design). In 1942, Lloyd enlisted in the Navy Air Forces and joined the Torpedo Bomber Fighting Unit. Elizabeth Nicholas Johnson remembers her brother: *He was an artist and went to art school. Lloyd aspired to belong to the Navy Air Corps as he believed that they were the top of the rung. He was laid back and self contained, never pushy. We all looked up to him.*[1, 7]

During World War II, the Japanese occupied Truk Lagoon, a base located north of New Guinea with a full complement of airstrips and support for Japan's massive naval fleet. Once the American forces captured the Marshall Islands, they ordered carrier-based planes, including Lloyd Nicholas's Torpedo Squadron 10, to launch a night attack on February 16 and 17, 1944, against Japanese shipping in the lagoon. At 0410, 12 Grumman Avengers, including one piloted by Lieutenant Lloyd Nicholas, launched from the USS *Enterprise* for a night low-altitude bombing attack led by Lieutenant Van Eason. Each aircraft carried four 500-lb. bombs and used radar to release their bombs at 250 feet. That night, 13 of the 48 bombs dropped from VT-10 sank two oilers and six cargo ships, and damaged another six cargo ships.[2] Only one aircraft, flown by Lieutenant Lloyd Nicholas on his second mission, and his two crewmembers, Len Thornton and Wilbert Docktor, did not return from the attack. The cause of the loss is unknown, and the aircraft and crew were never found.[3]

Lieutenant Lloyd Nicholas was awarded the Distinguished Flying Cross: *For heroism and extraordinary achievement in aerial flight as pilot of a torpedo bomber during a vigorous attack on enemy shipping inside the Lagoon at Truk Atoll on February 17, 1944. Launched from his carrier to participate in an extremely hazardous night bombing mission, Lieutenant Nicholas pressed home his attacks at perilously low altitude relentlessly pounding the enemy's ships in the darkness despite intense, persistent anti-aircraft fire. His superb airmanship and indomitable fighting spirit maintained at great personal risk, contributed in large measure to the destruction and damage of an important number of Japanese ships and were in keeping with the highest traditions of the USNR.*[4, 5]

Following the successful strike, LCDR Bill Martin stated, "VT-10 specialized in night radar search and attack and specifically requested this mission. I believe that this was the first time our carrier forces launched a night, minimum altitude bombing strike."[2]

At the end of the mission, more than 45 Japanese ships and 270 planes lay at the bottom of the lagoon, making Truk the biggest ship graveyard in the world. The attack ended Truk as a major threat in the central Pacific and made it possible for the Allies to continue advancing toward Japan.[2, 6]

Lloyd K. Nicholas is memorialized at the Manila American Cemetery, Fort Bonifacio, Manila, Philippines. Prior to his enlistment in the navy, Lloyd Nicholas worked for the *Virginia Daily Enterprise* as a correspondent from Gilbert, Minnesota. His father, who was born in England, worked as a foreman in the mines and later, when the mines closed, he assumed the duties of a night patrolman. In all, four men from Elcor lost their lives in World War II: Robert Brady (page 95), Rudolph Indihar (page 55), LeRoy Veralrud (page 74) and Lloyd Nicholas.[5, 7]

Morris John Olson

U.S. Navy, VB-110/Navy Fleet Air Wing 7, Seaman Second Class
FEBRUARY 8, 1923–FEBRUARY 27, 1944—Air Crash over Skellig Michael, Ireland

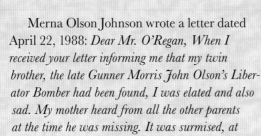

Merna Olson Johnson wrote a letter dated April 22, 1988: *Dear Mr. O'Regan, When I received your letter informing me that my twin brother, the late Gunner Morris John Olson's Liberator Bomber had been found, I was elated and also sad. My mother heard from all the other parents at the time he was missing. It was surmised, at that time, that the plane crashed at the "Great Skellig Rock," as the light keeper saw a plane crash and Morris' plane was in that area patrolling for German submarines. His best friend, Earl Inman from Kentucky, wrote to me and said it was a very stormy night, visibility very bad, but they had to go out anyway. He said, "We get very close over here, these are very difficult times." I corresponded with him for a few months and then did not hear anymore so he possibly was killed in the war, also.*[1, 2]

Skellig Michael is a island that rises 700 feet high from the Atlantic Ocean, located 6 miles off the coast of County Kerry in southwest Ireland. Home to a monastery that was literally carved out of rock during the seventh or eighth century and occupied until the twelfth century, it's now a world-famous site.

On February 27, 1944, Seaman Second Class Morris Olson and ten other crewmembers left Dunkeswell Airfield in Devon, England, for an anti-German submarine patrol when their Liberator aircraft struck the highest point of Skellig Michael at 1:03 a.m. The rock had appeared to be a submarine on their radar. When the aviation fuel and ammunition on board exploded, a lighthouse keeper on Skellig saw the aircraft burst into flames and sink into the sea. Deep water and thick fog hampered the search for the plane, and no survivors were found.[3]

Then in 1989, Gerard O'Regan from Cork, Ireland, heard the story of the missing plane and crew and launched an investigation. He started a nonprofit organization, which researches wartime plane crashes in that area and arranges memorial visits for family and friends. Irish military archives recorded that the day after the crash, a lightkeeper climbed to the highest point of the Skellig and discovered a long streak of white paint on the rock. Later that day, he plucked a lifejacket from the water with the wording "VPB-110." Using the information, Mr. O'Regan contacted the U.S. military for information. He tracked down Morris Olson's sister, Merna Johnson, by

sending a letter to *The next of kin of S2c M.J. Olson, United States Reserve (RIP) 1st known address RR@ Deer River.* O'Regan personally contacted the members of all 11 crew and in 1990, 33 relatives and friends attended a private memorial service on the north side of Great Skellig rock. Morris Olson's three sisters, Gladys, Viola and Merna; two brothers-in-law; Donald Johnson and Harry Scofield; a nephew, Harry Scofield; and a niece, Carolyn O'Brien, and her husband, Robert O'Brien, all attended the service. A lone piper played the haunting, "Abide With Me." Morris John Olson is memorialized at American Cemetery, Cambridge, England.[1, 2, 3, 4, 5, 6]

Merna Olson Johnson continues in her letter: *Morris and I shared our 21st birthday on the 8th of February, 1944, and we received the telegram that my twin brother was missing on the 29th of February, 1944. I will never forget the day we received the telegram. I was staying at their farm in rural Deer River as my husband was at Guadalcanal. My brother, Randy, and I went to Deer River the day the telegram came. Everyone in town knew Morris was missing when we got to town and I was given the job of bringing this telegram to my folks. I will never forget the look on my mom's face when I handed her the telegram–Dad was in the hospital at the time. She never really did get over it because she did not know for sure where her son met his death. A year later, Morris was declared dead and all his personal belongings were sent home, even his hammock. Also, some V-mail letters he had started to my mother and me. I still have his Navy blanket.*[1]

Skellig Michael is immortalized forever in the last scene of the movie *Star Wars: The Force Awakens*, released in December 2015. As you watch Rey ascend the stone steps to pass the light saber to Luke Skywalker, you can imagine the monks ascending the rock centuries ago.

Alvin George Probasco

Fifth Army, 3rd Infantry "Rock of the Marne" Division, 751st Tank Battalion, 1st Battalion, D Company, Technician Fifth Grade

MAY 3, 1920–FEBRUARY 29, 1944—Battle of Anzio, Italy

When President Franklin Roosevelt and Prime Minister Winston Churchill decided to invade North Africa, their army chiefs selected the renowned 3rd Division to land in French Morocco and capture Casablanca. The 3rd Division's reputation in World War I preceded them. Along the Marne River in 1918, the 3rd held their ground while two German divisions attacked from three sides. When the 3rd forced the enemy to retreat and saved Paris from attack, they earned the name "Rock of the Marne" Division.[1, 2, 3, 4]

Alvin Probasco enlisted in the army in Los Angeles, California, on December 3, 1941, four days before the attack on Pearl Harbor, and joined the 3rd Infantry Division, 751st Tank Battalion. He left for overseas duty in the fall of 1942, moving from Africa to Sicily to mainland Italy.[5] On November 25, 1943, the day before Thanksgiving, Alvin wrote to his brother Dan: *Received your most welcome letter a few days ago and sure was glad to hear from you. This letter leaves me just fine and hope everyone there is OK. I'm also very thankful today too. How about you? I'm glad you and mother live close enough so as to read the letters like you do. Boy, I bet that rifle will do the trick, won't it? Write and tell me how many deer you shot with it. We had chicken for dinner today and I think steak tonight. Boy oh boy, do I fill myself. Sometime tomorrow we will have our turkey and then I will fill myself again. You wrote a very good letter, Dan. Do it more often. All my love, your brother, Alvin* [6]

Two months later on January 22, 1944, Technician Probasco landed south of Anzio where 36,000 Allied troops began the Battle of Anzio, codenamed Operation Shingle. Commanded by Major General John P. Lucas, the Allies planned to break through Germany's Winter Line and attack Rome. After securing the Anzio beachhead 2–3 miles deep, the 3rd Infantry attacked the town of Cisterna on January 30, while the British moved toward Campoleone. Both regiments failed to take Cisterna.

By February 3, German forces outnumbered the Allied forces, over 100,000 men to 76,400, and the Allies moved back to defend the beachhead. Frustrated by the lack of success, General Mark Clark replaced General Lucas with General Lucian Truscott. Once again, the Allies made a move toward the Winter Line near Cisterna on February 29, where three German divisions waited for them.[1, 2, 3, 4] According to a daily report by the 751st Headquarters Company, when Alvin Probasco and D Company, in support of the 509th Parachute Infantry, moved their tanks toward the German line near Cisterna, German Mark VI Tiger tanks knocked out two American tanks, killing Probasco and two other men. Several other men were wounded. The "medium" tanks of D Company could not stand up to the larger and more powerful German tanks.[5]

Under constant artillery bombardment and making little headway, General Truscott suspended operations until spring, when American forces led by General Clark captured Rome on June 5, 1944.[1, 2, 3, 4]

Alvin Probasco's family moved from Nebraska to Hillman, Minnesota, by covered wagon shortly after his parents, Roy and Margaret (Wood) Probasco were married in 1904.

When the War Department requested a burial site, overseas or stateside, for Alvin Probasco, his father, Roy, expressed the family's strong faith in a handwritten letter: *We are Protestants and wish the service to be of our faith. We do not know where would be the best cemetery so we wish the Government to decide that and then let us know. The one where he lies now is a beautiful place and if it's kept as a permanent military cemetery, it would be alright with us to leave it as it now is. When the dead in Christ are raised, he can be raised again over there just as well as here. Thanks for your interest.* Alvin Probasco is buried at the Sicily-Rome American Cemetery, Nettuno, Italy.[7]

Robert Leslie Harju

Wolf Lake (Becker County)

Fifth Army, 3rd Infantry Division, 30th Infantry Regiment, 3rd Battalion, I Company, Staff Sergeant

AUGUST 12, 1919–MARCH 8, 1944—Operation Shingle, Italy

Robert Harju's sister, Olga Maki, 98 years old, recalls her brother: *Bobby was a homebody, a good guy who worked on the farm and was always smiling. He liked to ski and skate and loved jokes and stories. Even though he had the chance, Bobby never came home on furlough even when his motorcycle hit a mine and he was injured. When he enlisted, he said that he would stay until the job was done. What I remember most about the war is waiting for a letter from Bobby. My brothers, Bennie and Tom, were also in the war and times were really tough.*[1]

One of the first men to enlist from his township, Staff Sergeant Harju joined the army on October 19, 1940. He trained at Fort Lewis, Washington, Fort Ord, California, and the Presidio of San Francisco, both training centers for the 3rd Infantry Division. By the end of 1943, Germany occupied most of Europe and the Allies experienced high casualties against well-trained German forces. Desperate to break through the German-controlled Mediterranean, the Allies landed 6 divisions with 36,000 American, British and French troops at Anzio, an obscure fishing port 30 miles south of Rome. The 3rd Division, with Staff Sergeant Robert Harju, landed on Anzio beach on January 22, 1944. Operation Shingle's goals were to secure the Anzio beachhead, advance north to capture Rome and push the Germans back to their homeland.

Once on the Anzio beachhead, the Allies took German troops by surprise but lost their momentum when General Lucas ordered the units to stop the advance. On January 29, Robert Harju, with the leading 3rd Battalion, moved at night to Cisterna di Loretta, fighting until January 31, when Germans overwhelmed their attack. However, on February 16, when the Herman Göring Division fought to reach the beachhead, fresh American reinforcements stopped them. By March 3, Staff Robert Harju and the 30th Infantry Regiment secured the beachhead and the battle ground to a halt. During April, May and June, a constant barrage of air and ground artillery, including shelling from "Anzio Annie," a German railway gun, injured and killed many men.[2, 3]

On March 8, 1944, Staff Sergeant Robert Harju led a patrol mission north of Carano, Italy, and failed to return. He was missing in action until the family received a letter dated January 6, 1947, stating that his remains were identified and that he was buried in the Sicily-Rome American Cemetery, Nettuno, Italy.[4]

Robert's father operated a dairy farm near Wolf Lake and his grandfather built Harju House, an inn for travelers in the early years of the township's history. The son of Finnish immigrants, Robert and his family loved to dance and frequently attended dances in Wolf Lake. Neighbors frequently gathered for weekly saunas followed by tea and Finnish flatbread.[5, 6, 7]

Robert Dean Kanne

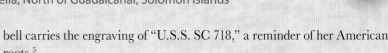

U.S. Navy, USS SC-700 (Submarine Chaser), Fireman Second Class
DECEMBER 28, 1924–MARCH 12, 1944—Vella Lavella, North of Guadalcanal, Solomon Islands

At the outset of World War II, German U-boats sank merchant vessels with thousands of tons of cargo throughout the Atlantic. Something had to be done quickly to stop the submarines, because in the summer of 1942, U-boats sank more ships and took more lives than the Japanese at Pearl Harbor. The U.S. Navy subsequently designed 110-foot, wooden-hulled boats to stop the German U-boat threat along the Atlantic. Agile and well-armed, over 40,000 men served on subchasers, the smallest commissioned warships of the U.S. Navy in World War II.[1]

The subchasers earned their workhorse reputation by performing a wide range of tasks as ships' escorts, search and rescue missions for downed airmen, and attacks on enemy submarines and barges.[2] Three chasers with Norwegian crews, "The Shetland Bus," ferried both civilians and armed forces in and out of Norway.[5]

By the time Robert Kanne enlisted in the navy on July 22, 1943, the navy mainly used subchasers to escort convoys and patrol harbors for submarines, as larger destroyers and destroyer escorts maintained the first line of defense.[1] During March 1944, Robert Kanne was stationed with his subchaser on Vella Lavella, an island north of Guadalcanal. Lois Kanne, who married Robert's brother, recalls the day that Robert's ship was sunk from shore gunfire: *Robert's parents received a letter from the chaplain who stayed with Robert in the hospital on the day that he died. On March 10, 1944, in Guadalcanal, Robert was tending his subchaser as the ship refueled from a tanker offshore. Most of the men had left the ship for liberty onshore and Robert was left to watch the fueling process. All the ships were roped together for fueling when the ship caught fire. While cutting the ropes, he caught fire and dove into the water. Two days later, Robert died in the hospital from severe burns.*[3, 4]

Only a handful of subchasers have survived through the years. But in 1981, the director of the Royal Norwegian Navy Museum discovered a photo of the downed *Hitra*, one of three subchasers loaned to Norway, submerged in a Swedish ships' graveyard.

Now fully restored to its former glory, the *Hitra*, based in Bergen, Norway, is used for exhibits, reunions and educational purposes. Her ship's bell carries the engraving of "U.S.S. SC 718," a reminder of her American roots.[5]

Robert Kanne is buried in Big Fork Cemetery, Big Fork, Minnesota. Survivors included his parents, Earl and Nora (Engebretson) Kanne and a brother, Captain Earl (Lois) Kanne, M.D.

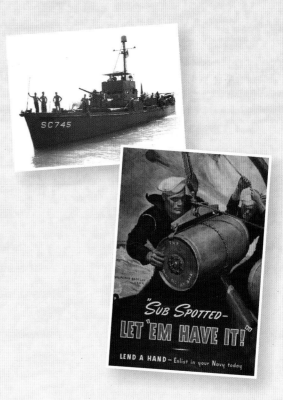

Waldo Lue Engholm

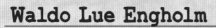

Evan (Brown County)

Fifth Army, 3rd Infantry "Rock of the Marne" Division, 3rd Quartermaster Corps, Private First Class
NOVEMBER 8, 1918–MARCH 16, 1944—Battle of Anzio, Italy

Private First Waldo Engholm entered the service on January 6, 1942, and trained as a truck driver with the Quartermaster Corps, 3rd Infantry Division. As army ground forces moved across Africa, France and Germany, the men in the Quartermaster Company traveled close behind, supplying the division with water, food, ammunition and fuel for their vehicles. No company was more appreciated or needed than the Quartermaster Company.

When the 3rd Infantry Division landed on the beachhead in Anzio on January 22, 1944, only two German battalions stood between them and Rome. However, after initial success on the beaches, the commanders hesitated for nine days, which allowed the Germans time to move eight German divisions into place along the Allied perimeter.[1, 2] One soldier, Bill Mauldin, wrote about the exposed beachhead: *There was no place in the entire beachhead where enemy shells couldn't see you out. Sometimes it was worse at the front, sometimes worse at the harbor. Quartermasters buried their dead, and amphibious truck drivers went down with their craft. Infantrymen, dug into the Mussolini Canal, had the canal pushed in on top of them by armor-piercing shells, and Jerry bombers circled as they directed glider bombs into Tank Landing Ships and Liberty Ships Wounded men got oak leaf clusters on their Purple Hearts when shell fragments riddled them as they lay on hospital beds. Nurses died. Planes crash-landed on the single airstrip.*[3]

Once the division moved off the beachhead, Major General Lucas ordered the 3rd Division to take Cisterna and cut off Highway 7, but as the men moved across the flat Anzio plain, they were cut down by fierce German fire. As the men dug into foxholes filled with icy rain, Reporter Ernie Pyle wrote about life in Anzio: *Around the outside perimeter line, where the infantry faced the Germans a few hundred yards away, the soldiers lay in foxholes devoid of all comfort. But everywhere back of that the men dug underground and built themselves homes. On that beachhead there must have been tens of thousands of dugouts, housing from two to half a dozen men each.*[4]

Atkinson recounts how the miserable conditions and prolonged shelling compelled a soldier to fall on his knees and pray: *God, help us. You come yourself. Don't send Jesus. This is no place for children.*[1] In an effort to further break the men's spirit, German aircraft dropped propaganda leaflets claiming that American soldiers were sleeping with British wives and girlfriends and that Jews in America were making money from the war. Over the radio, the propagandist known as "Axis Sally" described Anzio as "the largest self-supporting prisoner-of-war camp in the world."[1]

Colonel Haegelin wrote in the 3rd Quartermaster journal on March 16th: *Artillery has been going on intermittently all day. About a steady hour of it this morning, but since then intermittent. They were apparently 170 mm, have one dud and some detonators. We have 3 quartermasters killed, 1 engineer killed, 1 engineer in hospital, 7 quartermasters in hospital, several other scratched a bit but still on duty. Private First Class Waldo Engholm was one of the three quartermasters killed, and his best friend, Ernest Heitmanek, who was with him at the time, lost his right leg.*[5, 6, 8, 9]

The Engholm family moved from Fort Dodge, Iowa, to Evan, Minnesota, in 1921 when Waldo was three years old. His mother, Anna (Becker) Engholm, died when he was seven, leaving his father to raise seven children. Before entering the army, Waldo farmed with Lester Berkner, a local farmer.

Waldo Engholm is buried in Sicily-Rome American Cemetery, Nettuno, Italy. Before leaving for Italy, he was granted a six-day furlough where family and friends surrounded him on September 26, 1943, as most of the time was spent traveling to and from home. On March 6, 1944, just ten days before he died, he wrote a letter home stating, "The going was tough."[5, 8, 9, 11]

Robert Lloyd Goudy

Seaforth (Redwood County)

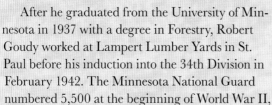

Fifth Army, 34th Infantry "Red Bull" Division, 135th Infantry Regiment, 1st Battalion, E Company, 2nd Lieutenant

OCTOBER 5, 1914–MAY 24, 1944—Battle for Anzio and Rome, Italy

After he graduated from the University of Minnesota in 1937 with a degree in Forestry, Robert Goudy worked at Lampert Lumber Yards in St. Paul before his induction into the 34th Division in February 1942. The Minnesota National Guard numbered 5,500 at the beginning of World War II, and 3,800 of its members belonged to the 34th Division. The college graduate headed to Camp Robinson, Arkansas, for medical corps training. However, Robert was drawn to the infantry and requested a transfer to Camp Shelby, Mississippi, where he was selected for officer candidate school at Fort Benning, Georgia.[1]

In September 1943, Lieutenant Goudy landed with the 34th Division in North Africa and arrived in Italy in time to join the First Battle of Monte Cassino from January 24 to February. While there, Lieutenant Goudy was hospitalized for two months for trench foot, a major problem for infantrymen. After rest and rehabilitation, the 34th Division arrived on Tank Landing Ships from March 23 to 24, in Anzio, Italy. By March 27, the regiment occupied positions held by the 3rd Infantry Division around Cisterna di Littora and Campo Morto. The Germans had views over the entire beachhead, and unleashed a constant rain of artillery, tank, and small arms fire, as well as nightly air raids. This kept men of the 34th pinned in their foxholes and dugouts during daylight. The Allies countered with fire from tanks and artillery to the extent that they could, and both sides carried out aggressive raids and regular patrols. The 168th Regiment relieved the 135th from this defensive position on April 27.[2, 3]

On May 11, 1944, the Fifth Army took the first steps toward the liberation of Rome. The Allies successfully broke through the enemy's "Gustav" and "Hitler" Lines and set the stage for an assault on the German perimeter around Anzio beach. On D-Day, May 23, Operation Buffalo began, the first task to cut supply routes to the German army by capturing main roads and the Cisterna-Albano railway. The offensive, which started at 0630, caught the Germans by surprise, as they had expected an earlier, pre-dawn attack, and many of them had gone back to sleep in their pillboxes. A 35-minute artillery barrage and the thunderous detonation of 4 "snakes," 352-foot-long metal casings filled with 1,400 pounds of explosive charge, caused shock and chaos among even the most seasoned German defenders. Allied forces continued their success in the battles that followed. Despite costly counterattacks and setbacks, this resulted in high numbers of German casualties and prisoners.[2]

The regiment secured the railroad track west of Cisterna under heavy artillery and mortar fire from the enemy, which cost the 1st Battalion six officers and commanders. 2nd Lieutenant Robert L. Goudy, a platoon leader, received the Silver Star for brave leadership: *For gallantry in action on 23 May 1944, in the vicinity of Anzio, Italy. Boldly leading his platoon over flat open terrain and through intense hostile machine gun fire, Lieutenant Goudy's platoon took forty prisoners and killed several more. Continuing their advance, the platoon encountered an enemy strong point consisting of several machine gun emplacements. Inspired by his previous actions, the platoon followed Lieutenant Goudy in an attack on the enemy positions. While leading the assault, Lieutenant Goudy was fatally wounded. The men, well organized, continued the attack and drove the enemy from their emplacements. The courage and leadership displayed by Lieutenant Goudy gained for him the respect and admiration of the men in his platoon.*[3]

On June 4, the Germans withdrew from battle, and the 135th Infantry Regiment marched to Rome along Highway 7. Joyful civilians lining the streets embraced the footsore, exhausted men of the 135th, the first infantry unit to march to Rome.[2, 3, 4]

2nd Lieutenant Robert Goudy was buried in Sicily-Rome American Military Cemetery, Nettuno, Italy, and later reinterred in Redwood Falls Cemetery, Redwood Falls, Minnesota. His older brother, Francis, died in France during World War I. Goudy's mother died April 12, 1944, just one month before her son's death. Robert's father managed the Farmer's Grain and Feed Company in Seaforth, Minnesota.[1]

Rolland Russell Rowe

3rd Infantry Division, 15th Infantry "Can-Do" Regiment, 1st Battalion, Headquarters Company, Sergeant
FEBRUARY 20, 1917–JUNE 1, 1944—Battle for Anzio and Rome, Italy

One of the more famous regiments in the United States Army, the 15th "Can-Do" Regiment, organized during the Civil War, also had a 26-year presence in China when they guarded Chinese citizens during the Boxer Rebellion in 1900. The regiment returned once again in 1912, to protect the Pekin-Mukden Railway between Tientsin and Chinwangtao. On March 2, 1938, the 15th Infantry resumed duty the in the United States and joined the 3rd Infantry Division, known as a first-rate unit for their fighting skills in North Africa (Operation Torch) and in Sicily (Operation Husky).

Once again, on January 22, 1944, Sergeant Rolland "Red" Rowe and the division demonstrated their battle-honed skills during Operation Shingle, the assault on the Anzio-Nettuno beachhead and the advance to Rome.[1, 2, 3]

On May 21, General Mark Clark ordered his forces at Anzio to break out of the beachhead, fight their way inland, and block both highways to Rome. The men would link up with Allied armies at Valmontone, where they planned to circle and destroy the German army. Sergeant Rowe and the 15th Regiment spearheaded the fighting on May 23, shooting their way into the ruined village of Cisterna, and flushing out 100 Germans hidden in caves. Hardin wrote that while the 7th Regiment fought house-to-house, street-to-street in Cisterna, the 30th and 15th encircled the town. All three regiments suffered heavy casualties before they finally secured the town on May 25. Just two days later the town of Artena, overlooking Highway 6 and Valmontone, fell to the 15th Regiment, and this placed Highway 6 under direct observation by Allied artillerymen. However, counterattacks by Germany's Hermann Göring Division near Artena stalled the Allied advance to Valmontone. After 6 difficult days of fighting and heavy losses, the 3rd Division ran low on men and welcomed 150 to 200 replacements in each battalion.[4]

The division resumed the attack to secure Highway 6 and Valmontone on June 1, as the 15th Infantry attacked along the Artena-Valmontone road, including the Artena railroad station. A thick mist and five German Mark IV tanks located at the railroad station slowed the 15th's advance, and intense fighting resulted in the loss of many men, including Sergeant "Red" Rowe.[1, 2, 4] Red's sister, Shirley, recalled: *The soldier in front of my brother stepped on a land mine and it killed my brother.*[6] For conspicuous gallantry and intrepidity in action, Sergeant Rowe was awarded the Silver Star on June 1, 1944, the third-highest decoration below the Distinguished Service Cross and the Medal of Honor.[5, 6, 7, 8] The next morning Valmontone fell to the 3rd Division, 133 days after the beginning of Operation Shingle. Only a rapidly retreating enemy stood between the Allies and Rome.

On June 7, Major General John W. O'Daniel, 3rd Division Commander, received a telegram from George C. Marshall, Chief of Staff, U.S. Army: *Please give to my old Division, the Third, my thanks, and to my first regiment in the army, The Thirtieth, and the Seventh of my Vancouver days and especially to my old China regiment, the Fifteenth, for cutting Highway Six.*[1]

Sergeant Rolland Rowe, son of Benjamin and Phoebe (Welch) Rowe, is buried at Fort Snelling National Cemetery, Minneapolis, Minnesota. Red's mother had tragically died in childbirth and his father died on May 30, 1944, just a few days before his son.[6] During World War II, the 15th Infantry Regiment earned 16 Medals of Honor, more than most divisions. Lieutenant Audie Murphy, the most highly decorated soldier in World War II, served in the 15th Infantry Regiment, 1st Battalion, with Sergeant Rolland Rowe.[1, 2, 3]

Herman Jerome Sundstad

Perley (Norman County)

5307th Composite Unit, "Merrill's Marauders," 3rd Battalion, Headquarters, 1st Lieutenant
JUNE 6, 1917–JUNE 5, 1944—China-Burma-India Theater, Burma

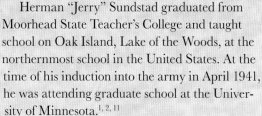

Herman "Jerry" Sundstad graduated from Moorhead State Teacher's College and taught school on Oak Island, Lake of the Woods, at the northernmost school in the United States. At the time of his induction into the army in April 1941, he was attending graduate school at the University of Minnesota.[1, 2, 11]

In 1942, President Franklin Roosevelt and Prime Minister Winston Churchill created an American commando force officially called the "5307th Composite Unit" and code-named Operation Galahad.[3, 4] Their mission was to invade Japanese-occupied Burma (now known as Myanmar), cut communication and supplies, and reopen the Burma Road to allow supplies into China. When President Roosevelt appealed for applicants to participate in a "dangerous and hazardous mission," 3,000 men volunteered from stateside units. A *Life* magazine correspondent dubbed the unit "Merrill's Marauders" after their commander, Brigadier General Frank Merrill, who trained his men in guerilla warfare in the jungles of India. 1st Lieutenant Herman Sundstad was not part of the initial force, but arrived as an infantry replacement at the end of May 1944.

On February 24, 1944, three battalions of "Merrill's Marauders" and two Chinese divisions began the 1,000-mile trek over a portion of the Himalaya Mountains and into the jungles of Burma behind Japanese lines, often with the essential cooperation of local scouts. All supplies were carried either on their backs or mules, and any additional supplies arrived during airdrops in the jungle. Many mules slipped and fell over the steep mountain trails, taking valuable equipment with them.[5, 6]

As the unit advanced across Burma, most of the men became deathly ill with scrub typhus, malaria, amoebic dysentery, malnutrition and fatigue. Chinese troops did not get dysentery, because they boiled their water, rather than relying on halizone tablets. Communication problems and Japanese attacks added to hundreds of non-battle casualties.

Reduced from around 3,000 men to fewer than 1,400, the men desperately needed rest, but General Stillwell ordered the "Marauders," along with several Chinese regiments, to attack the unsuspecting Japanese at the Myitkyina Airfield. On May 17, the depleted "Marauders" secured the airfield for a base to supply forces in jungle warfare in Burma and China, but now needed replacements to fend off Japanese attacks from the nearby town.

Initially the War Department had not planned to send additional men, as they accurately predicted an 85 percent casualty rate and the end of the "Marauders" after three months in Burma. However, in April 1944, the War Department called for 2,600 volunteers, and on May 25, 1st Lieutenant Herman Sundstad arrived by ship in Bombay Harbor. Carlton Ogburn wrote about the green American troops who received instruction in artillery in the plane on the way to Myitkyina, and how upon arriving at the airfield, they dove for cover as Japanese fire covered the airfield.[3, 5, 6, 7, 10]

On June 4, the inexperienced men practiced with machine guns and mortars; the next morning, they were ordered to advance and attack. Just ten days after his arrival on Myitkyina, 1st Lieutenant Herman Sundstad was awarded the Bronze Star Medal: *For gallantry in action near Burma, on 5 June, 1944. Lieutenant Sundstad displayed courage and combat efficiency of a highly commendable nature while in command of a forward reconnaissance unit. Ordered to secure an objective, the group was temporarily stalemated and forced to establish a position. The enemy launched a barrage of heavy mortar and small arms fire, which considerably enhanced the danger of the situation. Lieutenant Sundstad, without regard for personal safety, advanced to reconnoiter positions for heavy machine guns, and was forced to expose himself to the enemy. As a result, he was mortally wound by enemy fire.*[8]

By June 5, only 200 surviving members of the original "Marauders" remained and only 2 men had never been hospitalized with wounds or illness.[9] After the city of Myitkyina fell to the "Marauders" on August 3, the 5307th Composite Unit was awarded the Distinguished Unit Citation and every member of the commando force also received the Bronze Star, an unusual award for an entire unit.[3, 5, 7, 9]

1st Lieutenant Herman Sundstad is memorialized on the Tablets of the Missing at the Manila American Cemetery and Landstad Cemetery, Hendrum, Minnesota. His daughter Dianne, born six weeks after her father died, stated: *I look just like my dad. Although I never met him, I have always felt his presence throughout my life. The best memory I have of my Dad is in my heart.*[10]

Walter Timothy Kostrzewski

29th Infantry "Blue and Gray" Division, 116th Infantry Regiment, A Company, Private First Class
MAY 1, 1919–JUNE 6, 1944—Operation Overlord, Normandy, France

Every man who set foot on Omaha Beach that day was a hero.
—General Omar Bradley[1]

What happened at Omaha Beach on June 6, 1944, is the subject of many books and films, including the Oscar-winning movie *Saving Private Ryan*. The movie accurately portrayed the series of high bluffs that looked down on Omaha Beach, where the Germans erected concrete bunkers with guns and artillery. Unlike some of the other Allied landing beaches on D-Day, Omaha Beach was well-defended, with around 10,000 troops of the 352nd Infantry Division opposing the Allies.[2]

Two units were selected to land on Omaha Beach on D-Day: the 1st Division, a veteran division in action since 1943, and the 29th Division, a National Guard unit with little experience. Private First Class Walter Kostrzewski entered the service November 11, 1942, and belonged to the 29th Infantry Division, specifically A Company, 116th Infantry Regiment, nicknamed "The Stonewall Brigade." At approximately 6:30 in the morning on June 6, the *Empire Javelin* containing A, E, G and F Companies, part of the "Stonewall Brigade," landed on Omaha Beach. Later, William Geroux, reporter for the *Richmond Times-Dispatch*, called them the "Suicide Wave."[3] Seven survivors of the landing recorded the events in Group Critique Notes for A Company, 116th Infantry: *They crumpled as they sprang from the ship, forward into the water. Then order was lost. It seemed to the men that the only way to get ashore with a chance for safety was to dive head first into the water. A few had jumped off, trying to follow the standard operating procedures, and had gone down in water over their heads. They were around the boat now, struggling with their equipment and trying to keep afloat.*[4]

A third of the men drowned, either shortly after leaving the boats or after lying on the beach, wounded, and were caught by the rising tide. Those who made it to the sand found a hail of bullets. The survivors either made it back to the water up to their necks and worked their way up with the tide, or dug into the sand and moved once the tide caught up to them.[2, 3, 4, 5]

The survivors continue: *Within 7 to 10 minutes after the ramps had dropped "A" had become inert, leaderless and almost incapable of action. The company was entirely bereft of officers. … German machine gunners along the cliff directly ahead were now firing straight down into the party. … Within 20 minutes of striking the beach, "A" had ceased to be an assault company and had become a forlorn little rescue party bent on survival and the saving of lives. Orders were no longer being given by anyone; each man who remained sound moved or not as he saw fit.*

It is estimated by the men that one third of "A" remained by the time "B" hit the beach. One hour and forty minutes after the landing, six men from the boat which had landed on the far right flank (Boat No 23) … from "A" had worked up to the edge of the cliff.[4,6] Two of the men joined the 2nd Rangers in a cliff assault, and the remaining handful joined the battalion that night.

The 116th Infantry Regiment suffered 341 casualties that day, including 155 of the men from A Company.[2, 3, 4, 5, 6] Private First Class Kostrzewski was declared missing in action on June 6, 1944; his body was recovered on September 10, 1944.[7] Unaware of her son's status, Rose Kostrzewski wrote a poignant letter to the army on October 27, 1944: *Dear Sir, Could you please find out how my son, Private First Class Walter T. Kostrzewski, met his death? Was there anything found of him? If there was anything found, I would like to have it for remembrance. I am a broken hearted mother. Yours truly, Mrs. Rose Kostrzewski, Strandquist, Minnesota.*[8] Walter's parents had received a letter from their son dated May 30, a week before he died.

Walter Kostrzewski is buried at Normandy American Cemetery and Memorial, France. Private Ellsworth Onger (page 47), another Strandquist soldier, died the same day.[9]

Ellsworth Helmer Onger

Strandquist (Marshall County)

101st Airborne, 501st Parachute Infantry Regiment, 2nd Battalion, D Company, Private

OCTOBER 3, 1919–JUNE 6, 1944—Operation Overlord, Normandy, France

As in all wars, some of the finest men who served were killed before their time—we can only speculate on what miraculous contributions they might have made to the world, had they survived. Among the 101st fallen were artists, musicians, writers, skilled athletes, scientists, mathematicians, architects and builders. Above all, there were sons, brothers, lovers, friends, (and in some cases), husbands and fathers, whose caring and vibrant personalities are missed by those they left behind. The human race is diminished by their loss.

—Historian Mark Bando[1, 2]

The first men to see action on D-Day were 18,000 airborne troops who entered Normandy by glider and parachute. All men volunteered for the parachute infantry and were promised an extra $50 a month pay if they signed up for the dangerous duty. Private Ellsworth Onger left a quiet farming community to join the elite 501st Parachute Infantry Regiment, named the "Screaming Eagles," a unit trained to jump behind enemy lines in preparation for Allied troop landings on Normandy beaches. Each C-47, called the workhorse of the army, carried 18 paratroopers and 100 pounds of equipment for the planned attack.[1, 2, 3]

On June 5, 1944, at 2245 hours, the 501st Parachute Infantry Regiment left Merryfield Airfield in England to cross the English Channel for their first combat jump five hours prior to the amphibious landing. Men formed a line in the middle of the plane and attached their static lines to a steel cable, which ran the length of the cabin near their heads. Once over the drop zone, the troopers waited for the red light to turn green and jump. The 501st planned to drop near the town of Carentan, where they would seize key canal locks and destroy bridges over the Douve River. However, the detailed plans failed because of low clouds and enemy fire, which scattered the troop carrier formations and paratrooper jumps. Units were separated and many of the men had no idea where they had landed. Luckily, this haphazard landing confused the Germans and gave Colonel Howard R. Johnson, Commander of the 501st, time to collect a small force and capture the La Barquette Lock, which controlled the flooding of the Douve River.[1, 2, 3, 4]

Private Ellsworth Onger never made it off the plane. As his C-47 "Skytrain" approached drop zone-D, German anti-aircraft shot down the plane near Varenguebec on the French Cotentin Peninsula. Lieutenant Ian Nicholson, D Company platoon leader and jumpmaster, and his entire crew of 17 men, including Ellsworth Onger, never had a chance to use their parachutes. If the jump had gone as planned, the jumpmaster would have been the first jumper out the door. History shows that this strategic area was especially effective at destroying Allied aircraft. Of the 432 planes carrying the 101st Airborne, 38 Troop Carrier C-47s crashed or were shot down in the initial parachute drops.[1, 2, 5]

A model of a C-47 aircraft in Picauville, France, pays tribute to crews of the 9th U.S. Army Air Forces and the paratroopers killed in crashes near here on June 6, 1944. Private Ellsworth Onger is buried in the Normandy American Cemetery, France. His mother died while giving birth to twins when Ellsworth was four years old; this left his father to raise seven small children, the oldest just eight years old.[5, 6, 7]

Another Strandquist soldier, Private First Class Walter Kostrzewski (page 46), died the same day.

Arnold Walter Wilsing

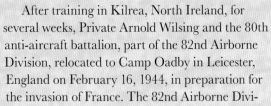

Coast Artillery Corps, 82nd Airborne "All American" Division, 505th Parachute Infantry Regiment Combat Team, 80th Anti-Aircraft Battalion, Battery A, Private

JULY 13, 1921–JUNE 7, 1944—Operation Neptune, Normandy, France

After training in Kilrea, North Ireland, for several weeks, Private Arnold Wilsing and the 80th anti-aircraft battalion, part of the 82nd Airborne Division, relocated to Camp Oadby in Leicester, England on February 16, 1944, in preparation for the invasion of France. The 82nd Airborne Division, commanded by Brigadier General Matthew B. Ridgway, invaded Normandy behind enemy lines on the beaches, along with the 101st Airborne Division and the British 6th Airborne Division.[1]

The men would soon travel overseas by the combat glider, a new development in World War II. This fragile, flammable, but silent craft could bring soldiers, heavy weapons, jeeps, and medical supplies to men on or behind enemy lines. Exposure to anti-aircraft or even small arms fire could disable or down these "flying coffins." The American Waco CG-4A was 48 feet long, built with steel, wood, canvas and no armor, contrasted with the longer British Horsa composed of plywood.

They were towed to their destinations by C-47s; on these dangerous missions they often had to fly low to stay under the radar, leaving the "flying coffins" vulnerable to anti-aircraft fire, as they were on D-Day. Pilots with no experience towing gliders often missed the drop zones, leaving the battalions dangerously scattered in enemy territory.[1, 2, 3, 4, 5, 6]

Captain Dwain Luce, whose first glider crashed when its nylon towrope snapped, recalled landing the aircraft: *So instead of landing slow, we landed at the highest rate of speed. I remember I was sitting up next to the pilot and I leaned over his shoulder and looked and when we dove over those trees we were doing over a hundred and ten miles an hour and I thought, "This is no speed to land." But it was too late to change. That's why so many of the gliders crashed.*[4]

On the evening of June 5, 1944, Batteries A (including Private Arnold Wilsing) and B rode Waco gliders across the channel to their landing zone west of Sainte-Mère-Église. Horsa gliders carried Battery C, and ships transported Batteries D, E and F. Hampered by fog and flak and landing in tiny fields separated by tall hedgerows, many gliders crashed and sustained casualties. Landing after the paratroopers, the first of 52 gliders crash-landed at 0404 and, like the paratroopers, were scattered in small groups. By late that afternoon, Batteries A and B had six 57 mm guns in position, but only 30 percent of the 82nd Division's forces were assembled by that evening.[1, 2]

On the morning of June 7, three German infantry battalions moved north of Sainte-Mère-Église. When the Germans sent a self-propelled gun down the road toward the 505th Parachute Infantry Regiment, Battery A, led by John C. Cliff, knocked out the vehicle. As the crew moved their gun to the side of the demolished vehicle to gain better visibility, a second self-propelled gun killed the entire gun crew from Battery A, including Private Arnold Wilsing.[6] His nephew Gary Nellis stated, "We were told that Arnie was hit by shrapnel from an exploding shell."[7, 8]

By the time the "All American" Division returned to England, they had lost 5,245 troopers killed, wounded, or missing in 33 days of combat. Masters points out that glidermen were never advised of the huge risks of their operation, didn't know about "Rommel's asparagus" networks of poles and mines that had been planted in the landing fields, and were not told that British generals predicted disaster and a 70 percent casualty rate.[3]

Brigadier General Ridgway's post battle report stated: ...*33 days of action without relief, without replacements. Every mission accomplished. No ground gained was ever relinquished.* In all, combat gliders were only used for about a dozen years.[9]

Private Arnold Wilsing is buried in Fort Snelling National Cemetery. Arnold's wife remarried Leonard A. Fell in 1947. The author of this book also has a connection to Private Wilsing: my high school English teacher, Arnold Nellis, was named after Arnold Wilsing, his uncle.[7, 8, 10, 11]

William David Wendt

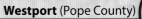

Royal Canadian Air Corps, 19 Royal Air Force Squadron, Pilot Officer
MAY 6, 1916–JUNE 7, 1944—Battle for Normandy, Normandy, France

Dave Schroeder recalls his Uncle Bill: *This story starts way back in 1941. Germany had occupied France and the Germans were bombing England into oblivion. Naturally, England had declared war on Germany, and by default, that included Canada. The United States had not entered the war and hoped to stay out of it. Many Americans thought it was our war and either we fight the war over there or over here, so they went to Canada and volunteered. They did this knowing it was against policy and could be imprisoned for serving in a foreign military. About 10,000 of them went anyway. William David Wendt was one of them. Nearly 1,000 were killed—Uncle Bill was also one of them.*[1]

By February 1941, William "Bill" Wendt knew that America would eventually be forced into the European war. His heart set on being a pilot, Bill volunteered for the American air force but was denied due to his height. Bill was over six feet tall and the United States did not accept pilots that tall. However, the Canadian air force gladly accepted the striking young man, and William Wendt left his job as an assistant manager at a car dealership to earn his wings in November 1941 from No. 14 Service Flying Training School, Aylmer, Ontario, Canada. The recruiting officer assessed Wendt: *"Good type of American lad. Keen to fly. Feels this is their war as much as ours. Definitely sincere as to purpose."* [2]

When word arrived that more flyers were needed at Malta, Pilot Officer Wendt landed there on October 15, 1942, to join daily bombing missions over Sicily, Lampedusa and Pantelieria, Italy.

On November 30, 1942, as Pilot Officer Wendt's squadron flew over Sicily, he experienced engine problems and dropped back in formation when two German fighters attacked. Described as a daring and resourceful flier, Pilot Wendt shot down one of the planes before his own plane caught fire, and he had to bail out. Pilot Wendt later reported: *I took off from Malta on 30th November 1942 in a fighter-bomber to bomb Biscari. After having reached my objective and dropped my bombs, I developed trouble as I came out of my dive. My engine caught fire and I was compelled to bail out. I came down about 5 kilometers west of Mount Calvo. I slashed my chute to the best of my ability, hid it under some trees, and started to walk in a westerly direction. I saw a man and a boy in a cart, and rode along with them for about half an hour. When their route turned away from the direction in which I wanted to travel, I got off and*

approached a woman standing outside a house, asked her for a drink and she gave me some food and wine. I was just finishing my meal when three Carabinieri and a civilian came to the house and rounded me up. William's nephew Dave remembers well the story: *I remember him telling of this lady giving him something to eat. When the soldiers showed up and attempted to arrest him, she flew into them like a wet hen and made them wait outside while he finished his meal.* Just four hours after landing in an orange grove in Sicily, the Italian police took him prisoner. The Germans wanted Wendt, but he successfully bargained to be a prisoner of the Italians and ended up in Chieti, Italy, along with 1,100 prisoners, of which 350 were American airmen.[1]

While imprisoned, Pilot Wendt was not sitting around waiting for action. After several attempts to escape through a man-made tunnel, Wendt and a group of prisoners finally escaped and traveled 6 weeks and 150 miles before arriving at the British lines. Following their sensational escape, Wendt returned to England, then Canada, and finally home for Christmas Eve with his family in Westport. While home he shared his story with the Glenwood Lions Club and WCCO Radio before returning to Europe.[1, 3]

His luck ran out the second time. On June 6, 1944, No. 19 Squadron provided fighter cover and air support for ground troops on Normandy. The next day Wendt and his Mustang fighter plane went down over Montfort, France, after bombing railway yards. Everyone dared to hope that once again, he was a prisoner of war. Squadron leader W.C.H. Gilmour sent a letter to Wendt's mother: *Bill called up by wireless to say his engine had stopped. Hit by flak or blast from his own bombs.* His fate remained a mystery until August 27, 1945, when the Canadian War Department wrote to Mrs. Wendt: *The report states that a fighter aircraft crashed on the side of the road between Rouen and Port Audemer, France. By the number on the aircraft it is known that your son was the pilot. He was buried as "unknown" at the cemetery of Eturgueraye, which is located 10 miles east of Port Audemer.* Later, the family heard from an unofficial source that Wendt parachuted into a burning plane that crashed just below him.[1, 4, 5, 6]

Pilot Officer William David Wendt is buried in Eturgueraye Churchyard, Eure-et-Loir, France. On July 31, 2011, the city of Eturgueraye, France, held a celebration in remembrance of him; over 200 people attended the ceremony.[1]

Carl Robert Emery

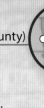

526th Ordnance Heavy Maintenance Tank Company, Detachment B, Private First Class
MARCH 22, 1921–JUNE 9, 1944—Invasion of Normandy, Normandy, France

Carl "Bob" Emery entered the service on September 25, 1942, and was assigned to the 526th Ordnance Company, a tank repair company. Earlier, his family lost a son, Jack Emery, at Pearl Harbor, and were unhappy to see him leave for training at Camp Bowie, Texas. Carl, the sole remaining son, unsuccessfully requested an early discharge to return home and help on the farm.[1]

In December 1943, the unit moved to Berkshire, England, to train for the Invasion of Normandy. As the men prepared for the invasion, the 526th Ordnance organized into two Detachments: A and B. On D-Day, June 6, 1944, Detachment A landed on Omaha Beach with 5 officers and 100 enlisted men. Their Tank Landing Ship carried the V-Corps assault force as well as parts for trucks and other vehicles. Private First Class Carl Emery and Detachment B were assigned to join Detachment A several days later.

Although scheduled to be on single transport on June 9, for unknown reasons Detachment B was boarded on Tank Landing Ship 1006 with the 3422nd Ordnance Medium Automotive Maintenance Company. As the Tank Landing Ship traveled 11 miles from the transport area in the English Channel to Omaha Beach, a German E-boat torpedoed the ship in the early morning. Lost were the entire 3422nd Company and 27 enlisted men of Detachment B, including Private First Class Carl Emery. Eleven men and two officers of Detachment B were rescued by a British destroyer and returned to England. All the company's equipment went down with the ship.[2,3]

Carl "Bob" Emery's life may have been spared had he enlisted after the death of the five Sullivan brothers who perished when their ship sank on November 13, 1942. The brothers, George, Frank, Joe, Matt and Al, from Waterloo, Iowa, entered the service with the stipulation that they serve together. Although the navy had a policy of separating siblings, this was not strictly enforced, and all five were assigned to the light cruiser USS *Juneau*. While patrolling in Guadalcanal, the ship was struck by torpedoes from a Japanese submarine, and all five brothers drowned. Their deaths resulted in the "Sole Survivor" policy, enacted by the United States military in 1948.[4] Carl Emery was drafted and sent overseas before the tragedy received national attention, and before Congress passed the law forbidding the sole

surviving son from being drafted. Carl was 23 years old, the same age as his brother, Jack.

In a newspaper interview 70 years after Pearl Harbor, Betty Emery Halvorson recalled her mother—a conservative, Swedish woman proud of her American citizenship—wish that her boys had been conscientious objectors, because their prison terms wouldn't last forever: *It was a strange thing for her to say. She was very patriotic and supportive of the war effort. But I suppose you change after you lose two sons. The worst part is not knowing, not having a body to bury. The worst part is that it just keeps going on, even after all these years. I still miss Jack and Bob. They were my brothers.*[1]

Eugene Dennis Lusk

Mizpah (Koochiching County)

82nd Airborne "All American" Division, 507th Parachute Infantry, 1st Battalion,
Headquarters Company, Staff Sergeant

SEPTEMBER 21, 1922–JUNE 14, 1944—The Battle of Carentan, France

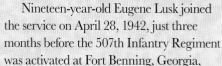

Nineteen-year-old Eugene Lusk joined the service on April 28, 1942, just three months before the 507th Infantry Regiment was activated at Fort Benning, Georgia, under the command of Lieutenant Colonel George Millett. In March 1944, Staff Sergeant Lusk and the 507th Parachute Infantry moved to Nottingham, England, to train for D-Day. Attached to the 82nd Airborne, the 507th and 508th were ordered to capture the city of Sainte-Mère-Église, secure important bridges, seal off the Cotentin Peninsula and capture the port city of Cherbourg.[1]

Tension filled the 82nd Airborne as D-Day approached. Soldiers studied maps, charts and drop zones on sand tables, and then drew it on paper from memory. Every soldier needed to know his job and the job of his unit so well that he would automatically respond in battle.

More than 13,000 paratroopers jumped on D-Day, including 2,000 from the 507th Parachute Regiment. The last airborne unit to land in Normandy on June 6, 1944, Staff Sergeant Eugene Lusk and the 507th experienced D-Day very differently from other parachute regiments. The 507th flew from airbases farther north in England and as a result, they arrived over Normandy two hours later than other units, which gave the Germans enough time to prepare for their arrival.[1,2,3,4] Staff Sergeant Lusk experienced combat for the first time when both the 507th and the 508th Parachute Infantry Regiments were dropped near the west bank of the Merderet River. On June 6, 1944, General Ridgway reported: *The first elements, the 1st Battalion, jumped at 0232 hours, and by 0312 hours the entire regiment was on the ground generally east of the Merderet River and was fairly dispersed. Small groups assembled to form small task forces until such time as the regiment could assemble completely. One such force on the west bank of the Merderet River attacked Amfreville but was forced back by overwhelming superiority in enemy strength to Flauk. A patrol was sent to the western end of La Fiere Bridge and contact was made with elements of the 505th Parachute Infantry on the eastern end at 1430 hours. The enemy recaptured Flauk and drove this patrol from the western end of the La Fiere Bridge. Another force of the regiment joined with Force "A" Headquarters and at 1130 attacked to secure the Chef Du Pont Bridge meeting extreme resistance. The eastern end of the bridge was finally secured by nightfall. Leaving one company to hold the bridge, the remainder of this second force moved to an assembly area at 1715 hours in the vicinity of the railroad overpass. Still another group, led by the regimental commander, landed on or near the scheduled drop zone but had no contact with other elements of the Division during the day.*[5]

The report doesn't state that several troopers overshot the drop zone and ended up in the Merderet River where troopers loaded with heavy equipment drowned in the river and surrounding marshes. Poor visibility and heavy fire in the early hours of D-Day left troopers spread out over a 20-mile area, often unable to connect with their unit. Even Colonel Millet, the commanding officer of the 507th, could not find his troops and ended up a prisoner three days later. The 507th never had a chance to fight together as a regiment, and became known as the "forgotten regiment," a unit that fought in small mixed groups led by commanders they did not know.[4]

Eugene Lusk survived the jump and landing. After securing Sainte-Mère-Église and Chef-du-Pont on D-Day, the 507th took the La Fiére Bridge Peninsula three days later. Historian Pat Curran describes the drive to capture the port city of Cherbourg: *On Wednesday, 14th June the attack to take St. Sauveur-le-Vicomte began from a jump off west of Etienville. This phase of the 505th Normandy campaign lasted four days. The attack commenced at 9:30 a.m. with the 507th in the lead and the 505th following behind. The two paratroop regiments advanced westward on the north of Etienville to St. Sauveur-le-Vicomte Road. To the 507th's right was the U.S. 9th Infantry, which overall was an experienced division, having seen action in North Africa. However, some of its regiments had no battle experience at all. The 507th had suffered huge losses prior to this attack. Its 1st Battalion numbered just over 100 men, and fewer still by the time it reached the eastern outskirts of La Bonneville that night.*[2]

On June 14, Staff Sergeant Eugene Lusk was killed in action during the drive to take Cherbourg. Following D-Day, the determined and well-trained paratroopers of the 82nd Airborne fought for 33 days, secured La Fiére Bridge and cut off the Cotentin Peninsula. Although over 2,000 soldiers from the 507th Parachute Infantry parachuted in on D-Day, only 700 returned to England a month later.[1,2,3] Initially buried in the United States Military Cemetery, Sainte-Mère-Église, France, Eugene Lusk was reinterred in Fort Snelling National Cemetery in 1948. The Mizpah American Legion and Auxiliary Curb-Lusk Post 541 honors Technical Sergeant Cyril Curb (page 21) and Staff Sergeant Eugene Lusk.[6]

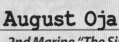

August Oja

2nd Marine "The Silent Second" Division, 18th Marine Regiment, 1st Battalion, D Company, Private First Class

FEBRUARY 2, 1920–JUNE 15, 1944—Battle of Saipan, Mariana Islands

While Allied forces advanced through Normandy in mid-June of 1944, the 2nd Marine Division fought their way through Guadalcanal and Tarawa. The men were ordered to seize Saipan, an island in the Mariana Islands chain; other Mariana islands include Guam and Tinian. Japan controlled Saipan in 1920 following World War I and was fiercely determined to hold onto the Marianas, home to their vital air and sea bases. The United States needed those bases to strike other Japanese bases in the Philippines, Formosa, China and the Japanese homeland.[1]

In preparation for the invasion of the Marianas on June 15, 1944, August Oja and the 2nd Marine Division trained in an area of Hawaii that closely resembled volcanic Saipan. Three divisions were ordered to lead the invasion: Private August Oja and the 2nd Marines under Major General Thomas Watson; the 4th Marines under Major General Harry Schmidt; and in reserve, the 27th Infantry Division under Major General Ralph Smith. August Oja served in the 18th Marine Regiment, a regiment composed of only engineers and Seabees, and an important support unit in all 2nd Marine Division battles.

Although intelligence reports placed enemy troop strength at 19,000, nearly 30,000 Japanese soldiers waited for the Americans on Saipan, an island filled with mountains and hills that were perfect for enemy cover.

On June 11, heavy Allied air and naval bombing hit Saipan in preparation for the marine landing, but the enemy remained intact. On D-Day, the 2nd and 4th Marine Divisions, many of the men combat-experienced from the Gilbert and Marshall Islands, headed for Saipan on 32 amphibious vehicles, including brand-new LVT-4s, which were equipped with rear ramps and 75 mm guns. As the vehicles approached the beaches, the enemy unexpectedly fired heavy automatic weapons, artillery and mortars, sinking 20 of the landing craft. Despite the barrage of fire, 8,000 men landed in 20 minutes, including the entire 2nd Marine Division, which landed north of the planned beaches and lost contact with the 4th Marine Division.[1, 2]

Although both divisions made it ashore, the marines lost over 2,000 men during the confusion and congestion on the beaches. Private First Class August Oja was one of them and was listed as lost at sea.[2, 3]

By July 8, the marines had pushed the Japanese north to the rocky ridges of Marpi Point, where hundreds of civilians and Japanese soldiers jumped to their deaths rather than surrender. The cost to secure Saipan was high; numbers soared to 16,500 American casualties, including 3,500 killed, but Saipan became the primary U.S. air base in the Pacific, with many B-29 flights originating there.[1, 2]

August Oja is buried at the National Memorial Cemetery of the Pacific, Honolulu, Hawaii.

Fernly Everett Bush

Myrtle (Freeborn County)

**29th Infantry "Blue and Gray" Division, 175th Infantry Regiment, 1st Battalion,
Headquarters Company, Medical Detachment, Private First Class**
DECEMBER 29, 1924–JUNE 16, 1944—Invasion of Normandy, Normandy, France

On Friday, July 28, 1944, Cleve and Freda (Fleischer) Bush received the telegram that every parent feared in World War II. Their 19-year-old son, Fernly Bush, was killed in action during the invasion of France while serving as a medic with the 175th Infantry.

Fernly Bush entered the U.S. Army in June 1943, just 18 years old and a recent graduate of Albert Lea High School.[1] Following induction at Fort Snelling, he trained in the medical corps at Camp Barkley, Texas, the largest medical replacement training center in the country. Medics learned first aid under fire, knowledge of wounds and diseases, and the evacuation of wounded over impossible terrain. Although designated non-combatants, medics were trained to protect themselves and their patients. After a furlough in November 1943, Private First Class Bush traveled to England, and then on to France.

On June 7, 1944, D-Day plus 1, Private First Class Fernly Bush and the 175th Infantry landed on Omaha Beach and advanced west to the city of Isigny. Two days later, the 175th captured Isigny and secured the bridge over the Vire River near Hait, an important objective to connect the Omaha and Utah beaches. That same day, the regiment marched southeast to secure the city of Lison, and on June 12, the task force crossed the Vire River. On June 14, the 29th Division, led by Fernly Bush's 1st Battalion, 175th Infantry, received a monumental order: attack and secure St.-Lô, a small city of strategic importance where all the major highways converged. Despite fierce opposition and minefields, the regiment cut off the road east of La Meauffe and continued their advance to St.-Lô.[2, 3, 4]

The After Action Report for the 175th Infantry Regiment states: *The morning of 13 June, a battalion of paratroops came up on the right of the task force relieving the pressure on their right flank. Later in the day, these were forced to withdraw, leaving the task forces again to face the enemy alone. Rations and ammunition were dropped from the air. An enemy Panzer Division was reported to be approaching Montmartin en Graignes and it was consequently felt that in spite of the fact that the task force was on the high ground of Montmartin en Graignes, the village must be shelled. The battleship Texas shelled the town with its 16-inch batteries, without hitting the task force. At 1205, 13 June, Company "G"* re-crossed the River Vire, having run into stiff enemy opposition. Colonel Goode *was missing, having been wounded or killed in this action. The morning of 14 June, the Division Commander ordered the task force to withdraw across the River Vire and rejoin the regiment. They fought their way back to the river and returned late that night. On the 14th of June, a new division attack order was issued. The objective: St.-Lô. This plan hinged on the 30th Division coming on line for a coordinated attack with the 1st Battalion leading, 3rd Battalion and 2nd Battalion to its rear, echeloned to the right to protect the right of the division. The attack started on schedule. By 1118, the 3rd Battalion had captured its objective, in the vicinity of Amy, despite determined opposition. The 1st Battalion also encountered stiff opposition being hindered by apparent minefields, which proved to be dummy mines. By 1305, it had cut the road east of La Meauffe.*[2]

During the advance to St.-Lô on June 16, Private First Class Fernly Bush was with the leading battalion in the 29th Combat Area where he was hit by fire, later dying from his wounds. Two days later, his battalion won both a Presidential Distinguished Unit Citation and the French Army's Croix de Guerre with a Silver-Gilt Star for refusing to yield Hill 108 just outside St.-Lô. From June 16 to 19, the 175th Infantry suffered more than 600 hundred casualties, including 164 killed.[1, 5, 6]

Fernly Bush is buried in Normandy American Cemetery, France. On August 20, 1944, a memorial service was held at Bethlehem Lutheran Church, south of Myrtle. The Bush family moved to Myrtle in 1938. There, Cleve Bush, Fernly's father, worked as section foreman for the railroad for 41 years.[7]

Robert Lawrence Forsberg

Tintah (Traverse County)

U.S. Navy Hospital Corps, 2nd Marine "The Silent Second" Division, 8th Marine Regiment, 2nd Battalion, Headquarters, Hospital Corpsman, Pharmacist's Mate First Class

APRIL 22, 1923–JUNE 16, 1944—Battle of Saipan, Mariana Islands

Just 19 years old, Robert Forsberg enlisted in the service on July 8, 1942, and later transferred to the marines Medical Field School. Stationed in San Diego, he wrote home on April 21, 1944: *Dear Mother, Well, how are you feeling? I'm feeling fine. The weather sure is severe here. We were going to ship out last Thursday but they held us up so I don't know when we'll be going now. But it won't be too long. We went on a hike the other day; it wasn't so good. We had to wade in the ocean up to your neck. It was a little bit chilly. I guess I'll go to the show tonight. They're out in the open. They have pretty good shows out here. There sure is some nice country out here—a lot of mountains. Well, I don't know of anything else to write so I guess I'll have to quit.—Bob*[1, 2]

When Robert trained as a Hospital Corpsman, he joined an elite group of navy medical personnel. During World War II, Hospital Corpsmen gave heroic service to their marines under harrowing conditions, and marines held the highest respect for their "docs." The bond between marines and their corpsmen remains strong today.

U.S. forces were determined to capture the Mariana Islands, as doing so would allow Allied B-29 bombers to strike all the way to Japan. Saipan, an important supply base 1,250 miles from Tokyo, was top priority. On D-Day, June 15, the 2nd and 3rd Marine Battalions, 8th Marines, arrived on Saipan to face intense fire from 25,000 well-concealed Japanese.[3, 4, 5] Navy Corpsmen Robert Forsberg and Samuel Culotta were among the first wave of marines to land on shore, where they found the beach littered with dead and wounded men. The corpsman's job, Culotta explained, was to stabilize the wounded until they could be taken to hospital ships: *That's what we were trained to do. We corpsmen had a saying: 'If you were alive when we got to you, you stayed alive.' I still think about Saipan, because it was the worst one.* Culotta survived nine Pacific landings.[4]

Casualties were extremely high the first day with over 1,300 men killed or wounded in action and 300 men missing in action. The next day, Corpsman Forsberg and his 2nd Battalion renewed their attack and during the battle, he was killed.[6] On May 15, 1945, Pharmacist's Mate First Class John Kelley wrote to Robert's mother: *I became acquainted with Bob at New River, early in November of forty-three, and found him to be the type of friend one seldom finds, but always looks for. A great sense of humor but what I liked most, he wasn't afraid, if you'll pardon my slang, to call a spade a spade. If you've got the details as to how it happened I'm positive that it was in helping a buddy with absolute disregard for himself.*[2, 7]

Colonel Joseph Alexander wrote about the navy surgeons and corpsmen who traveled with the assault units in anticipation of heavy casualties. Off shore, three Tank Landing Ships, used as provisional hospital ships, and four regular hospital ships, including USS *Solace*, took care of the wounded men, but: *As usual, it was the navy medical personnel ashore who paid the highest price for this support. A total of 414 surgeons and corpsmen were killed or wounded at Saipan, 8 times the number for Tarawa.*[3]

Robert Forsberg is memorialized at Courts of the Missing, National Memorial Cemetery of the Pacific, Honolulu, Hawaii; at the American Memorial Park, Saipan, Northern Mariana Islands, which is overseen by the U.S. National Park Service; and at St. Gall's Cemetery, Tintah.

Tintah American Legion J.F.B. Post is named in honor of Pharmacist's Mate First Class Robert Forsberg, Machinist's Mate Second Class Clayton Johnson (page 18), and Private First Class Sylvester Beckman (page 113). Robert's sister, Marie, and her husband Herman Gronwold later owned and operated the Blue Castle Café in Tintah.[2, 9, 10, 11, 12]

Rudolph J. Indihar

9th Infantry "The Old Reliables" Division, 47th Infantry "Raiders" Regiment, Third Battalion, K Company, Staff Sergeant

MARCH 2, 1917–JUNE 22, 1944—Normandy Campaign, Normandy, France

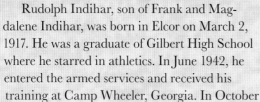

Rudolph Indihar, son of Frank and Magdalene Indihar, was born in Elcor on March 2, 1917. He was a graduate of Gilbert High School where he starred in athletics. In June 1942, he entered the armed services and received his training at Camp Wheeler, Georgia. In October of that year, he was sent overseas and took part in the invasion of Africa where he served with the Commandos. From there he saw action in Sicily and Italy. On D-Day he was shipped to Normandy, France, where he was killed in action on June 22, 1944. Staff Sergeant Rudolph Indihar was awarded the Silver Star and Purple Heart for bravery, which was presented to his mother by a representative of the U.S. Army from Fort Snelling at a ceremony, which was held at the Gilbert Community Center.[1, 2, 8]

While training in England in 1944, Staff Sergeant Rudolph Indihar and the 9th Infantry Division knew that an invasion was imminent when they were placed on alert status and ordered to marshaling areas on June 3. As they watched a steady stream of planes head south across the English Channel on June 5, the men understood that D-Day, the invasion of Normandy, had arrived.

Exhausted from extensive battle in Africa and Sicily, the 9th Infantry Division sat out the invasion on June 6th, 1944. The 9th waited to hit Utah Beach until June 10, when they moved rapidly toward Cherbourg, a strategic port on the Cotentin Peninsula. Here the 47th and 60th Infantry Regiments reached the east coast near St.-Lô and blocked the last German escape route in the Cotentin Peninsula. The enemy desperately attempted to break out near Saint-Jacques-de-Néhou, but the 9th destroyed the force and then turned north on June 19 to capture the port of Cherbourg.

During the drive to Cherbourg, Staff Sergeant Rudolph Indihar was killed in action. His nephew, Anthony Urick, recalls family discussions: *Rudy and a friend from Gilbert entered the army together. They served together in North Africa, Sicily, Italy and Normandy. The story is that after D-Day, Rudy's officer was killed and Rudy was in command. The objective was to wipe out a machine gun nest and he sent out a group to do so, but they were killed. A second group demurred, so he went out himself. He eliminated the machine gun nest and on the way back, a German sniper killed him. My mom claimed that the bullet grazed his temple, killing him but leaving little physical damage.[4]* Both the 2nd Battalion and Staff Sergeant Indihar's 3rd Battalion received Distinguished Unit Citations for their gallantry and heroism in the seizure of the city. Rudolph Indihar also received the Silver Star. Just three days later, men from Indihar's own 47th Infantry Regiment became the first Allied troops to enter Cherbourg.[3]

After the Germans surrendered on June 29, the 9th Division captured two senior commanders of the Cherbourg area: Army Lieutenant General Karl Wilhelm von Schlieben and Navy Rear Admiral Hennecke. Famed war reporter Ernie Pyle recounted their photo session: *Bob Capa, Life magazine photographer, appeared at the division commanders tent to take pictures of the captured officers. But the Germans definitely had other notions. "I am tired of this picture taking," he snapped. Capa, who spoke German, sighed and lowered his camera momentarily, "I too, am tired General," he pointed out, "I have to take pictures of so many captured German generals!"[5]*

The son of Austrian immigrants, Staff Sergeant Rudolph Indihar was survived by his parents and six siblings. He is buried in Calvary Cemetery, Gilbert, Minnesota. Elcor lost four men in World War II: Robert Brady (page 95), Lloyd Nicholas (page 37), LeRoy Veralrud (page 74) and Rudolph Indihar.[1, 2]

Ray Sherwood Lound

Denham (Pine County)

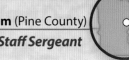

91st Infantry "Wild West" Division, 361st Infantry Regiment, 1st Battalion, A Company, Staff Sergeant
JANUARY 14, 1921–JULY 2, 1944—Battle for Casole d' Isola, Italy

The 91st Infantry Division, known as the "Wild West" Division, was organized in 1917 at Camp Lewis, Washington, with the majority of its men from western United States. Under the command of Major General Alexander M. Patch, the 91st Division landed in Oran, Algeria, on April 18, 1944, to train for the planned invasion of Italy. Staff Sergeant Ray Lound and the 361st Infantry, one of three divisions in the 91st, began training on May 3 at a special Invasion Training Center in Port aux Poules where the men learned wire breaching, demolition, flame-throwing, boat debarkation and dozens of other invasion techniques.[1]

Robbins wrote about the transition to Algerian life. Aside from the daily routine in military training, the men of the 91st were immersed in Algerian culture. Intrigued by Islamic shrines, veiled Arab women and colorful French Colonial architecture, the soldiers provided their families with fascinating snapshots and stories in letters sent home. The common sight of elderly Arabs riding ancient donkeys while their barefoot wives walked behind them amused the men to no end. However, that amusement did not extend to the petty theft that occurred on a routine basis: *Articles of clothing and equipment began disappearing into thin air. … One regimental intelligence officer's face was mighty red when he woke up one morning and discovered that his shoes and trousers had been neatly lifted from under his sack during the night.*[2]

Commanded by Colonel Rudolph W. Broedlow, Staff Sergeant Ray Lound and the 361st Combat Team completed their training in Africa and landed on Anzio, Italy, June 1, 1944. The first unit of the 91st Division to enter combat, the 361st Regiment detached from the 91st and attached to the 36th Infantry Division upon arrival in Italy. The regiment took up positions on the ridge four miles northwest of Velletri, and on June 3, the 361st experienced their first enemy fire. Once again the unit was reassigned, this time to the 34th Division, where they relieved the 133rd Infantry and began their advance along Highway 1, north of Rome. Although delayed by mines and enemy artillery, the 361st captured several cities including Tarquinia, Montalto di Castro, Nuxiatello and Orbetello.[1]

The rapid move north to the Italian front continued until June 19, when the regiment settled near Batignano. All battalions, minus the 2nd Battalion, were attached to one of three motorized combat teams with orders to ride the tanks, deploy and attack the enemy.[1, 2]

During the following two weeks the 361st Infantry saw continuous action. Staff Sergeant Lound was killed on July 2, 1944, as the regiment battled fiercely at Casole d'Elsa from July 1 to 4, before securing the town. After a full month of continuous fighting, the 361st Regimental Combat Team returned to the control of the 91st Division.[1]

Staff Sergeant Ray Lound is buried in Florence American Cemetery, Via Cassia, Italy. A musically talented family, his father played the violin and his mother played the concertina. The family raised capon chickens and Mr. Lound drove the school bus. Ray's parents and ten siblings survived his death.

His beautiful girlfriend, Ramona Peterson, grew up in nearby Willow River, Minnesota. Staff Sergeant Lound enlisted in the armed forces October 8, 1942.[3, 4, 5] His personal effects sent home to his family included a Good Conduct Ribbon, a Sharpshooter Medal, $3.51, a pipe, a Bible, a sewing kit and a writing kit.[6]

Stanton Johnson Shefveland

Perley (Norman County)

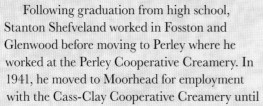

6th Infantry "Sightseeing Sixth" Division, 63rd Infantry Regiment, 3rd Battalion, L Company,
Private First Class

DECEMBER 3, 1910–JULY 5, 1944—Maffin Bay Campaign, New Guinea

Following graduation from high school, Stanton Shefveland worked in Fosston and Glenwood before moving to Perley where he worked at the Perley Cooperative Creamery. In 1941, he moved to Moorhead for employment with the Cass-Clay Cooperative Creamery until his induction into the army on August 3, 1942. After induction, Private First Class Shefveland trained at Fort Leonard Wood, Missouri, and Camp Luis San Obispo before transferring to the Hawaiian Islands with the 6th Infantry Division.[1, 2]

The 6th Infantry Division, called the "Sightseeing Sixth," moved to Oahu, Hawaii, in July 1943 for training in jungle warfare in preparation for the New Guinea Campaign. From January to June 1944, the division trained in Milne Bay, New Guinea, and landed on Maffin Bay on the northern coast of New Guinea to begin combat. Historian Thomas Price pointed out that if they were to seize the strategic Japanese installations still under construction at Maffin Airdrome, they would have to take Lone Tree Hill and others that overlooked the base. On June 20, 1944, the 6th infantry took over the battle against 8,000 Japanese troops.[3, 4]

U.S. maps depicted Lone Tree Hill as a single tree. In reality, the hill, formed from coral and covered with dense tropical foliage, extended much farther and straddled a steep slope and stream. On June 26, Private First Class Stanton Shefveland and the 3rd Battalion of the 63rd Regiment relieved two 20th Infantry Battalions, exhausted from days of battle on Lone Tree Hill. Mop-up of the remaining Japanese positions was dangerous and slow. Shefveland's L Company was exposed to snipers and machine gun nests hidden in the hollows of the coral, and artillery fire caused several casualties on June 29. Though Shefveland survived that assault, over 150 men of the 6th died from June 20 to 30, 1944, and Japanese casualties numbered well over a thousand.[3]

Following the capture of Lone Tree Hill, Japanese forces had largely abandoned defensive positions in the hills around Maffin Airdrome, where the Americans captured a large amount of equipment. On July 4, the 63rd Infantry occupied Hill 225 and on the next day seized the crest of Mt. Saksin, which still held some Japanese fighters. During the assault on the hills, Private First Class Stanton Shefveland died on July 5 from wounds to the abdomen, only one week before the 6th's departure from Maffin Bay.[3, 4, 5]

Private First Class Stanton Shefveland, youngest child of Johan and Ricka (Johnson) Shefveland, was buried in Maffin, New Guinea, and reinterred in Audubon Cemetery, Audubon, Minnesota. Both parents preceded him in death, his mother just nine months earlier on September 28, 1943.

The local newspaper described Stanton J. Shefveland as: *...a very honest, upright, hard-working young man with a happy disposition and a cheerful smile for everyone. He will be sadly missed by all who knew him in that community."*[1, 2, 6]

Edwin Joel Iverson

McGrath (Aitkin County)

27th Infantry "O'Ryan's Roughnecks" Division, 105th Infantry Regiment, 1st Battalion, Headquarters Company, Private

APRIL 7, 1923–JULY 9, 1944—Battle of Saipan, Mariana Islands

Evon Pearson recalls her Uncle Edwin: *My Uncle Albert told me that Edwin had a girlfriend, Adeline Ruud, and that he had a car. Albert advised Edwin to join the navy thinking he would be safer. Soon Edwin was drafted and the rest is history.*[1]

Approximately 1,300 miles south of Japan, the small island of Saipan in the Marianas chain held tremendous strategic value for Japan. Not only did Saipan operate as a major supply route between Japan and the central Pacific, the airfields there also provided a base for air attacks on American fleets. The Americans set their sights on Saipan for precisely the same reason: they needed a base to launch the new gigantic B-29 Superfortress bombers for air attacks against Japan. The importance of securing Saipan and the Marianas was fully understood in August 1945, when the nearby island of Tinian launched the planes that dropped atomic bombs on Hiroshima and Nagasaki, effectively ending the war.

Three divisions were assigned to secure Saipan: the 2nd Marine Division, the 4th Marine Division and the army's 27th Infantry Division, including 19-year-old Private Edwin J. Iverson, who entered the army on February 12, 1943. On June 11, 1944, the U.S. invasion force, consisting of 535 ships carrying more than 127,000 troops, bombarded both coasts of the island. Despite several days of naval and air bombing, the 2nd and 4th Marines met fierce Japanese artillery and mortar fire upon landing on June 15. More than 2,000 marines were killed or wounded.[2, 3, 4, 5] When Admiral Raymond A. Spruance, commander of the Saipan invasion, discovered that the Japanese fleet was approaching the Marianas, he went after the fleet and committed his reserve, the 27th Infantry Division, to the battle. Led by Lieutenant Colonel William O'Brien, Private Iverson and the 105th Regiment cleared the southern point of Saipan, held by over 1,200 Japanese defenders, and joined the rest of the 27th Division and the marines for a bloody assault on Mt. Tapochau, the island's main Japanese defense.[3, 4]

While the marines cleaned up the coasts, the 27th Division continued its attack up the center of the island. Near the end of the battle, the desperate Japanese mounted the largest banzai attack of the war. As Francis O'Brien said, this was more than a usual banzai attack; this was effectively a mass suicide of the entire unit. On July 7 more than 4,000 soldiers, including wounded men on crutches and men armed only with rocks, charged like madmen. The Japanese swept down the railroad track along the beach, overrunning the 105th Infantry, who bore the brunt of the charge. Rallying the troops before he died, Lieutenant Colonel William J. O'Brien's last words were, "Don't give them a damned inch!"[4, 5] That day, the 1st and 2nd Battalions of the 105th Infantry alone killed 2,295 Japanese, and 3 soldiers from the 105th were awarded the Congressional Medal of Honor. Division historian, Captain Edmund Love, wrote: *On the morning of July 7, its members were to stand in the face of the greatest single enemy Banzai raid of the Pacific War. They were to die almost to a man in one of the more courageous struggles of American military history.*[4, 5] Japanese commanders committed suicide before the charge, and their soldiers fought to the death. Hundreds of civilians, frightened by propaganda by the Imperial Japanese Army that depicted American troops as monsters, leapt to their deaths from cliffs at the northern end of Saipan.[2, 5]

Private Edwin Iverson survived the banzai attack only to die from sniper fire on July 9, four days before the island was declared secure. He was buried two days later in the Army Cemetery on Saipan Island.[6]

During the war, Private Edwin Iverson and his best friend, Marine Private First Class Ervin Buck from McGrath, were separated when Edwin was sent to Saipan. Following the battle for Saipan, Ervin was sent to Saipan to help recover the bodies of the servicemen, and he found Edwin's body.[7] Private Edwin Iverson was later re-interred at Holden Cemetery in Isle, Minnesota. All five of the Iverson brothers served in World War II.[8]

Herman Ingvar Holmstrom

9th Infantry "The Old Reliables" Division, 47th Infantry Regiment, 3rd Battalion, I Company, Private
FEBRUARY 16, 1911–JULY 12, 1944—Battle of the Hedgerows, France

On June 10, 1944, (D-Day plus 4), Private Herman Holmstrom and the 47th Regiment landed on Utah Beach between St. Martin and Saint-Germain-de-Varreville. As the men traveled from the beach to the countryside, they entered bocage country: solid walls of impenetrable hedgerows, 12 feet high and 8 feet deep. Designed as living fences to keep dairy cows from the road, the hedgerows now hid German soldiers and their artillery from the Allies.

When the 47th Infantry crossed the Merderet River on June 14, the marshy and flooded river caused serious problems for Allied soldiers and paratroopers. On the other side of the river, the Germans fought hard until June 16 when the Allies cut off their last escape route, boxing the enemy into the Cotentin Peninsula. Despite persistent German fire looking down on the Allies, the "Raiders" of the 47th entered Cherbourg on June 25 and joined in the victory celebration when the city fell three days later.

After a much-needed rest, commanders sent the 47th back into action on July 9 to once again face the merciless terrain at the "Battle of the Hedgerows," near St.-Lô.[1, 2, 3] Bob Bearden wrote: *Never in our instructions about the terrain of the Normandy countryside did we ever hear the word hedgerow. Twenty-foot high hedges, so impassable that not even tanks could penetrate them. Used to divide farming acreage, most often pasturage for cows, the hedgerows had often grown together to form a canopy over somewhat sunken, sandy roadbeds, where no sunlight ever penetrated.*[2]

During the battle for St.-Lô, Private Herman Holmstrom was killed by shrapnel and buried in Sainte-Mère-Église U.S. Military Cemetery in Normandy, France.[3] The Action Report for July 12 states: *The 1st Battalion continued their attack to the south, at 0830 they had two companies clear of the road junction moving against stiff resistance. Heavy machine gun fire from the west and southwest, direct 88 mm fire from the south, and enemy tanks operating from the front forced the lead companies to stop at 1130. By late afternoon they were able to push their way down to the road junction. The 3rd Battalion attacked to the south to the towns of La Haye and La Hogue. At 1145 the leading companies had cleaned up both places and were moving slowly along the road 200 yards south of La Hogue. At 1930 the 3rd Battalion was ordered to hold their present position until the 1st Battalion was able to catch up. They were to send one company,* (E Company), *into Le Glinel, blocking all roads around the town with tank destroyers and anti-tank mines. Toward evening an unusual amount of activity and movement was heard and observed behind the enemy lines, especially tanks and armored vehicles.*[4]

Herman Holmstrom was reinterred September 11, 1948, at Marmrelund Cemetery, Marshall County, Minnesota. He was survived by his father, two sisters, his wife and a four-month-old daughter.[5, 6]

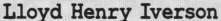

Lloyd Henry Iverson

Goodridge (Pennington County)

U.S. Army Air Forces, 8th Air Force, 95th Bomb Group, "Justice with Victory,"
336th Heavy Bomb Squadron, Sergeant
APRIL 2, 1923–JULY 12, 1944—Bombing Mission 469, Munich, Germany

Judy Iverson Skogerboe remembers her father: *My mom and dad went out with another couple on a double date, and ended up with each other at the end of the evening. My mom taught in the St. Hilaire School when my dad enlisted. He wanted to be in the navy but the navy quota was full and the recruiter placed him in the Air Force. When my mom visited my dad in Gulfport, Mississippi, they married there and moved to Texas before my dad shipped out for England. My dad was 5 feet, 4 inches tall, the right size for a tail gunner in an airplane. After his plane crashed on his third mission, the Red Cross recovered his body and returned my mom's class ring. My mom never remarried. She had other suitors after his death, but she loved and respected my dad so much that no one else could measure up to him.*[1,2]

After graduating from Goodridge High School in 1941, Lloyd Iverson worked at a defense plant in Michigan. He was inducted into the army in March 1943 and graduated from aircraft gunnery school where he was promoted to sergeant. While stationed at Gulfport Field, Mississippi, Lloyd married Pearl Limesand and in May 1944, he traveled to England with the 8th Air Force.[3,4]

Sergeant Lloyd Iverson was one of over 8,000 servicemen in the 95th Bomb Group, a unit that completed 320 missions for the 8th Air Force, losing 157 bombers and destroying 425 German fighters during the war. Sergeant Iverson's Squadron, the 366th, was one of four bomb squadrons in the 95th Bomb Group, which flew B-17 Flying Fortresses out of Horham, England.[5]

On July 12, 1944, 1,271 bombers and 803 fighters were dispatched on Mission 469 to bomb Munich and Enstingen, Germany. Sergeant Lloyd Iverson, tail gunner, left along with his ten-man crew. While flying their B-17 Flying Fortress over Munich, enemy anti-aircraft fire hit the plane. Headquarters for the 95th Bomb Group gave this account: *B-17, 42-97856, piloted by 2nd Lieutenant. James M. Redin, was seen to be hit by flak just after bombs away. The flak over the target was intense and accurate. The aircraft went into a steep dive and disappeared into the clouds. The tail section was hit and was breaking up as it disappeared into the undercast. No chutes were seen to leave the ship prior to this time. All ten crewmembers were initially listed as Missing in Action and later declared killed in action when the crashed plane was identified in Neubiburg, Germany.*[5,6,7,8]

Judy Iverson Briski recalls Lloyd Iverson: *My dad, Irvin Iverson, was Lloyd's cousin, and I remember this photo of Lloyd's bomb crew—Lloyd is the far right in the back row. Lloyd's parents were Henry and Christine (Bundhund) Iverson of Goodridge. Christine's father, Nick Bundhund, was a banker in Goodridge. Lloyd's siblings were Janice and Raymond. He was married to Pearl (Limesand) Iverson of Goodridge, and had one child: A daughter, Judy, whom he never met. My dad passed away two years ago at age 96, but his sister, Edna McNelly, is 102 and lives in the Warroad Nursing Home. Edna remembers that Pearl was quite pregnant at the church service. Edna had the luncheon after the service at her house, so she did not go to the funeral.*

Sergeant Lloyd Iverson is buried in Goodridge Cemetery, Goodridge, Minnesota, next to his wife, Pearl. Lloyd's daughter, Judy Lenee, born after her father's death, was crowned Miss Aquacade 1963 in Thief River Falls, Minnesota.[1,2,3]

Harold E. Winjum

Strathcona (Roseau County)

U.S. Army Air Forces, 12th Air Force, 57th Bomb Wing, 340th Bomb Group, 489th Bomb Squadron, Technical Sergeant

JULY 27, 1915–JULY 12, 1944—Bombing Mission over Chiavari, Italy

In the early morning on July 12, 1944, B-25 Mitchell medium bombers from the 489th Bomb Squadron left the French island of Corsica in the Mediterranean Sea on a bombing mission against the railroad bridge in Ferrara, Italy. Technical Sergeant Harold Winjum and his crew of six flew on *Flak Fodder II*, a bomber with two photographers aboard to photograph the target after the formation dropped the bombs. On the mission, a group of 6 to 8 German fighter planes broke away from a flight of 16 planes and attacked the lone camera plane trailing far behind the tight bomber formation. Gunners Winjum and Staff Sergeant Hertel shot down one German plane and a second "probable" plane. The *Flak Fodder* successfully returned to base and the two men happily posed for photographs.[1, 2, 11]

Later that day, another mission assigned 18 B-25 bombers from the 489th Bomb Squadron to strike the railroad bridge at Chiavari, Italy. Sergeant Winjum and Sergeant Hertel were part of the attack, serving aboard the *Legal Eagle*.

They missed the target, but hit the nearby marshaling yards. Shortly before reaching the target, the *Legal Eagle*, piloted by Lieutenant John Mitchell, developed left engine trouble. Despite the trouble, the pilot continued on to the target and the bombardier dropped the bombs. Just after turning off the bomb run, the right engine failed, forcing the pilot to ditch the plane in the Gulf of Genoa, about 50 miles southeast of Genoa. Both Technical Sergeant Winjum and Staff Sergeant Wallace MacRitchie apparently parachuted out of the plane; the rest of the crew stayed with the aircraft when it ditched in the water.[1, 2, 3]

What exactly happened to them is something of a mystery. On November 23, 1945, Captain John Mitchell wrote to Major William Sanders: *Dear Sir, Regarding Harold E. Winjum and circumstances of his disappearance, I submit this information to be true to the best of my knowledge. On July 12, 1944, on a mission over Chiavari, Italy, at about 10,000 feet the right engine necessitated feathering approaching the target. We dropped our bombs and came away from the target and when losing altitude at about 8,000 feet, the left engine was feathered and I called Sergeant Winjum and instructed him to throw overboard all*

excess weight. At about 6,000 feet I called again to see what progress was being made and he answered all was well. That was my last contact. I called again, but because of no answer, I presumed he was busy. After we crashed, I counted noses in the raft and discovered my tail gunner and radioman, Sergeant Winjum, were missing and immediately returned to the inside of the rear of the airplane, but even on a second try beneath the water in the rapidly flooding ship, I discovered nothing. Returning to the raft and just before it went down, I took notice of the disappearance of the emergency escape hatch of the tail gunner's position. I learned later from intelligence that both of them had bailed out at about 4,000 feet having been seen by a circling airplane. The fright of landing in water is the only possible reason I can see for bailing out because there were no instructions from me to do such a thing. Because of darkness coming on, the circling planes left and we were picked up the next morning by a PBY and of the two who bailed out, I know not.[4]

The bodies of Winjum and MacRitchie were never recovered.[5]

In addition to normal combat losses, the 340th Bomb Group lost more aircraft than any other medium Bomb Group during World War II due to two devastating events. In March 1944, Mount Vesuvius erupted when the 340th was based at nearby Pompeii Airfield near Terzigno, Italy. The eruption destroyed 88 B-25 Mitchell bombers, based on estimates at the time. Disaster struck again on May 13, 1944, when a surprise German air raid wiped out at least 60 aircraft on Alesani airfield at Alesani, Corsica.[1, 2, 3]

Technical Sergeant Harold E. Winjum is memorialized on the Tablets of Missing, Sicily-Rome American Cemetery, Nettuno, Italy, and in Poplar Grove Cemetery, Strathcona, Minnesota.[6, 7, 8, 9, 10]

Herman Eiben Hoffrogge

Third Army, 35th Infantry "Santa Fe" Division, 137th Infantry Regiment, 3rd Battalion, L Company, Private First Class

OCTOBER 21, 1921–JULY 14, 1944—Battle of the Hedgerows, France

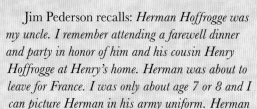

Jim Pederson recalls: *Herman Hoffrogge was my uncle. I remember attending a farewell dinner and party in honor of him and his cousin Henry Hoffrogge at Henry's home. Herman was about to leave for France. I was only about age 7 or 8 and I can picture Herman in his army uniform. Herman helped me assemble a wooden model airplane that he gave me during his farewell party. I very much remember Herman helping me with the airplane.*[1]

On July 4, 1944, Private First Class Herman Hoffrogge and the 137th Infantry Regiment, 35th Infantry Division, left England and landed at Omaha Beach near Colleville-sur-Mer, France. Upon seeing the beach destruction and row after row of white crosses, every infantryman asked the same question, "How did anyone survive?" By July 9, all three regiments of the 35th Division were on the lines west of St.-Lô, Normandy, the entry to central France and the core of German defenses.

The 35th "Santa Fe" Division had orders to replace the 29th and 30th Infantry Divisions on the front around St.-Lô and secure the town. However, there were major obstacles to overcome. The American line, under German observation from Hills 192 and 122 overlooking St.-Lô, faced large hedgerows surrounding each field. The highly trained German army used the hills and impenetrable hedgerows to pick off the advancing American infantry. With obstructed views in every direction, the men fought in close hand-to-hand fighting where the best, or luckiest, soldier prevailed. Another major obstacle was the loss of many highly skilled officers and infantrymen who had served in the army since 1940. Replacements who followed the original men rarely had more than 13 weeks of infantry training.[2, 3, 4]

Fortunately, U.S. soldiers had learned a lot about hedgerow fighting since landing in France in June. The "Culin Hedgerow Cutter," a four-pronged plow device on the front of the tank, developed by Sergeant Curtis Culin, could cut and lift the hedgerows, while protecting the tank's underside. This new invention and improved air support combined for a victory at St.-Lô. After the 2nd Division captured Hill 192 on July 12, Herman Hoffrogge and the 137th Infantry Regiment attacked Hill 122. Two days later, the 137th Regiment and the 737th Tank Battalion moved down the east bank of the Vire River and pinned the Germans down. This enabled the 134th Division to take Hill 122 overlooking St.-Lô and to be the first division to enter the city.[2, 3, 4]

During the advance on St.-Lô, Herman Hoffrogge lost his life. The Battle History Report of the 137th Infantry for July 14, 1944, states: *The regiment attacked again at 0800, with one platoon of medium tanks in support of each battalion. By 1300 the 1st Battalion had advanced up to 300 yards, but were meeting stiff resistance at la Pte Ferme. By 1630 the 1st Battalion was attacking the enemy stronghold at La Marelle, where German troops had assembled in the stone buildings in that area. The 3rd Battalion, on the right, had established contact with forces on the strongly held road junction of Highways 2 and 3. All elements were encountering heavy minefields and 88 mm fire. Casualties in the regiment totaled 127. Of these, 17 were killed, 106 wounded and 4 missing. Lieutenant Garthwaite and Lieutenant Kennedy were killed. Forty prisoners were taken. Some of the prisoners reported that many German soldiers wanted to surrender, but were being closely watched by officers and non-commissioned officers.*[3, 5]

Private First Class Herman Hoffrogge grew up on a farm northeast of Revere, Minnesota. He attended grade school in Revere and high school in nearby Lamberton. He joined the army in September 1942 and is buried at Normandy American Cemetery, Colleville-sur-Mer, France.

Originating from the Kansas, Missouri, and Nebraska National Guard, the 35th Division's shoulder patch, the Santa Fe cross, was a symbol used to mark the Santa Fe Trail, an area where the unit trained when it was first incorporated in 1918.[1, 6, 7]

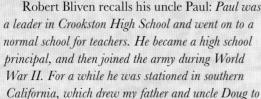

Paul Gulliford Bliven

8th Infantry "Golden Arrow" Division, 121st Infantry "The Gray Bonnet" Regiment, 2nd Battalion, Headquarters Company, 2nd Lieutenant
SEPTEMBER 7, 1912–JULY 15, 1944—Normandy Campaign, Normandy, France

Robert Bliven recalls his uncle Paul: *Paul was a leader in Crookston High School and went on to a normal school for teachers. He became a high school principal, and then joined the army during World War II. For a while he was stationed in southern California, which drew my father and uncle Doug to move to California. Tuberculosis swept through the Bliven household in the early 40s, which gave my father and Doug exemption from military service. They came here and joined the workforce in aircraft manufacturing plants. Probably the weather was better for their condition, too. I didn't hear a lot of stories about Paul. But once I was ironing a shirt and my dad told me not to let the sleeve touch the floor. It turns out that dad had a lot of experience ironing shirts because when Paul was in college; he sent home his dirty clothes by mail, to be washed, ironed, folded and mailed back to his school. The Bliven family lived in downtown Crookston next to the Red Lake River. During the Depression, they supplemented my grandfather's pay by growing and selling flowers. My dad did beekeeping too, so they also sold honey. My grandfather was a traveling sewing machine salesman. My grandmother was German, so they made sauerkraut in the cellar.*[1]

On July 1, 1944, the 8th Infantry Division steamed out of Belfast Harbor, Ireland, and on July 4, landed on Omaha Beach on the Cherbourg Peninsula. Burns recounts a common question on the minds of men, arriving just 28 days after D-Day: *How in God's name did those men make it on the first day through those barriers?* On a miserably hot day, the men, wearing fatigues, wool army socks, and underwear treated for lice, began a 22-mile march to Montebourg, where final preparations were made for battle.[2]

A month after D-Day, the Allies held only a few square miles in France. When the crucial port city of Cherbourg fell, the Germans were driven south to La Haye-du-Puits. Now the 8th Division planned to rout the Germans out of La Haye-du-Puits, but first they had to reach the Ay River.

Early morning on July 8, the 8th Division launched the first attack in France with 2nd Lieutenant Paul Bliven and the 121st Infantry on the front lines in a drive to the Ay River. The Germans mounted a strong defense of the river, and the division only advanced a few hundred yards at a time. On July 12, 1st Battalion relieved 2nd Lieutenant Paul Bliven and his 2nd Battalion after they had taken Hill 112, referred to as "Purple Heart Hill."

Despite heavy German machine gun fire from hedgerows and snipers in trees, they reached the north bank of the Ay River on July 14 and held their position for 11 days to plan their river crossing. Casualties were heavy, as expected among troops in combat for the first time, and artillery crashed in regularly at the same time each morning in the "Ten O'Clock Express." Every night German planes dropped flares and bombed and strafed Allied troops.[2, 3, 4]

Roseanne Barrett recalls her aunt telling her about her father's death: *My mother never talked about my father. She taught in a parochial school in St. Paul and would tell me stories of school, but nothing about my father. My aunt told me that dad was driving a truck and when night arrived, the soldiers slept in the truck. A bomb dropped from a plane and killed them all while they were sleeping. My mother never remarried. It was always just the two of us.*[5]

2nd Lieutenant Paul Bliven, son of Floyd and Rosella (Hauser) Bliven, married Rose Dolan from Danvers, Minnesota, in November 1941. Rose's brother, Private Vincent J. Dolan (page 104), died six months after her husband at the Battle of the Bulge, Germany. Both families requested that Paul and Vincent be returned together from France, and buried side by side in the Church of the Visitation Cemetery in Danvers, Minnesota.[6, 7, 8]

Verlyn DeBlonde Hegna

Sargeant (Mower County)

9th Infantry "The Old Reliables" Division, 60th Infantry Regiment, 1st Battalion, C Company, Private
OCTOBER 20, 1923–JULY 16, 1944—Normandy Campaign, Battle of the Hedgerows, France

Verlyn's sister, Wandah, seven years old at the time, remembers: *My brother, was a kind, thoughtful and loveable man. One day, while seated at my desk in school, Verlyn arrived home on furlough, and in full uniform, he surprised my class with a visit. I also remember the day my parents received the news of Verlyn's death. My family had moved from their farm near Sargeant to an apartment above the café they purchased in Hayfield in 1943. One night, the train unexpectedly stopped in Hayfield and the conductor left the train to deliver the telegram to my parents who were working at the café.*[1]

The 9th Division had proved their worth in Africa, Italy, and now in France. On June 11, 1944, five days after D-Day, Private Verlyn Hegna and the 60th Regiment landed at Utah Beach, Normandy, France, to lead the American advance from the beachhead to cut off the Cotentin Peninsula. They began a coordinated attack on the Douve River with the 82nd Airborne Division against strong German opposition. Once they bridged the river on June 16, they moved quickly across the peninsula and cut all the major roads by the next day. Near Cherbourg, when A and C companies failed to rout a determined group of Germans from their pillboxes with small arms and mortar fire, a lineup of American tanks convinced the remaining 350 Germans to surrender the next morning. While the 39th Regiment (including Private Herman Holmstrom from Strandquist and Staff Sergeant Rudolph Indihar from Elcor) and the 47th Infantry Regiment captured the Port of Cherbourg, the 60th cleared Cap de la Hague, northwest of Cherbourg.[2, 3, 4]

After cutting off the Cotentin Peninsula and capturing Cherbourg, Beckers described the 9th Infantry Division as they moved south into Norman hedgerows where: *Each man was on his own, and a gain of 300 yards was a good day's work.* Battlefields divided by solid banks topped with hedges and trees, steady rain and tanks backed up along the roads greeted the weary soldiers as they moved toward St.-Lô, 48 miles south of Cherbourg.[2]

As the 9th Division advanced across France to St.-Lô with the 4th and 83rd Infantry Divisions bordering on either side, they crossed the Canal de Vire and moved through the Hommet Woods before reaching St.-Lô on July 21. Private Verlyn Hegna was shot by a sniper on July 16 during the drive to St.-Lô and buried in Sainte-Mère-Église American Cemetery.[5]

Four soldiers who served with Verlyn Hegna in the 60th Regiment and survived the advance across France, wrote a letter on October 4, 1944, to their commanding officer: *Dear Sir: We four men who are lucky enough to still be here since the landing in French Morocco, November 8, 1942, through the entire Tunisian Campaign, the Sicilian Campaign, the hedgerows of France, through Belgium and now somewhere in Germany we ask if it would be possible to relieve us from active combat duty. All of us have been wounded at least once and feel that you could do something to help our cause.*

Staff Sergeant Grover C. Yonce, Staff Sergeant Charles M. Rose
Private First Class Harold M. Turley, Staff Sergeant Edward A. Roberts
Company G, 60th Infantry

Their request was denied. The four infantrymen were well aware that their odds of survival were low given that the average soldier remained in active front service 48 to 64 days before he was killed, wounded or taken prisoner. Beating the odds, all of the men except Staff Sergeant Roberts survived the war.[6, 7]

Private Verlyn Hegna, son of Oscar E. and Fern (Pederson) Hegna was survived by his parents and siblings: Twylah, Wandah, LaFaye and Corporal Robert Hegna.

Veryln Hegna enlisted in the armed forces November 2, 1943. In 1949, Corporal Robert Hegna wrote to the army to request that he be allowed to escort his brother Verlyn's body back to Minnesota from France: *I have been informed by my parents that my brother's body, Private Verlyn Hegna, is to be shipped home shortly, which is now in France. And therefore, I would very much like to be an escort of his body to my home in Hayfield, Minnesota. I am now serving in the Air Forces and am stationed at 3535th Installation Squadron Mather Field, California. Your help would mean so much to me.*

Following the approval of his request, Corporal Robert Hegna witnessed the reburial of his brother, Private Verlyn Hegna, in Evanger Lutheran Church Cemetery, Sargeant, Minnesota.[5]

Leon Gilmore Anderson

Hazel Run (Yellow Medicine County)

28th Infantry "Keystone" Division, 109th Infantry Regiment, 1st Battalion, Headquarters Company, 1st Lieutenant

MAY 25, 1919–JULY 31, 1944—Battle of St. Lô, France

Erling Anderson recalls his brother: *Leon was a typical Norwegian and well-known and well liked. He helped out on the family farm as a youngster but really loved to play football.*[1,2]

Following his graduation from Hazel Run High School, Leon Anderson attended State College in Brookings, South Dakota, a land-grant college where all men were enrolled in the Reserve Officer's Training Corps. An outstanding athlete, Leon played college football for three years and in 1941 the North Central Conference named him both honorary captain and All-Conference guard. He also claimed the school's heavyweight boxing championship. That same year he married his college sweetheart, Vivian Ray, a fellow student at South Dakota State College, who graduated with a degree in pharmacy. After graduation from the School of Agriculture in May 1942, Leon entered the army in 1943 as a Second Lieutenant from State College's ROTC program, having also served as an officer in the National Guard.[3,4]

1st Lieutenant Leon Anderson joined the 28th Infantry "Keystone" Division, formed from the Pennsylvania Army National Guard and named for its home state. As the 28th battled through World War II, the Germans called them the "Bloody Bucket" Division due to the red insignia on their sleeve and their furious fighting. After training for ten months in Wales, 1st Lieutenant Leon Anderson and the 28th Infantry Division landed in Normandy, France, on July 22, 1944, just six weeks after D-Day. Held within 20 to 30 miles from the beach, General Omar Bradley designed Operation Cobra, a plan to break through the German defense at St.-Lô in the Cotentin Peninsula and move inland to German-occupied territory.

On July 25, the Allied Air Forces launched a massive attack along the St.-Lô-Périers road in an effort to stun the German forces. Over 2400 aircraft dropped 4,000 tons of bombs; unfortunately, many landed on U.S. ground troops. The Americans lost 111 men and 490 wounded by friendly fire.[5,6,7] Despite the tragic loss of American lives, the Germans suffered more. Historian Martin Blumenson wrote: *Bombs buried men and equipment, overturned tanks, cut telephone wires, broke radio antennas, sent messengers fleeing for foxholes or the nearest crater. Communications with forward echelons were completely disrupted. The bombardment transformed the main line of resistance into a frightening landscape of the moon. No less than a thousand men must have perished in the Cobra bombardment.*[5,6]

After surviving the American bombardment, the "Keystone" Division moved quickly northwest of St.-Lô, and entered combat on July 30 where they functioned as a backstop while other divisions advanced east to stop German forces. The next day, the Americans broke through the Cotentin Peninsula and began to surround the enemy. Operation Cobra, the great breakout at St.-Lô, turned the war's direction to the Allies.[5,6] At the end of the campaign, while driving a jeep near St.-Lô, 1st Lieutenant Leon Anderson hit a land mine and died of wounds on July 31, 1944.[8]

Survivors included his parents, Gilbert and Mathilda Anderson; his wife, Vivian Ray Anderson, and seven siblings. In an interview in 2002, Vivian Ray Distad said of her former husband, *"He was an ambitious athlete and a scholar."*[3]

Leon Anderson is buried in Hazel Run Lutheran Cemetery, Hazel Run, Minnesota. The Hazel Run American Legion Anderson-Tongen Post 559, located in the old school, honors the memory of 1st Lieutenant Leon Anderson and Staff Sergeant Jerald Tongen (page 136), two local farm boys who didn't return home.[3,4]

Jack E. Berger

83rd Infantry "Thunderbolt" or "Ohio" Division, 453rd Anti-Aircraft Artillery Automatic Weapons Battalion, Battery D, Private First Class

FEBRUARY 22, 1920–AUGUST 5, 1944—Battle for Saint-Malo, France

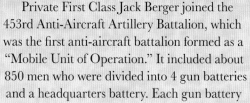

Private First Class Jack Berger joined the 453rd Anti-Aircraft Artillery Battalion, which was the first anti-aircraft battalion formed as a "Mobile Unit of Operation." It included about 850 men who were divided into 4 gun batteries and a headquarters battery. Each gun battery had 40 anti-aircraft guns and 50 machine guns transported by trucks and trailers.

On February 1, 1944, the 453rd left Camp Shanks, New York, on the *Dominion Monarch*, a British refrigeration ship where men in hammocks replaced cows hanging in the coolers. After intensive training in England to prepare the unit for the pending baptism of fire, Private First Class Jack Berger and his battalion landed on Normandy beach on June 18, 1944, to begin their advance into France. Upon arrival in France, the battalion was permanently assigned to the 83rd Infantry "Thunderbolt" Division. Initially named the "Ohio" Division as most personnel were from Ohio, the 83rd's shoulder patch has a downward-pointing black triangle and the letters "OHIO" within a gold circle.[1, 2, 3]

The 83rd Division entered the hedgerow struggle south of Carentan on June 17 and relieved the 101st Airborne. Stephen Ambrose quotes one of the men of the 101st Airborne, who witnessed the arrival of the 83rd: *They were so clean looking with a full compliment of men in each unit. Even the paint on their helmets looked as if they had just been unpacked.*[1] The fate of the soldiers changed quickly during warfare in the hedgerows as noted by Colonel James Shonak, Anti-Tank company/331st Infantry: *God we lost a lot of men. My worst nightmares are still in those rows.*[2]

As the 83rd fought their way through swamps that the Germans created by flooding the fields, the enemy, hidden beneath the hedgerows, fired on the advancing GIs with machine guns, mortars and artillery. Private First Class Jack Berger and the 453rd used their artillery to clear out the pillboxes in the hedgerows, so the infantry could improve their chances to gain ground. Later they used "Rhino" tanks for this purpose. Meanwhile, soldiers from the Engineer Corps picked their way through minefields to create supply routes through the hedges. On July 8, the 83rd fought through the hedgerows to the village of Auxais, and finally on the 10th, the 331st

Regiment captured Sainteny. As the 83rd regrouped along the Ay River, they viewed one of the largest air-ground operations ever attempted by American forces. Just 1,500 yards in front of the American line, Operation Cobra began on July 25 as 2,400 heavy bombers dropped 4,000 tons of bombs over the entire target area. Another 500 fighters provided cover and strafed enemy lines. The earth-shaking bombardment turned the enemy positions into a cratered wasteland.[1, 2, 3]

On July 27 the 83rd cut the St.-Lô-Périers road and forced their way into Le Mesnil-Vigot, a total of eight miles beyond their starting point. The 83rd moved out of the Cotentin Peninsula on August 3 with orders to capture the port towns of Saint-Malo and Dinard. The 453rd After Action Report dated September 7, 1944, described the events of August 5, 1944, the day that Private First Class Jack Berger died: *All batteries of the Organization were subjected to heavy shelling and small arms fire as they gradually worked with their respective Field Artillery Battalions towards St. Malo, their objective at the time. Battery "D" of this Organization had the only fatal casualty for the month on the 5th of August; one enlisted man was killed by a German sniper.*[4, 5]

Private First Class Jack Berger, son of Charles and Ida (Bostrom) Berger, joined the service October 20, 1942. He was buried in Brittany American Cemetery, Saint-James, France. Survivors included his parents and three brothers. All four boys served in the armed forces during World War II. One, Dorance Berger, received a purple heart for wounds received in action in Germany.[6]

In 1948, Truman Anderson, Jackie's good friend, donated land for the Jackie Berger Memorial Park in Duquette, Minnesota. Truman and Jackie grew up together and played baseball on the same team. The park, filled with beautiful pine trees, expanded in 1985 to 23 acres.[7]

Gerhard Burton Petersen

Perley (Norman County)

1st Infantry Division, 743rd Tank Battalion, C Company, Staff Sergeant

MAY 1, 1917–AUGUST 8, 1944—Battle of Mortain, France

After graduating from high school in 1935, Gerhard Petersen, known as Burton, worked as a farmhand before induction into the army on April 30, 1942. He moved to the Armored Division at Fort Lewis, Washington, and attended Gunnery School followed by ten months in the Mojave Desert Training Camp in Arizona.[1,2]

Originally a Minnesota National Guard unit, his 743rd Tank Battalion, like all tank battalions in World War II, did not stand alone but was attached to an infantry unit as needed. In November 1943, the 743rd left for England in preparation for D-Day on June 6, 1944, in France.

Two tank battalions arrived on Omaha Beach on D-Day: the 741st and the 743rd. Staff Sergeant Burton Petersen, in command of a section of two duplex drive amphibious tanks, landed with three companies in support of the 116th Regimental Combat Team. Journalist Earl Mago wrote in *Stars and Stripes*: *This unit fought its way ashore 10 minutes before H hour on D-Day.*[3]

As the 741st Tank Battalion attempted to launch their tanks 6,000 yards offshore from Omaha Beach, officers in the 116th Regimental Combat Team watched four-feet-high waves and high winds swamp the tanks. Captain Ned Eldar, commander of Petersen's C Company, decided not to risk the rough water, so all 32 tanks of the 743rd landed directly on the beach.

Once on shore, the tankers found a beach cluttered with men and equipment and flanked by cliffs defended by Germans. One soldier described the scenario for the 743rd Tank Battalion: *About the only type of direct fire that the enemy did not hurl at the tanks was bazookas. The bazookas were to be met later inland. The beach line was a maelstrom of shells [including] heavy artillery up to 155mm. Down from the cliffs came the direct fire of anti-tank guns. Mortar shells dropped down. Light and heavy machine guns spewed lead, and there was the crack of small arms. While four of the five men in each tank crew were not immediately concerned with the hail of machine gun and small-arms bullets, the fifth man—the tank commander with his head out of the turret—stood exposed to constant danger in the storm of splattering slugs and whistling shell fragments.*[4]

At 2200, the 743rd made it across the beach to an area near Vierville-sur-Mer, but lost 16 tanks during the day. The entire 743rd Tank Battalion received the Presidential Unit Citation for heroic action on D-Day, and Staff Sergeant Petersen was also awarded the Distinguished Service Cross.

Captain Ned Elder witnessed Staff Sergeant Petersens's extraordinary bravery: *Staff Petersen landed with the DD tanks in the assault wave on Vierville beach. He landed his section under heavy hostile fire, both small arms and artillery, and established liaison with the infantry in order to support them in their advance. In spite of strong hostile fire, he directed and coordinated the fire of his section against enemy installations, which were delaying the advance of the infantry. When the forward advance of his tanks was stopped by an anti-tank ditch, he dismounted under heavy fire and without regard for his personal safety, assisted in the preparation of a crossing of the obstacle.*[5,6]

Shortly after the battle, a commander of the 116th Infantry, who saw some of the worst fighting on the beach at Les Moulin, stated, "The tanks saved the day. They shot the hell out of the Germans, and got the hell shot out of them."[7]

Following the successful invasion of Normandy beach, the tank battalions had to work their way through the hedgerows, and after a tortuous, violent slog through them, only the city of Mortain stood between the Allies and deep, German-held territory. On August 7, the 743rd Tank Battalion, attached to the 30th Infantry Division, deployed C Company to protect the division's left flank. The next day, Staff Sergeant Petersen died when Royal Air Force Hawker Typhoons mistakenly bombed two C Company tanks. On August 8, the 743rd Journal reported: *1st platoon bombed by friendly aircraft. Two tanks set on fire...Sergeant Petersen died of wounds in hospital.*[8]

Staff Sergeant Petersen is buried in Brittany American Cemetery, Normandy, France. Memorial services were held at Bethania Lutheran Church and a marker honors him in Bethania Cemetery, Perley, Minnesota.[1,2]

LaVern Walter Nelson

Wilder (Jackson County)

30th Infantry "Old Hickory" Division, 120th Infantry Regiment, Private
SEPTEMBER 13, 1917–AUGUST 9, 1944—Battle of Mortain, France

LaVern Nelson's sister, Muriel, now 100 years old, recalls a story her mother told the family: *When LaVern left for the service, my mother told him that his dog, Snookie, would not remember him when he came home. LaVern said he would. And the story goes that when LaVern came home on furlough and got into his farm clothes, Snookie was right by him the rest of his furlough.*[1, 2]

LaVern graduated from Wilder High School in 1937 and entered the service on April 24, 1942. After training at Camp Chafee, Arkansas, Private Nelson worked as a military policeman for over a year before completing infantry training at Fort Jackson, North Carolina, and Camp Atterbury, Indiana. As of March 1943, he belonged to C Company, 423rd Infantry Regiment, 106th Infantry Division, but after a furlough at home in April 1944, LaVern traveled to the replacement center at Fort Meade, Maryland, and transferred to the 30th Infantry Division, which takes its nickname "Old Hickory" from President Andrew Jackson, who was known for his toughness and aggressiveness in the War of 1812 when he successfully led his troops from Tennessee and the Carolinas.

LaVern arrived in England on June 1, 1944, and landed in France on July 19, 1944, to begin the Battle of the Hedgerows.[3, 4]

After fighting hedgerow to hedgerow against Germans hidden in the dense foliage, the 30th Division captured the area overlooking St.-Lô, France. Known for their military strength and experience, the 30th Infantry Division, along with the 4th and 9th Divisions, was selected to lead Operation Cobra, the drive to break through St.-Lô and open the way to northern France. Despite Allied casualties from friendly bombers who dropped their bombs on Allied troops by mistake, the attack succeeded and the 30th continued south until they arrived in the Mortain-Sainte-Barthélemyon August 6. Here the 30th found four German Panzer divisions determined to hold their positions.

From August 7 to 12, the 30th succeeded in pushing the Germans out of Mortain by destroying several German tanks and killing hundreds of enemy soldiers.[5] In his personnel file, Private LaVern Nelson was listed as missing in action on August 8 and was buried on August 13, 1944, in the American Cemetery, Marigny, France. He died from chest wounds.

On December 4, 1944, Mr. and Mrs. Walter Nelson wrote a letter to the Quartermaster General in Washington D.C: *Dear Sir, I am writing you to get some information about our son, LaVern W. Nelson, who died for his country on August 9, 1944. Would like to know where he was in battle and where he is buried. It has been a comfort to know he was hospitalized and had some care. But would like to know where his wounds were. Don't think knowing would be any worse than thinking and that don't answer the problem. His personal effects we would like to have sent home if it is possible. I know he has some things we would like to have and keep. Any information you can give us will be greatly appreciated.*[6]

In 1948, LaVern Nelson was reinterred in Lakeview Cemetery, Windom, Minnesota.

Survivors included his parents, Walter and Iva (Christensen) Nelson, and a sister, Muriel. Iva Nelson did see her son before he went overseas. In August 1943, she traveled to Fort Smith, Arkansas, to visit LaVern on furlough and his girlfriend, Hazel Chitwood.

LaVern's parents lived two houses down from Harry and Ellen Lundgren whose son, Myril, died February 25, 1945, while fighting in Germany. Two other Minnesota men died during the Battle for Mortain: Gerhard Burton Petersen (page 67) and Sergeant Vernon Hoff (page 69). Both men were from Perley, Minnesota.[1, 2, 3]

Vernon Julian Hoff

Perley (Norman County)

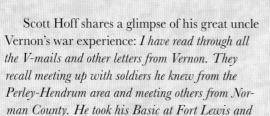

Third Army, 35th Infantry "Santa Fe" Division, 134th Infantry Regiment, 737th Tank Battalion, C Company, Sergeant

APRIL 29, 1914–AUGUST 10, 1944—Battle of Mortain, France

Scott Hoff shares a glimpse of his great uncle Vernon's war experience: *I have read through all the V-mails and other letters from Vernon. They recall meeting up with soldiers he knew from the Perley-Hendrum area and meeting others from Norman County. He took his Basic at Fort Lewis and spent a good amount of time training in Oregon and Yakima as well. He liked Yakima; its tents held six men and was much warmer than the raw rains of Oregon. He also traveled a bit to see his sister and family in Seattle and Uncle Art in the area also. He was engaged at the time to a local girl, Phyllis Hutchinson. There is a veiled acknowledgement of a girl he met when he was stationed in Washington, but later letters always talk about his marrying Phyllis when he would return home. He did make one comment about enjoying truck driving more than driving a tank, but acknowledged the safety and utility of the tank for their missions. They were sent by train from Seattle to the East Coast and from there off to Europe.*[1]

Vernon Hoff entered the service on April 30, 1942, and trained as a tank commander with the armored division at Fort Lewis, Washington. His unit, the 737th Tank Battalion, C Company, transferred to England in January 1944 before landing on Omaha Beach on July 12 and 13, 1944, to help capture St.-Lô in France.[2]

On July 22, 1944, Vernon wrote to Anna Hoff: *Dear Mother, This is Sunday once again, and it's been very quiet for us. I slept all afternoon, now I won't sleep so good tonight, oh well, what's the difference. Went to church this morning, the chaplain gave a very nice talk, too bad we don't get the chance to know him more often. He is good, but not as good as Rev. Anderson back home. We haven't been getting our mail, and I can tell you, mom, it's very disappointing not to hear from home, especially as how we've been chasing the Jerries around all day. We may get some tonight, at least I've heard a few rumors to that effect. Some of the boys have gotten purple hearts. I myself don't want any. All I want is to get out with my whole hide with no glory or glamour attached. Well, mom, I haven't much time anymore, so I guess I'll be stopping along here someplace. I'd sure like to see you for a few minutes tonight. You and Phyllis could sure help me a lot right now. Your loving son, Vernon.*[3]

After the capture of St.-Lô, the 737th battalion transferred from the First Army to Patton's Third Army, known as the "Spearheaders," on August 6, 1944. The 2nd Battalion had become separated from the 30th Infantry Division during their advance on Mortain and were now stranded on Hill 314. This "Lost Battalion" kept up a stream of artillery on the Germans, who were trying to split the Allied forces with an advance to the sea, but they now were running out of food and ammunition. On August 9, Sergeant Hoff and the 737th Tank Battalion led the way for the 320th Infantry, as they set out to rescue the "Lost Battalion."[4, 5, 6]

The leading M-4 Sherman tank had advanced only 100 yards before taking three rounds from a 50 mm anti-tank gun. Sergeant Hoff's tank pulled around the disabled tank and scored a direct hit that killed the entire crew of the anti-tank gun.[6, 7] Mark Reardon wrote: *As Task Force Gillis pushed further east, Sergeant Vernon Hoff's tank fell victim to another hidden 50 mm anti-tank gun. Two Sherman tanks immediately to the rear of Hoff's stricken vehicle knocked out the opposing gun.*[6]

By the time the 2nd Battalion was rescued on August 12, over 300 out of 700 men in 2nd Battalion were killed or wounded. In 2 miles from their line of departure, 13 of 38 tanks were destroyed. After rescuing the "Lost Battalion," the 737th Tank Battalion moved to liberate Mortain, France, and to secure Mortain Road.[4, 5, 6]

Estimates of Americans killed in action from August 6 to 13 varied from 2,000 to 3,000, with an unknown number of wounded. On August 21, more than 50,000 German troops surrendered, effectively ending the German 7th Army. The heroic 737th Tank Battalion participated in all of the five major battles including Normandy, northern France, Ardennes-Alsace, Rhineland, and Central Europe and saw 299 days of combat.[6]

Vernon Hoff was buried at Brittany American Cemetery, France, and memorialized at Landstad Lutheran Cemetery, Perley, Minnesota. Vernon's cousin, Jan Kjesbo, remembers playing tag with Vernon on their farmstead, where the big trees were safe zones.[1, 8]

James Clifford Graba

Nimrod (Wadena County)

U.S. Army Air Forces, 8th Air Force, 569th Bomb Squadron, 390th Heavy Bomb Group, 1st Lieutenant
SEPTEMBER 4, 1921–AUGUST 26, 1944—Air Collision over Hertfordshire, England

On the morning of August 26, 2007, a small group of people, including relatives, witnesses, and an aviation archaeologist, traveled to the woods near a small village in Hertfordshire, England, to remember an accident that occurred there 63 years earlier on August, 26, 1944. On that tragic day, 2 B-17s on a bombing mission collided and 14 American airmen and 2 civilians died.

2nd Lieutenant Paul Bellamy and 1st Lieutenant James Graba, pilot and co-pilot for their B-17 Flying Fortress, took off from Framlingham, England, to assemble into group formation at 10,000 feet with their plane leading the low squadron. A second B-17 Flying Fortress, *Ding Dong Daddy*, piloted by 1st Lieutenant George E. Smith, flew in #6 position in the lead squadron. The group proceeded to Luton, 30 miles north of London, when two hours later at 14,000 feet, Pilot Smith's plane dropped out of position directly down onto Bellamy and Graba's unnamed Flying Fortress. Their B-17 lost the right wing, started on fire, and exploded a few seconds later. The plane on top also caught fire and spiraled to earth, killing two civilians.[1]

Remarkably, four crewmen of the nine-man crew on Bellamy and Graba's plane parachuted to safety. Sergeant Conser, who survived, gave the following statement: *We were climbing for altitude and heading for the splasher to leave the English coast. The first alarm came when the top turret gunner called over interphone to the pilot that the man above us in the lead squadron was coming down pretty close. Then he said, "better drop down." He had no response from the pilot and the ship kept coming down. I looked up out of the left waist window and at the same time reached for my chute. The ship was about ten feet above us at the time and the top turret was calling "dive it, dive it," over interphone. It seemed that nobody in the cockpit heard his warnings and about a second later, we collided. It seemed to me #3 engine from the ship hit us in the fuselage around the bomb bay and the #1 and #2 engines went in our wing. By that time, I had my chute on one side and was through to the top of the waist. Next thing I knew, I was on my hands and knees on the floor and a big ball of fire came down the waist from the radio room. In the explosion I was thrown against the side of the fuselage and everything went black. I don't know how long I was there, but came to when the ball turret gunner called my name. I jumped up and at the same time hooked the other part of my chute. I went over to the ball gunner, who was standing in the*

end of the waist, where it had broken in two. He had lost his chute, so we looked around for it for a second. Then he said, "Let's get out," and I said "OK" So we jumped together. He locked his arms through my harness and his legs around mine, but when I pulled the ripcord he came off of me so quickly I didn't realize he was gone. While I was still in the air, one of the ships hit the ground and exploded. I was right above it at the time and it threw pieces for a mile or two and broke windows in the house I landed near, about a half mile from the explosion. We were at about 14–15,000 feet at the time of the collision.[2]

Unfortunately, 1st Lieutenant James Graba, son of Clifford and Bertha (Platten) Graba, didn't survive the crash. He is buried at Cambridge American Cemetery, Cambridge, England. Survivors included his parents, his wife, Dorothea, and six siblings. Graba flew 25 missions, the majority in a B-17 Super Fortress named *Dottie III*, later renamed the *Green Banana*. He graduated from Sebeka High School in Sebeka, Minnesota.[1,2]

Back Row L to R:
Ray E. Cook, Ball Turret; William W. Combow, Waist; Ground Crew Chief unknown; Herbert W. Harms, Tail Gunner; Unidentified Crewman; Francis T. McDermott, Radio; Charles W. Blackmon, Engineer/ Top Turret
Front Row L to R:
John W. Stearns, Navigator; Robert M. Buckley, Co-Pilot; James J. Graba, Pilot; Unidentified Crewman

Leroy Elmer Johnson

Revere (Redwood County)

U.S. Army Air Forces, 15th Air Force, 5th Bomb Wing, 2nd Heavy Bomb Group, 20th Bomb Squadron, 240 Headquarters Company, Sergeant

MARCH 24, 1925–AUGUST 29, 1944—Air Battle over the White Carpathian Mountains, Czech Republic

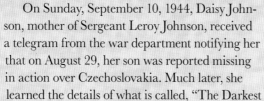

On Sunday, September 10, 1944, Daisy Johnson, mother of Sergeant Leroy Johnson, received a telegram from the war department notifying her that on August 29, her son was reported missing in action over Czechoslovakia. Much later, she learned the details of what is called, "The Darkest Day—A Squadron Lost," when an entire squadron was wiped out.[1]

The events that occurred on August 29, 1944, for Mission 263, were disastrous for the 2nd Bomb Group. That day, 28 B-17s left Amendola Air Base, Foggia, Italy, and dropped 49 tons of bombs on the Privoser Oil Refinery in Moravská Ostrava, Czechoslovakia. Not all the aircraft made it to the oil refinery. On the way to their target, 89 German fighters attacked the 20th Bomb Squadron and shot down all 7 of its planes in 20 minutes. Two other squadrons, the 49th and 429th, each lost one plane. It was the second-largest, one-day loss of aircraft for that Bomb Group and its greatest loss of life. A total of 90 young men were shot down; 40 lost their lives, another 46 were captured, and 4 men escaped.[2, 3, 4]

Sergeant Leroy Johnson, a right waist gunner, flew on *Lovely Ladies* with Pilot Merrill Prentice and a crew of nine others when they were hit by German fighters and knocked out of control. Only the navigator, 2nd Lieutenant Charles McVey, parachuted to safety, remaining a prisoner of war until the end of the war. He wrote: *It was around 10:40 a.m. and we were around 24,000 feet. Our ship was the last in the formation of our formation, the last in the wing that day. At that time our formation was attacked by about 90 planes, and our plane was immediately hit by 20 mm flak.*[1, 3]

The 2nd Bomb Group historians report that two men bailed out and one, tail gunner Sergeant Robert E. Fitch, died of injuries. The other eight were apparently still in the plane when it crashed into a farmer's house near Vyskovec and exploded.[2]

After his liberation, 2nd Lieutenant McVey wrote to Daisy Johnson on August 3, 1945: *Dear Mrs. Johnson, As Mr. Prentice has already informed you, I was navigating the plane on which Leroy was flying on our last mission. Due to the fact that we were attacked so suddenly and unexpectedly, our ship was almost instantly damaged and we were ordered to bail out. Under ordinary circumstances, I would not see your son bail out, since we use different escape hatches. On this occasion I did not see any other crewmember on the ship bail out, nor did I either see any other parachutes in the air, see any of the crew members on the ground, or see or hear about them after my capture. Mr. Prentice has indicated that he is trying to get information from people in the vicinity of our trouble near Trencin, Slovakia, through other sources. It is possible that he will receive either good news or at least conclusive information that way, and I suggest that you keep in touch with him. May I express my deepest regrets that you have not yet heard from Leroy. I do hope that you may still receive good news in the future. If I can be of any assistance, please call on me to answer any further questions.*[5, 6]

The Czech and Slovakian citizens will always remember the day when so many planes and men fell out of the sky. On August 28 and 29, 2004, the Czech Republic and Slovakia commemorated the 60th anniversary of the "Air Battle Over the White Carpathian Mountains." Hundreds of citizens visited seven memorial sites, where seven planes from the 20th Bomb Squadron were shot down. Loy Dickinson, survivor from the 2nd Bomb Group, attended the ceremony.

Sergeant Leroy E. Johnson and his eight fellow crewmembers were initially buried in the Slavičín Cemetery, Slavičín, Czechoslovakia. Although residents were forbidden by the Germans to put flowers on the graves, fresh flowers appeared on the graves each morning.[7, 8] In 1951, Sergeant Leroy Johnson, son of Elmer and Daisy Ellen (Hegwood) Johnson, was reinterred at Jefferson Barracks National Cemetery, St. Louis, Missouri.[9]

Joseph Rudolph Hogetvedt

Borup (Norman County)

U.S. Marine Corps, 1st Marine "The Old Breed" Division, 5th Marine Regiment, 3rd Battalion, I Company, Private

MARCH 3, 1925–SEPTEMBER 17, 1944—Battle of Peleliu, Present-Day Palau

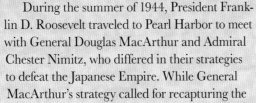

During the summer of 1944, President Franklin D. Roosevelt traveled to Pearl Harbor to meet with General Douglas MacArthur and Admiral Chester Nimitz, who differed in their strategies to defeat the Japanese Empire. While General MacArthur's strategy called for recapturing the Philippines and Okinawa before attacking Japan, Admiral Nimitz argued for skipping the Philippines, seizing Okinawa and Taiwan, and then invading Japan. MacArthur's strategy won, and the 1st Marine Division was chosen for the mission. However, before MacArthur could retake the Philippines, U.S. forces were ordered to capture Peleliu, a small island six miles long and two miles wide. The island's airfield could be used to launch future bombing attacks on Japan.[1, 2, 3, 4]

When Major General William Rupertus, commander of the 1st Marine Division, assured newspaper correspondents that the invasion would be a "quickie, three days, maybe two," 30 of the 36 correspondents planning to sail with the 1st Marines chose to cover other landings, leaving a handful to report the horrific battle.[1]

On September 4, 1944, 30 Tank Landing Ships, including one carrying Private Joseph Hogetvedt and the 1st Marine Division, shipped off from Pavuvu, just north of Guadalcanal, and traveled 2,100 miles across the Pacific to Peleliu, Palau Islands. On September 15, more than 5,000 men from the 1st, 5th, and 7th Marine Regiments landed on the western side of the island. They discovered that heavy Allied bombardment two days earlier had not damaged 11,000 Japanese soldiers protected inside a network of concrete bunkers and natural coral caves. Steel doors on the gun emplacements would open just long enough to shoot and then slam shut. The marines also faced razor sharp coral, extensive minefields and roads covered by Japanese artillery. Private Joseph Hogetvedt and the 5th Marine Regiment progressed the farthest due to protection from guns guarding the left and right flanks. As the 5th Regiment moved toward the airfield, Japanese Colonel Kunio Nakagawa's armored tanks rushed across the airfield to stop the marines' advance. However, Allied tanks, artillery and dive-bombers overpowered Nakagawa's tanks and infantrymen.

The next morning, Hogetvedt's regiment was ordered to attack the enemy on a hill overlooking the airfield called Bloody Nose Ridge. Here they fought in hand-to-hand combat under fierce artillery fire and extreme temperatures up to 115 degrees, with many casualties due to heat exhaustion. The airfield was in Allied hands at the end of the day, and now the marines faced the Umurbrogol Mountain, where the retreating Japanese hid in 500 caves and pillboxes.[1, 2, 3, 4]

As the marines advanced on the mountain on September 17, gunfire hit and killed Private First Class Joseph Hogetvedt.[5, 6] Private First Class Eugene B. Sledge, a fellow marine in Private First Class Hogetvedt's battalion, wrote of the sacrifice made on Peleliu: *We suffered so much for our country. None came out unscathed. Many gave their lives, their health, and some their sanity. All who survived will long remember the horror that they would rather forget. But they suffered and they did their duty so a sheltered homeland can enjoy the peace.*[3, 4]

After six weeks of combat, the 1st Marine Division was nearly wiped out after losing 6,526 men (1,252 dead and 5,274 wounded). The remaining men of the 1st Marines left the island and were replaced by the 81st Infantry Division. The expected two-day battle turned into two months of hell. By the end of November 1944, the entire Japanese force of 11,000 men was destroyed and the island secured by U.S. forces. Only 202 known prisoners survived the battle; 19 Japanese and the rest Korean or Okinawan workers. The Peleliu Campaign formally ended on April 27, 1947, when Lieutenant Tadamichi Yamaguchi led 26 survivors out of hidden caves and surrendered his samurai sword.[2, 3]

Private First Class Joseph Hogetvedt, 19-year-old son of Swen and Isabella (Askelson) Hogetvedt, was initially buried in Manila USAF Cemetery and later reinterred at Salem Lutheran Cemetery, Hitterdal, Minnesota.[5, 6]

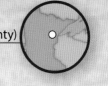

Vernon Lawrence Pearson

Wright (Carlton County)

Royal Canadian Air Force, No. 48 Squadron Coastal Command, Pilot Officer
JUNE 2, 1918–SEPTEMBER 18, 1944—Disappearance of a Douglas C-47 over the North Sea

Prior to the entry of the United States in World War II, thousands of Americans found a way to enter the war through the Canadian and British Armed Forces. Rejected by their country's air force program due to height, weight or other restrictions, the men found an opportunity to prove their ability as pilots and servicemen in other countries.

Vernon L. Pearson left Minnesota to enter the British Commonwealth Air Training Plan for training as a pilot in the Royal Canadian Air Force. He and about 800 other American citizens died while serving with the Royal Canadian Air Force and the Royal Air Force Volunteer Reserve during World War II. Many others joined other branches of the Canadian armed services.[1]

The Canadian World War II Registry states: *Vernon Lawrence Pearson: Killed in action with his entire crew at the age of 26 while attached to No 48 Squadron, Royal Air Force (Coastal Command) when his homebound Douglas C-47 was lost over the North Sea during a supply drop to Arnhem, the Netherlands, on September 18, 1944. Commemorated on the Panels of the Missing at the Commonwealth Air Forces Memorial at Runnymeade, Englefield Green, Surrey, England.*[2, 3]

A mystery surrounds the disappearance of Pilot Vernon Pearson, his crew, and his plane on a routine cargo trip from Down Ampney Airfield in England to Melsbroek, Belgium. Flying in support of the ill-fated Operation Market Garden offensive, their Douglas C-47 landed in Arnhem, Netherlands, on September 10, 1944, but was reported grounded with a defective tail wheel. On September 19, a replacement part was flown to the base, but by then No. 48 Squadron was reportedly involved in Market Garden. Not until September 26, after the Allied withdrawal from the area, did the commanding officer realize he had lost track of the plane and its four crew. Without any trace of the plane or men, the commanding officer of No. 48 Squadron wrote on October 23, 1944: *It can only be assumed that the Captain took off again without booking out or warning the responsible authorities, and that some kind of accident occurred on the return flight. The possibility of enemy action seems remote, but no message was received from the aircraft indicating that they were in difficulties.*[3, 4, 5]

Miss M. Stredder, Flight Officer Albert Lavoie's fiancé from Quebec, Canada, sheds some light on the mystery of the flight in a letter to Henk Welting: *On September 10th, the plane KG592 took off from Down Ampney on a 'dummy' run to Belgium. The purpose was to make a run to Belgium to pick-up casualties from a base hospital and bring them back to England. On board this plane were two nurses accompanying them for this purpose. They landed at Melsbroek, Belgium. Upon landing, they had a flat tail wheel. They were not equipped with gliders, and they did not carry petrol for a petrol run. After they landed, they immediately requested a tire replacement. In that evening the crew and the nurses went to a concert in Ghent. Ghent was where anyone landing at Melsbroek was billeted. The nurses were billeted at Lille. Now, after waiting 2 to 3 days for the replacement, up to around September 13th, without receiving it, the two nurses decided to hitch a ride back with whatever was leaving. So they did. After returning to England, one nurse took her leave in October and found that her parents had received a telegram saying she had posted 'missing.' As for the plane, the replacement part arrived in due course—before Operation Market Garden—and the plane had now disappeared. According to one English researcher, they would not be able to leave or land without a tire on the rear wheel. Also, being the crew they were, they would not leave or land without signaling—for sure. If they had, the signals either could have been silenced for security purposes or they could have also been ordered not to signal because the Germans could pick them up, one of the nurses felt. And others think that they took off for England and were electronically sabotaged by the Germans and their route changed from their course, to instead flying in error over Calais where they would have been shot into the Channel.*[5]

The son of Swedish immigrants, Per Gustave and Alma Sophia (Norell) Pearson, Vernon was survived by his parents, his wife Mary Jane (Carlson), who he married on October 2, 1942, in Chicago, and a brother, James Robert "Bob" Pearson. On his application to the Canadian Royal Air Force, Vernon stated his occupation as a baker and listed his hobbies as ski jumping, hockey, baseball and football. He belonged to the Brainerd Ski Club.[3]

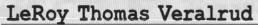

LeRoy Thomas Veralrud

Third Army, 80th Infantry "Blue Ridge" Division, 317th Infantry Regiment, 3rd Battalion, K Company, Private

JUNE 7, 1925–SEPTEMBER 2, 1944—The Crossing of the Moselle River, France

An excellent student and athlete, LeRoy Veralrud graduated from Gilbert High School in 1943, winning the coveted American Legion Award and membership in the National Athletic Scholarship Society. He entered the army on September 16, 1943, and joined the 80th Infantry Division, called the "Blue Ridge Division" a unit initially composed of draftees from the mid-Atlantic states of Virginia, West Virginia, Pennsylvania and Maryland.[1, 6]

On July 4, 1944, Private Veralrud and the 80th Infantry Division set sail on the SS *Queen Mary* for the Firth of Clyde, Scotland. After additional training in Norwich, England, the 80th, named the workhorse for General Patton's Third Army, landed on Utah Beach in Normandy on August 2, 1944. The 80th secured the Falaise Pocket, near the town of Falaise, by August 21, 1944, which trapped 60,000 Germans and civilians inside. Four days later, Paris was liberated and by August 30, the remaining Germans had retreated across the Seine, ending the battle for Normandy.[2]

On September 1, the 80th Division advanced to Commercy where the 317th and 318th crossed the Meuse River and seized the town of Apremont.

The Morning Report on September 2 for K Company states the fate of Private Veralrud and the 317th Infantry Regiment: *Vicinity of Bouconville-sur-Madt, France. Marched toward town. Were ambushed by enemy at 0610. They immediately pinned us down with machine gun fire, then placed artillery and mortar fire on us, plus some tanks firing on us inflicting many casualties on us.*[3]

Major General Ulio replied to a letter from Private Veralrud's father: *The distress you have suffered since you received the sad announcement of your son's death is most understandable and realizing your desire to know the attending circumstances, I wish to advise you that an additional report has been received in the war department. This report states that on 2 September 1944, the rifle company of which Private Veralrud was rifleman was advancing on the enemy held town of Pont-à-Mousson, France. On this advance, an enemy delaying force was encountered in the vicinity of Bouconville-sur-Med, France. During this advance, your son was instantly killed as the result of enemy automatic weapons fire. The report further stated that at the time of his death, your son was serving with the Third United States Army.*[4]

The Veralruds were one of 35 families who lived in Elcor, a small mining community near McKinley, named for the Elba and Corsica mines. LeRoy's parents, born and married in Oslo, Minnesota, moved to Elcor in 1926, where his father drove truck for Corsica Mines. When the mine reclaimed the land in 1955, all the families were forced to leave, and today Elcor no longer exists.[5, 6]

Survivors included his parents, Thomas and Julia (Tinnes) Veralrud, and two sisters. Initially buried in France, Private Veralrud was reinterred in 1948 in Gilbert Cemetery, Gilbert, Minnesota. Elcor lost four men in World War II: LeRoy Veralrud, Rudolph Indihar (page 55), Robert Brady (page 95) and Lloyd Nicholas (page 37).[1, 6]

Another soldier from Minnesota, Corporal Norbert Bruns from St. Rosa (page 103), served with Private LeRoy Veralrud in K Company. Corporal Bruns died four months later on December 26, 1944, in Luxembourg at the Battle of the Bulge.

Gordon R. Maxa

U.S. Army Air Forces, 8th Air Force, 384th Bomb Group, 546th Bomb Squadron, Staff Sergeant
JUNE 22, 1923–SEPTEMBER 25, 1944—Bombing Mission over Frankfurt, Germany

On New Year's Day in 1945, Staff Sergeant Gordon Maxa's wife, Betty, unaware of the fate of her husband, wrote a letter to Doris Anderson, wife of Corporal Frank J. Anderson, who flew on the same crew with her husband:

Dear Doris, You are the only one I know on the crew. We were always going to write each other but I guess most people need an address and we both forgot it, but I'm glad we can write each other especially under the present circumstances. All I've heard about Gordon is that they went on a combat mission over Frankfort, Germany, about 10:50 a.m. and were hit by enemy anti-aircraft fire and went down. Mrs. Findlay said some of you have the above info but am telling you just in case you didn't. Mrs. Findlay has probably also told you that her son was the tail gunner. I do hope and pray and pray and hope we all hear good news soon. I'm sorry to hear Frank is a prisoner but am glad to hear he isn't wounded and is alive. I guess there isn't much chance of any of them escaping and eventually getting back to their own company. Gordon is my whole world. I'd like to see your little girl. She is at such a cute age and I bet she keeps you on the run. I've been thinking of going to work if I can only get started. At present I'm almost in bed with a severe cold. Please forgive the delay in writing but I visit around so much that I have my mail come to one place and try to get it every week. I'm visiting my aunt in the country at present. Gordon was radio operator on the ship and also aerial gunner. He has a brother two years older that has been a prisoner of war for 18 months in Germany. I feel certain you'll hear from Frank soon so keep your chin up, kid. I got a telegram from Mrs. Carl Hart and probably have more waiting for me so I hope I get to town soon. This gas rationing is a deal all right. If you care to, write in between information. When I think back to Ardmore, Oklahoma, I still feel as though if I pinch myself I'll find out it is all one bad dream. As for me getting out to Jersey, wouldn't you be surprised to see me pop in some day? But seriously, are you near a big defense plant—just curious. I guess I've out done myself again. Most sincerely, Betty[1]

Doris's husband, Staff Sergeant Frank Anderson, was one of the lucky ones. On September 25, 1944, Betty's husband, Staff Sergeant Gordon Maxa, and a crew of eight boarded *The Spirit of '96* for an industrial bombing mission over Frankfurt, Germany. In all, 53 Boeing B-17 Flying Fortresses left that morning from the air base in Grafton Underwood, England, and only one plane, *The Spirit of '96*, failed to return.

This was the fifteenth mission for Corporal Gordon Maxa and his crew. On that ill-fated morning, anti-aircraft flak hit their B-17 and blew the tail off the plane. Three witnesses reported that the plane *"nosed over straight down out of control and was lost in the clouds."*[2]

Amazingly, three of the crew opened their parachutes at the last possible moment as the Germans fired at them and survived as prisoners of war until the war ended. The other six crewmen went down with the plane.[2,3]

Staff Sergeant Gordon Raymond Maxa, son of Edward and Alvina (Glassman) Maxa, is buried at Fort Snelling Cemetery. Survivors included his parents, his wife, Emma Jane "Betty," and nine siblings.

Gordon's brother Vernon recalls: *My family lived on the top floor of a house next to the dance hall and had a perfect view of the dancers. Gordon was an outstanding high school basketball guard and catcher for the baseball team, and went on to attend Mankato State College. Four of my brothers served in World War II: Gordon; Neil, a prisoner of war for two years in Stalag 7A and Stalag 17B; Russell in Iwo Jima; and Donald with the ground forces in the Middle East. My father served as a sergeant in France during World War 1.*[4]

Following the crash of *The Spirit of '96*, the wives and parents of the crewmembers wrote to each other seeking information of their loved ones. Staff Sergeant Frank Anderson's daughter, Jean Anderson, preserved all the letters that her mother received over the years, including the letter from Betty Maxa.[4]

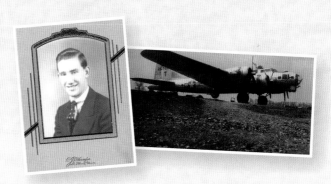

John Paul Sersha

Leonidas (St. Louis County)

82nd Airborne "All American" Division, 325th Glider Infantry Regiment, 2nd Battalion, F Company
APRIL 29, 1924–SEPTEMBER 27, 1944—Operation Market Garden, Netherlands and Germany

The day that John Sersha left for overseas duty, he told his brother Paul, "I don't think I will ever see you again." The family never expected that John would not return home until 72 years later.[1]

John's nephew, Dick Lohry, recalls his uncle's photo on his grandmother's dresser and John's footlocker, which was returned to the family after he was declared missing in action. In 2005, Dick's friends gave him a photograph of a panel on the Wall of the Missing in the Netherlands American Cemetery, in the village of Margraten, with 21 names on it, including Private John Sersha. The photo initiated a several-year investigation by Dick of John's military service. Over the years, Paul Sersha also tried to locate surviving veterans who may have served with John. John was named again, this time on a memorial paver in the veterans war memorial in Virginia, Minnesota, in November 2013. The following day, Dick received a phone call from Danny Keay, a retired U.S. army sergeant, who is also an amateur archeologist in Germany. From military files and records, he believed that John's remains were discovered in 1948.[2]

John Sersha grew up in Leonidas, a small mining community on the Iron Range just west of Eveleth. He attended the Leonidas School followed by employment with the Duluth, Missabe, and Iron Range Railroad Company. After induction into the army at Fort Snelling on November 17, 1943, John trained at Camp Fannin near Tyler, Texas, and at Fort George Mead, Maryland.[1, 2] At Fort Mead, John joined the 325th Glider Infantry Regiment of the 82nd Airborne Division, a regiment sent into battle by glider planes. Unlike paratroopers and equipment dropped by parachute that often ended up scattered for miles in a drop zone, gliders held troops and equipment intact as long as the glider held together. Glider assaults were extremely risky as the gliders and their tow planes moved slowly and lacked armor for protection. Landing in a glider was simply a controlled crash on ground covered with fences, ditches, tree stumps, and enemy-placed obstacles, all conducive to flipping a glider.[3, 4, 5]

Private Sersha did not land with the 325th during the Normandy invasion on June 6, but was among the replacements who arrived at Camp Scraptoft near Leicester, England, in July to prepare for Operation Market Garden in the Netherlands.

The largest single airborne operation of the war, Market Garden launched on September 17, 1944. Due to bad weather, Private Sersha and F Company from the 325th Glider Infantry Regiment arrived six days later in their wood and fabric Waco CG-4A gliders near Overasselt, six miles west of Kiekberg. Initially, F Company planned to land near Groesbeek, north and west of the Kiekberg Forest, but heavy German troop concentration in the area altered the company's position. The men were ordered to attack from the northeast in an effort to gain the high ground in the Kiekberg and wrest control of the forest from the Germans.[3, 4, 5, 6] On September 27, Private Sersha and two other men, called "Bazooka Men," left with a platoon from F Company to assault German positions led by the formidable 190th "Hammer" Infantry Division.[1, 2, 3]

None of the three Bazooka Men returned to their unit, and several soldiers in F Company reported Sersha's death. Following the war, he was declared killed in action. Then, in 1948, three sets of remains were recovered from two isolated graves in the Kiekberg Forest. Dick Lohry believes that German soldiers buried his uncle. However, positive identification could not be made and the remains were declared "non-recoverable" following a further investigation in 1950. For several decades, Private Sersha's remains, identified as X-7429, lay in the Ardennes military cemetery in Belgium until December 2015, when an exhumation order was obtained for DNA analysis to confirm his identity. Mr. Lohry, who was a one-year-old when his Uncle John was killed, gratefully acknowledges the many individuals who helped bring John home and the U.S. government, which honored him after so many years.

On May 28, 2016, Private John Sersha was buried next to his parents in the Eveleth Cemetery, Eveleth, Minnesota, with full military honors. His brother Paul and sister Julia attended the service. Dick Lohry stated, "My message at the Memorial Day graveside service was 'God Never Forgets' based on Isaiah 49:13–16.[1, 2, 3, 4, 7, 8]

Walter Otto Kurth

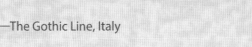

Fifth Army, 34th Infantry "Red Bull" Division, 135th Infantry Regiment, 3rd Battalion, I Company, Staff Sergeant

SEPTEMBER 17, 1914–SEPTEMBER 27, 1944—The Gothic Line, Italy

Walter Kurth entered the service on April 22, 1941, and served his entire three-plus years with I Company, 135th Infantry, originally the Madison Minnesota National Guard unit. The unit participated in the original invasion of North Africa on November 8, 1942, and fought through the entire North African campaign.[1,2]

When the 135th Infantry Regiment landed on the beachhead in Anzio, Italy, on March 25, 1944, steady artillery fire by the enemy positioned on higher ground pinned the men down in their foxholes and dugouts. On April 26, Staff Sergeant Kurth and the 3rd Battalion ended the standoff when they executed the "Charlie" plan: a tank and infantry raid on a house where the Germans were all killed or captured.

On May 11, 1944, the soldiers began the drive for Rome, and on June 5, the 135th Infantry was the first infantry unit to march into Rome. One of the soldiers wrote: *The civilian population of the "Eternal City" lined the streets, throwing flowers and fruit to the troops and embracing and kissing the men. Because of this emotional welcome, the movement of vehicles and foot soldiers was slow. Our infantrymen were footsore, dusty and weary, but the greeting of a liberated people helped greatly in reviving their spirits.*

After liberating Rome, Staff Sergeant Walter Kurth and the 135th Infantry Regiment were ordered to break the enemy's heavily fortified Gothic Line, a defensive line drawn across Italy.[3] Walter Kurth's family received a final letter from their son on September 9 where he wrote that he "had been out of the fighting but was expecting to go back to the front."[1] As the 2nd and 3rd Battalions passed through the 168th Infantry near Barbarino on September 12, they discovered a German minefield where multiple soldiers became casualties, including 1st Lieutenant Leslie Vensel, the commander of Kurth's company.[4]

The next day, as the regiment moved forward toward Ciragnano, German prisoners stated that their troops had reached the perimeter of the Gothic Line, an area defended by the 4th German Parachute Division. On September 14, Staff Sergeant Kurth and the 3rd Battalion attacked Hill 671 where the enemy used minefields, barbed wire, concrete pillboxes and dugouts in an attempt to stop the Americans. During the attack on the hill, the 135th broke through the Gothic Line but suffered many casualties. I Company alone lost 18 men wounded and 5 killed.[3]

From September 26 to 27, the 3rd Battalion launched an attack against Bruscoli, Italy, where Staff Sergeant Kurth received the Silver Star: *For gallantry in action on 27 September, 1944, in the vicinity of Bruscola, Italy. When Sergeant Kurth's platoon became pinned down by an enemy machine gun, which could not be located because of dense underbrush, he immediately began maneuvering up a hilly slope in an effort to spot it. Although his action attracted vicious fire, he succeeded in locating the gun and engaged it with his rifle at close range. Sergeant Kurth killed one of the enemy and by distracting their attention enabled his platoon to advance over a better route. While engaging the enemy gun Sergeant Kurth was fatally wounded, but his courageous action so inspired his comrades that they swept forward and took their objective. Sergeant Kurth's intrepidity and devotion to duty was outstanding and reflects great credit on himself and the Armed Forces of the United States.* Just two days later, the 135th Regiment passed into division reserve and off the front lines.[5]

Survivors included his parents, Paul and Emma (Buhman) Kurth and six siblings. Walter lived his entire life on his parent's farm except for one year, 1936, when he attended the University Agricultural College. Initially buried at Castelfiorentino, Italy, Walter Kurth was reinterred in 1947 in St. John's Lutheran Cemetery, Cedar Mills, Minnesota. Another Minnesota man, Sergeant Harold Meyer (page 36) died February 4, 1944, and served in I Company with Staff Sergeant Walter Kurth.[1,2]

William Jennings Talberg

Hillman (Morrison County)

6th Corps Combat Engineers, 345th Engineers General Service Regiment, Corporal
MAY 21, 1905–SEPTEMBER 27, 1944—Rome-Arno Campaign, Italy

I heard everyone from Generals to Privates remark that "this is certainly an engineers' war"— and indeed it was.
—*Ernie Pyle in* Brave Men[1]

In March 1943, Corporal William Talberg and the 345th Engineers General Service Regiment, without any previous experience in building pipelines, built a 160-mile gasoline pipeline from Casablanca, Morocco, to Marrakesh to supply both the Army Transport Command and the North African Training Command.[2]

Nine months later, on October 10, the 345th Engineers joined the Fifth Army "Peninsular" Base Section. The first base engineer construction unit in Naples, they rebuilt the bombed Port of Naples for use as a supply and maintenance base for further operations.

For their fearless work, Corporal William Talberg and the 345th General Service Regiment received the Meritorious Service Unit Award: *345th Engineer General Service Regiment, for superior performance of exceptionally difficult tasks and outstanding devotion to duty in the Peninsular Base during the period 1st January to 6th August 1944. This regiment performed a major portion of the rehabilitation of Naples and the surrounding country. It repaired an extensively damaged sewer system, promptly opened cratered and debris clogged streets and roads and reconstructed important parts of the railroad system, thus insuring an early and unrestricted flow of supplies urgently needed by combat troops. In addition, this regiment was assigned numerous tasks of construction and reconstruction, all of which were accomplished in a minimum of time and in an outstanding manner in spite of great handicaps of extensive mine fields, inclement weather and lack of materials, equipment and manpower. The achievements of the 345th Engineer General Service Regiment during this period were in the highest traditions of the military service.*

As the Allies prepared for the push to Rome in early spring 1944, men in the 345th General Service Regiment became power-line experts in a few weeks as they repaired damaged power lines and towers destroyed by the Germans. That same spring, the leaders decided to establish a recreation area for battle-weary GIs near Agropoli in southern Italy. However, the Germans mined the area prior to landings in the Gulf of Salerno, and the beautiful beaches were full of concealed mines. The 345th assumed the dangerous task of digging out several thousand mines along miles of beach.[2]

When the Allies occupied the city of Florence in September 1944, the 345th Engineers built top-notch hospitals and supply depots in the city. Concerned that heavy fall rains would drain into the Era and Arno rivers near Florence and flood the supply depots, river patrols watched river levels, cleared demolished bridges and rebuilt levees. Unfortunately, hazards still existed. On September 27, Corporal William Talberg died of wounds when he stepped on a land mine.[3, 4]

The son of Swedish immigrants, Lars and Anna (Olson) Talberg, Corporal William Talberg enlisted in the army on April 6, 1942. Survivors included his six siblings. His mother died when William was two years old and his father died in 1940. He was initially buried in Florence American Cemetery, Florence, Italy, and reinterred in Minnesota State Veterans Cemetery, Little Falls, Minnesota. The Hillman American Legion Wojciak-Talberg Post 602 is named in honor of Private John A. Wojciak and Corporal William J. Talberg.[3, 4]

Harland Hermann Friedrich Mittag

Myrtle (Freeborn County)

Fifth Army, 34th Infantry "Red Bull" Division, 133rd Infantry Regiment, 2nd Battalion, E Company, Honor Guard, Private First Class

AUGUST 4, 1913–OCTOBER 6, 1944—Italian Campaign, Italy

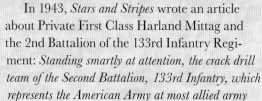

In 1943, *Stars and Stripes* wrote an article about Private First Class Harland Mittag and the 2nd Battalion of the 133rd Infantry Regiment: *Standing smartly at attention, the crack drill team of the Second Battalion, 133rd Infantry, which represents the American Army at most allied army functions, prepared to go through practice paces to maintain its record as the smartest performing Yankee drill team in the Algiers area. The team is made up of 60 six-foot-tall soldiers, chosen for their expert drilling abilities. The team was formed early this year (1943) when it was ordered that an American drill unit be organized that could out-perform other allied teams. The team has drilled at practically all of the important Allied celebrations of recent months and has been the guard of honor for General Dwight D. Eisenhower, General Charles de Gaulle, General Henri Giraud and Admiral Sir Andrew Cunningham.*[1]

After the liberation of Rome on June 5, 1944, Harland Mittag and the 2nd Battalion Honor Guard left their drilling skills behind to push north toward the Gothic Line, a defensive line extending along the Apennines Mountains of Italy. The history of the 133rd Infantry Regiment recorded their struggles: *On September 11, the attack began, and for 9 days the 2nd Battalion battled the enemy through concrete bunkers and pillboxes protected by barbed wire and surrounded by minefields covered by machine gun fire. Over 170 mules transported the wounded men and supplies on narrow, slippery trails in the mountains, where as many as five mules per night slipped off the steep trails. Any available intact men, including cooks, Service Company and Anti-Tank Company personnel, served as litter-bearers, carrying their wounded over a relay chain that stretched for 7½ miles.*[2]

As the Allies penetrated the Gothic Line, the Germans withdrew to the north and the 133rd Infantry Regiment moved to the Mount Venere area in a drive to reach the Po Valley before winter. Early on October 4, in miserable cold and endless rain, the 2nd Battalion, minus company E, rode on medium tanks to Mount Venere, secured the mountain, and advanced to Monzuno. Meanwhile, Private Mittag and Company E rode light tanks and assisted in clearing the town of the enemy.[2]

As the division drove toward Bologna, Italy, the gateway to the Po Valley, German resistance intensified. Documents for the 133rd Infantry

Regiment reveal the events on October 6: *At daybreak on 6 October, all our troops were meeting ever-stiffening resistance: they did not advance appreciably through the night. Supply and evacuation difficulties had grown in severity since midnight and became even more critical as the day wore on. Rain fell almost continuously. Our one attached Company A of the 109th Engineer Combat Battalion was hard pressed to maintain trails treacherous even under normal conditions. No more engineers were available for our use, as bad roads were general in this region. Soldiers of the 133rd Infantry fought alone this day in the entire rugged sector, for at a suggestion from Division, elements of the 135th Infantry had not been committed, as previously planned. Nevertheless, at the end of this day we had won ground in the face of strong enemy opposition on a wide front. The 1st and 2nd Battalions, in particular, weathered heavy artillery, mortar, self-propelled and machine gun fire besides small arms. The latter unit experienced a number of casualties.*[2]

The latter unit included Harland Mittag, and when the 2nd battalion was finally relieved on October 7, he was one of 32 men who had died in action since the beginning of October.[3] Son of August and Emma (Zarling) Mittag, he is buried in Pilgrim's Rest Cemetery, Myrtle, Minnesota. Survivors included his parents and four siblings.[1]

Albert Otto Longhenry

Nassau (Lac Qui Parle County)

45th Infantry "Thunderbird" Division, 179th Infantry Regiment, 1st Battalion, D Company, Private First Class

SEPTEMBER 29, 1917–OCTOBER 11, 1944—The Vosges Mountains Campaign, France

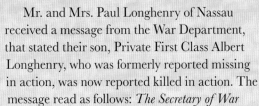

Mr. and Mrs. Paul Longhenry of Nassau received a message from the War Department, that stated their son, Private First Class Albert Longhenry, who was formerly reported missing in action, was now reported killed in action. The message read as follows: *The Secretary of War asks that I assure you of his deepest sympathy in the loss of your son, Private First Class Albert Longhenry, who was previously reported missing in action. Report now received states he was killed in action 11 October in France. –Dunlop, acting Adjutant General*

Private First Class Longhenry left for service March 5, 1942, and was home on his last furlough in March 1943. In May 1944, he left for overseas duty in France, and the last letter he wrote home from southern France was dated October 9.[1]

Upon his induction into D Company, 179th Infantry Regiment, 45th Division, Albert Longhenry joined a heavy weapons company with six squads of machine guns and two squads of mortars. After fighting their way through Africa and Italy, the experienced 45th Division landed in Sainte-Maxime on the Riviera in southern France on August 15, 1944. The men were ordered to secure routes to Germany through the treacherous Vosges Mountains in France on their way to the ultimate objective, Berlin.[2, 3]

Munsell detailed the events after September 19, when Private First Class Longhenry and the 179th led the 45th Division north to secure a bridgehead across the Moselle River near Epinal, a strongly defended and strategically important city: *Patrols scouting along the Moselle reported that the enemy destroyed all bridges from Arches to Epinal on the 80-foot-wide river and that roadblocks covered the entrances to the city. The 179th finally completed a bridge at Arches and crossed the river, moving quickly against heavy fire and a fast-flowing current. Other elements of the 45th crossed the Moselle and attacked Epinal. A few days after the advance on Epinal, a signpost appeared on the road: "Sainte-Tropez 430 miles, Berlin, 430 miles."[2]*

As the division cleared one pocket of resistance after another, the 45th moved farther into the densely wooded forest of the Vosges foothills. Despite stubborn enemy resistance, heavily mined fields, and mounting casualties, on September 23, Albert Longhenry and the 179th attacked northeast into the lower Vosges Mountains. Warren Munsell wrote: *The fighting grew ever more savage. The Germans, old men and fanatical Hitler youths, fought like madmen. Snipers along the route of advance had to be attended to individually. Tanks were ineffectual, artillery observation limited. There was no guessing where the enemy was, his strength, the depth of his defense, or in which shadowy growth he lurked.*

On September 30, Albert Longhenry and the 1st Battalion fought house-to-house in Grandvillers, a village straddling the highway, until October 2 when they pushed the Germans out. For the next two weeks, the 170th fought for every yard in the woods as they worked their way to Bruyéres.[2] On October 11, during the advance to Bruyéres, Private Longhenry was killed in action.[4] The War Journal report for October 11, 1944 states: *Small arms and grenade fights occurred sporadically throughout the darkness in the Sector. At 0810, A Company laid down a barrage of grenades as strong patrols moved out against the enemy. F Company took over B Company's positions. At 1040 a C patrol with one tank knocks out an enemy machine gun. K's platoon on Hill 392 moved down the ridge attempting, but upon meeting with heavy small arms and mortar fire, it withdrew to its original positions. Around 40 enemy attacked I Company, but the attack was repulsed. At 11:45, L Company elements moved to the nose of Hill 392 where E had been heavily engaged, and despite a heavy artillery preparation it at once ran into strong enemy fire. At 1325 E Company was under enemy machine gun fire and K Company continued to suffer casualties from steady mortar fire from enemy positions in Brouvelieures.[5]*

Private First Class Albert Longhenry is buried in Trinity Lutheran Cemetery, Nassau, Minnesota. Survivors included his parents, Paul and Margaretha (Geotsch) Longhenry and seven siblings.[1]

45th Infantry Division Landing at Ste. Maxime, France
15 August 1944
(National Archives)

Donald James Doyle

Danvers (Swift County)

U.S. Army Air Forces, 9th Tactical Air Group, 71st Fighter Group, 422nd Night Fighter Squadron, 1st Lieutenant

JANUARY 25, 1920–OCTOBER 12, 1944—Bombing Mission over Ostheim, Germany

Major General William Kepner, commander of strategic bomber operations from England in 1943 and 1944, wrote the commander of IV Fighter Command, who was in charge of training night fighters:

Night fighter pilots must be picked for their ability to operate at night and that means able to use a lot of instruments, and of course they must be fed and prepared physically to have good eyesight at night. You must have a willingness to fly alone long distances at high altitude with low temperatures. In other words, they should combine all the aggressive and dogged fighting characteristics with a somewhat phlegmatic disposition that bores in like a bulldog without any other idea than getting the job done. Their courage and resourcefulness will have to exceed, if possible all that any pilot has ever had before. This is some guy and you have to produce him.[1]

1st Lieutenant Donald Doyle met all the requirements. On March 7, 1944, Doyle and the 422nd Night Fighter Squadron arrived at Charmy Down, a Royal Air Force base just north of Bath, England. There, they trained on a new aircraft, the P-61 Black Widow, which was developed by aviation designer Jack Northrup. Named for the American spider, the Black Widow was designed specifically for night interception of enemy aircraft and the first designed around the use of radar. The P-61 had a crew of three: a pilot, a gunner and a radar operator.[2, 3]

Warren Thompson described the fighter in detail: *Equipped with the latest radar, multiple gun turrets, and an eight-hour airtime, the twin-engine Black Widow fighter held an advantage over enemy craft and could shoot down German V-I "buzz bombs" that attacked England at night. Although Allied forces used the P-61 against Japanese bombers in the Pacific, the Royal Air Force's Mosquito fighter was thought to be superior, and the U.S. Army Air Forces kept the 422nd P-61 squadron from combat. Eager to prove the Black Widow's abilities, the 422nd challenged the Royal Air Force's Mosquito to a fly-off, and chose Lieutenant Donald Doyle as their test pilot. The Army Air Forces finally agreed, and on July 5, Lieutenant Doyle and the Royal Air Force pilot took off, "balls to the wall," each pushing his aircraft to the limit. The P-61 Black Widow won every test, and by mid-July was taking out enemy bombers over France and V-1s over the English Channel.*[2]

By early spring, 1st Lieutenant Doyle and the 422nd operated near the front lines in Maupertus, France. Some models of the P-61, fitted with rockets and bombs under the wings, were used when the squadron began attacking targets on the ground in so-called "intruder missions." On October 12, 1944, 1st Lieutenant Donald Doyle, pilot, and 2nd Lieutenant Norman Williams, radar operator, normally assigned the *Husslin' Hussey*, took off in the *Laura Lil*, on an intruder mission to the Ostheim Airdrome in Germany. They were last heard from at 1945 hours when 1st Lieutenant Doyle reportedly said, "Hot target, see you later." Their location at that time was south of Bonn, Germany.[4] After the Missing Air Crew Report was filed, German forces discovered the crashed plane on the Autobahn near the bridge at Wiedmuhle. Both 1st Lieutenant Doyle and 2nd Lieutenant Williams died in the crash.

1st Lieutenant Donald J. Doyle, son of William and Elizabeth (O'Donnell) Doyle, is memorialized at Henri-Chapelle American Cemetery, Belgium, and Church of the Visitation Cemetery, Danvers, Minnesota. Survivors included his parents and four siblings. He enlisted on April 13, 1942 and was awarded the Air Medal with two Oak Leaf Clusters and the Purple Heart.

Donald Olaf Bollum

Farwell (Pope County)

Third Army, 79th Infantry Division "The Cross of Lorraine" Division, 315th Infantry Regiment, 2nd Battalion, E Company, Technician Fifth Grade

JULY 5, 1914–OCTOBER 13, 1944—Battle of Foret de Parroy, France

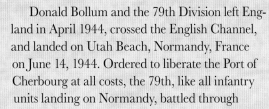

Donald Bollum and the 79th Division left England in April 1944, crossed the English Channel, and landed on Utah Beach, Normandy, France on June 14, 1944. Ordered to liberate the Port of Cherbourg at all costs, the 79th, like all infantry units landing on Normandy, battled through impenetrable hedgerows used for defense by the Germans. After the division secured Cherbourg and the peninsula on June 27, the men drove down the west coast of the Cotentin Peninsula in driving rain and captured La Haye-du-Puits on July 8, 1944.

On September 25, the 79th Division crossed the Meurthe River in northeast France and attacked Foret de Parroy, a heavily wooded forest where a young Adolf Hitler had fought in World War I. Just beyond the forest lay the Vosges Mountains near the border and a point of entry into Germany.[1, 2, 3] Donald Bollum wrote to his wife, Jeannette, on October 6, 1944: *Dearest Wife, It's quite some time since I have had a chance to write but I hope you haven't been worrying too much. I know how you feel, darling, and I hope the war will soon end so you need not worry about your husband who loves you more than anything in the world. I need you so much and can hardly wait for the day when we can be united again. Things have been rather rough lately, but I trust in God to bring me through okay. I haven't been getting mail very regularly, but yesterday I received about seven from you, one each from Rolf, Helen and George. It surely was great to get all of that at once. I finally received the package of soap you sent but having no place to carry it, I had to give most of it to the other fellows. Thanks, darling, for going to all the trouble of wrapping it and sending it off. You need not send any more soap, tooth powder, etc, because we don't have a chance to wash often anyway. I'm glad that Bernard has a chance to send a cable off once in awhile, so Dad gets to hear he's OK. I haven't heard from Bernard for a long time, but I guess he doesn't get a chance to write often either. It's nice that Rolf came to see you because that shows that he thinks a lot of you. Of course, dear, I don't mind you going out with any of my brothers because we are all one big family. I am sure Rolf had a big time on his furlough and I would have liked to have been with him. Just about a year ago since you and I were having a wonderful time hunting pheasants, visiting around the country and making love in between times. That really was a perfect furlough and I don't know that I have ever had a better time*

in all my life. Just being with you is all I need for a perfect life. It still rains quite a bit but the past few days have been quite nice. George seems to be getting along fine in New Guinea, and it is good that there are only two of us here in France. I'm way behind in letter writing, and I don't know when I'll be able to catch up again. Darling, I'm writing every chance I get, so when you don't hear for a few days, please don't worry too much. We must have faith in the Lord to pull us through this war, and I'm sure he will unite us again. I hope your folks are well, and be sure to greet all of the family for me. Darling, remember always that I love you as much as it is possible for a man to love a woman. All my Love and Kisses, Your Adoring and Faithful Husband, Don[4, 5]

As Technician Bollum and the 315th Regiment advanced through the forest toward the Vosges Mountains, they came under heavy fire at the edge of the woods. On April 7, 1945, Captain Bernard Deutchman wrote a letter to Jeannette Bollum: *Dear Mrs. Bollum, On October 13, 1944, Company "E", of which Donald Bollum was a member, was located in the vicinity of Forest of Parrot, two miles northeast of Luneville, France, where a battle was raging for possession of the forest. The enemy taking full advantage of the difficult terrain had mined every conceivable route of approach and kept the entire area held by our troops under a constant rain of artillery and mortar fire. The clearing of the forest was the focal objective in the freeing of the entire Alsace region in France. At 8:00 a.m., the company, in the face of strong enemy resistance, moved out in a combined attack on enemy positions. The platoon in which Tec 5 Bollum was a member was one of the leading elements. At 9:00 a.m., as it was proceeding over an area approximately 100 yards west of a small dirt road in the forest, Donald Bollum stepped on an enemy mine and the explosion killed him instantly.*[5, 6, 7]

Donald Bollum, son of Olaf and Ella (Belgum) Bollum, is buried in Epinal American Cemetery, Lorraine, France. In April 1943, a year after entering the army, he married a teacher, Jeannette Kiera. Survivors included his parents; a sister, Helen; and three brothers, all in the army: Rolf, George and Bernard. Jeannette Bollum never remarried. She remained close to Donald's family until her death in 2012.[8, 9]

Earl Richard Burger

U.S. Naval Reserve, USS LST-277, Seaman Second Class
JULY 29, 1907–OCTOBER 23, 1944—Battle of Leyte Gulf, Philippines

Gary Burger was one year old when his father died. He wrote: *My father, Earl Richard Burger — U.S.N—was killed in October of 1944 in the South Pacific during the Battle of Leyte Gulf, Philippines. He was on an LST and he was the only casualty on that ship during the entire war. He was 36 years old at the time of his death and so he didn't have to be there, but, he had 3 younger brothers (all survived) who went off to war and he felt guilty to be at home and so was compelled to go. He was initially buried in the Philippines but was later brought home. He now rests in Bemidji.*[1]

Following his enlistment on January 27, 1944, Earl Burger served on a Tank Landing Ship fleet, which could deliver men, tanks, trucks and other equipment to landing zones on enemy beaches. Although the 1942 design featured flat bottoms and lurched and bobbed in rough seas, the sides were buoyant and the vessels were durable and hard to sink. Navy men say that, "When the weather's bad, nobody sleeps on an LST."[2] Famous for the Normandy beach landings, the 1,000 Tank Landing Ships built during the war brought men and material to beaches all over the South Pacific.

After surviving Saipan, Seaman Second Class Earl Burger and USS *LST-277* headed for Leyte Gulf, near the Philippines.[2, 3] When the Japanese captured the Philippines in 1942, General Douglas MacArthur, the commander of the American forces in the Philippines, fled the island with his wife and four-year-old son. He vowed to reclaim the Philippines, and arrived along with the Sixth Army on October 20, 1944, the first day of the invasion. With a landing force of 175,000 borne largely by Tank Landing Ships, MacArthur waded ashore in the third wave. Later he recalled the landing: *It took me only 30 or 40 strides to reach dry land, but that was one of the most meaningful walks I ever took. When it was done, and I stood on the sand, I knew I was back again—against my old enemies of Bataan, for there, shining on the bodies of dead Japanese soldiers, I saw the insignia of the 16th Division, General Homma's ace unit.*[4] Two days later, he announced, "People of the Philippines: I have returned," in one of the most famous radio speeches during World War II.

The Japanese fought back hard, knowing this was their last chance to win the war. On October 23, as the Allied troops secured Tacloban, then the temporary capital of the Philippines, and the former government was

restored, Earl Burger died from head wounds following an accidental fall.[5]

Earl's sister, Myrtle, recalls her brother and the story of the accident: *Earl was a baker on a Navy ship in Leyte Gulf. When they men were called to their station, he went up the ladder through the hatch and the hatch fell on his head. He died later on a hospital ship from the head injury. Earl was a great guy with a wonderful sense of humor. He loved to dance and always won first place at the Halloween Dance in Turtle River. I remember when he came home on leave and took my mother to the liquor store for a beer. My mother was Irish and dark skinned, what they called "black Irish." The bartender thought she was American Indian and refused to serve her as it was then against the law to serve liquor to any American Indian.*[6]

Survivors included his parents, George and Etta Burger; his wife, Helen (Coleman) Burger; three children, Barbara, Derrill and Gary; and seven siblings.

Earl had a hobby farm near Turtle River and worked for a seed company in Bemidji. His son Gary, the Mayor of Turtle River from 2006 to 2014, was a well-known musician and filmmaker.

During World War II, Earl's wife, Helen, worked in two shipyards: first in Portland, Oregon, and later, the Todd Pacific Shipyards in Tacoma, Washington, where she was one of two female mechanics.

Initially buried at the U.S. Air Force Cemetery at Leyte in the Philippine Islands, Earl Burger was reinterred in Greenwood Cemetery, Bemidji, in 1948.[6, 7, 8]

Ferdinand Vincent Kuznia

Strandquist (Marshall County)

U.S. Army Coast Artillery Corps, 59th Coast Artillery Regiment, 1st Battalion, Headquarters, Corporal

JANUARY 22, 1922–OCTOBER 24, 1944—Prisoner of War on the "Hell Ship" *Arisan Maru*

Less than a year before the Japanese attacked Pearl Harbor, Ferdinand "Freddie" Kuznia, a farmer from Strandquist, enlisted in the army in January 1941, and shipped out to Corregidor Island in the Philippines. The island protected Manila Bay, the finest natural harbor in the Far East and crucial to Japanese expansion. Freddie Kuznia was assigned to the 59th Coast Artillery Regiment, one of four regiments organized into the Harbor Defense Force composed of 5,700 men. On November 8, 1941, Freddie wrote to his family from Fort Mills, Philippines: *Boy, I got some real news for you in this letter. Now hold yourself, I was made corporal two weeks ago and now wear two stripes on my arms. Not bad, eh, and I hope to have one more before I leave the Philippines. About fighting, well I had to break up some fights and I had to hit a few guys over the head with my club but I never went out to look for one, you see keeping peace is one of my jobs here. So if I lay a guy up for a few days in the hospital, that doesn't mean anything. Oh ya, I shot at a guy once when I was on duty but I didn't shoot to kill him, just to scare him a little.*[1]

The day after the Bataan Peninsula fell on April 9, Corregidor, just two miles away from Bataan, stood alone against the Japanese. When Corregidor fell on May 6, Ferdinand Kuznia joined 11,000 Americans and Filipinos as Bataan prisoners of war. The prisoners from Corregidor were marched through the streets of Manila, and then moved by train to Prison Camp Cabanatuan in the Philippines. After a long year, his mother finally received a brief postcard in September that stated: *Please do not worry as I am in the best of health. Give my regards to all of my friends. All my love and best wishes. As ever, Fred V. Kuznia.*

On October 11, 1944, the Japanese loaded 1,783 prisoners of war, including Ferdinand Kuznia, on the *Arisan Maru*, a 6,886-ton Japanese cargo ship, one of the infamous "hell ships." Typical of POW transports, prisoners were packed into the cargo hold so tightly that they all had to stand. The next day half of them were moved to another hold, but their captors provided no water, and many died from heat and dehydration. Dysentery and even asphyxia (from the close quarters) took many lives on other ships. The *Arison Maru* left Manila on October 21, bound for a slave labor camp in Takao, Formosa (present-day Taiwan).[2]

Three days after it departed, torpedoes hit the ship as it entered the Bashi Straits between Luzon and Taiwan, stopping it cold. After cutting the rope ladder to the hold, the Japanese abandoned ship. Some prisoners managed to escape and threw ropes and rope ladders into the holds. Grabbing life jackets and anything they could cling to, the men jumped into the ocean. As Japanese destroyers pulled away from them, men attempted to reach nearby vessels, but were beaten back with clubs. Most men stayed on the ship, awaiting their fate. They gorged themselves on food, water and cigarettes from the galley and sang "God Bess America."[3]

For many years, the families of the prisoners of war did not know that an American submarine, the USS *Shark*, commanded by Commander E. Blakely, was the ship that torpedoed and sank the *Arisan Maru*. The Japanese did not mark their cargo ships indicating that POWs were aboard; there was no way for American forces to know what the ships held. During the engagement, Japanese destroyers sank both the USS *Shark* and another submarine, the USS *Snook*.[2]

Only 9 American prisoners of war survived the sinking, which occurred 200 hundred miles off the coast of China. Five men rigged a sail on an abandoned lifeboat, and after several days Chinese fishermen picked them up and brought them to an American base. Japanese vessels picked up four survivors and took them to the prison camp in Formosa.[2, 4, 5]

The family held out hope that Ferdinand had survived, when well after the reported sinking of the *Arisan Maru*, his brother John received a card from Ferdinand thanking him for the Christmas package. (Unfortunately it was just a letter that took a long time to reach home.)

Corporal Ferdinand Kuznia, son of Frank and Rosalia (Kasprowicz) Kuznia, was survived by his mother and three sisters and four brothers. Corporal Ferdinand Kuznia is memorialized on the Tablets of the Missing, Manila American Cemeteries, Philippines, and Assumption Cemetery, Florian, Minnesota.[4, 6]

Alfred Peter Bruns

St. Rosa (Stearns County)

Fifth Army, 85th Infantry "Custer" Division, 337th Infantry Regiment, 2nd Battalion, G Company, Private

JULY 26, 1921–OCTOBER 24, 1944—Italian Campaign, Italy

The War in Italy was tough. The land and the weather were both against us. It rained and it rained. Vehicles bogged down and bridges washed out. The country was shockingly beautiful and just as shockingly hard to capture from the enemy.
—Ernie Pyle in *Brave Men*, 1944[1]

On May 15, 1942, just a few months after the United States entered World War II, the 85th Infantry Division was reactivated at Camp Shelby, Mississippi. Named the "Custer" Division after George Armstrong Custer, the 85th had three infantry regiments: the 335th, 337th and 338th. On March 24, 1943, Private Alfred Bruns joined the 337th, the "Wolverines," and trained in desert warfare until he shipped overseas on December 24, 1943, for Casablanca, Morocco, and the Italian Campaign. Upon arriving in Naples, Italy, on March 27, 1944, the 85th Infantry Division set about to capture Rome, break the Gothic Line in the North Apennines and secure the Brenner Pass in the Italian Alps.

After the road inland from Anzio Beach opened in mid-May, the 85th entered Rome on June 5, an objective that soon paled in comparison to D-Day and the invasion of France that dominated all the headlines. Following the capture of Rome, the 85th motored to a rest and training area near Lido de Roma, a resort town on the sea for men just out of combat. Part of their training involved mountain warfare and how to pack a mule for the treacherous mountain trails that were to come.[2]

On September 13, the division broke through the Gothic Line and advanced through driving rain, wind and cold to reach Mt. Mezzano overlooking the Po River Valley on October 24.

The Army Report of Operations relays the action of Private Alfred Bruns and his G Company: *The day of 24 October was mainly spent in patrolling in preparation for a night attack. Company "G," with an effective strength of 44 men, inched forward toward Hill 444. For the attack at 2200, a different approach was used; instead of attacking north up the road, the draw southwest of the objective was used as a line of departure, with three companies attacking abreast. Division sent word that it was vital that this objective be taken as soon as possible. The operations against Hill 444 and Mezzano continued during* the night. *The commanding officer of the 1st Battalion reported the capture of the Mezzano hill, but requested reinforcements to assist in holding it. Company "K" was sent to C. Rovine and attached to the 1st Battalion. Company "G" was still short of Hill 444 despite reinforcement by an "E" Company platoon. On this day the Army Commander ordered present positions strongly defended for an indefinite period, the work to be expedited and completed as soon as possible. During the period the enemy increased the tempo of his artillery and mortar fires. Supplying the regiment became a most difficult problem as the rain continued, bridges washed out, and trails turned into quagmires of mud. Mule trains were the only means of getting equipment to the front line troops. Evacuation of casualties, because of the long, backbreaking hand carries, was necessarily slow and sometimes impossible.*[3]

Private Alfred Bruns died that night in the 32nd Field Hospital from wounds in the abdomen and right leg and was buried in Florence American Cemetery, Italy.[4] Survivors included his parents, Lambert and Mary (Zimmerman) Bruns, and three siblings: Norbert, Evelyn and Marian. Two months later on December 26, 1944, his brother, Corporal Norbert Bruns (page 103), was killed in action in Luxembourg. Private Henry Kroll from Gully, Minnesota (see 141), served with Alfred Bruns in the 337th Infantry Regiment, and died on April 22, 1945, in Italy.

Malcolm James Gordon

Fort Ripley (Crow Wing County)

U.S. 7th Fleet, Task Unit 77.4.3 "Taffy 111," Composite Squadron VC-3, Aviation Radioman First Class

OCTOBER 17, 1921–OCTOBER 25, 1944—Battle off Samar, Philippines

On September 14, 1944, the escort carrier *Kalinin Bay* arrived in southern Palau, Micronesia, to provide air support for the landing forces on Peleliu, Angaur and Ngesebus. Crewmember Malcolm Gordon flew on an Avenger torpedo bomber, which was launched from the *Kalinin Bay*. Cox outlines the ship's battle history: *After flying nearly 400 missions against Japanese shipping and ground forces, the squadron moved on to Leyte Island in the Philippines on October 17. Kalinin Bay was part of Rear Admiral Sprague's "Taffy 3" (Task Unit 77.4.3) with 6 carriers, 3 destroyers, and 4 escorts. Through October 24 her planes flew 244 missions to support landing operations on Leyte, Samar, Cebu, Negros and Panay Islands.*[1, 2, 3, 4, 5]

On October 25, 1944, Japanese Vice Admiral Takeo Kurita's fleet (4 battleships, 8 cruisers and 12 destroyers) opened fire on "Taffy 3," in the Philippine Sea near Samar and the Battle off Samar began. Under heavy fire the *Kalinin Bay* launched ten Avengers with orders, "to attack the Japanese task force and proceed to Tacloban airstrip, Leyte, to rearm and re-gas." Each Avenger had three crewmembers. On this flight the crew consisted of Lieutenant Patsy Capano, Ensign Paul Hopfner and Aviation Radioman First Class Malcolm Gordon. They were in lead formation and attacked the leading Japanese cruiser, and then joined Lieutenant Commander Keighley for a strafing run on another Japanese cruiser. Unable to land back aboard *Kalinin Bay*, Lieutenant Capano and his crew flew to Tacloban, a base on Leyte, to refuel and reload ammunition. The aircraft action report states that Lieutenant Capano's plane was not in condition to fly after landing at Tacloban, so Capano, Gordon and Hopfner left in an another Avenger borrowed from aircraft squadron VC-65. The plane and crew were never heard from again and were declared missing in action.[1, 2, 3, 4, 5, 6, 7]

During the Battle off Samar, 13 poorly armed, slow, outdated U.S. ships faced 24 superior Japanese ships and courageously sank 3 enemy heavy cruisers. The Americans lost 5 ships, several aircraft and over 1,580 lives. However, the battle disrupted Vice Admiral Kurita's plan to move into Leyte Gulf, and he withdrew his remaining ships to Japan, ending the threat to Allied forces. In *Great American Naval Battles*, Thomas Cutler wrote: *But the moment of truth, the instant when victory was indeed snatched from the jaws of defeat, occurred when*

Taffy 3's escorts and all three Taffies' aircraft threw themselves headlong into harm's way, upholding the finest traditions of the United States Navy in a selfless act of courage that has sometimes been equaled, but never surpassed.[8]

The son of Daniel and Ruth (Gates) Gordon, Aviation Radioman First Class Malcolm J. Gordon is memorialized at Manila American Cemetery, Philippines, and Pine Tree Cemetery, Crow Wing County, Minnesota. Survivors included his parents and five siblings.

The Gordon family farmed in Fort Ripley, and Malcolm and his brother Dudley drew straws to see who would go to college and who would stay on the family farm. Malcolm went to Brainerd Junior College and Dudley stayed on the farm. Malcolm entered the service on June 9, 1942.[9]

The most famous man to fly an Avenger was George H.W. Bush, later the 41st President of the United States. On September 2, 1944, he was shot down over Chichijima. Bush parachuted to safety after bombing his target, but both of the crewmen aboard perished. Actor Paul Newman also flew on the Avenger as a rear gunner.

John Joseph Reardon

Johnson (Big Stone County)

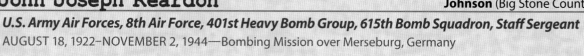

U.S. Army Air Forces, 8th Air Force, 401st Heavy Bomb Group, 615th Bomb Squadron, Staff Sergeant

AUGUST 18, 1922–NOVEMBER 2, 1944—Bombing Mission over Merseburg, Germany

Following graduation from Graceville High School in 1940, John Reardon worked for the Lockland Aircraft plant at Burbank, California, before enlisting in the Army Air Corps on September 30, 1942, at age 20. He completed his basic training at Big Springs, Texas, and earned his wings the following February in Las Vegas, Nevada.[1,2] In June 1944, Staff Sergeant John Reardon trained in England with the 401st Bomb Group, a force trained to fly B-17s with the mission to destroy enemy oil refineries and industrial complexes.

On November 2, 1944, Staff Sergeant John Reardon and the 401st left on Mission 164, a force of 210 B-17 bombers ordered to drop 469 tons of bombs on the Leuna synthetic oil refinery at Merseburg, Germany. As they approached the refinery, enemy flak hit 27 planes, causing major damage to 2. Only one plane, *Wolfpack*, piloted by 1st Lieutenant Herbert Oas Jr., failed to return. Staff Sergeant John J. Reardon served as tail gunner. Army personnel eyewitness accounts reported that the plane was hit by anti-aircraft fire and went down in a spiraling dive. Three parachutes were seen leaving the plane and of those three, 1st Lieutenant Herbert Oas survived the jump, was captured by the Germans and later returned to U.S. control.

Pilot 1st Lieutenant John Udy of the 615th Squadron reported the loss of 1st Lieutenant Oas' crew: *"The target was the oil refineries at Merseburg, Germany, and I was flying on Lieutenant H.L. Oas' wing. He received a direct hit in his No. 3 engine causing his aircraft to pitch up into mine. I pulled back on the control column and managed to miss him. This caused a loss in airspeed and I fell behind the formation. As I applied full power to get back into formation, and as we watched Lieutenant Oas' aircraft spin down suddenly, we were hit from behind by three FW-190s. I was doing some evasive action to avoid the flak and I think that prevented us from being shot down. The 20 mm shells fired by the 190s went through the right wing and burst in little white puffs approximately 100 yards in front of the aircraft. Our gunner opened up on the 190s and thought they had hit them but could not confirm this. We got back in formation and completed the mission."*[3]

On August 19, 1948, almost four years after the air crash, the Search and Disinterring Team arrived in Kriegsdorf, Germany, to determine the fate of the crew. They located three local men who removed the bodies from the plane and buried them. The men told the following story: *On the 2 of Nov. 1944 one American bomber crashed on the road to Wallendorf, just outside the village. The villagers were the first ones at the crash. One witness said he recovered six remains from the wreckage: one from the cockpit, two outside the plane by the motors, 2 in the middle of the plane, and one from back further in the fuselage. These were buried in the Kriegsdorf Cemetery. No list of the names was made and what identifications were on the remains were buried with them. The tail of the plane crashed in Wallendorf, and the tail gunner, Staff Sergeant Reardon, was buried in Wallendorf, and two days later, his grave was destroyed by a bomb in an air raid.*[4]

Staff Sergeant John Reardon had completed 27 of the 35 missions required to earn a furlough home. His parents, Thomas and Frances (Conway) Reardon, who owned the grain elevator in Johnson, received a letter from their son dated October 24. Their hopes were dashed on January 6 when the war department confirmed his death via telegram.

Staff Sergeant John Reardon is memorialized at Henri-Chapelle American Cemetery in Belgium. His mother wrote several letters to the War Department seeking information on her son. Survivors included his parents; two sisters, Catherine and Constance; and one brother, Private First Class Richard Reardon.[2]

Only a very small number of 401st Bomb Group B-17s achieved the magical number of 100 missions. One 615th Squadron B-17, the *Morning Star*, recorded a total of 112 missions before returning to the United States on Operation Home Run in June 1945.

In 2008, Andy Swinnen from the Netherlands adopted Staff Sergeant Reardon's grave. He places flowers three times a month on John Reardon's name on the wall of the missing at Henri-Chapelle.[5]

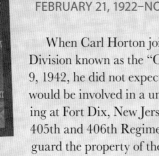

Carl Richard Horton

Squaw Lake (Itasca County)

102nd Infantry "Ozarks" Division, 406th Infantry Regiment, 1st Battalion, B Company, Private
FEBRUARY 21, 1922–NOVEMBER 6, 1944—Attack on the Siegfried Line, Baesweiler, Germany

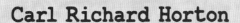

When Carl Horton joined the 102nd Infantry Division known as the "Ozarks" on November 9, 1942, he did not expect that his regiment would be involved in a union strike. After arriving at Fort Dix, New Jersey, in June 1944, the 405th and 406th Regiments were deployed to guard the property of the Philadelphia Transit Authority during a union strike, which shut down the entire city of Philadelphia. The strike, fueled by a racist reaction to efforts to end job discrimination for African-Americans in the Philadelphia Transit Authority, paralyzed several industries vital to the war effort. When other efforts failed, 5,000 troops arrived to guard rail installations, bridges and highways. Machine guns bristled from major intersections and army riflemen rode in the rail cars to enforce the action and also to protect African-American drivers from violent strikers and protestors.[1, 2, 3, 4, 5]

Philadelphia settled with the transit workers on August 9, and by September 12, 1944, the "Ozarks" were on their way to Cherbourg, France. There they boarded the trucks and trains of the "Red Ball Express," bound for the Roer River in northern Germany. By the end of October 1944, Allied armies drove the Germans from France and planned a full-scale attack against Hitler's Siegfried Line, a defensive fortification with ten-foot-thick cement walls, heavy artillery and minefields. Allied forces at Aachen had already breached the defensive line, and now plans called for the 102nd Infantry Division to break the Siegfried Line at Geilenkirchen, 14 miles north of Aachen.[6]

Private Carl Horton and the 406th Regiment entered battle on November 2 while attached to the 30th Infantry Division. The following day, the 102nd Division began their drive through the Siegfried Line, and during the battle, Private Carl Horton was declared missing in action on November 6. His body was recovered December 4 near Baesweiler, Germany.

In response to a letter written by Ellen Horton requesting information on her son's death, Major General Edward Vitsell replied on October 21, 1946: *Your desire to learn as much as possible regarding the death of your son is most understandable. Information available in this office reveals that Private Horton was killed in action on 6 November 1944 in Baesweiler, Germany. I regret that I am unable to furnish you complete facts concerning his death but I feel confident*

that you will understand that full details covering each heroic deed in which our men fought the enemy could not always be told, as the movements of many men and machines in battle were over large areas and involved great numbers.[7]

The 102nd reached the Rhine River in early March 1945, and drove eastward to the Elbe River, less than 50 miles from Berlin, by mid-April. Moore recalls the events of April 14, 1945, when the 102nd discovered a barn outside the town of Gardelegen, where the German SS burned 1,016 camp prisoners alive. *When prison guards discovered that Gardelegen had fallen to the Allies, they murdered the prisoners to prevent their turning on the guards in the event of liberation. However, two men, buried under a shield of dead bodies, survived and crawled out from the debris. Major General Frank Keating, commander of the 102nd, ordered civilians from Gardelegen to properly bury the prisoners. The 102nd erected a monument at the burial site: "The people of Gardelegen are charged with the responsibility that these graves are forever kept as green as the memory of these unfortunates will be kept in the hearts of freedom-loving men everywhere."*[8]

Private Carl R. Horton, son of Oliver and Ellen (Maish) Horton, was initially buried in Margraten Military Cemetery, Holland, and reinterred in 1949 in Lakeview Cemetery, Blackduck, Minnesota. He was awarded the Expert Infantryman Badge and the Purple Heart.

The Ozarks patch includes a large, golden "O" on a field of blue with the letter "Z" within the "O." Original plans called for unit personnel to be drawn from the Ozark Mountains area of the United States.

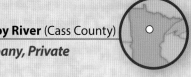

Otto William Peterson

Boy River (Cass County)

28th Infantry "Keystone" Division, 112th Infantry Regiment, 1st Battalion, A Company, Private
APRIL 16, 1925–NOVEMBER 8, 1944—Battle of the Hürtgen Forest, Germany

After training in England and Wales, Private Otto Peterson and the 28th Infantry Division arrived in Normandy, France, on July 22, 1944, in time to enter the hedgerow struggle northwest of St.-Lô. Inching their way through fierce opposition, the men of the 28th rolled across France to Paris. By August 19, the 28th Division had killed hundreds of Germans and captured 833 German prisoners, earning the division the name *Blutiger Eimer* or "bloody bucket." The Germans interpreted the division's "Red Keystone" shoulder patch as a bucket filled with blood.

As the Allies approached Paris, they found the French Resistance rising up against the Nazis. When Allied forces broke through German defenses on August 25 and claimed Paris, Major General Dietrich von Choltitz defied Hitler's order to destroy Paris and surrendered the city intact. On August 29, 1944, the 28th Infantry Division, along with other Allied troops, marched down the Champs-Élysées in Paris during a victory parade where the 28th received the honor of the only division chosen to march by General Charles de Gaulle's reviewing stand.[1, 2]

As jubilant Parisians greeted the men with wine, flowers and affection, one soldier, Ralph Johnson remarked, "My feelings as we marched along in the parade were that surely the war must be nearly over. I could not have been more wrong. So many of my friends and comrades would be killed before that happy moment would arrive. Hitler just would not give up."[3]

After parading through Paris, the 28th continued to drive through France and Luxembourg in a race with the Germans for possession of the Siegfried Line, a series of pillboxes and steel barriers running along the German border. If the Allies could break through the Siegfried Line, only the Rhine River prevented the American forces from entering Germany.

On November 2, 1944, the 28th Infantry Division prepared for battle in the Hürtgen Forest in Germany. As Weaver pointed out, this was a dense forest heavily defended by the Germans with minefields, barbed wire and booby traps hidden in the snow. An area of 50 square miles, the terrain was a horrible nightmare filled with dark forests, stone ridges and deep gorges. The mission was to attack and secure critical villages, specifically Vossenack, Kommerscheidt and Schmidt. Initially, the 112th Regiment held the villages, but bad weather and poor planning left the soldiers to defend the area without protection from aircraft or tanks.

On November 5, 1944, German soldiers, heavily supported by tanks, attacked the American troops. Although the soldiers of the 112th fought bravely, they could not hold their positions against the Germans' superior firepower. By November 8, the regiment had fallen back to their assembly area and suffered heavy casualties with over 2,000 men killed, wounded or captured. Over 200 missing soldiers, including Private Otto Peterson, were absent on reorganization of the company. No search could be conducted as the area in which they were missing belonged to the enemy. Private Otto Peterson was listed as missing in action on November 8. Someone discovered his body on March 4, 1945, near Kommerscheidt, Germany, with a gunshot wound in his back. The Battle of Hürtgen Forest cost the 28th Infantry Division 6,184 casualties. Private Otto Peterson's 112th Infantry Regiment sustained 2,316 casualties out of 3,100 soldiers.[1]

Private Otto Peterson was initially buried in Henri-Chappelle Military Cemetery in France and later reinterred December 10, 1947, at Fort Snelling National Cemetery.[6]

Otto's mother kept a journal when both her sons served in World War II: *Oct 2: Got first overseas letter from Otto. He was in France (12). He was in Belgium. Nov. 27, 1944: Got letter Otto is missing. Oh Ottie you have to be alright. Jan. 7, 1945: It will be 2 months tomorrow Ott is missing. Wonder if he has enough to eat and if he is warm. Mar. 8: Ott has been in the army a year and missing 4 months of that. Mar. 19: Got the telegram saying Ott's been killed in action Nov. 8, 1944. How can it be our Ott? Why is it Ott? Jan. 10, 1947: Received a picture of the cemetery Ott is supposed to be buried in. April 8: 2 Years ago, had service for our Ott. Sent a letter today asking to have him brought back. April 16: Ott's 22nd birthday. Oct. 25: Got telegram saying Ott was in the States. Dec. 10: Got to Minneapolis at 10. Started home at 2, got home at 8 that night. Now Otto is with us again.*[6, 7]

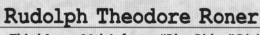

Rudolph Theodore Roner

Strandquist (Marshall County)

Third Army, 80th Infantry "Blue Ridge" Division, 318th Infantry Regiment, Third Battalion, I Company, Private First Class

JULY 18, 1924–NOVEMBER 8, 1944—Lorraine Campaign, France

Harriet Lindstrom remembers the day her Uncle Rudolph boarded the train for the army: *Rudy left for the army right after graduating from high school in 1943. We had him home after six weeks, or maybe six months, of basic training. We saw him off at the train station in Strandquist.*

Rudolph's mother, Marie, died in 1929. She had been pregnant and had the flu. She lost the baby and died.

Afterwards, my mother (Marie's sister) raised some of the children. The day before Marie died, my mother had a dream in which Marie told her she was crossing the river and would she please take care of her children. The next morning she had a call that her sister had died, and that was when the youngest children, Rudolph, Kenneth, Hazel and Florence, came to live with us.[1]

Private First Class Rudolph Roner and the 80th Division set sail aboard the SS *Queen Mary* on July 4, 1944, and arrived three days later at the Firth of Clyde, Scotland. After training in Northwich, England, they landed on Utah Beach, August 3, 1944, and prepared to chase retreating German units east across France. On August 10 they took Évron and Sainte-Suzanne, and traveled on through isolated skirmishes until they encountered their first serious resistance in Argentan. There, they faced off against the Seventh German Army from Argentan, inflicting severe damage to that division before it retreated. Moving rapidly, the 80th crossed the Moselle, and on October 8 the 318th captured Manoncourt-sur-Seille on the west bank of the Seille River, where they stopped to prepare for the drive to the Saar Valley.[2, 3, 4, 5, 6]

Lieutenant John Bier, commander of Private First Class Roner's I Company, relays the events of November 8, 1944: *At the time of the attack to cross the Seille River, the 3rd Battalion. 318th Infantry was in regimental reserve. They crossed the river at 0830 in the zone of the 2nd Battalion and went into Rouves. That afternoon they were given the mission to take the high ground northwest of Nomeny and to take the town from the rear. Resistance from the town was not expected. I Company moved toward Nomeny but was held up by enemy infantry dug-in on the high ground north of the town. A platoon of tanks from B Company, 702nd Tank Battalion arrived to support the company at about 1700. The tanks and infantry drove the enemy off the high ground and the remaining Germans*

withdrew into Nomeny. Heavy casualties were suffered by I Company; in the fighting the CO was wounded and there were approximately 75 other casualties. The next morning 9 Nov., I Company reinforced by other elements of the battalion moved in and took Nomeny against very light resistance. The town was mopped up and 200 PWs were taken by about 1200. Private First Class Rudolph Roner was one of the casualties.[7]

Initially buried in United States Military Cemetery, Limey, France, Rudolph Roner was reinterred in 1948 in Fort Snelling. After the death of Rudolph's mother in 1929, his father, Theodore Roner, moved his family from the country to Strandquist and built Roner's Store, the social center of the community. On cold winter nights, residents would gather around the old woodstove to discuss local news, politics and religion. During the lively discussions, you could hear the cracking of peanut shells, an inexpensive treat at five cents a pound. Theodore also showed silent movies in the new town hall and broadcast a Sunday afternoon radio show from the back of his store.[1, 9]

Ernest Raymond King

Seaforth (Redwood County)

24th Infantry "Victory" Division, 21st Infantry Regiment, 3rd Battalion, L Company, Staff Sergeant

SEPTEMBER 16, 1914–NOVEMBER 10, 1944—Battle of Breakneck Ridge, Philippines

Ernest King grew up on the family farm near Seaforth with his parents, Herbert and Clara (Winslow) King and seven siblings. His niece, Gertrude Witschen, recalls her mother telling her: *Ernest was a very kind son and caring brother. After our dad died, he stayed home to take care of mom on the farm until he was called into the service.*[1]

Following his induction into the army February 3, 1942, Ernest joined the 24th Infantry Division and trained as a machine gunner.

The 24th Infantry Division, among the first to see combat in World War II, was stationed on Oahu during the bombing of Pearl Harbor, December 7, 1941. After building a system of defense on northern Oahu, the 24th transferred to Australia to train for the invasion of New Guinea. After occupation duty there, the 24th Division landed on Red Beach on Leyte, October 20, 1944, and drove up Leyte Valley.

On November 7, Staff Sergeant Ernest King and the 21st Infantry Regiment moved to the mountains above Carigara Bay where the Japanese 1st Division, hidden behind heavy logs and trenches known as Breakneck Ridge, waited for them. A typhoon, with heavy rains and mudslides, hit the area on November 8 and made it nearly impossible to dig the Japanese out of their trenches on the ridge. Despite adverse weather and counterattacks, the American forces captured and then recaptured hill after hill before finally securing Breakneck Ridge on December 14.[2]

Captain Kermit Blaney wrote about L Company on November 10, 1944, the sixth day on Breakneck Ridge, when Staff Sergeant Ernest King died: *The brief period Company L was in reserve was ended with orders attaching the company to the 2nd Battalion to attack at 0900 hours and take the high ground at point "H." Once again the movement was slow and treacherous due to the rains during the night. The company had to move mostly in a column and employing human chains to ascend...the slippery sides of the gulches. The company could not deploy to any extent beyond platoon column and it was with the supporting fires of G and F Company, close artillery and mortar support that made it possible for Company L to take the high ground by 1120 hours...During the afternoon, L Company's position was under direct heavy artillery fire from short range.*

Staff Sergeant King was buried on Leyte Island and two days later, the ridge was secured. From November 5 to 16, the 21st Infantry Regiment advanced 2,000 yards over a series of 6 ridges, each being occupied by both forces several times. Major General Fredrick Irving commented on Breakneck Ridge, "The terrain is the toughest I ever saw."[2]

Memorial services for Ernest King were held at First Presbyterian Church assisted by the Ralph Lamb Post Legionnaires of Seaforth. Legion Commander Frank Smetak presented the U.S. flag to his mother. On October 8, 1945, Clara King wrote to the War Department: *Dear Sir, I am writing to see if I can get my boy's body brought home. His name is Staff Sergeant Ernest King. He was killed on Leyte Island, Philippines on Nov. 10, 1944. I sure want him brought home. Don't ask the government to do it all, I'll do my part whatever it cost to get him brought back as quick as I can get him here. Please write back and tell me if he can be brought back soon and if there is anything I can do to get him here.*[3, 4]

Ernest King was reinterred in Redwood Falls Cemetery, Redwood Falls, Minnesota.[5, 6]

Roy Merle Lee

Perley (Norman County)

Seventh Army, 100th Infantry "Century" Division, 399th Infantry Regiment, 1st Battalion, A Company, Private First Class

MARCH 5, 1923–NOVEMBER 17, 1944—Drive Against the German Winter Line, France

On October 6, 1944, Private First Class Roy Lee and the 100th Infantry Division, consisting of men from all 48 states, left the lights of Manhattan to board the SS *McAndrews* for the voyage to Marseilles, France. Life on the ship allowed plenty of time for talking, reading, playing poker and chess, and attending nightly movies and variety shows. When the ship docked in Marseilles on October 20, the setting changed to one defined by wet, cold and mud. The first morning on the wet ground, more than one man woke up to find himself floating in a pup tent. On October 29, the division traveled in open trucks up the Rhone Valley for the battlefront near Fremifontaine, located in the northeast corner of France and the foothills of the Vosges Mountains. French citizens happily welcomed American soldiers all along the route.

Behind their front line on the night of October 31, Private First Class Roy Lee and A Company heard American artillery for the first time. Inexperienced, frightened and just 26 days away from Manhattan, A Company relieved the 179th A Company of the 45th Division on November 1, near the small village of LaSalle, France, in the Vosges Mountains.[1,2] Bruner wrote that here the men met: *the real 'Combat Joes, the beaten-up dogfaces, the characters who have learned by experience and misery just what combat fighting means.*[2] While advancing to St. Rémy, the men discovered the ravages of combat when the enemy shelled the town, causing many casualties.

On November 12, the 100th Infantry Division joined other divisions for the drive down the Meurthe River to secure Raon-l'Étape, which was a key city protected by Germany's Vosges Winter Line. German forces erected the Winter Line by thinning the thick Vosges forest for 200 yards, placing barbed wire and digging in on the high ground behind the wire. During the advance on Raon-l'Étape, Private First Class Roy Lee and the 1st Battalion received a Presidential Unit Citation: *Overlooking the important Meurthe River city of Raon-l'Étape, in the thickly forested foothills of the Vosges Mountains, is a hill-mass known as the Tête des Reclos. This high ground, affording perfect enemy observation, barred an assault upon the vital communications city. On the rainy morning of 16 November, the 1st Battalion launched an attack to clear the enemy from those strongly fortified hill positions. Fighting through the dense pine forest, under intense enemy artillery, mortar, machine gun and automatic-weapons fire, the 1st Battalion, after three hours of effort, drove across a trail circling the base of the hill-mass. A withering, 45-minute artillery preparation at this point proved ineffective against the deep, concrete and log-covered enemy bunkers, and it soon became evident that basic infantry assault was the only feasible method for driving the enemy from their positions. In a fierce, close-in, small arms firefight, which increased in fury as they climbed the precipitous slopes, the 1st Battalion wormed its way toward the top of Hill 462.8, key to the enemy's defenses. Battling against fanatical enemy resistance, it finally reached the crest. Bitter, hand-to-hand fighting developed as the enemy hurled repeated counterattacks against the inspired infantrymen. Once, the 1st Battalion was driven from the hilltop, but rapidly regrouping, it regained its positions. At dark, the enemy finally withdrew, leaving the 1st Battalion in possession of the high ground. Throughout, supplies had to be hand-carried up the steep slopes under continuous enemy fire. Only the teamwork, coordination, and determination of all elements in the heroic 1st Battalion made the success of this attack possible.*[3]

The writer of *Able Company* mentions Private First Class Roy Lee in his narrative on November 17: *The hill went straight up into the sky. It was buddy with buddy, squad-by-squad, platoon with platoon. Some fired into German foxholes, others climbed to the next tree. Sergeant Clarence Sutton and Lucian Zarlenga reached the top first and Able fanned out to fight on two knobs. Lieutenant Ballie's 3rd platoon got surrounded on the right knob and Captain Young took Sergeant Buss's 2nd platoon up to retake it, with light machine gunners Joseph Hoffman, Roy Lee and William Pondrom leading the attack. The cream of the 1st Battalion died on that hill.*[1] By November 26, the Vosges Mountains Campaign was over and the 100th advanced north to break the Maginot Line near the city of Bitche, heart of the entire German defense system.[1,2]

Private First Class Roy Lee enlisted in the army on June 24, 1942. In 1948, Private First Class Lee was reinterred at Prairie Home and Riverside Cemetery, Moorhead, Minnesota.

Arthur Eugene Gooselaw

St. Vincent (Kittson County)

Ninth Army, 95th Infantry "Victory" Division, 377th Infantry Regiment, 3rd Battalion, K Company, Private

JULY 2, 1921–NOVEMBER 15, 1944—Battle for Metz, France

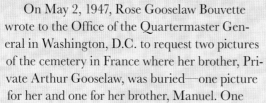

On May 2, 1947, Rose Gooselaw Bouvette wrote to the Office of the Quartermaster General in Washington, D.C. to request two pictures of the cemetery in France where her brother, Private Arthur Gooselaw, was buried—one picture for her and one for her brother, Manuel. One year later, on August 2, 1948, Rose wrote a second time: *Dear Sir, I thought I'd write again to ask you if you could send me one more photograph of the United States Cemetery, Limey, France, where my dear brother, Arthur E. Gooselaw, is buried. I have an Uncle who would so much like to have it to frame, and I was wondering if there are any photographs where my other dear brother, Jerome, is buried and if you have any. I'd sure love to have them. Thanks so much. Mrs. Lawrence Bouvette, St. Vincent, Minnesota*[1]

The Gooselaw family endured much tragedy during World War II. When Adele Gooselaw's husband died in 1942, she could not imagine that she would lose two sons in battle in World War II: Jerome in the New Georgia Campaign in 1943, and Arthur in the battle for Metz, France, in 1944. Three other sons: Lewis, Edmund and Nazareth, also served in the army during World War II.

Arthur Gooselaw, of Cree and French Voyageur ancestry, was inducted into the army on July 3, 1942, and trained as a paratrooper before transferring to the 95th Infantry Division.[2, 6] On September 15, 1944, the 95th Division moved to France to prepare for combat and to capture Metz, which *Stars and Stripes* described as: *a city that had withstood all attacks by military forces since 451 A.D. The original city fortifications, consisting of an inner ring of 15 forts and an outer perimeter of 28 steel-and-concrete bastions, had recently been reinforced with high-powered weapons placed in revolving steel turrets.*[3]

Army historian Hugh Cole downplayed the "outdated fortifications" as overrated, and attributes the strong defense of Metz to a combination of elite troops, "the moral and physical strength derived from steel and concrete," and high ground favoring defense.[4]

With Patton's Third Army, the "Victory Division" captured forts in the Moselle region south of Metz and prevented the Germans from attacking across the river. Their determined actions earned them the name "The Iron Men of Metz." On November 8, the offensive on Metz began, with multiple divisions crossing the Moselle River during the next week and storming the towns surrounding Metz. On November 15, Private Arthur Gooselaw and the 377th Infantry attacked two areas in Operation Casanova, a deceptive, small-scale operation. The 1st Battalion crossed the river east of Uckange that night, as the 2nd and 3rd moved south against an enemy post on the west bank of the Moselle near Maiziéres-lés-Metz. There the 3rd ran into "vast minefields," which could blow all at once if someone hit a trip wire. The explosions attracted enemy mortar and artillery fire, delaying their crossing of the swollen, turbulent river.[3, 4, 5] Although artillery and mortar fire rained on the advancing troops, the 2nd and 3rd Battalions continued their drive south, and by twilight, the 3rd Battalion held La Maxe, just four miles north of Metz.[4]

Private Arthur Gooselaw died from gun shrapnel wounds during the advance, near Maiziéres-lés-Metz. Three days later, he was buried at 2:00 in the afternoon at the U.S. Cemetery in Limey, France. And in 1949, the remains of Arthur and his brother, Private Jerome Gooselaw (page 27), who died in New Georgia in 1943, were sent back via the USAT *Lawrence Victory* and the Great Northern Railroad for side-by-side burial in St. Vincent Cemetery, St. Vincent, Minnesota.[1, 2, 6]

Oscar Thorvald Hanson

U.S. Army Air Forces, 8th Air Force, 93rd Combat Bomb Wing, 34th Heavy Bomb Group, 391st Bomb Squadron, Captain

FEBRUARY 18, 1918–NOVEMBER 30, 1944—Bomb Mission 95 over Merseburg, Germany

Captain Oscar T. Hanson started his military flying career as a flight instructor with the Royal Canadian Air Force in 1941, and a year later, he transferred to Perrin Field, Texas, as a flight instructor for the U.S. Army Air Forces. At the end of 1943, the 34th Bomb Group converted to B-24 Liberator aircraft in preparation for assignment to the 8th Air Force in England in April 1944.[1] Captain Hanson flew a B-24 on his first mission on D-Day June 6, 1944, when the 34th Bomb Group supported the Allied invasion of Europe. They also attacked German forces at St.-Lô on July 24 and 25. By the fall of 1944, Eisenhower surrendered control of heavy bombers to the 8th Air Force and the 34th Bomb Group switched to the B-17 Fortress for the remainder of the war.

On November 30, 1944, the 8th Air Force launched Mission 95 where 36 bombers from Mendlesham air base joined forces with 1,200 bombers and 946 escort fighters over southern England to destroy an oil refinery in Merseburg, Germany. Leading the low squadron and just after bombs away, Pilot Captain Oscar T. Hanson and his eight-man crew in their B-17, named *Chesty-V,* took a direct hit in No. 2 engine, causing a major fire. The aircraft slid violently under the formation, losing 2,000 to 3,000 feet of altitude. Minutes after the crew bailed out at 27,000 feet, the left wing broke off, sending the bomber into a dive over Bad Kosen, Germany. Five crewmembers, Staff Sergeant Joe Burton, 1st Lieutenant Lindsey Liscomb, Staff Sergeant Paul Shull, 1st Lieutenant Donald Topping, and Staff Sergeant Sidney Brown, survived the parachute jump out of the flaming aircraft and remained prisoners of war in Germany until liberation. Staff Sergeant George Simpson and Staff Sergeant Lawrence Layton were captured by German civilians and killed. Pilot Hanson and Co-pilot 1st Lieutenant Roy Keirn, died on impact when thrown from the aircraft as it broke apart over Bad Kosen. Captain Hanson's bomber was the only one out of 36 from the 34th Bomb Group lost to flak.[1, 2, 3]

Jim Hanson remembers his Uncle Oscar Hanson: *Over the years, from talking to surviving crew members and other former pilots in the 34th Bomb Group, I found out that he was one of the better pilots in the group and always had very high regards for the enlisted men in his crew. As a lead pilot, he instructed the replacement pilots in his squadron to fly missions, and most of them survived. A few years ago, by a stroke of luck, I came into contact with a co-pilot who saw Oscar get shot down, as they were flying behind him. He had Oscar's "fifty mission hat" as pilots called them and Oscar tossed it to him the night before he got shot down. As he put it, "Captain Hanson came into the officers club the night before, rather agitated, and threw the cap to me. I had never seen him that upset, as it wasn't in his nature. Maybe the stress of all the missions had built up in him, but later in the hut, I tried to give it back to him as it had gone on most of his combat missions. It fit me better than my own cap, so I took it with me on the mission the next day. We saw him get shot down and felt the heat from the wing fire for a second as he swung past us. The cap was under my seat and when we returned back to the base shot full of holes, I noticed a flak hole, just inches from his cap. If he hadn't tossed me the cap, it would have gone down in his bomber! I decided it must be lucky, so it went along with me on all of my 33 missions and I survived. I brought it home and have kept it in the same box since 1945, along with a pair of my pilot wings." I visited the co-pilot a few years ago and got to see the frail cap, that Oscar had bought at Perrin Field, Texas. Oscar had written his name on the inside band. This co-pilot and I became good friends and when he passed away, his family sent me the cap, as he wanted me to have the cap along with his wings because of our friendship.[1]*

Captain Oscar Hanson, son of Thomas and Clara (Severson) Hanson, is buried in Fort Snelling Cemetery. Survivors included his parents; seven siblings; and his wife, Clara; and three young sons, Jerry, Eric, and Dwight, who was born a month after Oscar died. His wife, Clara, grew up in High River, Canada, and worked at the base canteen where Oscar met her and fell in love. After Oscar's death, Clara gave the children to family members: Mavis adopted three-year-old Jerry, Norman adopted two-year-old Eric and Amy adopted one-year-old Dwight. In 1991, the brothers were reunited with their mother in Texas.[1, 4, 5]

Robert H. Brady

McKinley/Elcor (St. Louis County)

Ninth Army, 95th Infantry "Victory" Division, 379th Infantry Regiment, 1st Battalion, B Company, Staff Sergeant

MARCH 22, 1917–DECEMBER 3, 1944—Rhineland Campaign, Germany

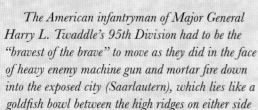

The American infantryman of Major General Harry L. Twaddle's 95th Division had to be the "bravest of the brave" to move as they did in the face of heavy enemy machine gun and mortar fire down into the exposed city (Saarlautern), which lies like a goldfish bowl between the high ridges on either side of the Saar. This battle-tried division had crossed the Moselle to help capture Metz and was now up against the principal river between the Moselle and the Rhine.

—Joseph Driscoll, *The New York Herald Tribune*[1]

As Staff Sergeant Robert Brady and the 95th Infantry Division approached Metz on November 14, 1944, they faced Saarlautern, a fortified city long known for withstanding foreign attacks. Germany had reinforced the inner ring of 15 forts and the outer ring of 28 in 1941, to make the city impenetrable from anything other than a direct strike. The 95th crossed the Moselle River and took Metz, forcing the Germans to surrender fort-by-fort on November 21st only after bitter hand-to-hand combat had wiped out all resistance. Their efforts earned them the name "The Bravest of the Brave" from war correspondents, and "The Iron Men of Metz" from the Germans.[1,2] The 95th Division crossed the German border on November 28 where the 379th Regiment received orders to advance to the Saar River and seize Saarlautern before crossing the river and capturing Rehlingen. On December 3, air reconnaissance spotted an intact bridge across the Saar River in the city of Saarlautern. Under cover of the noise of an American artillery barrage, Sergeant Brady and the 1st Battalion quietly slipped across the river in boats and seized the bridge, cutting demolition wires and fending off counterattacks by scattered parties of soldiers and tanks.[1,2,3]

Captain Albert Kinslow wrote about Sergeant Robert Brady's B Company: *As soon as the bridge was captured, the 1st Battalion began clearing that part of Saarlautern north of the river. One platoon of Company B surprised Germans in a two-story bunker almost at the same time the first shot was fired. This bunker had no outside security, and the effects of a hand grenade dropped into it persuaded the Germans to surrender. Just after daybreak, the Germans apparently realized that they had lost the bridge. Enemy artillery and mortar fire began* pounding the bridgehead about 0900 and increased throughout the day. The artillery fire was the heaviest ever received by the first battalion. Trees and buildings were gradually destroyed. Movement was reduced to a minimum, but casualties began to reach a high figure. Only the strongly constructed stone buildings prevented the casualties from being much higher.[3] During the battle for Saarlautern, Staff Sergeant Robert Brady was killed in action.[4]

Although the enemy resisted with all its power, the Americans had firm control of the bridgehead by December 19. At this point, the division learned of the German army's advance into Belgium and Luxembourg—the Battle of the Bulge had begun. Part of the division deployed to the Bulge, while the rest remained to defend Saarlautern.[1,2,3]

Staff Sergeant Robert H. Brady is buried in Saint-Avold, Lorraine, France. Robert graduated in 1942 from Eveleth Community College. His father, a Swedish immigrant, worked as a driller, pumpman, and watchman for the Pickands Mather Company.[5] In all, Elcor lost four men in World War II: Lloyd Nicholas (page 37), LeRoy Veralrud (page 74), Rudolph Indihar (page 55) and Robert Brady.[6]

95

Arthur A. Hackbarth

7th Infantry "Hourglass" Division, 184th Infantry Regiment, 1st Battalion, D Company, Private First Class

MARCH 26, 1913–DECEMBER 15, 1944—Battle for Leyte, Philippines

Following his induction into the army on March 24, 1942, Private First Class Arthur Hackbarth completed basic training at Camp San Jose, Camp Obispo and Camp San Francisco, California. In July 1943, Private First Class Hackbarth and the 184th Infantry Regiment left San Francisco for the Aleutian Islands, and participated in Operation Cottage, a plan to recapture the last Japanese-held island in the Aleutians.[1] Daniel Sebby wrote that the 13th Canadian Infantry Brigade arrived with the Americans and upon landing in Kiska, Colonel Curtis O'Sullivan ordered the regiment's band to play, "California, Here I Come," and "The Maple Leaf Forever." To their surprise, the regiment found that the Japanese had evacuated the island on July 28, "in such a hurry, that they left mess tables still set with meals and blankets soaked in oil, but not lit." Nevertheless, the 184th Regiment is the only National Guard regiment to reclaim American territory from an enemy in World War II.[2]

After four months of further training on Oahu, the 184th headed for the Marshall Islands, Japanese territory since World War I and a mystery to the outside world. On January 31, 1944, the 7th Division landed at Kwajalein, one of the world's largest coral atolls and the center of dozens of other islands. The next day, Private First Class Arthur Hackbarth and the 184th Infantry Regiment, along with the 32nd Regiment, attacked the heavily defended island. Five days later, when the battle for Kwajalein ended, the 7th Division counted 176 killed, but it cost the Japanese more than 8,000 soldiers. The 184th earned another trip to Hawaii for rest and more training.

For their third campaign, Private First Class Hackbarth and the 184th infantry landed near Dulag, Leyte Island, prepared to face the Japanese 34th Army. Stationed on Leyte for three years, the 34th was very much at home in the jungle, and the troops there included the 16th Division, which claimed the Bataan Death March and Rape of Nanking on its resume.

All of the U.S. divisions lost many men on the push through the swamps and rain forests of the Dulag Valley. At one point they relieved the exhausted and hard-hit 32nd Infantry Regiment along Shoestring Ridge, and were charged by 50 Japanese. Within ten minutes the attack was over, and the ridge was cleared.[2, 3, 4, 5]

The 7th Division regrouped at Bambay on the west coast of Leyte, and in early December the 184th and 17th began a move north to Ormoc City, the port to a key valley on the west side of the island. In preparation of the advancing regiments, American tanks positioned west of Balogo along the Leyte coast, blasting the hills. Both regiments encountered heavy enemy fire from Hill 918, a position overlooking the entire coast to Ormoc. By December 8, American forces had taken Hill 918, two other hills, plus surrounding ridges.[2, 3, 4, 5] As the 7th Division made contact with the 77th Division at Ormoc City on December 10, Arthur Hackbarth wrote his last letter home, penning it on the day he was wounded. He wrote of leaping into his foxhole every time the bullets started flying, and that excessive rain made foxhole fighting very uncomfortable.[1, 7] Arthur Hackbarth died five days later from wounds.

A year later, his parents wrote a memorial for their son: *In memory of Arthur Hackbarth who died one year ago, December 15, at Leyte in the service of his country. Our home tonight is lonely, the reason you can see. For our thoughts are slowly going far across the deep blue sea. On the tenth day of December, the lonely message read: "Your son is wounded seriously," Yes, that is what it said. Oh how we longed to be with him, to kiss his aching brow; to tell him how we loved him, too, more so than ever, now. On the 15 of December came more lines that didn't seem true: "Your soldier son will not come back, no, he'll never come home to you." So that's why our hearts are sad tonight, as our thoughts go over the sea. To a lone white cross and a soldier's grave, who died for you and me.*

—Sadly missed by parents, Mr. and Mrs. C.H. Hackbarth, Hazel and Irene

Private First Class Arthur Hackbarth is buried in Oakland Cemetery, Hutchinson, Minnesota. Arthur lived on the family farm three miles southwest of Cedar Mills until he entered the service.[1]

Larry Arthur McNew

11th Airborne "The Angels," Division, 511th Parachute Infantry, 1st Battalion, C Company, Private First Class

AUGUST 24, 1923–DECEMBER 16, 1944—Leyte Campaign, Philippines

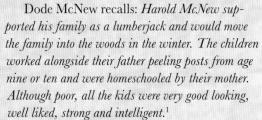

Dode McNew recalls: *Harold McNew supported his family as a lumberjack and would move the family into the woods in the winter. The children worked alongside their father peeling posts from age nine or ten and were homeschooled by their mother. Although poor, all the kids were very good looking, well liked, strong and intelligent.*[1]

When the 511th Parachute Infantry Regiment selected Private First Class Larry McNew for training, he joined an elite corps of men chosen by strict criteria for intelligence and toughness; eventually, only a third would make the cut. Private First Class McNew made it through basic training at Camp Mackall, North Carolina, and parachute jump training at Fort Benning, Georgia, where Kocher notes that with the selection process and intense training: *No 511th PIR soldier who boarded a C-47 refused to make the jump.* The men went back to Camp Mackall for advanced training, then on the Camp Polk, Louisiana, for more rigorous exercises.[2]

After over a year of intensive training, the 11th Airborne had their chance to prove their mettle. On May 8, 1944, Private First Class Larry McNew and the 511th boarded the SS *Sea Pike*, bound for yet more training in New Guinea, while on strategic reserve through October. Some paratroopers were to be sent in to the beaches or overland, so they learned how to handle amphibious landings and jungle warfare, as well as airborne maneuvers. They found time for fun, which included live bands, USO shows with entertainers like Jack Benny, and sports. Although the 511th football team claimed the top spot, author Edward Flanagan wrote that the troops especially loved boxing. *Madison Square Garden boxing spectators were less avid than we when witnessing one of the weekly cards.*[2, 3]

On October 24, 1944, Larry McNew, now a new father, wrote home: *Dear Mom, Been a little lax in answering letters so guess I'd better catch up a little. Don't get the idea that I am working too hard or that there's too much entertainment, the fact is I'm just lazy. Haven't heard from you since you returned from Cille's (his wife). Would like to get your opinion of the situation. Bet Dad was pretty glad to see you back. Does he still spend most of his time listening to news broadcasts? Bet he never worked a day during the playing of the World Series. The weather is still sticking close to the usual unpleasantries of the New Guinea* *climate. Rain and heat. It wouldn't be bad if it wasn't for the G.I. rules and regulations dress. But then the heat often overrules the fear of catching a tropical disease. Bonnie is over a month old now. Before I realize it I'll be home with her on my knee. Do you think I possess any fatherly qualities? Pretty near six months since I went under that San Francisco bridge, all I'm living for now is to make another trip under her in the opposite direction. My urge to travel has been fully satisfied, and I must soon begin concentrating on how to become a family man. Married at twenty, father at twenty-one, things happen fast these days, don't they? Write more often Mom. Lots of love, Larry.*[4]

Torrential rains welcomed the paratroopers of the 11th Airborne upon their arrival on Bito Beach, Leyte Island, on November 18, 1944, and continued almost every day during the Leyte Campaign. Just four days later, the 11th Airborne received Field Order No. 28, a directive that made the division famous: *The 11th Airborne Division will relieve the 7th Infantry Division along the line Burauen-La Paz-Bugho and destroy all Japs in that sector.* Here on Leyte Island, the 11th Airborne would not be used as paratroopers but as light infantry ordered to mop up after the six divisions that had gone ashore earlier.[3]

By December 5, Private First Class Larry McNew and the 1st Battalion of the 511th, plus Regimental Headquarters, were en route from Anonanag to Manonag on the Middle Trail to cut off a main Japanese supply road at the base of the Mahonag Mountains. Between December 10 and 20, the 511th cleared the entrenched Japanese on Rock Hill. (Flanagan). While securing Rock Hill, Private First Class Larry McNew was killed by shrapnel and buried on Rock Hill.[3] In 1949, his body was reinterred at Fort McKinley United States Military Cemetery, Manila, Philippine Islands, at the request of his father who wrote: *It was his wish to be interred where he was at the time of his death with the rest of his buddies, and that his identification bracelet and flag be sent to his mother, Mrs. Isabell McNew.*[5]

Survivors included his parents, Harold and Isabell, his wife, Lucille "Cille" (Carrigan) McNew, and a three-month-old daughter, Bonnie Louise.

The 511th Parachute Infantry Regiment lost 289 men killed or missing in action during the Leyte and Luzon Campaigns. Technical 4 Rod Serling, Radioman for Regimental Headquarters and later famous for his work in radio and writing the television series, *The Twilight Zone*, served with Private First Class McNew during the campaign.[6]

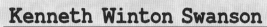

Kenneth Winton Swanson

Comstock (Clay County)

U.S. Army Air Forces, 20th Air Force, 73rd Bomb Wing, 499th Bomb Group, 878th Very Heavy Bomb Squadron, Sergeant

JUNE 24, 1923–DECEMBER 18, 1944—Attack on Mitsubishi Aircraft Factory, Nagoya, Japan

Following his graduation from Comstock High School, Kenneth Swanson enlisted in the Army Air Corps at Fort Lewis near Tacoma, Washington. After basic training, he completed B-29 aircraft combat crew training at Smoky Hill Army Airfield near Salina, Kansas. In October 1944, he deployed from Mather Field, California, to Isley Field on Saipan in the Mariana Islands. Assigned to the 20th Air Force, 73rd Bomb Wing, 499th Bombardment Group, 878th Bomb Squadron, Ken belonged to one of three squadrons, with 20 crews in each squadron.[1,2]

By the time the Allies claimed victory on Saipan on July 9, 1944, many men had given their lives to secure the island for an air base within bombing distance of Japan. When Sergeant Kenneth Swanson and the 499th Bomb Group arrived, construction crews were rapidly constructing Isley Airfield in honor of Commander Robert H. Isley, the first American pilot to die in the Battle of Saipan. The 73rd Bomb Wing had recently trained on the new Boeing B-29 Superfortress, an improvement over the B-17 except for the engine failures that could occur on long flights. In an effort to improve efficiency, General Curtis LeMay, nicknamed "Bombs Away," ordered all guns and ammunition removed from B-29s and missions flown at lower altitudes. Crews flying at 28,000 to 34,000 feet faced high winds, low bombing accuracy and overheated engines when climbing to higher altitudes. Dropping the altitude to 8,000 to 12,000 corrected many of the problems.[3,4]

On November 24, 1944, the 499th flew its first combat mission over Tokyo. The mission was unsuccessful due to high winds, but no crews or planes were lost. A second mission to Tokyo three days later, hampered by heavy cloud cover, caused the bombers to miss the primary target, but they did hit other targets. Upon returning to Saipan, the crews returned to a damaged air base, which had been attacked by 17 enemy Zeke fighters, destroying one B-29, and damaging the facilities. The 499th lost their first aircraft in combat on December 13 during an attack on the Mitsubishi Heavy Industries Company and Aircraft Engine Plants near Nagoya, Japan. Enemy flak downed a B-29, which crashed into Magicienne Bay near Saipan, killing all aboard.[3,4,5,6]

Bad luck hit the 878th Squadron again on December 18 when Lieutenant Leo Conway and Crew One, including radio operator Sergeant Kenneth Swanson, left on a bombing mission to Nagoya, Japan. That day 63 out of 89 B-29s of the 73rd Bomb Wing flew from Saipan to bomb the Mitsubishi aircraft factory near Nagoya. Caleb Dana in the 73rd Wing, whose diary was discovered in a used bookstore in New Orleans, wrote about that day: *On the 18 December our alternate crew, our closest buddies, took our ship back to Nagoya. They did not return to base. The last time they were seen, which was with the 498th Group, they were under heavy fighter attack and slightly behind the formation. Leo dropped the bombs, peeled off and dove down into the clouds, where they shot down a fighter. At the time they disappeared, all engines were running, although some of the gunners reported that they were smoking.*[7]

Two witnesses who last saw the plane, Technical Sergeant Russell Sandquist and Sergeant Norman Roberts, stated in the Missing Crew Report: *The plane was first observed about 30 minutes south of the coast and never got into a tight formation with the lead squadron of the second element. Sergeant Sandquist observed the plane under attack by enemy aircraft and saw it go into a very steep wing over to the left with the forward bomb bay closed and on fire, which he believed to be coming from the forward bomb bay. At the time he last saw it, the plane was not under attack and, because of the steepness of the dive, he felt the fire was not coming from the turret. Sergeant Roberts saw smoke trailing from the plane, which could have come from fire in the bomb bay or smoke from the #2 engine. Two enemy fighters were observed by Roberts following the plane as it disappeared through the cloud cover, which was estimated at 20,000 feet.* The plane and crew were never recovered and declared killed in action after the war ended.[8]

Sergeant Kenneth Swanson, son of Sander and Othelia (Jorgenson) Swanson, is memorialized on the Courts of the Missing, Honolulu Memorial, Honolulu, Hawaii. Survivors included his father, his wife, Doris (Mosciell), and three siblings, one of whom, Lloyd G. Swanson, served in the army in the Pacific.[1,2]

Helmer Mathias Eichten

Wanda (Redwood County)

Seventh Army, 103rd Infantry "Cactus" Division, 411th Infantry Regiment Service Company, Private

JUNE 24, 1910–DECEMBER 24, 1944—Battle for Climbach, France

Doug Eichten remembers: *My uncle Helmer was known as "Turk." I was told that he drove troop trucks in the army in France. His unit came under fire, and like a good Eichten, he went back to drive the truck to a safer area and was killed. A non-family member also told me that he was the most handsome of the Eichten boys.*[1]

On October 20, 1944, just a few months after the Allied invasion of Normandy on D-Day, Private Helmer "Turk" Eichten and the 103rd Cactus Division landed at Marseilles, France. They entered combat on November 16 and began their advance through the Vosges Mountains into Germany. A member of the 411th Infantry Regiment Service Company, Private Eichten provided transportation services and maintained all equipment, ammunition and weapons.

Within 11 days the "Cactus" Division battled through the Saverne Gap, fought across the Vosges Mountains and moved into Alsace Plain.[2] Turk wrote on December 2: *I guess we got the Germans on the run and it shouldn't take too long before it's over with, I hope. Yesterday was the first day we had sunshine since we've been here. I was beginning to wonder if they had sun here in France. Most of the people in France talk just as much German as they do French, so I can understand them when they talk German and we get a lot of wine and cognac from them, ha. Merry Xmas to you all, cause it will probably be about Xmas time when you get this. I've got an idea what I'll be doing on Xmas Day.*[3]

By December 4, the division captured the cities of St. Die, Diefenbach and Selestat against heavy German fire. As the 411th drove deeper into France near the German border, the German army fought harder to stop the Allies from entering their homeland. On December 13, the 411th attacked the city of Climbach, located near the Maginot Line in northern Alsace. Although the Germans fought furiously, the 411th broke through the line to capture the town on December 14 and forced them to retreat behind the Siegfried Line.[2, 6, 7, 8]

Private Helmer Eichten never made it into Germany. On December 14, he was wounded by shrapnel and died from peritonitis on Christmas Eve at the 59th Evacuation Hospital in Mutzig, France. His Bronze Medal citation states the circumstances: *For heroism in action. On 14 December 1944, Private Eichten, driver of a two and a half ton truck, was transporting foot troops of a task force en route to France. Several times heavy enemy artillery and mortar barrages made it necessary for the men to detruck and seek cover. During a particularly heavy barrage, Private Eichten, at the order of his truck officer, supervised the detrucking of the foot troops, and then found cover. Realizing that the intense army shelling would probably result in the destruction of his vehicle, Private Eichten, with utter disregard for his life, was determined to move the truck to a position of safety. Leaving his sheltered position, he valorously succeeded in driving the truck to a less exposed area when a burst of enemy fire mortally wounded him. Private Eichten's display of outstanding courage was in accordance with the highest traditions of the military service.*[4, 5, 9] By the time the 103rd Infantry Division captured the city of Innsbruck in Austria on May 3, 1945, total battle casualties numbered 4,558 and total deaths in battle were 834.

Private Helmer "Turk" Eichten, son of William and Margaretha (Backes) Eichten, was buried in Lorraine American Cemetery, Saint-Avold, France. Survivors included his mother and eleven brothers and sisters.[10]

Marlys Shelby wrote about her uncle: *After graduation, Turk had a number of occupations including working for the Fairmont Novelty Company. He was a self-taught piano player and also played the drums. For a while, he had his own band that played at various dances in the area. The band was viewed as a chance to met girls. His brother Ole played trumpet in the band and the story goes that throughout the evening, various band members would go down into the crowd to dance with the girls and grab a little moonshine (this was during prohibition years). Unfortunately, they often never returned to the stage. So, on one occasion, Ole claimed that the only person left on the state was Turk, playing the drums.*[3]

The legacy of the 103rd also lives on in the memory of survivors of the Holocaust; the United States Holocaust Memorial Museum recognizes the 103rd as an official liberating unit for liberating Dachau's Kaufering subcamp at Landsberg, Germany, on April 17, 1945.[6, 8]

Almon

Warren

Harold

Lloyd

Almon Lee Armbrust

Federal Dam (Cass County)

U.S. Naval Reserve, USS Spence *(DD-512), Seaman Second Class*

FEBRUARY 4, 1926–DECEMBER 18, 1944—Typhoon Cobra

Warren Irvin Hakenson

Norcross (Grant County)

U.S. Naval Reserve, USS Spence *(DD-512), Fireman First Class*

OCTOBER 23, 1923–DECEMBER 18, 1944—Typhoon Cobra

Harold Donald Kaufman

Nassau (Lac Qui Parle County)

U.S. Naval Reserve, USS Spence *(DD-512), Seaman Second Class*

FEBRUARY 10, 1926–DECEMBER 18, 1944—Typhoon Cobra

Lloyd Otto Lundgren

Norcross (Grant County)

U.S. Naval Reserve, USS Spence *(DD-512), Seaman First Class*

AUGUST 20, 1922–DECEMBER 18, 1944—Typhoon Cobra

On December 18, 1944, Seaman First Class Lloyd Lundgren, Fireman First Class Warren Hakenson, Seaman Second Class Harold Kaufman, and Seaman Second Class Almon Armbrust, washed overboard when their ship, the destroyer USS *Spence*, capsized during powerful Typhoon Cobra. The USS *Spence*, part of Task Force 38, Third Fleet, operated 300 miles east of Luzon in the Philippine Sea and conducted air raids against Japanese airfields in the Philippines. Despite deteriorating weather conditions on December 17, the ships of the fleet remained in their stations until Admiral Halsey sailed the Third Fleet into the typhoon. The USS *Spence*, low on fuel, was unstable in the huge waves. High seas, torrential rain and 100-mile-per-hour winds sank 3 destroyers: the USS *Hull*, USS *Monaghan* and USS *Spence*, all part of the Little Beaver Squadron. A total of 790 lives were lost, and only 24 out of 336 men survived on the USS *Spence*. The survivors spent 39 hours hanging on life rafts, and fighting off sharks and barracuda, before the USS *Tabberer*, despite orders from Admiral Halsey to return all ships to port in Ulithi, rescued 55 survivors in a 51-hour search. She picked up 41 men from *Hull* and 14 from *Spence* before the destroyer *Brown* arrived to rescue 7 survivors from *Monaghan* and 13 sailors from

Hull. Over the next 3 days, other ships from the Third Fleet rescued 18 more survivors from *Hull* and *Spence.*[1, 3]

Lieutenant Gerald Ford, future President of the United States, recalled nearly going overboard on the carrier USS *Monterey* that night. The rolling seas caused aircraft below decks to careen into each other, igniting the *Monterey* on fire. He and a fire team fought fires all night, saving the ship from destruction.[1, 3]

On March 8, 1945, the *Grant County Herald* printed a letter addressed to Mrs. Ada Hakenson of Norcross from a shipmate of her son: *My dear Mrs. Hakenson, It is with deepest sorrow that I, as senior survivor of the USS Spence, write to you concerning the loss of your son, Warren I. Hakenson, who following the capsizing and sinking of that vessel on 18 Dec. 1944, was listed as missing at sea.*

The circumstances surrounding the disaster in which his life was lost are as follows. The Spence was carrying out a mission of war with other vessels, which included the ill fated Hull and Monaghan. There was little warning of the vicious typhoon, which struck us with great violence. The seas were mountainous and the wind was estimated to be about 110 knots. There was no indication of the ship capsizing until it was caught in the trough of the huge swells. The tremendous waves were beating us unmercifully with water washing over the entire main deck. The men had been advised to seek shelter several hours before the disaster to prevent their being washed overboard. The ship, unable to combat the sea any longer, rolled over on her side and continued until she was turned completely over, thereby trapping all the men below the main deck and those who were in such enclosures as the engine room, fire room, radio room, etc. Only those who were topside were able to jump into the water. The violent seas pounded us terrifically. We were at the mercy of the seas for two to three days before being picked up.

At the time of capsizing, Warren was not able to get off his ship into the water. He was not seen by any of the survivors at any time after the ship rolled over. Extensive and careful searches were made the following by surface vessels and aircraft for survivors. Since there was no land for several hundred miles, it was quite impossible that anyone could have survived if he were not picked up.

The USS Spence had been a member of the "Little Beaver Squadron," which after many hectic encounters with the enemy during the early stages of the South Pacific operations, molded strong ties of friendship and understanding. During the past few months, the kinship of the men and officers of the USS Spence and its sister ship, the USS Dyson, became more binding during an operation which separated us from the rest of the "Little Beavers." At 9:30 a.m. 22 December 1944, services were held aboard the USS Dyson in honor of the men and officers
of the USS Spence, who lost their lives in honor of their country. All men and officers of the Dyson attended these services and wish to extend their sympathies and share your great sorrow.

The knowledge that your son lost his life in the service of his country fighting a war against brutal and unprincipled enemies must be of some consolation to you in your great loss. Please accept my sincerest sympathy in your great sorrow. Very sincerely, A.S. Krauchunas, Lieutenant (jg), S.C.U.S.N.R., Senior Survivor.[3]

Best friends Warren Hakenson and Lloyd Lundgren from Norcross enlisted in the navy together in November 1942. At their request, they were assigned to duty together aboard USS *Spence* and remained constant companions for two years.[5] Warren Hakenson, son of Louis and Ada (Schoonover) Hakenson, was survived by his mother, and siblings: Private First Class Lloyd Hakenson, Lester, Melvin, Cheslie, Luella, Milo and Grace.

The son of Carl Otto and Anna (Johnson) Lundgren, Lloyd was survived by his father and siblings Arvid, Mae, Carl, Roy and Edith (Carl) Williams.[3]

Almon Armbrust, son of Edwin Armbrust and Hazel (Clark) Croskrey, enlisted April 18, 1944. Survivors included his parents and a brother, Lloyd Wayne.[4]

Harold Kaufman enlisted in the navy January 29, 1944. Irvin Kaufman, now 93 years old, remembers his brother: *Harold was a lot of fun. He loved to hunt gophers and fish, and he used a kerosene lantern to check his ten-mile trap line. We were both stationed in Hawaii and I asked my sergeant for permission to spend time with my brother. Harold and I had three weeks together. We played a lot of cards. I am so glad that I had those three weeks with him.* Survivors included his parents, Charles and Theresa (Christianson) Kaufman, and nine siblings.[8, 9, 10, 11, 12]

All men are memorialized at Manila American Cemetery and Memorial, Manila, Philippines.

In *The Caine Mutiny*, author Herman Wouk explores the moral and ethical decisions made at sea by the captains of ships. The novel developed from Wouk's personal experience and survival aboard a destroyer-minesweeper during Typhoon Cobra.[13]

Victor Adin Malmrose

Delhi (Redwood County)

Seventh Army, 12th Armored "Hellcats" Division, 495th Armored Field Artillery Battalion, Battery B, 1st Lieutenant

JUNE 15, 1915–DECEMBER 26, 1944—Battle of the Bulge, France

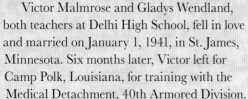

Victor Malmrose and Gladys Wendland, both teachers at Delhi High School, fell in love and married on January 1, 1941, in St. James, Minnesota. Six months later, Victor left for Camp Polk, Louisiana, for training with the Medical Detachment, 40th Armored Division. Victor spent the summer of 1942 in Fort Sill, Oklahoma, for field artillery officer training before moving to Camp Campbell, Kentucky, followed by Abilene, Texas. When Victor went overseas, Gladys returned to Bellingham, Minnesota, to live with her brother, Leonard Wendland.[1, 2, 5]

On October 2, 1944, the 12th Armored Division, including 1st Lieutenant Victor Malmrose, a forward observer with the 495th Armored Field Artillery, landed at Liverpool, England. Pitching and rolling across the English Channel on flat-bottomed Tank Landing Ships, the division arrived on November 11 at Le Havre, France. On December 6, 1st Lieutenant Malmrose and Baker Battery fired their first round in combat near Sarreinsburg, where they also had a few close calls with Bouncing Betty mines. They advanced against the Maginot Line through mud, snow and cold, all within a week. The 12th then assisted in liberating the cities of Rohrbach and Bettviller, France. Utweiler, Germany, followed on December 21st. While stationed near Bining, the unit's doctor delivered a baby girl for a local civilian who named the baby Marie and paid the doctor with three shots of schnapps.[4]

In the regimental history of the 495th Armored Field Artillery Battalion, 1st Lieutenant Clinton Seitz wrote about the death of 1st Lieutenant Victor Malmrose following the liberation of Utweiler: *Lieutenant Croker radioed that he and Lieutenant Branson were now in the 17th in the town of Utweiler. Krauts were still dug in several yards outside, deployed along tree line on a slope. Thus the town was pretty hot from small arms and mortar fire. Lieutenant Seitz at night had set up an OP with the 92nd Calvary on a high hill southwest of Utweiler. On the high ridge just south of town was Lieutenant O'Brien's observation post from which could be seen both Kraut infantry and a self-propelled 75 or 88 in an orchard on the creek bank. The day before Christmas, Lieutenant Malmrose was sent up as relief for Lieutenant Branson. On Christmas Day while attempting to locate the most advantageous spot from which to fire upon Krauts, Lieutenant* *Malmrose and his sergeant were seriously wounded when a Kraut patrol caught them with machine pistol fire. During the night 25-26 December 1944 at a Field Hospital in Diemeringen, Lieutenant Malmrose succumbed to his mortal wounds after a valiant struggle.*

After Christmas, on December 28, the unit marched to Farebersviller where "in a bleak woods behind Baker Battery, where Vic was so much at home, Chaplain Dillon held memorial services for Lieutenant Victor L. Malmrose."[4] Lieutenant Malmrose received the Bronze Star Medal for Heroic Achievement and the Purple Heart. Survivors included his parents, his wife, Gladys (Wendland) Malmrose; his daughter Sandra Kay; and a brother, Pharmacist's Mate First Class John (Lillian) Malmrose, who served in the U.S. Navy.

Victor Malmrose is buried in Fort Snelling Cemetery, Minneapolis, Minnesota. Gladys married Albert Ramm in 1951, and they had two sons, Charles and William.

Norbert W. Bruns

St. Rosa (Stearns County)

80th Infantry "Blue Ridge" Division, 317th Infantry Regiment, 3rd Battalion, K Company, Corporal

APRIL 16, 1923–DECEMBER 26, 1944—Battle of the Bulge, Luxembourg

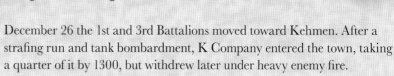

On October 24, 1944, Private Albert Bruns died in the Italian Campaign, and less than two months later, his brother, Corporal Norbert Bruns faced the Battle of the Bulge, the last major German offensive on the Western front in Europe.[1] On December 16, 1944, at 0530, guns blazed from German positions, "screaming mimis" shrieked overhead, artillery pounded Allied positions, and the creak of moving tanks was heard all across a 60-mile front in southern Belgium and northern Luxembourg. The Battle of the Bulge had begun. Atkinson vividly describes Hitler's massive counterattack to turn the tide of the war, capture Antwerp, Belgium, and force a stalemate. Hitting American and British troops with a surprise attack in terrible weather, Panzers and infantry smashed battalions and sent them reeling in retreat. Germany's strongest forces, like Colonel Peiper's brutal 1st SS Panzer Division, rolled north in a wave of destruction. At Malmedy, Peiper's troops machine-gunned 84 U.S. prisoners of war. German General Rundstedt "had told his legions in an order captured early in the battle: *Es geht um das Ganze.* Everything is at stake."[2, 3, 4, 5]

Following a contentious series of meetings with his generals, Eisenhower agreed with General Patton's plan to rush his divisions in from the south by December 22 to defend Luxembourg and begin attacking the salient from the southern side. Patton's order to "hold to the last man," committed Corporal Norbert Bruns and the 80th Division to head for Luxembourg City, with its valuable Radio Luxembourg, and secure it at all costs.[2, 3, 4, 5]

Adkins described the 80th Infantry Division's 150-mile journey to Junglinster, just north of Luxembourg City. As the 305th Engineers led the way sweeping mines, a stream of vehicles carried Corporal Bruns and three regiments, who huddled together for warmth through the cold, clear night. The men reported: *There were no rest stops and no delays of any kind. When we had to relieve ourselves, we did so off the back end of the truck while hanging on for dear life.*[2, 3, 4]

The 317th After Action Report describes the terrain of Luxembourg: *It features a great number of steep ravines, with successive high ground, making the maneuvering of tanks in the support of Infantry Operations practically impossible.* From Junglinster the 317th and 318th attacked a series of towns. On

December 26 the 1st and 3rd Battalions moved toward Kehmen. After a strafing run and tank bombardment, K Company entered the town, taking a quarter of it by 1300, but withdrew later under heavy enemy fire.

The Morning Report for K Company, 317th Infantry Regiment, for December 26, 1944 states: *Attacked town of Kehmen, Luxembourg, at 0915. Two tanks gave support part of the way. Heavy resistance with artillery and small arms fire. Entered town, behind first three buildings. Pinned down by small arms fire. We suffered heavy casualties. Withdrew to crest of hill. 2 officers wounded, 1 missing, 4 men killed, 32 men missing, 10 wounded. All casualties occurred in Luxembourg. Weather cold. Morale fair.* On December 29, the morning report listed Corporal Bruns as missing in action, but the report on January 26, 1945, changed his status to killed in action on December 26, 1944.[2, 3, 4, 6, 7]

President Franklin Roosevelt awarded the Silver Star posthumously to Corporal Bruns: *...for gallantry in action while serving with the 317 Infantry Regiment, 80 Infantry Division with connection with military operations against an enemy of the United States on 25 and 26 December 1944 in Luxembourg. On 25 December 1944, in the attack on Kehmen, Luxembourg, Corporal Bruns, by skillfully using rifle grenades, neutralized enemy strong points and personally captured an enemy machine gunner who had been delaying the attack. On the following day Corporal Bruns with rifle grenades destroyed two enemy machine gun positions and alone assaulted and destroyed another gun and crew. His bravery, aggressiveness, and sincere devotion to duty were in keeping with the highest traditions of the military service and reflect great credit upon himself, his unit and the United States Army.*[8]

Corporal Norbert Bruns is buried in the Luxembourg American Cemetery. Survivors included his parents, and siblings: Eveline and Marian. Private LeRoy Veralrud (page 74), from Elcor, Minnesota, served in K Company with Corporal Bruns, and died September 22, 1944, in France.[1]

Vincent Joseph Dolan

Danvers (Swift County)

Third Army, 35th Infantry "Santa Fe" Division, 134th Infantry Regiment, 2nd Battalion, F Company, Private

MARCH 21, 1915–JANUARY 1, 1945—Battle of the Bulge, Belgium

Private Vincent Dolan, a rifleman for the 34th Infantry Regiment, 35th Infantry Division, landed on Omaha Beach, Normandy, July 5 to 7, 1944 and fought his way through the hedgerows north of St.-Lô, the gateway to central France.

On July 18, the Division secured St.-Lô, and pushed the Germans across the Vire River on August 2. After breaking out of the Cotentin Peninsula, the 35th helped secure the Mortain-Avranches corridor and rescued the 30th Division's "Lost Battalion," August 7 to 13, 1944.

As the division continued their advance across France to the German border, the 35th captured the city of Nancy in northwest France. *The Oregonian* on October 19, 1944, and *Time* on October 30, published a heart-warming story of the 134th Infantry Regiment's compassion and courage, titled the "Baby Patrol." During the summer of 1944, 81 children, between ages 2 and 6, had been evacuated from Nancy to a chateau in Han, to escape bombing as the Allies drove through France. Han was now in German hands, and the Allies were about to attack. They knew not to shell the chateau housing the children, but feared that counterattacks might endanger the children. On the cold night of September 29, 1944, 11 volunteers from A Company crept across an exposed marsh and into the chateau in Han. Holding a baby under each arm and gathering the children who could walk, the soldiers carried and guided the frightened, half-clothed children across 1,000 yards of marsh. Germans heard them moving and opened up on the marsh with artillery and mortar fire. The baby patrol kept going, passed the children across a creek and finally reached trucks to bring them all safely back to their parents in Nancy.[1, 2]

After the division crossed the Saar and Blies Rivers, the 35th moved to Belgium on Christmas Day to fight the Battle of the Bulge, where Private Dolan in F Company fought on the front line. The Report of Action on New Year's Day states: *The first day of 1945 found the 35th Infantry Division pressing its drive into the German salient in the III Corps Zone southeast of Bastogne. In front of the division's riflemen, the opposition continued to be as fierce as it had been the last week of December. The enemy obviously was making an all-out attempt to hold its gains. In addition to the stiff resistance displayed by the enemy,* *front line men also had the elements to combat. Heavy snow and bitter cold took its toll of men through exposure and frostbite. The attacks still continued despite the weather and stonewall type of opposition. During the morning, the 134th had its battalions dig in to prepare positions for defense in case of a counterattack. In the afternoon it attacked at 1330. The 1st Battalion drove to positions beyond the crossroads about a kilometer south of Marvie and the 2nd and 3rd Battalions advanced toward Lutrebois, seizing part of the town by dark.*[3]

On March 27, 1945, Vera Dolan received a reply from Captain Raymond Anderson, 134th Infantry Regiment: *Dear Mrs. Dolan, Your letter addressed to the chaplain has been forwarded to this office for reply. We shall attempt to answer your questions concerning Private Vincent J. Dolan, insofar as possible. Vincent was a Rifleman in company F, and as you know, he was reported killed in action on 1 January, 1945. At the time your husband was killed, he was assisting his company in an attack on German positions in the vicinity of Bastogne, Belgium. This action occurred as General Patton's Third Army struck against the "bulge." This part of Belgium is a hilly, wooded area, and a heavy snowfall had made fighting unusually difficult. Your husband was struck by fragments from enemy mortar fire and death was immediate. He was buried in the United States Military Cemetery #1, in Grand Failly, France, and a Catholic chaplain officiated at the burial. It is hoped that the above information will be of comfort to you in this time of sorrow. May I also take this opportunity to express the sympathy of the commanding officer.*[4]

Prior to his enlistment on November 25, 1942, Vince Dolan worked for contractors in Dutch Harbor, Alaska. He married Vera Hinson of Mount Pleasant, Texas, while stationed at Fort Sam Houston, Texas. Vincent's sister, Rose, was married to 2nd Lieutenant Paul G. Bliven (page 63), who was killed in action in Normandy on July 15, 1944. The families requested that Vincent and Paul be returned from France together, and they are buried side by side in Church of the Visitation Cemetery in Danvers, Minnesota.[6, 7]

Bertil Quinton Gustafson

Viking (Marshall County)

17th Airborne, 82nd Airborne "All American" Division, 517th Parachute Infantry, 2nd Battalion, E Company, Private

JANUARY 28, 1922–JANUARY 3, 1945—Battle of the Bulge, Belgium

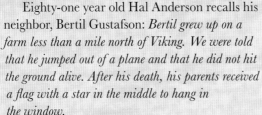

Eighty-one year old Hal Anderson recalls his neighbor, Bertil Gustafson: *Bertil grew up on a farm less than a mile north of Viking. We were told that he jumped out of a plane and that he did not hit the ground alive. After his death, his parents received a flag with a star in the middle to hang in the window.*

Following graduation from Newfolden High School in 1941 and two years at Concordia College in Moorhead, Minnesota, Bertil Gustafson entered the army on June 15, 1943 at Camp Roberts, California. Three months later he transferred to parachute school in Fort Benning, Georgia, where after jump training, all units, including the 517th, joined the 17th Airborne at Camp Mackall, Fort Bragg, North Carolina.[2] Weber wrote that while many men washed out of parachute training, no one from the 517th failed to meet the high standards for expert marksmanship and superb physical training. One day an inspection team from Headquarters Army Ground Forces arrived at Camp Mackall to test the unit's physical fitness. Individuals took the physical fitness test, which consisted of pull-ups, push-ups, timed calisthenics and running various distances. When the results were tabulated, the 517th took first, second and third in all tests, scoring higher than any unit tested.[3]

On May 17, 1944, Private Bertil Gustafson and the 517th Parachute Infantry boarded the *Santa Rosa* for Naples, Italy, to support the invasion of southern France. Named the "Battling Buzzards," the 517th experienced heavy fighting in Italy in June before transferring to southern France in August for Operation Dragoon where they completed their first combat jump. Following the liberation of France, the 517th was attached to the 82nd Airborne Division during the Battle of the Bulge.[3, 4, 5, 6]

Christmas 1944 found the 82nd Airborne stationed in Soissons, France, and about to endure one of the most horrific battles in World War II. Shortly after December 16, the day the German army decided to launch their final offensive in the Belgian Ardennes, Colonel R.D. Graves, combat team commander 517th Parachute Infantry, sent this letter to his regiment: *On the occasion of our first Christmas overseas, I would like to take this opportunity to extend my heartiest congratulations and greetings to all members of this*

command. Although we naturally miss being at home, we do not feel sorry for ourselves but take comfort in living under the best condition possible and also take comfort in being with the comrades with whom we have served and whom we trust. At this Christmas time I wish you all a Merry Christmas. May the New Year strengthen the ties of friendship and loyalty and keep us steadfast in our determination to serve our country well and honorably during the coming year.[7]

On January 1, 1945, the 517th Parachute Infantry Regiment posted the 2nd and 3rd battalions in an area north of Trois-Ponts (the northern shoulder of "the Bulge"), Belgium, with orders to secure the Salm River Line from Trois-Ponts to Grand-Halleux, a distance of three miles. Observation on high ground was impossible due to freezing weather, a thick snow 12 inches deep, and limited visibility of 100 to 200 yards in the low areas. On January 3, Private Bertil Gustafson and the 2nd Battalion were ordered to attack and seize Trois-Ponts and Mont-de-Fosse. The lead companies, D Company and E Company, suffered severe casualties, including Private Gustafson. Twenty soldiers died and 90 were wounded.[6, 9]

Private Bertil Gustafson was buried at Henri-Chapelle American Cemetery in Belgium, and on February 10, 1945, a memorial service for Private Bertil Q. Gustafson was held in Zion Lutheran Church in Viking.

Private Gustafson was reinterred in Fort Snelling National Cemetery.[2]

Truman Arnold Meling

Ihlen (Pipestone County)

101st Airborne "Screaming Eagles" Division, 401st Glider Infantry, 327th Glider Regiment,
1st Battalion, B Company, Private First Class
JANUARY 5, 1912–JANUARY 1, 1945—Battle of the Bulge, Belgium

Don Meling recalls the day that he learned of the death of his brother Truman: *On January 1, 1945, our brother, Truman Arnold, was killed in the Battle of the Bulge in Belgium. I was teaching in Lake County in South Dakota, when Dad and Don brought this message to the rural school. This began to reconcile the loss of Mother. This was something that she didn't have to bear. There was a memorial service in the Ihlen church. After the War, Dad had Truman's body repatriated. There was a funeral service and he rests in the Ihlen Cemetery. In my mind, he remains forever young.*[1]

On August 15, 1942, the army renamed the 327th Infantry Regiment as a Glider Infantry Regiment and assigned it to the 101st Airborne Division. The 327th Unit History states that some of the new arrivals had never flown in an airplane and went AWOL rather than get into the fragile-looking glider.

Private First Class Meling trained in the Waco CG-4A at Fort Bragg, North Carolina, along with other airborne units. Their first encounters with paratroopers from the 502nd Parachute Infantry Regiment didn't go well. The paratroopers didn't believe the glidermen had the "right stuff," and this sparked numerous fights. However, glider landings proved to be more dangerous than chutes, frequently leading crashes into trees or nosedives after touchdown.[2]

The 327th met their first action on D-Day, June 6, 1944, in Normandy. But instead of piloting gliders, the men landed on Utah Beach by amphibious landing craft due to a shortage of tow planes from other airborne drops that day. They moved on to take their objective, Carentan. In September, the 327th, along with other airborne units, led Operation Market Garden, the failed attempt to get troops across the Rhine and drive into the German heartland. The landings were successful, but the 327th remained embroiled with other Allied forces in the 73 days of continuous combat followed by another 48 days on the front lines. The 101st Airborne experienced 3,700 casualties during the operation. They withdrew by truck and then went back to France for rest.

On December 16, 1944, the Germans launched the Battle of the Bulge in the Ardennes Forest, with the 101st ordered to defend Bastogne, Belgium, at all costs. Following a 100-mile truck march, the 327th set up their position south of Bastogne on December 19. Three days later, the Germans completely surrounded Bastogne and the German commander offered terms of surrender to General McAuliffe, who replied, "Nuts!" The Germans said they did not understand. Colonel Harper explained to them, "The reply is decidedly not affirmative; in plain English, it is the same as 'Go to Hell.'"[2, 3]

On December 23, American C-47s dropped 334 tons of critically needed supplies to the 101st Airborne Division, and the following day, American Thunderbolts strafed German tanks and artillery. By this time, the 327th Glider Infantry Regiment with the 1st Battalion of the 401st Glider Infantry attached, moved to defend the west edge of Bastogne. The 401st Operations Report stated that on Christmas Day at 0710, German tanks and infantry, some men wearing American uniforms, attacked and: *by 0720 hours the enemy had rolled over A and B companies only to be repulsed by point blank artillery fire. … Savage fighting raged between the opposing forces the entire morning, but by midday the German attackers had been rejected and A and B companies of the 1st Battalion were disposed in their original early morning positions.*[4]

The 327th Regiment held for 9 days, took 750 prisoners, knocked out 144 Nazi tanks and 105 other enemy vehicles. The 327th's casualties were heavy, including Private First Class Truman Meling who was wounded on December 31. He died the following day in a hospital in Bastogne, Belgium, just four days before his thirtieth birthday.[2]

Truman Meling, son of Jacob and Clela (Naig) Meling, is buried in Ihlen Cemetery, Ihlen, Minnesota. Survivors included his father and five siblings. Truman enlisted in the service on June 9, 1942.

Andrew Richard Brummer

Hillman (Morrison County)

Third Army, 35th Infantry "Santa Fe" Division, 134th Infantry Regiment, 1st Battalion, B Company, Private
JANUARY 29, 1918–JANUARY 7, 1945—Battle of the Bulge, Belgium

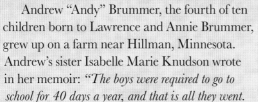

Andrew "Andy" Brummer, the fourth of ten children born to Lawrence and Annie Brummer, grew up on a farm near Hillman, Minnesota. Andrew's sister Isabelle Marie Knudson wrote in her memoir: *"The boys were required to go to school for 40 days a year, and that is all they went. Then they would leave school to hunt, trap or help out on the farm. My brothers always carried a 22 rifle with them. When they got to school, they just pulled the bolt out and gave it to the teacher. Before and after school they would hunt or check their traps. Herb and Andy were very close brothers. Herb was big and Andy was smaller, maybe 5'11", and finer boned. When they were hired out to work they always paid Herb and said, "Give the little one something if you want."*[1]

Following the draft in 1941, Andrew was sent to Trenton, New Jersey, for anti-aircraft training. Isabelle recalls that after serving in Europe, the army transferred her brother from artillery to the infantry, but without any infantry training. Andrew was now a soldier in the 35th Infantry Division, 134th Infantry Regiment, and lost his life fighting in the Battle of the Bulge. After days of fighting around the town of Lutrebois, Belgium, the division held positions along the Lutrebois-Lutremange road, four to five miles southeast of Bastogne. While on combat patrol, Private Brummer crossed a clearing into the woods, where enemy soldiers ambushed the patrol and killed Private Brummer. He was declared missing in action until July 8, 1945, when Mr. Gabriel, a citizen of Lutrebois, discovered his body.[2]

The After Action Report for January 7, 1945, states: *After an unsuccessful attempt to capture positions astride the Lutrebois-Lutremange road, the 2nd Battalion of the 134th Infantry held along a line short of the road. The 1st Battalion of the 320th Infantry, still trying to come abreast of the 1st Battalion of the 134th infantry, attacked during the afternoon but made no progress. The remainder of the day the Regiment continued to maintain pressure against the enemy.*[2]

Andrew's sister remembers the day the family found out about his death: *Ma and Pa were notified of Andy's death by Erwin and Mae Probasco, who ran the telephone office in Hillman. They tried to call us but the telephone lines were down. They had received a telegram and they brought the telegram to Ma and Pa. The telegram told us that Andy was missing in action, and having someone missing in action was bad. We all knew about the Belgian Bulge battle and knew that there had been*

so many casualties. Ma and Pa had all the hope in the world that Andy would come back alive, but Pa never said much. They then got a letter stating,that Andy had been killed by a small bullet. Sometimes death gives you a certain peace of mind. They knew he wasn't a prisoner of war and that he could not be hurt any more, tortured or left hungry. Ma and Pa never brought his body home because they said they would always wonder if they had the correct body.*[1] Ten months earlier, on February 29, 1944, Erwin Probasco, the telephone operator in Hillman, had received a telegram informing him that his brother, Technical 5 Alvin Probasco, had died in Italy on February 29, 1944.

Private Andrew Brummer is buried in the Henri-Chapelle American Cemetery in Belgium. Survivors included his parents and seven siblings. After visiting his grave in Belgium, Isabella commented: "I think Pa and Ma did the right thing when they allowed him to be buried over there, it seems right that he was buried where he died for his country."[1]

On September 14, 2002, four veterans from the 35th Infantry Division traveled to Lutremange, Belgium, to participate in the dedication of a monument in memory of the men who fought there. The mayor gave a very moving speech stating that the people of Belgium and particularly of that area would be forever grateful for the sacrifices that the Americans and the 35th Division made for them. Each veteran was given a medallion from the mayor of Lutremange.[7]

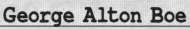

George Alton Boe

Seventh Army, 100th Infantry "Century" Division, 399th Infantry Regiment, Medical Detachment, Private First Class

JANUARY 17, 1923–JANUARY 8, 1945—Battle of the Bulge, France

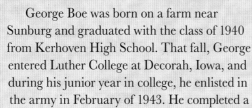

George Boe was born on a farm near Sunburg and graduated with the class of 1940 from Kerhoven High School. That fall, George entered Luther College at Decorah, Iowa, and during his junior year in college, he enlisted in the army in February of 1943. He completed a nine-month Army Specialized Training Program (ASTP) at the University of Minnesota, designed to train America's "best and brightest men" in technical military fields. George trained for another three months at a Medical Technician School at Fort Benjamin Harrison, Indianapolis, Indiana.[1,2]

The Army ended the ASTP, and in early 1944, Private First Class George Boe joined the 100th Infantry Division at Fort Bragg, where the division took over 3,000 replacements from the disbanded program for their infantry. On October 20, 1944, Private First Class Boe and the 100th landed in Marseille, France, where he served with the medical corps of field artillery on the front line.[3,4]

Following a victory against the German Winter Line in the Vosges Mountains in November, the division moved in December near the ancient fortress of Bitche, France. On January 1, 1945, the same day Private First Class Boe transferred to the Infantry Aid Station with the 399th Infantry Regiment, the Germans counterattacked with three divisions during Operation Nordwind. Some of the U.S. units fell back, but the 100th held their ground. A week later, Private First Class Boe died during a second counterattack.[3,4,5] In his book, *399th In Action*, the author wrote that during the attack near the small village of Reyersviller close to Bitche: *Medic George Boe ran around all afternoon of the 8th under fire caring for wounded. At twilight, 160 Krauts stormed up from the Reyersviller backslope to hit King and Item's precarious new holdings but they were driven back down.*[3]

For his selfless courage, Private First Class George Boe was awarded the Silver Star: *The President of the United States of America, authorized by Act of Congress July 9, 1918, takes pride in presenting the Silver Star (posthumously) to Private First Class George A. Boe, United States Army, for conspicuous gallantry and intrepidity in action against the enemy while serving with Medical Detachment, 100th Infantry Division, in action at Lambach, France during World War*

II. Private First Class Boe's gallant actions and selfless devotion to duty, without regard for his own safety, were in keeping with the highest traditions of military service and reflect great credit upon himself, his unit, and the United States Army.

Revered for their tenacity and courage near Bitche during the Battle of the Bulge, the men of the 100th Division became known as the "Sons of Bitche."[6] In March 1945, the 100th Infantry Division captured the Citadel of Bitche and passed through the Siegfried Line into Germany.

Private First Class George A. Boe is buried in Epinal American Cemetery, Dinozé, France. Memorial services were held April 15, 1945, at the West Norway Lake Lutheran Church. Stuart Gulsvig of the Lutheran Theological Seminary in St. Paul sang a solo, "The Great White Host," and the congregation sang "God Bless Our Native Land." Bugler C.G. Granoski played taps.[1]

Wallace Adolph Skaar

Nimrod (Wadena County)

83rd Infantry "Thunderbolt" Division, 329th Infantry Regiment, Private
MARCH 10, 1919–JANUARY 9, 1945—Battle of the Bulge, Belgium

On September 23, 1944, Private Wallace "Wallie" Skaar and the 329th Infantry Regiment traveled 300 miles out of France to the outskirts of Luxembourg where the unit joined Patton's Third Army. After battling through Luxembourg, the 329th crossed into Germany on December 10, where they relieved weary soldiers in the hellish Hürtgen Forest. The men groaned at the log structures and dugouts built by former units and the narrow roads with knee-deep mud. Just 6 days later, Field Marshall Karl Gerd Von Rundstedt ordered Germany's last major offensive—the Battle of the Bulge, where at the start 200,000 German soldiers faced off against around 83,000 Americans in a battle that raged for over a month in the Ardennes Forest in Belgium and Luxembourg.[1]

By December 18, the 329th had battled in Gürzenich and Birgel and fought their way out of the Hürtgen Forest, a deathtrap for the Allied forces, and landed on the eastern bank of the Roer River. The first American patrol, A Company, crossed the river into the town of Düren, the deepest foray into Germany by any American force in 1944.

On the last day of December, 1944, the regiment moved to Tohogne, Belgium, to continue the advance into Germany.[4, 5, 6] On January 2, 1945, Wallace Skaar wrote a letter to his close friend, Glen Shore: *Dear Glen, Well my friend, I'm at the present time somewhere in Belgium and assigned to a regular outfit now. I'm wondering how you like basic by this time. It's better than here, that's for sure, although the people are accommodating and glad to see us G.I Joes come to their towns and villages. I'm using a B.A.R. and may God strengthen me with my load. As for me, this war can end now or sooner. Ha. We had turkey for Christmas and yesterday also. A Red Cross truck came with fresh coffee and doughnuts, etc., visited by sure enough, American girls. Signing off with the best of luck. Your friend, Wallie*[2]

The 329th's first objective was to secure the town Petite Langlir. As the men advanced through the woods into the snow-covered fields surrounding the town, they drew heavy tank and machine gun fire. Forced to take cover back in the woods, the men spent a miserable night in sub-zero cold and with frozen feet. One week after Wallie wrote his letter, the 329th Combat Digest reported: *On January 9th we moved to Halt, Belgium. E and*

F Companies attacked down a road to the east of Petite Langlir. E Company met light resistance and gained their objective quickly. F Company was not so fortunate. As soon as they secured the crossroads, they became the target of a major counter-offensive by enemy panzer and infantry troops. Our men rose to the occasion, repulsed the attack and drove the Germans back along snow-covered roads to the roadblock.[4, 5]

By January 13, all but three German tanks had retreated and both the 329th and 331st Regiments occupied Petite Langlir. In the course of the battle, Private Wallace Skaar became a casualty.

Private Wallace Skaar enlisted in the service on June 17, 1944. Survivors included his parents, Norwegian immigrants Julius and Nora (Howe) Skaar, and a sister, Alice. Initially he was buried in Henri-Chapelle American Military Cemetery in Belgium and later reinterred in Bethlehem Cemetery, Pine River, Minnesota. On August 9, 1953, the Wallace Skaar Memorial Park opened in the Foot Hills State Forest on the shore of Spider Lake, Pine River, Minnesota.

Wallace Dean Colson

Merchant Marines, USS *Jonas Lie*, Merchant Marine Oiler
FEBRUARY 6, 1921–JANUARY 9, 1945—Bristol Channel, England

During World War II, shipyards turned out cargo vessels faster than they could be supplied with crews. Recruiters urged men to join the Merchant Marine, and men like Wallace Dean Colson, who had never seen the ocean, joined to run the ships that carried supplies through the North Atlantic and Pacific. There, Japanese and German U-boat submarines sabotaged Allied deliveries.[1, 2] Wallace Colson was assigned to the SS *Jonas Lie*, a 7,198-ton American cargo steamer built in 1944 and named for Norwegian-born American painter Jonas Lie, famous for his colorful paintings of the sea and ships.[3]

On January 29, 1945, the American Foreign Service reported the death of an American citizen, Wallace Dean Colson, an oiler on a U.S. ship off the coast of Wales. The master (captain) of the oiler, Carl L.V. Von Schoen, reported two men missing after an explosion on the vessel. The consul stated: *Consulate was advised by the Master of the American vessel in which the seaman was employed as oiler that an explosion occurred on the ship about 18 miles northwest of Milford Haven, Wales, at 5:20 pm on January 9, 1945, and that two members of the crew were reported as missing. There is no specified time that has to elapse before the court will officially presume death after a person is missing. Such time will depend on the circumstances of the case. It would be illegal for a surviving spouse to remarry within seven years of the disappearance of the husband and wife. Seaman was shipped at New York November 27, 1944.*[4]

During the war, it was not unusual for Merchant Marines who manned the engine rooms to die from explosions, but there is more to this story. On January 9, 1945, en route from Swansea and Milford for New York, German submarine U-1055 torpedoed the *Jonas Lie* at the entrance to the Bristol Channel in England. The torpedo blew a huge hole in the lower part of the ship, killing Colson and one other sailor. An armed trawler, MS *Huddersfield*, rescued 69 crew and guards, and the Norwegian ship *Fosna* picked up one survivor. The officers rode the crippled vessel into Milford Haven three hours later.[1]

On January 14, 1945, while being towed by the *Empire Sprite* and HMS *Stormking*, the towline parted and the SS *Jonas Lie* sank. The German submarine U-1055 that attacked the *Jonas Lie* was last heard from on April 23, west of Ireland. The U-boat was posted as missing by the war's end in Europe (May 8) when it failed to return to port. According to the U.S. Navy, a Catalina patrol plane sank her off the coast of France.[1, 2]

Merchant Marine Oiler Wallace Dean Colson, son of Waverly and Ethel (Denton) Colson, is memorialized at the East Coast Memorial, Battery Park, New York. The East Coast Memorial, which faces the Statue of Liberty across the New York Harbor, honors the 4,601 missing American servicemen who perished in the Atlantic Ocean in World War II. His father worked as a car inspector for the Great Northern Railway Company in Brookston. Survivors included his parents and a sister, Joyce.[5]

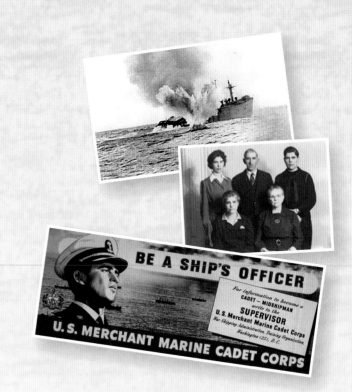

Russell J. Cummings

U.S. Naval Reserve, Construction Battalion Maintenance Unit 540, C Company, Seabees, Machinist's Mate First Class

JULY 15, 1915–JANUARY 12, 1945—Accident in Bermuda

The only trouble with your Seabees is that you don't have enough of them.
—General Douglas MacArthur[1]

Organized at Davisville, Rhode Island, Construction Battalion Maintenance Unit 540 arrived in Bermuda in October 1943. Called the "Seabees," these navy men were highly skilled craftsmen in the building and construction trade: electricians, carpenters, plumbers, and equipment operators. Their combined experience spanned virtually all construction and mechanical trades of the time. Most Seabee construction battalions were on or near the front lines of battle, landing after the marines to build airstrips, hospitals, housing and other base infrastructure. Maintenance Units would follow to operate and maintain the base.[1, 2, 3]

When Russell Cummings joined the navy on August 26, 1943, he was a perfect candidate for the Seabees. An experienced truck driver, he had also worked as a foreman at Breezy Point Civilian Conservation Corps Camp. When the men left their training grounds at Camp Thomas, Davisville, Rhode Island, they had no idea where in the world they were going. They only knew that their destination was "Island X." The Seabees had infantry training and were issued rifles before they embarked on their ship, so most assumed they were heading for Europe or the Pacific theater and active war zones. Seasick and apprehensive, they stepped off their vessel onto a construction base in Bermuda.

Seabees at rear bases did work that was little-known or appreciated by others on active duty near the front, but they worked long, grueling hours on vital construction projects with heavy equipment that often proved to be dangerous.[4]

Machinist's Mate First Class Cummings lost his life in such a situation. The accident report for January 12, 1945 states: *A crew of men was engaged in removing the outrigger on a Lorraine Moto-Crane. A steel cable led from the hood to the outrigger. Russel Cummings was standing on the ground and steadying the cable while slack was being taken up. The end of the crane came in contact with an overhead high tension line carrying 4160 volts. The medical officer who was summoned immediately to the scene failed to find any vital signs of life. Artificial respiration was instituted for two hours. Intra-cardian adrenalin and coramine were administered, all without avail.*[5]

Machinist's Mate First Class Russell Cummings was buried in Fort Bell Cemetery, Bermuda, and later reinterred in Pine Grove Cemetery, Cass Lake, Minnesota. Survivors included his parents, Melville and Lillian Cummings; his sister, Dorothy; his wife Lola; and his two-year-old daughter, Beverly.[6]

More than 325,000 men served with the Seabees in World War II; they fought—and built—in more than 400 locations before the war's end. And they represented more than 60 skilled trades.[1, 2, 3]

Arthur Ingvald Kolberg

6th Infantry "Sightseeing Sixth" Division, 20th Infantry Regiment, 2nd Battalion, G Company,
Staff Sergeant

MARCH 25, 1915–JANUARY 20, 1945—Battle of the Cabaruan Hills, Philippines

Arthur Kolberg worked on a farm near Kennedy, Minnesota, before his induction into the army in May 1941. He left Fort Snelling for Fort Leonard Wood, Missouri, for basic training and then traveled to Nashville, Tennessee, and San Luis Obispo, California, for desert maneuvers. After his furlough in July 1943, Staff Sergeant Kolberg joined the 6th Infantry Division in Oahu, Hawaii, to train for jungle warfare in New Guinea.[1]

As Thomas Price points out in the official history of the 6th Division, the "Sightseers" trained hard day and night to improve skills at fighting in the dark with the enemy a few yards or feet away. But fighting skills were not the only lessons they needed to learn to survive. The jungle was rife with diseases like scrub typhus, which could prove deadly. Also, the Japanese ignored Geneva Convention rules and did not respect or honor surrendering soldiers. After warfare in Burma and Guadalcanal, medics learned to remove their red cross, which was used as a target by the enemy.[2]

On D-Day, January 9, 1945, the division landed at Lingayen Gulf, Luzon, in the Philippines, where the 20th and 1st Infantry Regiments continued to move south toward Manila. On January 19, military leaders determined that the remaining Japanese defenders were centered in the Cabaruan Hills, a U-shaped ring of small hills west of the town of Cabaruan. The 3rd Battalion, including Staff Sergeant Arthur Kolberg, was ordered to rout out the remaining 200 to 300 Japanese concealed in foxholes and pillboxes. On January 20, as the battalion advanced slowly against fierce mortar and artillery fire, the soldiers overran the enemy and reached the last high ground between them and Cabaruan.[2,3] During the battle, Staff Sergeant Arthur Kolberg died of a gunshot wound.[4]

By the time the battle for the Cabaruan Hills ended on January 30, 1945, 81 men died and 198 had been wounded. Casualties for the Japanese included 1,432 men killed and 7 captured.[2,3]

Staff Sergeant Arthur Kolberg is buried in Bethania Cemetery, Greenbush, Minnesota, and is memorialized on the Kittson County Memorial. He was awarded the Combat Infantryman Badge, worn only by men who had experienced mortal encounters with the enemy, and the Purple Heart.[1]

Sylvester Michael Beckman

Tintah (Traverse County)

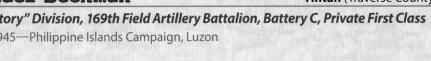

43rd Infantry "Winged Victory" Division, 169th Field Artillery Battalion, Battery C, Private First Class

JULY 6, 1919–JANUARY 21, 1945—Philippine Islands Campaign, Luzon

Sylvester "Jess" Beckman lived in Tintah, Minnesota, his entire life before he enlisted in the service in June 1942. After training at Camp Bowie, Texas, and Leesville, Louisiana, Private First Class Beckman left for the Pacific in November 1942. While fighting in New Caledonia, Beckman suffered a leg wound and was shipped to New Zealand for recovery.[1, 2]

Private First Class Beckman and the 43rd Division left New Zealand in February 1943 to mop up the remaining Japanese on Guadalcanal in the Solomon Islands. Five months later, the 43rd advanced to the Northern Solomons to secure Munda Airfield. In New Guinea in July 1944, the experienced veterans fought in the Aitape Campaign, where the enemy launched banzai charges that failed to break the division's line.

On January 9, 1945, the 43rd Infantry Division waded ashore on the beaches in Lingayen Gulf, Luzon, and secured the beach four days later. When Private First Class Beckman and the 169th Artillery Battalion moved to Hill 355 and Mt. Alava, they faced 5,000 Japanese east of the Pozorrubio-Rosario Road and north of the Rosario-Damortis Road. On January 21, the day the 169th captured Mt. Alava, Private First Class Beckman died trying to save the leader of his section.[3, 4]

Both Private First Class Sylvester Beckman and his leader, Sergeant John Cordeiro, received the Silver Star and the Purple Heart: *For gallantry in action against the enemy 21 January 1945 at Palguyod, Luzon, P.I. On the morning of 21st January, Sergeant Cordeiro's Battery was in position at Polguyod and was being shelled by enemy artillery. His battery was given orders to fire counter-battery. Rather than expose the whole section to enemy fire he ordered them to their dugouts and he proceeded to fire counter-battery single handed, but in the act of loading his gun was killed by enemy artillery. His outstanding courage and devotion to duty were an inspiration to his men. Private First Class Sylvester M. Beckman, a member of Sergeant Cordeiro's section, immediately and on his own volition, left the security of his foxhole and went to the assistance of his chief of section. Disregarding enemy shells that were landing nearby, he picked up a projectile and was in the act of loading the gun when an enemy shell landed in his howitzer position, mortally wounding him. Private Beckman's gallant courage and full devotion to duty are in keeping with the highest tradition of the army.*[2]

The 43rd Division spent six months fighting in the mountains of Luzon, securing the Ipo Dam and the water supply in Manila before Japan surrendered in August 1945. The men of the 169th Artillery Infantry received 4 Distinguished Service Crosses, 19 Silver Stars, 6 Legions of Merit and 2 Soldier's Medals, while 118 soldiers received the medal no one wanted, the Purple Heart for being wounded or killed in combat.[2, 3, 4]

Survivors included his parents and ten siblings. He is buried in Manila American Cemetery.

J.F.B. American Legion Post 610 in Tintah, Minnesota, is named in honor of Clayton Johnson (page 18), Robert Forsberg (page 54) and Sylvester Beckman.[2]

Private First Class Beckman, a promising writer, wrote "Bloody Hill" about combat experiences:

The sands of time are passing by—what has been done is gone. The deeds of American soldiers are forgotten in places. You read a little of the news, a magazine or two. Because they are so far away, it doesn't mean much to you.

New Georgia is a jungle trap, malaria runs deep, and mosquitoes and a million bugs rob you of your sleep. There are days when we go hungry, water couldn't be had, but the folks back home were eating, for that we were glad.

After the battle was over, I went over to look around, expecting to pick up trophies that were scattered on the ground. They named that place "Bloody Hill." And well they named it this for the scene I saw around me, my mind cannot dismiss—coastal guns were along the shore.

Field pieces lay there too; many blown to smithereens, with them went their crew. American and Japanese all mangled into one, friend or foe–Hard to tell after battle was done. From back of every tree and stump, in every bush and brook, the smell of death comes to you; it took plenty of guts to look.

The vision burned in my mind, it's something I can't forget. Years have passed since that day, but "Bloody Hill" is with me yet. I never took the trophies I tried so hard to get; I left them with the dead comrades as a token of respect.

Each night I say a prayer, that if I ever have a son, he'll never see what I have seen or do what I have done. I'll tell the stories of places I have been, but I swear I'll never tell what we went through to win.[7]

Howard Vern Hanson

4th Infantry "Ivy" Division, 12th Infantry Regiment, Private
JULY 19, 1915–JANUARY 22, 1945—Battle of the Bulge, Luxembourg

Howard Hanson Killed In Action

On Monday when it was reported that Private Howard Hanson had been killed in action on the German front, it cast a shadow of gloom over all the people of Taopi and community. Howard is the first Taopi boy reported giving his life in this war, and in the Taopi-Adams community there is genuine sorrow. He enjoyed a two-week furlough last August, which he spent with his family and friends. He was sent to France in October where he has been in active duty. In paying tribute to him we can but feel our unworthiness in the limitation of mere words to convey the loss and the sympathy of this his home community to his nearest of kin. Our thoughts cannot but wander back to last August when he spent a few short days at home. To the fine, strong, good-looking soldier that he was, and to remember how he radiated kindness, good will, sunshine and to his genial good-natured ways. He was devoted to his home and family where his loss will be the greatest. The sincerest sympathy of the entire community goes out to Mrs. Hanson, his children, and all members of his family. Howard Vern Hanson, son of Louis and Christina Hanson was born July 19, 1915 at Taopi on a farm in Clayton Township. Howard spent his entire life in and around Taopi and Adams up until the time he entered the service of his country December 28, 1943, receiving his training at Camp Blanding, Florida. He gave his life in action on the western front in Luxemburg on January 22, 1945. He went to school in Taopi and after that spent some time working around Taopi until July 30, when he started working for the Osmundson Brothers, road contractors of Adams. He was in their employ when he was called. On September 29, 1938, he was united in marriage to Margaret Marie Christensen of LeRoy. To them two children were born, a son Darrell, who will be five in April, and a daughter, Carol Ann, who was three in January who with their mother are left to mourn the passing of a loving husband and father. He also leaves his father, Louis Hanson, a sister, Mrs. Richard (Helen) Johnson; three brothers, Carl and Henry of Adams, and Martin of Waterloo, Iowa. One brother, Elmer, preceded him in death. He will be sadly missed by a host of other relatives and many friends.[1]

The 4th Infantry Division fought in five European campaigns through France, Belgium, Luxembourg and Germany. On D-Day, June 6, 1944, the 4th infantry Division led the assault landing on Utah Beach under the command of Colonel Russell "Red" Reeder. Between August 9 and 12, the 12th Infantry Regiment fought and defeated some of the famed 1st SS Panzer Division *Leibstandarte* SS Adolf Hitler near Mortain, France. When Private Howard Hanson arrived in France in September 1944 with other replacement soldiers, they were desperately needed to fill out the depleted ranks of the 4th Division after the two major battles.[2, 3, 4]

On November 6, the division engaged in the bloodiest battle of its history—the Battle of the Hürtgen Forest. They fought in cold, rain and snow in dense forests of massive pine and fir trees, with some trees as high as 150 feet. Army historians described the Hürtgen as "a dense, primordial woods of tall fir trees, deep gorges, high ridges, and narrow trails, terrain ideally suited to the defense."[2] The 4th inched forward yard by yard against German artillery and infantry resistance, and by early December, the various divisions had emerged from minefields and shredded trees, and the scene was reminiscent of a World War I battlefield. Casualties in the Hürtgen Forest were so high that Bradley's Twelfth Army was short 17,000 riflemen, and total First Army casualties exceeded 33,000.

With the Hürtgen Forest behind them, the 4th Division moved to Luxembourg in early December, hoping for a rest. On December 16 the Germans launched the Battle of the Bulge, and the 4th Division was right in their way. When the Allies stopped the Germans in the Bulge, the 4th Division resumed the attack and pushed through the Siegfried Line in their pursuit across Germany.[2, 3, 4, 5]

On January 22, 1945, Private Howard Hanson was killed near Longsdorf, Luxembourg, from a gunshot wound and is buried in Luxembourg American Cemetery, Hamm, Luxembourg. One year later, Dr. Blanche Woltz from Luxembourg adopted his grave and the graves of two other servicemen to ensure that the American sacrifices in the war would not be forgotten.[6]

Glenn Adolph Ranum

25th Infantry "Tropic Lightning" Division, 161st Infantry Regiment, 2nd Battalion, E Company,
Private First Class

NOVEMBER 18, 1923–JANUARY 27, 1945—Battle of San Manuel, Philippines

Elodee Ranum recalls her cousin Glenn:
Glenn's mother died in 1924 at the age of 36; she left
behind eleven children including one-year-old Glenn.
His father Alfred gave Glenn to his brother Otto and
his wife Lorine; they raised him until his teens, when
he returned to live with his father and his second
wife, Clara, on their farm in Viking. Lorine, who had cared for Glenn
all those years, was not happy to see him return to his father's home.[1]

Glenn worked with his uncle at Pioneer Land and Loan Company
Elevators prior to enlisting in the army on June 16, 1943, at age 19. He
trained at Camp Roberts and Fort Ord, California, before deployment
overseas with the 25th Infantry Division in January 1944. At the same time,
three of his brothers, John, Sanford and Lloyd, were all stationed overseas
with the army.[2, 3]

The 24th and 25th Infantry Divisions, stationed on Oahu, Hawaii,
were the first U.S. Army divisions to see combat in World War II when
the Japanese attacked Pearl Harbor on December 7, 1941. Following the
attack, the Division sailed for Guadalcanal in November 1942 and cleared
out the Japanese entrenched on Mt. Austen, earning the 25th the nickname,
"Tropic Lightning" for their speed and aggressiveness. Shortly after Glenn
Ranum joined the service, the 25th participated in securing the Solomon
Islands and moved to New Caledonia on February 8, 1944, to prepare for
the invasion of the Philippines.[4]

After intensive training in amphibious landings in New Caledonia,
Private First Class Glenn Ranum and the 161st Regiment returned to battle
on January 17, 1945, at Luzon Island in the Philippines. As the history of the
161st describes, both the 161st and the 27th Infantry Regiment were ordered
to capture three villages. At Binalonan Village, the 161st met fierce resistance as Japanese forces counterattacked with tanks and infantry; however,
the 161st prevailed and captured the town the next day. On January 19,
the 161st was ordered to clear the town of San Manuel of Japanese forces
and encountered heavy opposition three days later from over 1,000 Japanese troops, deeply entrenched and supported by 40 tanks. As Private First
Class Glenn Ranum and E Company advanced to the edge of town, the
Japanese counterattacked. In the two-hour battle, E Company, supported

by C Company, sustained 50 percent casualties in extremely close combat
but turned back the Japanese attack. C Company, equipped with 105 mm
howitzers, destroyed nine enemy tanks. On January 25, the 2nd Battalion
followed C Company into San Manuel and inflicted heavy casualties on
retreating Japanese forces. After slow house-to-house fighting on January 26,
over a dozen M4 Sherman tanks fired on the Japanese from a safe distance
and destroyed most of the enemy armor.[5]

Pushed back to the hills with no route for escape, the Japanese 7th Tank
Regiment planned a banzai attack for January 28th with their remaining
13 tanks. However, ten tanks were destroyed before reaching the American
lines, and the remaining three retreated to the hills. In the deadly fighting at
San Manuel, E Company of the 161st saw five company commanders killed
in four days.[4, 5] Just one day before the 161st liberated San Manuel, Private
First Class Glenn Ranum died from a gunshot wound.[7] His E Company
received a Presidential Unit Citation for valor, and Colonel James Dalton,
Commander of the 161st, was promoted to Brigadier General and Assistant
Commanding General of the 25th Infantry Division.

Private First Class Glenn A. Ranum, son of Alfred and Hulda (Johnson) Ranum, was initially buried on Luzon and reinterred in 1948 at Fort
Snelling National Cemetery. Survivors included his father; his stepmother,
Clara; his aunt and uncle, Otto and Lorine Ranum; and 14 siblings, half-
siblings and stepsiblings.[2, 3]

Wilbur Clarke Wright

Kinbrae (Nobles County)

82nd Airborne "All American" Division, 508th Parachute Infantry "Red Devils" Regiment,
2nd Battalion, F Company, Headquarters, Private
JULY 22, 1924–JANUARY 30, 1945—Battle of the Bulge, Belgium

Slogans on posters beckoned young men and women to "Join the Army and see the world!" After spending their initial time training, the men in the 508th Parachute Infantry complained that they had seen only the U.S. South and were eager to head overseas. On December 20, 1943, the men left Camp Mackall, North Carolina, and boarded the train for Camp Shanks, New York, where a week later, the 508th boarded the *James Parker* for Ireland to train for the Normandy invasion.[1]

Private Wilbur Wright was not in the original regiment of the 508th Parachute Infantry Regiment. A graduate of Fulda High School in 1941, Private Wilbur Wright was inducted at Fort Lewis, Washington, in July 1943, and assigned to Camp Roberts, California. Private Wright trained there until July 1944, when he transferred to Fort Meade, Maryland, and then traveled to Nottingham, England, in September 1944, thereby missing D-Day on Normandy's beaches.[2]

Private Wright first saw action in the Netherlands on October 6, when the 508th joined other forces that were already embroiled three weeks into Operation Market Garden. In the history of the 508th Infantry, William Lord recounts a misstep that occurred after they had been trucked over a bridge to the Arnhem-Nijmegen Island: *One of the drivers lost his way and drove his vehicle through British lines into German territory. The soldiers on the trucks found themselves staring down into German foxholes. The Germans were as surprised as the Americans, and the troopers quickly abandoned their vehicle and made their way back to friendly territory.*[2] When the war stalled in the Netherlands, the 508th marched 22 miles on November 11 from Oss, in the Netherlands, to Camp Sissonne, France, in the Reims area. Their rest in relative comfort ended on December 16, 1944, when 12 enemy divisions pushed through the Ardennes in Belgium. The Battle of the Bulge had begun. After enduring a month of cold, snowy combat, the 508th was ordered to the northeastern edge of the Bulge.[2, 3, 4]

On January 20, Private Wilbur Wright wrote an eloquent letter to his mother: *Dear Mother, I'm afraid it's way beyond the time when I should have written you a letter but that's something that I have a little trouble doing. Our facilities aren't quite the same as you would find in a drawing room, but at the present we aren't sleeping in foxholes, anyway. And I'm very happy for that because the weather,* to say the least, is inclement. *We've had quite a lot of snow and yesterday was a veritable blizzard. Of course, it can't compare with the snow and cold spells we've seen in Minnesota because if it did, we'd all be "hurtin'," as the saying goes. But even though the weather has been against us, the Boche are going back. An awful lot of them are surrendering and a lot have been killed. The prisoners especially seem glad to be out of it. I guess they know they'll get better food and treatment in our prison camps than they've had in their Army. And they're away from the shells and dangers. One day a group of prisoners was passing our squad positions and one said in English, "Hurry up and get the war over, Yank." He must have realized that was the quickest way to get back to the Fatherland. Those are the feelings of the Wehrmacht (or regular army) but the SS troops are something else. They are the brutal, fanatical Nazis that have been with Hitler since his start and were the original storm troopers who were so brutal in their persecution of the Jews. They put up a fair fight before they give up and when they do quit, they are a sullen bunch of boys. But they behave themselves darn good if someone points a gun at them. I guess they're afraid of getting the same treatment they give their prisoners. They undoubtedly deserve much harsher treatment than they get, but as the General says, "You guys are Yanks, not Nazis."*[5, 6]

On the 30th, at nightfall, the Allies began a major attack on the Siegfried Line at St. Vith. Lieutenant R.L. Daggett, Private Wright's commanding officer, wrote to Wilbur's mother: *He met his death instantly with two companions when they unexpectedly ran into a German machine gun emplacement. One of his best friends immediately knocked it out and killed the crew of the gun—and we're sorry it couldn't have been done before the damage was done.*[5]

Private Wilbur Wright, son of Clarence and Mabel (Clarke) Wright, grew up on a farm near Kinbrae. Survivors included his parents and four siblings. From letters he sent home, the family learned that Wilbur was engaged to a girl named Shirley, nicknamed "Spud," whom he met in Coeur d'Alene, Idaho, just prior to his induction into the army. They never found her after Wilbur died.[5] He is buried at Worthington Cemetery, Worthington, Minnesota.[1]

Edward Howard Engblom

U.S. Navy, U.S. Submarine Force, USS Canopus, Machinist's Mate Second Class
SEPTEMBER 7, 1921–JANUARY 29, 1945—Fall of Corrigedor, Prisoner of War in Bilibid Prison

The USS *Canopus* was not a famous warship, but rather a 20-year-old submarine tender that her crew nicknamed the "Old Lady." Nineteen-year-old Edward Engblom enlisted in the navy on November 28, 1939, in Minneapolis, Minnesota, and came aboard *Canopus* on October 19, 1940. The ship served as a floating service station and machine shop for submarines prior to World War II.

At that time the *Canopus*, along with the Asiatic Fleet, was held in the southern islands of the Philippines in preparation for war.

After the attack on Pearl Harbor, the navy pulled all ships but the USS *Canopus* out of Manila Bay. The *Canopus* remained behind, navigated around Manila Bay and docked the next morning at Manila. John Wepplo wrote: *When the essential equipment and personnel were evacuated, I believe the decision was made to keep* Canopus *in PI to perform maintenance and repairs on those vessels still operating e.g., PT boats and submarines. After the shipyards and docks were bombed,* Canopus *was the only viable maintenance activity available in the area.*[1]

Showered by bomb fragments while docked in Manila on Christmas Eve, the *Canopus* moved to Mariveles Bay on Bataan, where General MacArthur's troops were quickly withdrawing in the face of a Japanese advance.

Just a few days later, heavy bombers hit the submarine tender causing severe damage. She lost six of her crew in the attack, with another six wounded. Unharmed, Machinist's Mate Second Class Edward Engblom remained aboard the *Canopus* until February 28, 1942, when the ship's logbook states that he transferred with a group of 221 sailors from the *Canopus* to beach defenses on Corregidor with the 4th Marines. Stationed in foxholes along the beaches of Corrigedor, Engblom and the 1st Battalion were the first to face Japanese landings in the final battle for Corregidor and Manila Bay, where they fought fiercely, often in hand-to-hand combat.[2,3]

Meanwhile, during the five-month battle for Manila Bay, the Japanese attacked the *Canopus* several times before capturing Bataan on April 8. To make the ship appear abandoned, the remaining men would light pots of oil on deck during the day, making it look smoky, ruined and abandoned, and then resume their maintenance activities at night. The residual crew finally sank the ship off Manila Bay on April 9 rather than face capture by the enemy, and escaped in small boats to Corregidor where they joined the 4th Marine Regiment.[2,3]

When Corregidor fell on May 6, 1942, over 400 *Canopus* sailors, including Edward Engblom, were captured along with 70,000 other American and Filipino troops. After three weeks with little water or food, the Japanese loaded the Corregidor prisoners of war on freighters and transported the men to Manila.

There, the men were forced to march in a Japanese victory parade to Bilibid Prison, an abandoned military prison.

A large number of the *Canopus* crew died in the Philippine Islands during transport to prisoner of war camps in Japan or later in the camps themselves.[3,4] Edward Engblom was imprisoned in Camp 510, Batangas POW Camp at Lipa, Batangas, Philippines, and died at Bilibid Prison in Manila. The cause of death was listed as malnutrition.

Edward Howard Engblom, son of Gunnar and Ida Mae (Nygren) Engblom, was survived by his mother and two sisters. He was buried in Oakwood Cemetery, Mora, Minnesota. Edward Engblom received the Prisoner of War Medal and Purple Heart.[5]

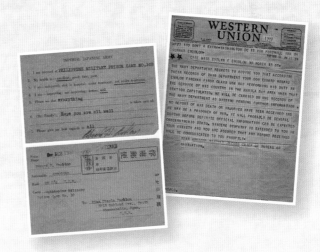

Emmett Truman Loucks

Third Army, 35th Infantry Division, "Santa Fe Division," 134th Infantry Regiment, 3rd Battalion, L Company, Staff Sergeant

OCTOBER 31, 1913–FEBRUARY 4, 1945—Battle of the Bulge, Belgium

Almost a year after he died, the *Itasca Iron News* reported the death of Staff Sergeant Emmett T. Loucks: *Word was received Thursday by Mrs. Emmett T. Loucks of Grand Rapids that her husband, Staff Sergeant Loucks, had died in Germany on February 4. He previously had been reported missing in action in Belgium since December 30. Apparently the young man had died a prisoner of war as the message to Mrs. Loucks came through the International Red Cross. He had been overseas since November, serving with Patton's Third Army. Three years ago he married Miss Judith Forseen of Squaw Lake, and it was shortly after this marriage that he went into the service. Mrs. Loucks is a member of the Cohasset school faculty.*[1]

On December 28, 1944, Staff Sergeant Loucks and the 3rd Battalion were ordered to attack through the woods and seize Lutrebois, a small town five kilometers south of Bastogne, with L Company in the lead followed by K and I Companies for support. As L Company swept into town, enemy groups of infantry began to filter through Allied lines. When the enemy struck back in a pre-dawn attack on December 30, with the Luftwaffe and tanks giving support to their ground forces, the fate was sealed for L Company. Holed up in a house in Lutrebois, surrounded, and without ammunition, the men continued to defend themselves in an increasingly impossible situation. Finally, unable to stop the tanks, L Company was forced to surrender. A German medic, a prisoner of the Allies, left the house and told a tank man parked by the house that a company of Americans hid inside. The 49 men of L Company, including Staff Sergeant Emmett Loucks, were lined up in the woods, marched off, and sent to prison camps. The Germans took their uniforms and winter coats and used them to infiltrate American lines.[2]

Letters from Staff Sergeant Loucks' wife and sister indicate that on January 9, 1945, they were notified that Staff Sergeant Loucks was missing in action. A second message on March 9, 1945, this time from the German Red Cross, stated that he died on February 4, 1945, from wounds while a prisoner of war in Germany.[3]

Back home in Itasca County, on December 1, 1946, Itasca County dedicated a parcel of tax-forfeited land in honor of two fallen war heroes: Staff Sergeant Emmett Loucks and 2nd Lieutenant Franklin Danyluk. One of four memorial forests in Itasca County, the Loucks/Danyluk Memorial Forest lands are managed for timber and wildlife and open to the public for hunting and other recreational purposes.

Sixty-six years later, when the county considered trading the land to a private party, James A. Loucks and Colin M. Loucks, nephews of Staff Sergeant Loucks, wrote a letter on June 2, 2012 to the *Grand Rapids Herald-Review*: *Emmett Truman Loucks was captured in the Battle of the Bulge and was subsequently murdered by the SS Nazis because he refused to give information to the Nazis on U.S. strength and movement. His murder galvanized the rest of the POWs not to give information to the SS. If we trade this memorial forest for the hunting pleasure of a few we certainly do not deserve our freedom and would be a disgrace not only to him, but to all veterans living and dead. Not only was he our father's brother but his best friend. While our father fought the Japanese in the Pacific his brother gave his life in the European Theater. This loss changed all his siblings forever. Our father could barely speak his name without tears the rest of his life, but he understood why Emmett gave his life willingly as a volunteer, so all other people could enjoy the freedom he loved so dearly that he bravely gave his last full measure of devotion and life willingly and without second thoughts. We were deprived of ever getting to know our uncle due to his murder in the defense of freedom. The Nazis murdered Emmett and other US soldiers so they could take their uniforms and identification to infiltrate the Allied forces so they could cause havoc and spy on the strength and positions of the United States military units that were thrust against them.*

The state has since ruled against trading the land to a private developer, and the Loucks/Danyluk Memorial Forest remains open for public recreation.[4]

Staff Sergeant Emmett T. Loucks, husband of Judith (Forseen) Loucks, and son of Albert and Annie (Clemens) Loucks, was reburied at Luxembourg American Cemetery, Belgium, in 1946. Survivors included his wife, his father and seven siblings. He entered the service on October 10, 1941.[1]

Donald J. Swenson

Perley (Norman County)

U.S. Army Air Forces, 15th Air Force, 55th Bomb Wing, 485th Heavy Bomb Group, 831st Bomb Squadron, 2nd Lieutenant

JULY 16, 1921–FEBRUARY 7, 1945—Bombing Mission over Pola, Italy

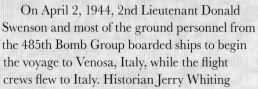

On April 2, 1944, 2nd Lieutenant Donald Swenson and most of the ground personnel from the 485th Bomb Group boarded ships to begin the voyage to Venosa, Italy, while the flight crews flew to Italy. Historian Jerry Whiting wrote about April 20, when Junkers JU-88 torpedo bombers attacked the convoy in the Mediterranean Sea, just off the coast of Algiers, and sank three ships. The liberty ship, SS *Paul Hamilton*, which carried 154 officers and men from the 485th Bomb Group, most from the 831st Squadron, exploded and sank in 30 seconds. All men aboard were lost. The remaining ground personnel, including 2nd Lieutenant Donald Swenson, stationed on other ships in the convoy, made it safely to Venosa, Italy.

One of four heavy Bomb Groups assigned to the 55th Bomb Wing, the 485th began combat operations on May 10, 1944, from their base at Venosa, Italy, by bombing the marshaling yard at Knin, Yugoslavia. On June 26, 1944, the 485th, in a formation of 36 B-24 Liberator aircraft, flew to Vienna, Austria, to attack the Floridsdorf Oil Refinery. Despite heavy flak and intense opposition, the Group inflicted massive damage to the refinery and crippled the enemy's fuel production during a crucial period of World War II. The 485th Bomb Group was awarded a Unit Citation for this successfully completed mission.[1, 2, 3]

On February 7, 1945, pilot Ken Wydler, along with 39 other planes and the 831st Bomb Squadron, flew a B-24 Liberator on a mission to Pola, Italy, to bomb an oil storage facility. Pilot Wydler's crew included 2nd Lieutenant Donald Swenson, who served as navigator. On the Pola mission, their aircraft received a direct hit in the nose section, instantly killing 2nd Lieutenant Don Swenson and blowing his body out of the aircraft. Both pilots were temporarily knocked unconscious from the hit, but miraculously recovered in time to save the aircraft and crew.[1, 2, 3]

Jerry Whiting, whose father trained with 2nd Lieutenant Swenson and Lieutenant Wydler's crew in Idaho, provides an eyewitness report from his father: *A few years ago, I was in touch with Don's sister. My dad and his crew trained with Lieutenant Wydler's crew in Idaho. Even though my dad was an enlisted man, he knew Lieutenant Swenson. I think he made the effort because my dad was from South Dakota right along the Minnesota border and spent a lot of time in the Ortonville area when he was growing up. My dad's crew was flying with him (in a different plane but the same formation) when he died and witnessed the tragic event. In summary, he was in the navigator's compartment and an 88 mm shell came through the bottom of the plane and exploded in his compartment. I'm sure that he died instantly, but his body was blown out of the plane. It really bothered those who witnessed it.*[1, 2, 3]

The son of Oliver M. and Emma (Hansen) Swenson, 2nd Lieutenant Donald Swenson was buried at Fort Snelling National Cemetery, and a memorial stone honors his memory at Immanuel Lutheran Cemetery, Hendrum, Minnesota. Survivors included his parents; his wife Betty Ann (Kromer) Swenson; and a sister.[4]

His father, Oliver, managed the DeCazinove bonanza farm between Perley and Hendrum, Minnesota. Donald was a senior at North Dakota State University, Fargo, North Dakota, when he entered the service in May 1943. His final mission over Pola, Italy, was his twelfth mission on a B-24 Liberator. Honors included the Air Medal with an Oak Leaf Cluster, a Presidential Unit Citation for a raid over Vienna and the Purple Heart.

Donald's wife worked as a stewardess for Northwest Airlines and later married Harold Van Allen Stewart, a navy man and a physics professor.

Approximately 3,500 men served in the 485th Bomb Group in Italy. According to official records, the 485th flew a total of 187 combat missions and lost 59 bombers in aerial combat and 62 others in accidents. The 485th lost 475 men who died in combat or from combat-related injuries.[1, 2, 3]

Archie Lind Olson

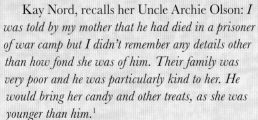

U.S. Army Coast Artillery Corps, 59th Coast Artillery Regiment, Headquarters Battery, Private First Class

OCTOBER 21, 1910–FEBRUARY 12, 1945—Prisoner of War, Fukuoka #3 Camp, Japan

Kay Nord, recalls her Uncle Archie Olson: *I was told by my mother that he had died in a prisoner of war camp but I didn't remember any details other than how fond she was of him. Their family was very poor and he was particularly kind to her. He would bring her candy and other treats, as she was younger than him.*[1]

Archie Olson, born in Trail, Minnesota, lived in Madison County, Illinois, when he enlisted in the army on January 30, 1941, at 31 years of age. Private First Class Olson was assigned to the Coast Artillery Corps on Corregidor Island, an island located at the entrance of Manila Bay on southwest Luzon Island in the Philippines. Coastal artillery defended the bay and the city of Manila, located 30 miles inland. Called the "Rock," Corregidor housed a complete tunnel complex with the army's underground hospital, barracks, headquarters and storage. Men and women on Corregidor believed that the island symbolized security and a less dangerous existence than life on Bataan. Here one could expect two meals a day, a hot shower and clean water.[2]

That sense of safety dissolved when Bataan fell on April 9, 1942, and the Japanese controlled all of the northern Philippines. Only the island of Corregidor, with its network of tunnels and defenses across the entrance to Manila Bay, prevented the Japanese from entering the harbor. On May 6, 1942, Corregidor fell to the enemy, and Archie Olson, along with 11,000 American and Filipino prisoners, joined their Bataan comrades at Camp O'Donnell. Private First Class Olson fought to survive as hundreds of men died from malnutrition, exhaustion, malaria and dysentery.

Archie Olson beat the odds at Camp O'Donnell, and on July 17, 1944, he left Manila on the Japanese ship *Nissyo Maru* with 1,539 prisoners of war on board, all headed for labor camps in Japan. Private First Class Olson survived the "hell ship" journey and arrived at the Fukuoka #3 POW camp, near Moji, Japan, on August 4, 1944, which held 79 other American prisoners of war. Most of the prisoners worked as slave laborers for the Nippon Steel Company.[3, 4, 5, 6]

His family did not learn of his death until a year later.[7] The local newspaper, *Fosston Thirteen Towns*, reported in March 1946: *Archie Olson of the Fosston-Trail area was the first man from this area to be taken prisoner during the war. Recently the family had word from the war department that he had died in a prison camp about a year ago. Last week the family received the following letter from the commanding officer: Dear Mrs. Quam: I was Archie's C.O. in Japan. We were at the Fukuoka No. 3 camp, which you can find on the map at a place called Moji, at the tip of the island called Kyushu. Archie was a grand big man, a man the men loved, he was quiet, easy going and happy. He did not suffer; he became ill, went into a coma and then passed away. I do not recall that he ever was a victim of beatings, and as for food, he received enough of what we had to normally get along. I believe that he just happened to be a victim of war. It was most likely from malaria that he died. His doctor was Captain Charles Armstrong of Fletcher General Hospital, Cambridge, Ohio. Dr. Armstrong was a very wonderful young officer, who worked hard for his men. He took care of Archie. With every wish I remain. Sincerely yours, John L. Curran, O.P.*[8]

The camp death roster lists the cause of death as beriberi, malnutrition caused by a deficiency of Vitamin B1 (thiamine).[5, 7]

Archie's capture was first reported to the International Red Cross on May 7, 1942, and the last report was made February 12, 1945. Based on these two reports, Archie was imprisoned for two years and ten months, one of the longest durations of captivity on record.

Private First Class Archie Olson is memorialized in Manila American Cemetery, Manila, Philippines, and at Salem Lutheran Cemetery, Gully, Minnesota. Survivors included his parents, Louis and Mary (Paulson), and seven siblings.[1, 8]

James T. "Todd" Knight

U.S. Army Air Forces, 12th Air Force, 57th Bomb Wing, 57th Fighter Group, 64th Fighter "Black Scorpion" Squadron, 2nd Lieutenant
NOVEMBER 8, 1917–FEBRUARY 18, 1945—Italian Campaign, Italy

Janice Knight Evensen recalls her family: *I come from a strong military family. My brother, Todd, a pilot, died in an air accident in Italy. My oldest brother was a scientist who was part of the Manhattan Project that split the atom and made the atom bomb. I also was a World War II veteran, serving in the Marine Corps. I taught pilots instrument flight and navigation. My younger brother was career military but did not go overseas during the war. I lost my niece's husband in Iraq.*[1]

James "Todd" Knight was born in Bustitown, near Effie, Minnesota. Following graduation from Big Fork High School, he attended Hibbing Junior College and St. John's University in Collegeville. On July 16, 1941, Todd enlisted in the Army Air Corps, entered pilot training in October 1943, and earned his lieutenant's commission and wings as a fighter pilot on April 12, 1944.[2]

On September 25, 1944, 2nd Lieutenant Knight and his squadron moved from Corsica to Grosseto, in northern Italy, to attack German-controlled railroads and main roads supplying their Gothic Line defenses. The "Black Scorpion" Squadron flew the P-47 Thunderbolt, a single-engine fighter/bomber, armed with .50 caliber guns and rockets. The fighter's long range, speed and heavy armaments made it ideal for this mission.

A member of the famed squadron, Pilot James T. Knight flew 50 missions, including an operation on November 6 called Bingo, to disable electrical transformers along the Brenner rail line. Here the pilots encountered some of the worst flak of the war against the heavily defended line.[3]

On February 18, 1945, 2nd Lieutenant James Knight, pilot of a P-47, collided with a fellow pilot, 1st Lieutenant Royce Maier, during takeoff for a dive-bomb mission from Grosseto Main airfield. A witness narrative from 2nd Lieutenant Charles Kitowski states: *As the second section was starting to form up, the leader with his wingman started to pull up to make a diamond formation. Coming up on the leader's section, which had already formed up, Lieutenant Royce Maier looked as though he had too much speed and was closing in rapidly on the lead section. It appeared that the yellow section leader had his ship almost in a vertical bank to bring it around, although he then popped his nose forward to keep from hitting one of the planes in lead section. As a result his own plane looked as if it sliced part of the left wing off of his wingman, Lieutenant James T. Knight. His own plane appeared to be out of control and hadn't gone far when it broke into flames and started into a spin. A fraction of a second later, the other plane, though not burning, started towards the ground. They both seemed to have gone down close together. The first ship hit nose first and the other went in on a wing. Both ships exploded on contact with the ground. In both cases neither pilot seemed to make an effort to abandon their ships. The collision occurred at about 900 feet above the ground.*[4]

Survivors included his parents, James and Esther Knight; two sisters, Sergeant Janice Knight of Marines Women's Reserve and Jean (Arvid) Burke. He also was survived by two brothers, Lieutenant William Knight, a fighter pilot instructor at Aloe Army air field, and Dr. Jere (Sylvia) Knight, a government researcher at Oak Ridge, Tennessee.

2nd Lieutenant James "Todd" Knight is buried at Florence American Cemetery, Italy.[2]

121

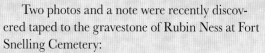

Rubin Leroy Ness

Holt (Marshall County)

33rd Infantry "Prairie" Division, 130th Infantry Regiment, 1st Battalion, C Company, Private First Class

DECEMBER 30, 1922–FEBRUARY 25, 1945—Battle of Baguio, Philippines

Two photos and a note were recently discovered taped to the gravestone of Rubin Ness at Fort Snelling Cemetery:

Rubin L. Ness is buried here. In 1945, Rubin was killed in action on Luzon, in the Philippines. He was buried there until 1948, when his remains were brought here. Rubin was 22 years when he died. He was the second of five children born to Olaf and Inga Ness. He was from Holt, a small town in northwest Minnesota. He was an Eagle Scout. All who knew him say he was a great guy. The family picture on the right was taken on the day he left home for the army (he is 2nd from the right). It was the last time he and his family were together. It is sad to consider how much life he never got to live: He never married his girlfriend. He never had a family of his own. His mother and father were grief-stricken by his death for the rest of their lives. His brothers and sisters all grew up, had families, and lived good lives. They all spoke often of the hole in their lives that his death caused. In grave #7720 are the remains of Rubin L. Ness, a real person who died on the other side of the world while serving our country.[1]

On the evening of February 9, 1943, Private First Class Rubin Ness and the 33rd Infantry Division, anchored offshore in Lingayen Gulf of Luzon near San Fabian, looked at shredded coconut palms on the now-quiet beach that the 43rd Division and others invaded and cleared one month before. Other elements of the Sixth Army had swept through the plains to the south and controlled most of Manila, while the exhausted 43rd was locked in a stalemate with Japanese forces in the rugged mountains that loomed above. As they relieved the 43rd and moved toward General Yamashito's headquarters at Baguio, they encountered a series of sharp ridges, perfect for the defenders who had three years of preparation to dig into bunkers and caves. According to military historian Robert Ross: *The 33rd Division would clear one side of a ridge nose, round the nose, and find the Japanese just as strong on the opposite side.* The process seemed impossible.[2]

Supply problems hampered the GIs in their initial attack on what became known as Question Mark Hill. Parched with thirst in the extreme heat and with wounded who desperately needed water, the men ran out of water. General Clarkson ordered a reluctant 100-man group of engineers to do the chore. *The Golden Cross* states: *No one wanted to sidestep a fight, but few relished the task of serving as pack mules in the oppressive heat.*[3] Once they saw the condition of the troops, they shouldered their heavy loads and did the job. After more fighting, a planned water airdrop drifted too far and landed on Japanese lines. The men wept.[3]

Following an intense artillery barrage on the morning of February 22, the Americans rushed the hill, firing small arms and blasting caves with grenades and flamethrowers. In half an hour the fight was over, and they took no prisoners. After days of struggle the men finally swept over Question Mark Hill, suffering heavy casualties.

As the division advanced toward Baguio, the men rooted the Japanese out of the hills from Pozorrubio to Rosario. Reconnaissance patrols, including Rubin Ness and the 1st Battalion of the 130th Regiment, still short of water, searched out and destroyed small bands of Japanese under the hot sun and in close, brutal combat. By evening, the area around the hill was secure.[3, 4, 5, 7] On the last day, near Pozorrubio, Private First Class Rubin Ness was shot in the back by an enemy sniper.[8]

Gladys Ness Erickson recalls her brother: *My brother Rubin was 7 years old when my parents moved from Mud Lake to Holt, where my father, Olaf Ness, managed a grain elevator. He also ran the only "Cattail Factory," which made life preservers for the navy when the usual materials were cut off during the war. There were five children in our family, with me the youngest. In later years, he loved to hunt and fish, anything outdoors. He was a Boy Scout and received the Eagle Scout and Bronze Palm. In the fall, he drove truck for the grain elevator hauling grain. In later years Rubin drove truck for Hartz at Thief River Groceries. Our family had just come home from church when my parents got the telegram that Rubin was missing in action.*[6] Private First Class Rubin Ness, son of Olaf and Inga (Johnson) Ness, is buried in Fort Snelling Cemetery. Survivors included his parents and four siblings.[9]

Following his induction on February 20, 1943, Private First Class Ness trained at Camp Roberts, California, followed by training in Hawaii and the Dutch East Indies. After his death, his parents received an inventory of his belongings, which included a cribbage board, prayer books, 50 seashells, 1 Neptunus Rex membership card (for crossing the equator), 111 photos, 2 cigarette lighters, 3 pieces of silk, and various badges.[8]

Myril Allen Lundgren

Wilder (Jackson County)

First U.S. Army, VII Corps Artillery, Headquarters Battery, Technical Sergeant

MAY 17, 1919–FEBRUARY 25, 1945—Crossing the Roer River, Germany

Myril Lundgren was born at home in Rushriver Township in rural Le Sueur, and graduated in 1938 from Le Sueur High School. After graduation, he worked as a farmhand on his uncle Ben's farm before enlisting in the service May 24, 1942.[1] Now a member of the VII Corps Artillery, Tech Sergeant Myril Lundgren's job description stated: *Field artillery is a supporting arm. It contributes to the action of the entire force by giving close and continuous fire support to infantry units and by giving depth to combat by counterbattery fire, fire on hostile reserves, fire to restrict movement in rural areas, and fire to disrupt command agencies.*[2]

In mid-December 1944, Hitler launched his last major offensive in the Ardennes region: the Battle of the Bulge from December 1944 to January 1945. The United States endured heavy casualties, but the attack was repelled. The Allies resumed their advance to Germany in February 1945. At that point, all that stood in the way were battered German forces and a series of rivers, the first of which was the Roer. On February 10, Technical Sergeant Myril Lundgren's unit, the VII Corps Artillery, provided the big guns to lead the infantry's Roer River crossing.

Operation Grenade called for six divisions to cross the Roer River between Roermond and Düren. The Allies expected strong enemy resistance as crossing the Roer would open the way to Cologne and the Rhine, deep into the heart of Germany. When the Germans destroyed the discharge valves on the seven dams, it flooded the Roer River, turning the area into a mile-wide lake, stopping the army's advance cold for two weeks.

Brief artillery firing on February 21 and 22 helped pinpoint enemy positions. On D-Day, February 23, Technical Sergeant Myril Lundgren and the VII Corps artillery unleashed a concentrated 45-minute barrage. As the first wave of assault boats crossed the swollen Roer River and hit the shore, casualties were light due to accurate artillery corps fire, which kept the enemy in their shelters. After the forces secured Baal, the infantry advanced to Doveren, where the Germans counterattacked by firing on the Roer River crossing sites.[3] Two days later, near Derichsweiler, Germany, Myril Lundgren died when his jeep hit a land mine. On March 2, he was buried in Henri-Chapelle American Cemetery in Belgium.[4]

On June 29, 1945, Axel Lundgren wrote to the War Department in Washington, D.C. for information on his son's burial: *Dear Sir: As my son is in the military service in France, he's requested us to write and ask you where his brother, Technical Sergeant Myril Lundgren, 37125685, Hq. Battery, VII Corps Artillery, is buried as he was killed in action in Germany on Feb. 25, 1945, and is supposed to be buried in Belgium in a Protestant Cemetery. His brother, Sergeant Russell Lundgren, has requested to know, as if he has the opportunity he would like to visit his brother's grave. Please do this for us, as it will be appreciated very much. Thanking you in advance, I am yours very truly, Axel Lundgren, father*[4]

Technical Sergeant Myril Lundgren was survived by his parents, Axel "Harry" and Ellen (Anderson) Lundgren, and three brothers, Private First Class Virgil Lundgren, Sergeant Russell Lundgren and Seaman First Class Sheldon Lundgren, all in the service at the same time. Sheldon, stationed on a ship when his brother died, was unable to return home to be with his family. Joyce Rossow recalls Myril: *He liked to tease and have a good time unlike his twin brother Virgil who was serious and quiet. The family was shocked when the servicemen showed up to tell us that Myril was dead, especially since all his brothers were in the service, too.*[5] In 1947, Technical Sergeant Myril Lundgren was reinterred in Clear Lake Swedish Lutheran Cemetery, Gibbon, Minnesota.

Myril's father operated the creamery in Wilder. Myril's parents lived two houses down from Walter and Iva Nelson, whose son, LaVern Nelson (page 68), died on August 9, 1944, while fighting in France.[1]

Glen Alfred Bixby

Richville (Otter Tail County)

U.S. Marine Corps, 5th Marine "Fighting Fifth" Division, 28th Weapon Company, 2nd Battalion, F Company, Corporal

NOVEMBER 23, 1918–FEBRUARY 26, 1945—Battle of Iwo Jima, Iwo Jima

Glen Bixby wrote to his family on August 30, 1944, from Camp Pendleton, California:

Dear Folks, Yes, I am still here in the continental U.S.A.- surprised? So am I! Today we had a "shoving off" parade. Quite a colorful event to say the least! The whole regiment was dressed in starched khaki. I wish that you could have seen us pass in review marching to band music. It gives you a thrill that is really unexplainable. We have a half grown lion cub for our mascot. Of course, he commands lots of attention. We also had a large inspection today. Outside of that, we have done considerable waiting for the ship. The majority of our equipment is packed so we haven't much to work with. Mother, will you do me a favor? Fine! Send the best one of my "dress blues" photos to this address: Miss Doris Vanderwall, 1700 University Avenue, St. Paul, Minnesota. Be sure that there are no markings on the photo. I expect to keep this photo in the family – if you get what I mean? Mother, I'm in love. I never was more sure of anything in my life. I've only been with her two short weekends and I can't get her off my mind even if I wanted to. Get ready for a daughter-in-law with dancing brown eyes when this war is over. O.K. Chuck, quench that chuckle. Love, Glen[1]

A month later, Glen Bixby left Miss Doris in California and headed for Hawaii with the "Fighting Fifth" Division to prepare for the assault on Iwo Jima, an 8-square-mile volcanic island located just 700 miles from Tokyo. Following the capture of Saipan and Tinian airfields in July 1944, American B-29s could now reach Japan, but Iwo Jima used their two airfields for attacks on Saipan and Tinian. Later described by Lieutenant General Holland Smith as the "most savage and costly battle in the history of the Marine Corps," the battle for Iwo Jima pitted 3 marine divisions against 21,000 well-entrenched Japanese defenders.

For 72 days American bombers pounded Iwo Jima, followed by 3 days of continuous naval bombardment. Then, early on February 19, 1945, the 4th and 5th marine divisions moved ashore. Veterans of Saipan, Tinian, and Peleliu, the seasoned soldiers climbed the steep beach in a strange quiet. Once the beach was filled with troops and equipment, all hopes that the pre-invasion bombardment had destroyed the enemy's defenses were quickly dashed. The Japanese, hidden in underground tunnels and bunkers, unleashed their fire on the men struggling onto the beach. Japanese Commander Kuribayashi ordered his men to make it their duty to: *kill ten of the enemy before dying.*

During the intense fire, Corporal Glen Bixby and the 28th Marines started their advance across the island to surround Mt. Suribachi on the southern tip of Iwo Jima, and by nightfall, they successfully isolated Suribachi from the rest of the island.[3, 4, 5] On February 21, the 28th rolled forward to the very foot of the mountain where Corporal Bixby was wounded, dying five days later. Bixby and many of his comrades were buried at the foot of Mt. Suribachi.

The 28th Marines remain famous for the most celebrated photo in World War II—Raising of the Flag on Iwo Jima—on top of Mt. Suribachi. when on February 23, the 28th Marines managed to surround Mt. Suribachi. Corporal Charles Lindberg remembered February 23: *We found a water pipe, tied the flag to it and put it up. Then all hell broke loose below. Troops cheered, ships blew horns and whistle, and some men openly wept. It was a sight to behold…something a man doesn't forget.*

Shortly after raising the flag, Colonel Chandler Johnson ordered the men to put up a larger flag: *. . . large enough that the men at the other end of the island will see it. It will lift their spirits also.*

By March 25, Americans held the island, but at great cost. In the end, the Japanese lost their entire force on Iwo Jima, but not before killing nearly 6,000 marines, 5 times the number of dead on Guadalcanal or Saipan and a third of all the marines killed in the Pacific.

Corporal Glen Bixby, son of Jacob and Emma (Bjornstad) Bixby, was survived by his parents, two brothers and two sisters. He enlisted in the marines on February 19, 1943. Corporal Glen Bixby was reinterred in Fort Snelling National Cemetery on April 26, 1948.

Steven Duerre remembers his uncle: *My mother, Rosalie, who was Glen's sister, passed away this August. He was the oldest and she was the second so they were very close. She adored him. The whole family did. Everyone expected great things from him and the whole family was devastated when he was taken at such a young age. They always spoke of him with such reverence that he has achieved almost legendary status among us who were not yet born and never had the chance to meet him. My middle name is Glen.*[6]

Palmer Clarence Ringstad

Gully (Polk County)

10th Armored "Tiger" Division, 11th Tank Battalion, C Company, Technician Fifth Grade
FEBRUARY 20, 1916–MARCH 5, 1945—Crossing the Rhine River, Germany

Richard Berg wrote about his Uncle Palmer Ringstad: *He was my mother's oldest brother. Uncle Palmer was born to Mabel (Dahl) and Alfred Ringstad on February 20, 1916, the oldest of eight children. The family lived in various places around northern Minnesota, mainly in the Gully, Gonvick and Clearbrook areas. Palmer grew up in a farming family and worked for the neighbors as soon as he was old enough to work. He was drafted into the army following the attack on Pearl Harbor and posted to the 10th Armored Division. The first US Army Division shipped to the European theatre and the 10th Armored Division landed directly in Cherbourg, Normandy, France without stopping in Great Britain. The division trained for a short time before being turned loose on the Nazi Germany war machine.*

The 10th Division was attached to fight in the Battle of the Bulge in Bastogne, Belgium, and following a brief rest, the division crossed into Trier, Germany on March 2, 1945. After crossing the Moselle River, they turned up a rather narrow valley in the mountainous regions and were restricted to stay in a single column. While harassed by German troops left behind to slow down the advancing US Army units, Uncle Palmer's tank was struck by a shot from a 88 mm gun and the whole crew perished. Palmer was buried in Belgium and later returned to the family and was reinterred in Lund Lutheran Cemetery in Gully, Minnesota. Uncle Palmer is still held in the hearts of the whole family.[1]

On March 10, 1945, the operations directive issued by the Headquarters Third Army confirms Richard Berg's story: *On 11 February 1945, 3rd U.S. Army attacked and cleared the Saar-Moselle triangle. Then without pause, the attack was continued across the Saar River and north to the capture of Trier by the 10th Armored Division on 2 March 1945. Meanwhile, other elements of 3rd Army were continuing the attack north of the Moselle to Coblenz.*

Multiple armored task forces had surrounded Trier and Mosel so quickly that defenses around the city collapsed on the second day of the assault, trapping 3,000 German soldiers and their commander. The action earned them a visit and congratulations from Generals Eisenhower and Patton. As the 10th continued their advance into Bavaria, they overran one of the many subcamps of the Dachau concentration camp in the Landsberg area on April 27, 1945. The U.S. Army's Center of Military History and the

United States Holocaust Memorial Museum recognized the 10th Armored Division as a liberating unit in 1985. As the 10th Division neared Innsbruck, Austria, on April 30, they were relieved from duty before the German surrender May 8, 1945.[2,3]

Technician Fifth Grade Palmer C. Ringstad entered the service in November 1942. Survivors included his parents and seven siblings.

Funeral services for Palmer Ringstad were held at Lund Lutheran Church, Gully, Minnesota, with the Gully American Legion Post and Auxiliary in charge.[4]

John William Parker

Kerrick (Pine County)

U.S. Marine Corps, 5th Marine "Fighting Fifth" Division, 27th Marine Regiment, 2nd Battalion, F Company, Private First Class

MAY 9, 1920– MARCH 6, 1945—Battle of Iwo Jima, Iwo Jima

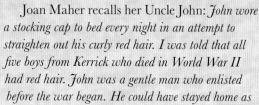

Joan Maher recalls her Uncle John: *John wore a stocking cap to bed every night in an attempt to straighten out his curly red hair. I was told that all five boys from Kerrick who died in World War II had red hair. John was a gentle man who enlisted before the war began. He could have stayed home as he was his mother's only means of support but a strong sense of duty compelled him to enlist. He belonged to an elite marine division called the Marine Raiders, similar to today's Navy Seals. John's mother told the family that John "helped raise the first flag on Iwo Jima."*[1]

John Parker enlisted October 13, 1941, and joined the Marine Raiders, activated from 1942 to 1944 for special operations forces operating behind enemy lines in the Pacific. When the Raiders were redesignated in 1944, John, diagnosed with malaria, returned home for a final furlough in November 1944 to attend his father's funeral.[2] Just two months later, Private First Class John Parker and the 27th Marines received their first combat assignment as a unit: the invasion of Iwo Jima, a small island 700 miles from Japan known only for its sulphur deposits. The capture of Iwo Jima's two airfields, which were being used to attack American-held Saipan would provide an excellent base for Allied fighter planes.

On February 19, 1945, the 27th Marines stormed ashore Iwo Jima through ankle-deep volcanic ash with orders to isolate Mt. Suribachi from the rest of the island. Despite fierce resistance from Japanese soldiers concealed in underground shelters, the marines pushed inland. As the 28th Marines surrounded Mt. Suribachi, the 27th and others took Airfield 1. Ordered to move north to continue the attack with their sister units, the marines advanced slowly as they faced rugged terrain and heavy enemy fire from the Japanese, who were deeply entrenched in a network of tunnels and caves. Hidden underground from air and artillery bombardment, the enemy would pop up in unexpected places during close combat. Only bazookas, grenades and flamethrowers could remove them from the underground network.[3, 4]

As the marines prepared for another assault on the Japanese on March 6, the day that Private First Class John Parker died of wounds, Private Dale Worley wrote in his diary: *There is a quiet deadly stillness in the air, the tension is strong, everyone is waiting. Some will die–how many, no one knows. God knows, enough have died already.*[3]

The After Action Report for March 6, 1945, reflects the tenacity of the Japanese: *The day's pre-assault bombardment was one of the heaviest so far in the battle for Iwo Jima with some 132 guns firing some 22,500 shells in just over an hour. Added to that, a battleship, a cruiser, and three destroyers added some 450 shells while Corsairs and Dauntless carried out ground attacks with bombs and napalm. The assault was staggered with the 5th Marine Division in the west attacked at 0800 while the 4th Marine Division in the east attacked at 0900. Resistance was as strong as ever. The 27th Marines (5th Division) and 21st Marines (3rd Division) attacked in the west but soon ran into trouble despite being supported by flamethrower tanks. An element of the 21st Marines led by Lieutenant William Mulvey reached the top of another ridge, to see what General Schmidt had been after for so long: the sea. The ocean was no more than a quarter of a mile away but the Japanese decided to remind the Americans that a quarter of a mile could still be a long way by pinning them down with mortar and machine gun fire. Although reinforcements tried to get through they were beaten back and Mulvey and his group had to wait until later in the day until they could make their way back to their lines. The day had seen advances of on average, around 200 yards, the best being 350 yards.*[3]

On March 16, Iwo Jima was declared secure, although resistance continued for another two months. The 27th Marine Regiment alone lost 566 men killed and another 1,703 wounded. The 27th Marines returned to Camp Tarawa in April to prepare for the invasion of Japan, but after the Japanese surrender, they ended up sailing there in September for occupation duty.[3, 4]

Private First Class John Parker was buried at the 5th Marine Division Cemetery, Kazan Retto, Iwo Jima, and reinterred in 1948 in Fort Snelling National Cemetery. The son of David and Myrtle Parker, survivors included his mother; two brothers and a sister. Private First Class John Parker's brother-in-law, Sergeant Rolland Rowe (page 44) from Kerrick, died on June 1, 1944, in Italy.[2]

Henry Martin Hunkins

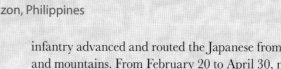

6th Infantry "Sightseeing Sixth" Division, 63rd Infantry Regiment, 1st Battalion, A Company, Staff Sergeant

JULY 21, 1917–MARCH 7, 1945—Battle for Luzon, Philippines

In 1942, after Japanese forces captured Luzon, the largest island in the Philippines, General Douglas MacArthur vowed, "I came through and I shall return" as he left it. MacArthur, who was in charge of defense in the Philippines, had to wait two years to fulfill his promise.

In December 1944, American forces secured the island of Leyte, followed by Mindoro, and later, Luzon.

On January 9, 1945, Staff Sergeant Henry Hunkins and the 6th Infantry Division landed at Lingayen Gulf, Luzon, to face General Yamashita and 250,000 experienced Japanese who were determined to defend the Philippines in order to prevent an Allied invasion of Japan. That morning the 43rd and 37th Infantry Divisions joined the 6th Division for a massive amphibious landing in the Pacific. Following hours of fierce naval bombardment, the Americans landed unopposed on the beaches of Lingayan Gulf.

As the 6th Division moved toward Manila, their main objective, Staff Sergeant Henry Hunkins and the 63rd Infantry Regiment were engaged in what became known by the men as the "Purple Heart Valley Campaign," by the men. Around 8,000 Japanese soldiers were hidden in tunnels and caves in the hills south of the Damortis-Rosario highway. Combat ensued, and from January 10 to 31, the 63rd suffered 489 casualties, 103 killed, and the Japanese lost 971 men.[1,2,3]

After securing the town of Munoz, the 20th Infantry Regiment and the 63rd drove east toward the coast, dividing Japanese forces. There, the 6th Division liberated the horrific Cabanatuan Prison Camp and completed their mission to recapture the Bataan Peninsula. Now the Division's regiments reunited on the Shimbu Line east of Manila where another 14,000 Japanese troops, hidden in caves, "were determined to fight to the death."[1]

On February 20, Staff Sergeant Hunkins and the 6th Infantry Division moved into the rolling hills east of Manila to capture the dams in the north Marikina Valley. As the unit traversed the valley, the troops ran into trouble in the hills, where Japanese waited with machine guns. The assault on Mt. Pacawagan stagnated near the crest on March 4, as the day and night battles ground on. On March 7, Staff Sergeant Henry Hunkins was killed near Montalban, Luzon, from shrapnel to the chest. Finally on March 8, the infantry advanced and routed the Japanese from their positions in the hills and mountains. From February 20 to April 30, more than 6,500 Americans died, including 107 from the 6th Division.[1,2,3]

Staff Sergeant Henry M. Hunkins, son of Sargent and Agnes (Connally) Hunkins, is buried at Manila American Cemetery, Manila, Philippines. A memorial stone in St. Mary's Cemetery, Breckinridge, Minnesota, honors his memory.

Staff Sergeant Henry Hunkins was awarded the Bronze Star and the Purple Heart. Survivors included his father, stepmother Mary, and two half-siblings. His mother died when he was only a year old.

Jim Gowin interviewed his father, Clarence, who married one of Henry's sisters: *My dad served in the Army. He really didn't know Henry too well. He met him once before he went to war and then while in New Guinea he got a call from Henry. He was on a ship that would be in port for a while and they got together for a two-hour visit. Henry was in the infantry and was shot about three months after that visit. Henry was not married. We don't have a photo or an obituary and don't know anything about his personal life.[4]*

Clarence Robert Lehner

Nimrod (Wadena County)

4th Infantry "Ivy" Division, 22nd Infantry Regiment, Private
NOVEMBER 7, 1925–MARCH 7, 1945—Rhineland Campaign, Germany

Jessica Wilson recalls her great uncle Clarence: *Clarence graduated from Sebeka High School in the spring of 1944, and enlisted or drafted by September. In January, he came home on a two-week leave from training. He was based in Kentucky, I believe. His leave was cut short when his orders arrived at the family farm saying he was headed overseas. He died March 7, 1945 at age 19. Originally, he was buried in an American Cemetery in Luxemburg, Germany. When the war ended, his mother requested that his body be returned home and he was buried at Fort Snelling on September 11, 1948.*[1]

When the war ended on May 8, 1945, the 4th Infantry Division had participated in all campaigns from Normandy Beach through Germany. By the time Clarence Lehner left his furlough on the family farm in January 1945 for duty overseas, the 4th had already battled through D-Day, the Hürtgen Forest and the Battle of the Bulge. After the Germans were stopped in Belgium on January 26, the Ivy Division continued to chase the Germans, who were now in full retreat, from Belgium. As they crossed the border, the 4th captured several German villages, while the 22nd Infantry Regiment took Brandscheid, a village that survived all previous attacks. Through rain, snow and mud, the 22nd pushed deeper and deeper into Germany where the Germans fought and retreated as each village fell to the Allies.[2]

Heavy enemy resistance temporarily stopped the 4th Division at the Prum River, but on February 9, the 8th Infantry Regiment broke through German fire and crossed the river. Just two days later, Private Clarence Lehner and the 22nd Infantry Regiment took the village of Prum. On March 7, the division moved quickly to the Kyll River, where Private Lehner was killed during the river advance and crossing near Scheuern, Germany.[2,3]

Robert Babcock relays the events of the 22nd Infantry Regiment on March 7, 1945: *There were no enemy lines established during the period. Our troops were opposed by rear guard elements. A determined resistance was put up by the enemy along the east bank of the Kyll River, and it was not until late in the period that our troops were able to dislodge the opposition from these positions. The 4th Infantry Division captured the towns of Dohn, Bolsdorf, Bewingen and Killescheid. Progress was impeded by lack of adequate bridging facilities across the Kyll River. The 3rd Battalion of the 22nd Infantry crossed during the night 6-7 March, the Kyll River in the vicinity of Ober Bettingen and relieved elements of the 11th Armored Division. The battalion received a slight counterattack after completion of the relief but repulsed it quickly. The 1st Battalion and the 2nd Battalion effected their crossing. During the hours of darkness, 6-7 March, Company E of the 2nd Battalion occupied the town of Hillesheim.*[4]

Clarence Lehner entered the army on September 9, 1944, soon after high school graduation. Survivors included his parents and nine siblings.

Melvin Daniels remembers a story told by Clarence's mother, Clara: *As a child, Clarence was very caring. One winter, he found a squirrel's nest where a squirrel was hibernating for the winter. He brought the squirrel into the house, warmed it up, and took it back to the nest. Later, when he believed the squirrel was cold again, he would bring the squirrel back into the house.*[1]

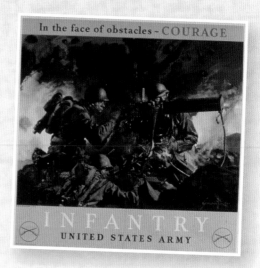

In the face of obstacles - COURAGE

INFANTRY
UNITED STATES ARMY

Milton Otto Stoll

6th Infantry "Sightseeing Sixth" Division, 1st Infantry Regiment, H Company, Medical Detachment, Technician Fifth Grade

AUGUST 15, 1912–MARCH 16, 1945—Luzon Campaign, Philippines

Milton Stoll joined the military on February 10, 1941, as an original member of Hutchinson, Minnesota's 135th Infantry Regiment, B Company. When Technician Fifth Grade Stoll transferred to the 1st Infantry Regiment, he joined one of the first armies in the United States. Organized in 1791, just three years after the adoption of the Constitution, the 1st Infantry Regiment participated in all major wars from the War of 1812 to World War 1. In 1939, the 1st Infantry became part of the 6th Infantry Division and brought with them the motto, *Semper Primus*—"Always First."[1, 2]

Historian Thomas Price describes their first camp on February 2, 1944, in Milne Bay, New Guinea: *The Division set up camp on a palm tree plantation owned by the Palmolive Palm Oil Company. The men were told that they would be fined if they cut down the trees.* But Japanese snipers in the trees put an end to that order.[1]

The division cleared the jungle and pitched their tents 12 inches above ground to keep out rain, mud and to avoid the organisms carrying deadly scrub typhus, dengue fever, malaria, yellow fever and elephantiasis. Battling the environment on New Guinea proved to be a close second to battling the Japanese. Technician Fifth Grade Milton Stoll, trained as a medic, treated jungle diseases and administered first aid to wounded soldiers, often under direct fire. Although Geneva Convention stipulated that no one fire on a medic while treating a wounded man, the Japanese targeted medics.[1]

As the 6th Infantry Division fought their way through New Guinea, Technical 5 Stoll survived two serious battle wounds. On January 9, 1945, he arrived with the 6th on Lingayen Gulf, Luzon, to spearhead the drive for the liberation of Manila, the "Pearl of the Orient." *The 6th Infantry Division in World War II* describes the robust defensive system that the Japanese, led by Lieutenant General Yokoyama Shizuo, prepared on the Shimbu Line. Forced Filipino labor carved caves and pillboxes into the hills of the Sierra Madre, which overlooked exposed, flat rice fields. A series of peaks—Mt. Oro, Mt. Pacawagan, Mt. Mataba and Mt. Batytangan—stood in the way of U.S. forces as they advanced toward Manila, 12 miles away.

On March 8, a new tactical plan called for a push through the center of the Shimbu Line by the 1st Infantry; this attack followed two days of artillery shelling to support the four battalions. A pattern emerged over the next few weeks as the men would attack Japanese positions in the ridges during the daytime, then retreat to a fortified position after dark. Banzai attacks destroyed their sleep nearly every night, as the Japanese struggled desperately to hold their ground despite heavy losses during these attacks.[3]

During the assault on the Shimbu Line, Technician Fifth Grade Milton Stoll, Medical Corpsman, was shot while attending to a wounded soldier. On March 16, he died of wounds at the 2nd Battalion Aid Station, Bayanbayanan, Rizal, Luzon.[4] Memorial services were held Sunday, May 6, at St. John's Lutheran Church in Cedar Mills, with burial in Emanuel Lutheran Cemetery, Fairfax, Minnesota. Survivors included his parents, his wife Reva (Kidd) Stoll, whom he married on November 14, 1942, and four siblings. His wife, Reva, remarried Berlin Walsh in 1946.[5, 6]

Frank Leopold Leitner

5th Infantry "Red Diamond" Division, 11th Infantry Regiment, 1st Battalion, B Company, Private First Class

DECEMBER 16, 1923–MARCH 23, 1945—Rhineland Campaign, Germany

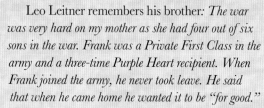

Leo Leitner remembers his brother: *The war was very hard on my mother as she had four out of six sons in the war. Frank was a Private First Class in the army and a three-time Purple Heart recipient. When Frank joined the army, he never took leave. He said that when he came home he wanted it to be "for good."*

Unfortunately, he never made it back home. He died of wounds received in action in the Rhine Valley in Germany on March 23, 1945, at age 28. He had a burial ceremony at the American Cemetery at Stromberg, Germany, and then his body was brought to France for burial at the U.S. Military Cemetery. In 2006, one of our sisters, Ann, was diagnosed with cancer and was dying. The Make-a-Wish Foundation wanted to grant her a wish. Her wish was to have Frank's body brought back home to be buried with his parents in McGrath. The Foundation was unable to fulfill the wish of bringing his body back home, but did have a headstone made and placed next to his parent's stone in the McGrath Cemetery. [1]

On July 9, 1944, the 5th Infantry Division and Private First Class Frank Leitner landed on Utah Beach, where they began their advance across 700 miles in France. They successfully fought their way though Vidouville and Angers, crossed the Seine in August at Fontainebleau, and then crossed the Marne to seize Reims at the end of August.

In September, the 5th Division, under the command of General Patton, prepared for the assault on Metz, a city in northeast France located between the rivers Moselle and Seille, by building a bridgehead across the Moselle, south of Metz.[3,4] Frank wrote home from "somewhere in France" on September 25, 1944: *Dear Folks, Just a few lines to let you know I am in the hospital and am getting along o.k. I only had a pain in the chest, which they call pleurisy so it wasn't a jerry that sent me here anyway. The nearest I came to getting hurt while up front was one time I was digging myself a hole and I wasn't near finished yet when some shells came over so I laid as flat as I could but a shell landed less than five feet along side of me about in line with my heels. One piece of shrapnel cut a slit in my hind pocket, another made about a five inch slit in my shirt just above my belt, and the third one made two holes in my shirt and one hole in my undershirt and scratched my skin by my shoulder blade just enough to give me a purple heart. I felt like it hit pretty hard but after the medic put a patch on it and told me how bad it was, I was good as new again...That's about all I know for this time so I'll close hoping to hear from you*

again soon. As always, Frank[1]

Metz finally fell in November after a hard-fought ten-day battle. After a period of relative calm, Patton's Third Army rushed north to meet the German Ardennes Offensive of December 16th. Following the collapse of the German offensive, a rapid advance kept German forces on the run, and by March 21 the 5th Division reached the Rhine River. In five days Patton's army captured 68,000 German prisoners. As Allied forces gathered in massive numbers on the west bank of the Rhine, the Germans knew the invasion into Germany was unstoppable. General Patton, who had been told to wait until British General Montgomery prepared for a crossing, did not have orders to cross the Rhine. Nevertheless, on March 22, 1945, assault boats carrying Private First Class Frank Leitner and the 5th Division silently shoved off from the bank of the Rhine River at Nierstein and Oppenheim. Under the command of 1st Lieutenant William Randle, Private Leitner and B Company were part of the first battalion to reach the east bank in spite of heavy resistance. The Rhine crossing was a tribute to the courage of these riflemen who paddled 800 feet into the thick of enemy fire. Within 30 minutes the battle was over, and the Third Army entered the final phase of the war through Germany.[2,3,4]

On April 7, 1945, Colonel Paul J. Black, 11th Infantry Commander, wrote to Frank's mother: *Frank was with his company on a river crossing when he was hit by small arms fire. He was evacuated to a hospital where expert surgeons did everything humanly possible for him.*[5,6]

Private First Class Frank L. Leitner, son of Frank Josef and Johanna K. (Mehlstaub) Leitner, is buried at Saint-Avold Cemetery, France. He was survived by his parents and nine siblings. His family remembers him as a gentle, sensitive man who they believe would have struggled with battle memories had he survived the war.[1,7]

Cecil Raymond Stevenson

Effie (Itasca County)

Seventh Army, 12th Armored "Hellcats" Division, 92nd Cavalry Reconnaissance Squadron, Troop C, Technician Fifth Grade

SEPTEMBER 15, 1921–MARCH 22, 1945—The Drive to the Rhine, Germany

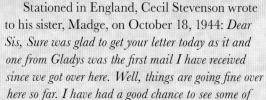

Stationed in England, Cecil Stevenson wrote to his sister, Madge, on October 18, 1944: *Dear Sis, Sure was glad to get your letter today as it and one from Gladys was the first mail I have received since we got over here. Well, things are going fine over here so far. I have had a good chance to see some of this part of England the past week as I was lucky enough to be among the few to take a couple of short trips. Both of them combined added to a little over 300 miles. The strangest thing that I have seen is that almost all the people ride bicycles. It is nothing to see a 50- or 60-year-old man or woman riding along. No matter how big or how small, they all make out. The trains are almost midgets according to what ours are in the U.S., but they really ride comfortable. Never a jerk or a bump. If you want to send me something, please send some candy. That's the only thing I can think of that the army doesn't have plenty of. Sis, I have a few words I want to write you and don't know exactly how to go about it but I will try. It has always been on my mind that something might happen to Gladys and that our baby would be alright. I want to be sure that he is taken care of until I get back. If something should happen, would you get him and keep him until I can take care of him? Please don't say anything of this so that Gladys would hear of it but don't you think it is better to be prepared? Time is really flying by now and the nearer it gets the more I think about her. The one comfort I have is to know that she has the best of medical care right there. Must close for now. Please answer soon. Love, Your Brother, Cecil*[1, 2]

Three weeks after writing to his sister, Cecil Stevenson and the 12th Armored Division arrived at Le Havre, France, on November 11, 1944, and began their advance across France, which was interrupted by the Battle of the Bulge. In March 1945, the 12th Armored Division prepared to drive the enemy across the Rhine River and deep into the heart of Germany. While held in reserve in Saint-Avold, France, from March 1 to 17, Technician Fifth Grade Cecil Stevenson and the 92nd Cavalry Reconnaissance Squadron maintained a protective screen west of the Saar River and south of the Maginot Line. However, in the middle of the night on March 17, the 12th Division received surprise new orders to join Patton's Third Army. For the second half of the month, the Seventh Army temporarily transferred the 12th Armored to Patton's Third Army to assist his drive into Germany to capture the Rhine cities of Ludwigshafen, Speyer and Germersheim. General Patton nicknamed the 12th the "Mystery Division," and ordered the soldiers to remove all identifying vehicle markings and 12th Armored patches. Officers wore Third Army insignias, as intelligence did not want the enemy to know that Patton had an additional armored division under his command, and Patton wanted the officers to know they were now in his army.[3, 4, 5, 6]

After completing the move to Patton's Army under strict security, Patton ordered the division to race to the Rhine River and seize all intact bridges. On the way to the Rhine, the speed and power of the 12th advance caught the Germans by surprise and thousands of German soldiers were captured along with their equipment and territory. Moving rapidly at 25 miles per day, prisoners were merely disarmed and told to keep walking toward the rear until some one picked them up. Only a route littered with abandoned German equipment, including Volkswagens and Tiger tanks, delayed the "Hellcats."[7]

Orders were followed to: *Keep going. When you hit the Rhine, search for a bridge intact at Ludwigshafen.* The 92nd spearheaded the division and closed in on Kleinkarlbach on March 20. The next day, they attacked the city of Speyer, a city of 50,000 on the Rhine River, and seized the city on March 24. During the attack on Speyer while riding in an armored scout car, Technician Fifth Grade Cecil Stevenson was killed when a mortar shell hit the vehicle.[6, 7]

In 1949, Technician Fifth Grade Cecil Stevenson was reinterred in Diehl Cemetery, previously part of his grandmother's farm, in Woodburn, Indiana. Survivors included his father, Vernon, and step-mother, Ella; his wife Gladys; a two-month-old daughter, Florence; and eight siblings. His mother, Amy, died in 1926. Cecil entered the service on November 12, 1942.[2]

Robert Edwin Horne

McGrath (Aitkin County)

Seventh Army, 12th Armored "Hellcats" Division, 56th Armored Infantry Battalion, C Company,
Private First Class

JANUARY 30, 1925–MARCH 23, 1945—Crossing the Rhine River, Germany

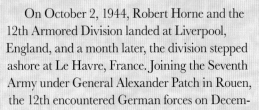

On October 2, 1944, Robert Horne and the 12th Armored Division landed at Liverpool, England, and a month later, the division stepped ashore at Le Havre, France. Joining the Seventh Army under General Alexander Patch in Rouen, the 12th encountered German forces on December 5 at Weisslinger and reached the Maginot Line two days later. After rolling through Rohrbach, Bettviller and Utweiler, Germany, the 12th Division attacked Herlisheim, a German post established during Operation Nordwind. Their efforts on January 8 were stopped by heavy fire, but another attempt on January 9 took a portion of the town. Numerous counterattacks against the depleted division, culminating on January 18, also failed. The division left and met French forces south of Colmar on February 5, and in a "lightning drive," successfully cut off Colmar and crushed German forces in the Vosges Mountains.

On March 17, 1945, the 12th Armored Division secretly transferred from the Seventh Army to General George Patton's Third Army to assist with the crossing of the Rhine River.[1,2] 2nd Lieutenant Elmer Bright wrote that "Mystery Division" soldiers were ordered to remove or paint over all unit markings on their vehicles, and officers were to wear their rank and Third Army insignia in plain view. This order disguised the fact that Patton had an additional tank division in the Third, and "Old George Patton wanted all officers to know they were now in Patton's Army."[3] As Private First Class Robert Horne and the 56th Armored Infantry Battalion led the Third Army toward the Rhine River, Bright wrote on March 20th: *We jumped off on the attack from Trier and headed for the Rhine River. It just so happened that the so-called elements of CCB were the 56th Armored Infantry Battalion, the first unit of the entire Third Army to reach the Rhine. We had raced down the Autobahn all night to finally enter Ludwigshafen on the Rhine.*

While the 56th advanced to the Rhine River, without any knowledge of what was ahead or on either side, the Germans retreated toward the Rhine and tried to cross the river. As the soldiers moved toward the river in their half-track, 2nd Lieutenant Bright continues: *We were ordered to pull back from the river and happened to halt near a large factory where there were many Polish displaced persons working. In a section of the battalion headquarters, there was a communications*

Sergeant named Henry Figurski who spoke the language. The Polish workers informed Henry this was a fruit-canning factory and there were large stores of canned peaches, pears, plums and other fruit locked away under the buildings. So we proceeded to remove the locks and remove cases of canned fruit. Everyone enjoyed the fruit to the fullest extent, but it had been a long time since we had eaten such sweet fruit in syrup. You can imagine the result of this binge; the latrines were visited more frequently for the next few days.[3]

After parking the half-tracks around a large mess hall near the factory, the 56th Battalion decided to stretch out on the tables in the mess hall. Their rest was brief, however, as all hell broke loose when the Luftwaffe attacked with machine guns and cannon fire falling through the roof. Elmer Bright continues: *Our real mission as a division was to find an intact bridge over the Rhine for General Patton who was itching to get a bridge like the Ninth Army had gotten at Remagen before it was blown. I think the closest that we came was at Speyer when we heard the bridge being blown when we were a very short distance away. The Germans had left a lot of troops on our side of the river and we had quite a fight to finally capture Speyer.*[3]

During the attack on Speyer, Private First Class Robert Horne died on March 23 from a shotgun wound to the thigh and abdomen.[4] The next day, the Allies secured the ancient cathedral city of Speyer, chief community of the Bavarian Palatinate, after a rough fight. On March 28, the 12th Armored Division crossed the Rhine River at Worms and near the end of April, they witnessed the horror of Nazi atrocities as they began the daunting task of liberating Nazi concentration camps, including Hurlag, Landsberg and Dachau.[1,2]

Robert Horne, born in Los Angeles, California, joined the Army on July 21, 1944, and trained at Camp Hood, Texas, for 17 weeks. Survivors included his mother, Neita (Roy) Sower; his father, Reginald Horne; and one sister, Delores. On May 27, 1945, a joint memorial service was held at Calvary Presbyterian Church in McGrath for Private First Class Robert Horne and his good friend, Private First Class Ira Bashore (page 143), who died a month later in Bad-Worishofen, Germany. At the request of their mothers, the men were buried side by side in Fort Snelling Cemetery.[4,5]

Elmer Willhelm Kittelson

Strandquist (Marshall County)

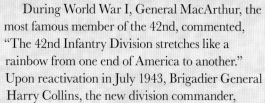

Seventh Army, 42nd Infantry "Rainbow" Division, 232nd Infantry Regiment, 3rd Battalion, I Company, Technician Fourth Grade

FEBRUARY 14, 1913–MARCH 25, 1945—Allied Invasion of Germany

During World War I, General MacArthur, the most famous member of the 42nd, commented, "The 42nd Infantry Division stretches like a rainbow from one end of America to another." Upon reactivation in July 1943, Brigadier General Harry Collins, the new division commander, echoed General MacArthur's sentiments, "The rainbow represents the people of our country." Once again, the 42nd would represent all of America, made up of men selected from each state in proportion to its population.[1] One of the men selected from Minnesota, Elmer Kittelson, grew up in Strandquist, located in the northwestern corner of the state. On April 29, 1942, Elmer entered basic training at Fort Lewis, Washington, and worked as a cook during his entire enlistment. Technician Fourth Grade Kittelson transferred to the 42nd Infantry Division in June 1944, at Camp Gruber near Muskogee, Oklahoma, before heading overseas.[2]

The 42nd, soon to be called Task Force Linden, landed in Marseilles, France, on December 8, 1944, and set up a tent camp in a storm. When the Germans launched the Battle of the Bulge, *Task Force Linden* (composed of three regiments: the 222nd, 232nd and 242nd) traveled by truck to positions in the Alsace area on the west side of the Rhine River, just north of Strasbourg, France. Elmer wrote to his sister in December: *Dear Agnes, I received your letter the day before yesterday and was glad to hear from home. In fact I have got all the letters now that you folks have written. Well I am here in France and the people are very nice to us they take us in to their homes and treat us so nice. It makes one feel so at home when someone does that for you. Well I must close now hoping this letter finds you all fine. Love from Elmer*[3]

In wet, cold and miserable weather, the 42nd relieved the 36th Infantry Division just two days before Christmas. Technician Fourth Grade Elmer Kittelson and the 232nd Regiment were ordered to defend a sector stretching 22 miles along the Rhine against veteran German paratroops and Panzer forces. That placed one soldier for every 40 feet, a very thin defensive force with no reserves. Fighting in the worst winter weather in 50 years, foxholes offered no protection against frostbite.[1] On January 26, 1945, Elmer wrote another letter to his sister: *Dear Agnes, I will drop you a few lines today to let you know I am just fine and feeling good every day. I will also mention that I got the box of candy you*

sent me. It was very good and I want to thank you all a lot for it. It is kind of cold here in France now but we have plenty of good clothes to use so the cold ain't hurting us any. I am doing the same kind of work as I have first doing and will continue to do so. In your next letter Agnes please tell me if you can read it or should I write large and plain. That will be all for this time. Write soon. Love from Elmer[3]

As the 42nd Division advanced through France and the Hardt Mountains, they moved into dugouts in the Hürtgen Forest. On March 15, the entire Allied front launched an attack that broke through the Siegfried Line and carried them over the Rhine into Germany. His niece, Corriene Jacobson, recalls her mom's story: *I remember my mom telling me that my Uncle Elmer, a cook for his company, left camp to look for firewood to make the meal and stepped on a land mine.*[3] Elmer Kittelson died from wounds on March 25, 1945, at 132 Evacuation Hospital, Hagenau, France.[2, 4] As his division continued their advance through Germany in April, the "rainbow" soldiers captured Wurzburg, Schweinfurt, Nuremberg and Munich.

On April 29, 1945, the 42nd Infantry Division, along with the 45th Infantry Division and the 20th Armored Division, liberated the Dachau concentration camp, the original concentration camp in Nazi Germany. They discovered more than 30,000 prisoners near death in the overcrowded camp and several railroad cars stacked with dead bodies. As they approached the main gate, a German officer along with another German soldier and a Red Cross worker, stepped forward with a flag of truce. General Linden officially accepted the surrender of the camp in the name of the "Rainbow" Division for the U.S. Army. The 42nd Infantry Division was recognized as a liberating unit by the United States Holocaust Memorial Museum in 1985.[5]

Technician Fourth Grade Elmer Kittelson was survived by his mother and eight siblings. Kittelson was buried in Lorraine American Cemetery, Saint-Avold, France. A memorial marker resides in Marmrelund Cemetery, Marshall County, Minnesota.[2, 3]

Sigwald Martin Anderson

6th Infantry "Sightseeing Sixth" Division, 20th Infantry Regiment, 2nd Battalion, F Company, Private First Class

OCTOBER 10, 1908–MARCH 28, 1945—Battle for Luzon, Philippines

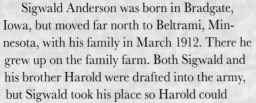

Sigwald Anderson was born in Bradgate, Iowa, but moved far north to Beltrami, Minnesota, with his family in March 1912. There he grew up on the family farm. Both Sigwald and his brother Harold were drafted into the army, but Sigwald took his place so Harold could stay home and take care of the farm. On June 3, 1941, Sigwald entered the service, and after basic training at Fort Leonard Wood, he was stationed at Little Rock, Nashville, Yuma and San Luis Obispo before arriving in Oahu, Hawaii, in September 1943. Following a stint in New Guinea and the Dutch East Indies, Private First Class Sigwald Anderson spent his last Christmas and New Year's Day on board a ship on the way to Luzon Island where the 6th Infantry Division faced their harshest campaign.[1]

Cracking the Shimbu Line, a heavily fortified line of defense 12 miles northeast of Manila, "proved particularly harsh and pitiless. The men fought around the clock and every night proved the power of the cult of Bushido as the Japanese launched banzai attacks."[2] The Japanese held strong defensive positions on Mt. Oro, Mt. Pacawagan, Mt. Mataba and Mt. Baytangan, all heavily wooded with weapons hidden everywhere. A member of the 20th Infantry Regiment and trained as a sniper, Private First Class Sigwald Anderson faced the same type of opposition as Technician Fifth Grade Milton Stoll (page 129) who also served there. The men of the 20th huddled in foxholes during the night to escape heavy artillery and repeated banzai charges, while by day they inched ahead, destroying enemy pillboxes and gaining ground, "one damn hill after another." By March 24, all three battalions, the 1st, 20th and 63rd, had reached their assigned areas on the southeast slope of Mt. Mataba and atop Mt. Baytangan.

On March 28, the 1st and 20th Infantries advanced slowly north, crossing ravines and climbing steep ridges to gain a few yards in their final drive against Mataba and Pacawagan. Again the men faced heavy enemy artillery, mortars and rockets, machine gun emplacements and repeated banzai attacks.[2,3] As Private First Class Sigwald Anderson and the 20th Infantry moved through the hill country to the base of Mt. Mataba, they dug in to escape enemy fire. That day, Private First Class Anderson was awarded the Bronze Star: *For heroic achievement in connection with military operations*

against the enemy in New Guinea. Without regard for his personal safety, he crawled under heavy enemy fire far beyond his own perimeter, assisted neutralizing enemy fire, which wounded one of his comrades and assisted in evacuating the wounded man to a place of safety. While rescuing his fellow soldier, a sniper shot Private First Class Anderson, who later died of his wounds.[4]

The 6th Division fought continuously for 112 days for the Shimbu Line, and lost 107 men with another 569 wounded. By June 12, 1945, the 6th Division had cleaned out the enemy in the Central Luzon area, securing Bataan and fulfilling General MacArthur's promise to return and recapture Bataan.[2,3]

While in the war, Sigwald carved "trench art" out of shell casings, a common pastime for soldiers who whittled away the hours while in the trenches. Before Christmas 1944, he wrote to his sister Lillian: *Dear Sis, Just a line, haven't anything to write and nothing to do. Been making a letter opener from a Jap 25 caliber shell and a strip of brass, and am sending it tonight to Gladys for Christmas. I sent Doreen a letter opener, a ring made from a shilling, and a cat eye that I shined up like a looking glass. A cat eye is a half round stone from some kind of a seashell. Some are brown, others are black, and the real nice ones are green. Running out of paper, so will sign off for this time, Sigwald.*[5]

The son of Andrew and Margaret (Iverson) Anderson, Sigwald is buried in Fort Snelling National Cemetery and memorialized at the Fertile Veterans Memorial, Fertile, Minnesota. Survivors included his parents and five siblings. Memorial services were held at Trinity Lutheran Church in Beltrami on Sunday, May 20, 1945. Sigwald Anderson American Legion Post 626 in Beltrami, Minnesota, is named in his honor.[1]

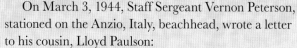

Vernon Russell Peterson

Sunburg (Kandiyohi County)

3rd Infantry Division "Rock of the Marne," 30th Infantry Regiment, 3rd Battalion, Medical Corps, Staff Sergeant

JULY 11, 1915–MARCH 26, 1945—Spearhead across the Rhine, Germany

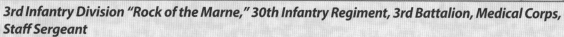

On March 3, 1944, Staff Sergeant Vernon Peterson, stationed on the Anzio, Italy, beachhead, wrote a letter to his cousin, Lloyd Paulson:

Dear Lloyd, At last I am permitted to tell you that I'm sitting on the Anzio beachhead. I guess the censors decided that since the Jerries know we're here, you might as well share the secret. Of course, nothing can be said about the fighting, but I can say that the fellows all have one eye cocked on Rome, which the right way will show you is not so far away. Mail started coming thru the very first week we were here. We were especially interested in seeing the Jan. issue of Life *magazine. In it the first six pages were devoted to sketches some artist made in our sector of the front during that 60-day grind last fall on the other side of the German's Winter Line. You'll learn more about the where and when of the outfit during the days by reading* Life *than I could ever put in a letter. As far as farm country is concerned, it is both good and bad depending on how much sympathy you have for the lot of a farmer caught in the middle of a battlefield. The farmer's livestock certainly has served us well on occasions. Every once in a while a chicken gets tangled up in barbed wire (tough break) or a cow steps on a land mine and we have a feast. Even at their toughest, a battlefield steak makes the mouth water.*

With the radio informing us that the third division is officially here ("enhancing our glory,") I think it safe to guess the old Rock of the Marne is getting a lion's share of newspaper space back in the States. While no one could ever accuse the G.I. of being prima donnish, and God knows nobody here'd ever say "enhancing glory" is any man's glamour job, we do like to read about ourselves. And the magazine or newspaper, which mentions the names of the Third or includes a photo of a dirt-stained doggy wearing our square blue and white striped patch, races thru the outfit like news of a victory. Speaking of newspaper pictures, we are easier to recognize now that we wear the patch on both sides of our helmets as well as on the left shoulder.

And speaking of….the happiest boys of the week were those who finally took off to the states on "rotation" for a month's furlough. The percentage is awfully small. So don't dream too much about me getting on the list for a long time to come. But somehow it helps just to touch a guy about to sail west over the Atlantic.

What's it like on our beachhead? Frankly, without revealing any secrets, it's quite like a night in hell. But then'll come a quiet spell and a flirtatious tank will rumble noisily down the road or one of my buddies will dig up a forgotten bottle of vino from some mud cellar and the world sits firmly on four legs again. And then there are those wonderful days where clear skies open up the way for our American big bombers. From our grandstand seats, we watch the show, wave after wave of them, horribly beautiful as they fly over us to pound the Krauts in the rear—where it hurts. Those airmen are never wholly real to us, slugging it out with the mud on the ground. They are part of another world—winged angels or devils, depending on whether they're hitting for or against us...My best wishes and good luck to you. Vernon[1]

After fighting their way through Tunisia, Sicily, Italy and southern France, the 30th Infantry Regiment, with Staff Sergeant Vernon Peterson in the Medical Corps, began the drive to break through the Siegfried Line, a fortified system of defense along the western border of Germany.[2] Historian James Dunigan describes their secret advance on March 15, 1945, from Nancy, a city in northeastern France, to be the first unit to breach the Siegfried Line. All vehicle numbers, shoulder patches and helmet markings were covered with adhesive.

Although slowed down by land mines, the regiment attacked through the Siegfried Line, and on March 20, the city of Zweibrucken fell. They advanced quickly to Worms, where the regiment crossed the Rhine on March 26, in the face of increased German artillery fire.[3] During the crossing, Staff Sergeant Vernon Peterson died, and a German citizen recovered his body weeks later in the Rhine River near Worms.

According to the Report of Investigation, the local burgermeister, a priest and an undertaker buried Staff Sergeant Peterson on June 3, 1945, in the cemetery in Nordheim, a city 3 miles northeast of Worms.[4] Staff Sergeant Vernon Peterson was reburied in American Military Cemetery, Saint-Avold, France, and reinterred in 1949 at West Norway Lake Cemetery, Sunburg, Minnesota.

Survivors included his parents, Elling J. and Molly (Jorgenson) Peterson, of Sunburg and three siblings; two brothers preceded him in death.

Jerald Ira Tongen

Hazel Run (Yellow Medicine County)

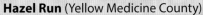

40th Infantry "Sunshine" Division, 185th Infantry Regiment, 2nd Battalion, G Company, Staff Sergeant
OCTOBER 19, 1918–APRIL 9, 1945—Battle of the Visayas, Philippines

On January 9, 1945, Staff Sergeant Jerald Tongen and the 185th Infantry Regiment along with the 160th Infantry Regiment, landed on Lingayen Beach on Luzon, Philippine Islands. After securing Lingayen Airfield, the 40th Infantry Division, relieved by the 43rd Infantry Division, left Luzon on March 15, 1945, for Panay Island in the Philippines. Determined to fulfill his promise to retake the islands from the Japanese, General Douglas MacArthur ordered U.S. troops to capture the Visayan Islands of Panay, Negros Cebu, and Bohol in the central Philippines. Over 30,000 Japanese troops controlled large coastal towns on these islands, including Cebu City on Cebu Island and Iloilo City on Panay. General MacArthur needed the two port cities in preparation for the anticipated invasion of Japan.[1, 2, 3]

Historian Stephen Lofgren outlined the events on Panay Island, the first objective. On March 18, 1945, the 40th Infantry Division, led by 185th Infantry Regiment, including Staff Sergeant Jerald Tongen, landed several miles south of Iloilo City, where a strong Filipino guerilla force held most of Panay. The friendly force greeted them on the beach and escorted them to Iloilo, which the Japanese had burned in retreat. The 185th secured Iloilo on March 20 amid "laughing Filipinos, throwing flowers."[1] They left for Los Negros Island on March 29 to prepare for an attack on the Japanese in the region. On April 9, all three regiments of the 40th Infantry Division, attached to the 503rd Parachute Infantry, pushed east into the steep mountains of the island. Initially the Japanese held their positions by using booby-trapped terrain and counterattacks at night, but despite this and torrential rain, the 40th drove the enemy from the ravines and cliffs.[1, 2, 3]

On April 23, 1945, Jerald's commanding officer wrote a letter to his father: *Dear Mr. Tongen, Your son, Staff Sergeant Jerald I. Tongen, on April 9, 1945, was struck by an enemy rifleman and died a few moments later. Staff Sergeant Tongen was advancing upon enemy held ground with other members of his platoon near Guimbalaon, Negros, Philippine Islands. You have the deepest sympathy of the officers and men of this company. Jerald had been with this company for a long time, as a result he had made many friends and was held in high regard by all members of his company. He was a splendid soldier and of outstanding character. His loss will be deeply felt by his many friends. Funeral services were conducted on April 10, 1945, by Chaplain S.M. Mulkey and Staff Sergeant Tongen was laid to rest in United States Armed Forces Cemetery Bacolod Number 1, Negros, Philippine Islands, Grave 34, Row 2. May I express my personal sympathy in your loss. Please feel free to call upon me for any additional information you may desire. Sincerely, John S. Colton, Jr., 1st Lieutenant, 185th Inf., Commanding*[4]

As the 40th Infantry Division drove the enemy deeper into the mountains of Negros, the Japanese forces scattered in the jungle and were largely ineffective by August 1945.[3]

Staff Sergeant Jerald Tongen grew up on a farm in Hazel Run, Minnesota. Survivors included his parents and four brothers. Initially buried in Manila, he returned to the United States aboard army transport *Dalton Victory* and was reinterred in Hazel Run Lutheran Cemetery, Hazel Run, Minnesota, a cemetery surrounded by lush farmland. The Hazel Run American Legion Anderson-Tongen Post 559 named after 1st Lieutenant Leon Anderson, who died in France on July 31, 1944, and Staff Sergeant Jerald Tongen, is located in the old schoolhouse from District 82.[5, 6]

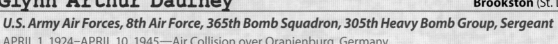

Glynn Arthur Daufney

Brookston (St. Louis County)

U.S. Army Air Forces, 8th Air Force, 365th Bomb Squadron, 305th Heavy Bomb Group, Sergeant

APRIL 1, 1924–APRIL 10, 1945—Air Collision over Oranienburg, Germany

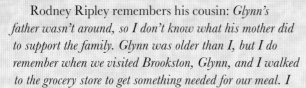

Rodney Ripley remembers his cousin: *Glynn's father wasn't around, so I don't know what his mother did to support the family. Glynn was older than I, but I do remember when we visited Brookston, Glynn, and I walked to the grocery store to get something needed for our meal. I think we even had some extra change to buy candy. Wow! Glynn and the others can no longer speak for themselves and need to be acknowledged for their very short lives, which paid for not only our freedom, but the freedom of those in other countries. Glynn's cousin, Clyde Borgers of Foxholm, North Dakota, was wounded the first day of the Battle of the Bulge and was a POW for the duration of the battle. He was shot in the back of the neck under his helmet by a German sniper who had snuck behind American lines. The bullet came out his open mouth. He should have instantly died, but obviously it wasn't his day to die. Miracles do happen. And he surrendered to a German unit that took care of him and left him and other wounded Americans in a safe place when the Germans retreated until the Americans returned.*[1]

On April 10, 1945, Sergeant Glynn Daufney, ball turret gunner for 2nd Lieutenant James Laubach's crew of nine, left Chelveston, England, for a bombing mission to Oranienburg, Germany. As the B-17 bombers were in formation near Oranienburg, witnesses reported: *The two ships collided and ship #4338803 went down, out of control, in a steep dive.* The Missing Persons Report expands on the circumstances of the crash: *Subject enlisted man was a crewmember of B-17 airplane which collided with another plane in same formation and crashed 60 miles northwest of Berlin, Germany. He was not seen to parachute out. One man, Lloyd E. Mueller, parachuted to safety and was a prisoner of war.*

Staff Sergeant Lloyd Mueller, tail gunner of the second plane involved in the collision, was the sole survivor of both planes. All nine men in Daufney's crew were listed as missing in action. Both B-17s crashed near Wilsnock, Germany.[2]

Glynn graduated from Brookston High School in 1942 and entered the service on December 20, 1943. His mother received his class ring from the army after his death. Initially buried by German civilians in the small town of Buddenhagen where their plane crashed, the Russian Commandant ordered the bodies of Daufney's crew and 36 other American flyers reburied by Russian authorities in the military cemetery in Meyenburg, Germany. At the head of each grave, a red Russian cubicle, four feet high, commemorated each man. In 1948, Glynn Daufney was reinterred in Ardennes American Cemetery, Neupre, Belgium. Sergeant Glynn Daufney, son of Louis J. and Lillian (Martin) Daufney, was survived by his mother and six siblings.[3, 4]

Jan Tester Backus, whose brother Private Rodney Tester (page 12) died in the war, recalls her neighbor Glynn: *I was so young when Glynn was a part of our family. I do know that his mom was a widow and I believe there were at least four children in the family. After watching* The Roosevelts *this week the war brought back all the old memories of sadness. He was a dear friend of ours, and especially of my brother, Bill, who also was in the military during the war. We knew the family very well and still have fond memories of Glynn.*[5]

Lawrence August Storch

Wanda (Redwood County)

83rd Infantry "Thunderbolt" Division, 331st Infantry Regiment, 3rd Battalion, L Company, Private First Class

MAY 17, 1915–APRIL 13, 1945—Crossing the Elbe River, Germany

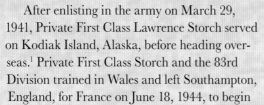

After enlisting in the army on March 29, 1941, Private First Class Lawrence Storch served on Kodiak Island, Alaska, before heading overseas.[1] Private First Class Storch and the 83rd Division trained in Wales and left Southampton, England, for France on June 18, 1944, to begin their fight across Europe. The 83rd covered 1,408 miles, from Omaha Beach in Normandy, through the Loire Valley of France, Luxembourg, Belgium, Holland and the Rhineland, to reach central Germany. Both Private First Class Storch and President Franklin Roosevelt almost survived the war.[2, 4]

On April 13, 1945, troops of the 83rd Signal Corps, responsible for radio news throughout the war, sent out this message: *Franklin D. Roosevelt, President of the United States of America, died at Warm Springs, Georgia, of a cerebral hemorrhage. Mr. Roosevelt was 63 years of age. The body will be interned at Hyde Park, New York on Sunday. Vice President Truman has been sworn in as President. The British Press speaking in tribute of President Roosevelt said that, "He gave his life for Allied Victory." An American Sergeant from the western front said, "Nobody has fought more mightily for victory than he did." The people of the United States will now know that they have lost more than a familiar and friendly person. In England, Parliament adjourned for the day in memory of Mr. Roosevelt. This is the first time that the House of Commons had adjourned for the death of a President from a foreign state.*[3]

On the day the 83rd Signal Corps broadcast the death of President Roosevelt, the 83rd Infantry Division had advanced 220 miles into the heart of Germany and were ordered to build and cross a bridge across the Elbe River, 65 miles southwest of Berlin. The 3rd Battalion After Action Report on April 13 states: *At 0600 a liaison officer from Task Force Biddle came to the Battalion CP and informed Major Sellers that the Battalion was again attached to the Calvary. Lieutenant Ashmore went to the Regiment to verify the message. At 0900 the Battalion moved back into Derenburg and "K" company reverted to Battalion control. Orders were received from Colonel Biddle to attack and capture Heimburg. At 12:00 "L" Company jumped off in an attack from Benzingerode with the mission of capturing Heimburg. One platoon of light tanks was attached to the "L" Company and one platoon of heavy machine guns were in direct support. At 1330 the leading elements of "L" Company were on the western edge of the town but were meeting heavy enemy automatic and mortar fire. A high ridge was on "L" Company's right flank and they were receiving fire from the ridge as well as from the town and from a high hill on their left flank. The enemy had well-prepared positions and had used the terrain to the utmost having constant observation on "L" Company. Due to the terrain, the tanks were not able to give close support to the infantry. At this time Major Sellers committed "K" Company around the right of "L" Company along the high ridge. "K" Company was able to reach the western edge of the town and the high ground surrounding the town. General Ferenbaugh, the Assistant Division Commander, was at the battalion CP all afternoon and at 2200 decided to withdraw both companies from the town. Although "I" Company had a platoon in the center of the town, heavy fire was still being received from all around the town. "K" and "L" companies were ordered to withdraw at 2230 and to outpost all approaches leading into Benzingerode.*[2]

Against fanatic enemy counterattacks, the 83rd Infantry Division erected the first and only Allied bridge on the Elbe River; 17 soldiers from the 3rd Battalion, including Private First Class Lawrence Storch, gave their lives during the battle near Heimberg, Germany, and 22 men were wounded.[4, 5] Sharon Coulter recalls the family story: *We were told that Lawrence died while going house-to-house, looking for people. He died the day before the battle ended.*[6]

Private First Class Lawrence Storch, son of John and Helena (Kratzke) Storch, is buried in Netherlands American Cemetery, Margraten, Netherlands. Survivors included his mother and five siblings and half-siblings.[1]

John Gray Stevenson

Delhi (Redwood County)

U.S. Marine Corps, 6th Marine "The Striking Sixth" Division, 4th Marine Regiment, 1st Battalion, B Company, Private

OCTOBER 8, 1923–APRIL 14, 1945—Battle of Okinawa, Okinawa

As a young man, John Stevenson played basketball for the Delhi basketball team and also specialized in raising purebred stock in the Redwood County 4-H Club. Following graduation from Redwood Falls High School in 1943, John enlisted in the U.S. Marine Corps on May 25, 1944. He trained in San Diego and at Camp Pendleton, California, before transferring to Guadalcanal in December to prepare for Okinawa.

The 6th Division, the last marine division formed during the war, was the only division that formed, fought and disbanded overseas. Created on the island of Guadalcanal in the southern Solomon Islands in September 1944, the 6th Marine Division was composed of three infantry regiments (the 4th Marines, the 22nd Marines and the 29th Marines), an artillery regiment (the 15th Marines) and several support units. John Stevenson's regiment, the 4th Marines, were originally known as the "China Marines," as they formed in 1911 and served many years in China prior to the war. Decimated on Bataan during early in the war, a "new" 4th Marines was established in time for the invasion of Guam in 1944.[2, 3, 4]

The 4th Marines, 6th Division headed for Okinawa in Operation Iceberg, the last major amphibious assault of the Pacific War. Okinawa lay only 350 miles from southern Japan, and if captured, the island would provide the United States with numerous air and naval bases to strike Japan's other home islands. American planes began attacking Japanese airfields on the island in October 1944 and continued intermittent, but intense, bombardment through the end of March. This culminated in several days of fierce bombing and shelling by American and British naval and air forces prior to the American landing.

On April 1, 1945, the 6th Division landed on Okinawa with Private Stevenson, and the 4th Marines among the first units to go ashore. Surprisingly, they met little resistance, and Yontan Airfield was swiftly taken on the first day. Far ahead of schedule, the division headed north and reached the Motobu Peninsula on April 7 where the 4th Marines were to secure Mt. Yae-take, while the 29th and 22nd Marines would seal off the Motobu Peninsula.

On April 14 at 0830, the 2nd Battalion of the 4th Marines and 3rd Battalion of the 29th Infantry Regiment began their assault on a 700-foot ridge on the rim of Mt. Yae-take. A few hours later, Private John Stevenson and the 1st Battalion arrived for the attack, where their commanding officer, Major Bernard Green, died in an ambush that afternoon. Marines destroyed the well-concealed Japanese, who fought on in spite of continuous attacks supported by sea and air bombardment.[2, 3, 4, 5] The authors of *In Okinawa: The Last Battle* wrote: *The marines met running opposition from small groups of machine gunners and riflemen. The enemy had good observation of the marines' movements; his machine guns and mortars covered the approach routes; and he followed his custom of allowing a few troops to pass across an open saddle and then firing on the group from behind. American officers were his favorite target. It was dangerous to hold a map, to wave a directing arm, or even to show a pistol rather than a carbine or rifle.[2]*

Private John Stevenson died during the attack on Mt. Yae-take, and he was buried in the 6th Division cemetery on Okinawa. Two days later, on April 16, the marines took the summit by bravely charging through heavy mortar fire and gunfire. The men captured Motobu Peninsula on April 20, and northern Okinawa declared secure a day later.

Despite the hopelessness of Japan's situation, the remaining Japanese on the island held out until late June in an attempt to slow down the Allied advance over this last stepping-stone to the main islands. The cost to the United States in total casualties was the highest in the Pacific, with over 49,000 killed, wounded, or missing. Over 110,000 Japanese forces were killed in action or committed suicide, including General Ushijima; only 7,800 surrendered. This fanaticism to commit suicide rather than surrender led the Americans to end the war with the atomic bomb.[3]

Private John Stevenson's survivors included his parents and five siblings. Private John Stevenson was reinterred in Redwood Falls Cemetery, Redwood Falls, Minnesota.[1]

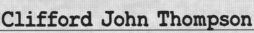

Clifford John Thompson

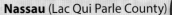

69th Infantry Division, 777th Tank Battalion, A Company, Sergeant

JUNE 13, 1921–APRIL 16, 1945—Advance to Leipzig, Germany

Activated September 20, 1943 at Fort Gordon, Georgia, Sergeant Clifford Thompson and the 777th Tank Battalion arrived in England on December 27, 1944, and after six weeks of training, the battalion landed at Le Havre, France, on February 6, 1945. Initially attached to the 28th Infantry Division, the 777th Tank Battalion marched to the Monschau Forest, where citizens waved and cheered them on through France until they arrived at the sign, *You are entering Germany.* "And then it was silent, hurrying people, who neither looked nor paused as we went by."[1, 2, 4] On March 26, the 777th Tank Battalion joined the 69th Infantry Division, crossed the Rhine River and advanced rapidly along the Lahn River, taking several towns before it began the drive east to Saxony.

Sergeant Clifford Thompson and his tank crew almost made it to Leipzig. After Action Reports on April 16, 1945 for A Company, Third Platoon stated that Sergeant Thompson was one of three crewmembers killed in Audigast: *Moved out at 1100 to Audigast with infantry on tanks, and received heavy small-arms fire. Infantry dismounted and town was subjected to artillery concentration. Infantry and tanks started to move in, and a panzerfaust knocked out platoon leader's tank, killing the platoon leader and seriously wounding two enlisted men. Platoon sergeant took command, and all tank weapons were used in marching fire, causing extremely heavy casualties among the enemy. Two tanks remained at Audigast to clear town, and two proceeded to Kobschutz. At northern end of town, the platoon sergeant's tank received 88 mm fire on the turret. The column proceeded, and a second tank received four direct hits from 88 mm at point-blank range, killing three crewmembers, seriously wounding one, and slightly wounding the fifth. The enemy gun position was destroyed, and an ammunition dump set on fire. Enemy opened up with heavy artillery concentration, and the remaining tank withdrew into Audigast and remained for the night.*[1, 2, 4, 6]

On April 18, elements of the 777th went on to support the 69th Infantry Division in their battle to capture Leipzig, with heavy machine gun fire, German Panzer units, and small arms causing heavy casualties among the infantry. On that day, at a small concentration camp at Thekla, German guards had herded 300 inmates into a barracks. As the 69th sped toward the camp, the SS guards set the building on fire, shooting anyone who tried to flee.[1, 2, 3, 4]

The United States Holocaust Memorial Museum posted this tribute to the 69th Division: *During the fierce battle for Leipzig, the 69th Infantry Division discovered Leipzig-Thekla, a sub camp of the Buchenwald concentration camp…Upon arriving at the camp, the 69th immediately began providing for the 90 to 100 survivors.…The swift advance of the 69th prevented the SS guards from committing a similar atrocity at a nearby camp housing some 250 women."* The Allies ordered the "local German mayor to provide 75 caskets for the dead prisoners, floral wreaths for each coffin, and crews of workers to bury the inmates at the entrance of the town cemetery, and 100 prominent citizens from Leipzig, … to attend the funeral services.* On April 27, 1945, another 1,000 German citizens attended the ceremony to bear witness to the atrocities in their backyard. The U.S. Army's Center of Military History and the United States Holocaust Memorial Museum recognized the 69th Infantry Division as a liberating unit in 1993.[3]

The son of John A. and Jessie (Martin) Thompson, Sergeant Clifford Thompson was survived by his sister, Lucille C. Thompson. Sergeant Thompson is buried in Netherlands American Cemetery, Margraten, Netherlands, the only U.S. war cemetery in the Netherlands. Grateful Dutch citizens adopted the graves of 8,301 American soldiers; another 1,722 names of missing soldiers are recorded on the Walls of the Missing.[5]

The American Legion Meyer-Thompson Post 536 in Nassau is named in honor of Sergeant Harold Meyer (page 36), who died on February 4, 1944 in Italy, and Sergeant Clifford Thompson.

A Company
777th Tank Battalion
Camp San Luis Obispo, California, 1945

Henry Louis Kroll

Fifth Army, 85th Infantry "Custer" Division, 337th Infantry Regiment, 1st Battalion, C Company, Private

SEPTEMBER 14, 1924–APRIL 22, 1945—Po Valley Campaign, Northern Italy

Henry Kroll, born in Blackduck, Minnesota, attended grade school in Bemidji and completed his schooling in Gully, where his family lived just north of the village. Raised in a faithful Lutheran family, Henry was confirmed on December 4, 1938, in the Gully Lutheran Church by Reverend O.A. Aaker. Following graduation from high school, Henry worked at the Louis Dow defense plant in St. Paul until he entered the service on August 3, 1943.[1] Henry trained at Fort Leavenworth, Kansas, and at Camp Wolters, Texas, where he received both the rifle marksmanship medal and good conduct medal.[2]

After a furlough home in April 1944, Private Henry Kroll left for two months of training in North Africa in preparation for the Italian campaign. Assigned to the 337th Infantry Regiment, 85th Infantry Division, Private Kroll fought under the command of Colonel Oliver Hughes across Italy in 1944 and into the Po Valley in 1945.

One well-remembered battle occurred from May 12 to 16, 1944, when Private Henry Kroll and the 1st Battalion advanced on Hills 69 and 66 north of Tremensuoli, Italy. Just one day into battle, the battalion was ordered to relieve the 3rd Battalion, 339th Infantry, who lost many men when fighting to take the strategic hills. As the 337th advanced through heavy enemy fire, two companies of the battalion were stopped, but Private Kroll and C Company kept moving and reached the hill. Although surrounded on 3 sides by the enemy and with only 18 men remaining in the company, C Company held their positions and pushed back the enemy. After the 337th cleared Hill 66, the German Gustav Line north of Minturno lost strength. For heroic action that day, Private Kroll and C Company received the Presidential Unit Citation.[3]

From September 1944 until January 1945, Private Kroll's family received no word or letter from Henry. Concerned that her son was either lost or separated from his detachment, Amelia Kroll wrote to the army to request information on her son. General Dunlop replied: *The records do show that during month of October, November, and December 1944, Private Kroll was in Caserta, Italy.*[2]

On January 6, 1945, the 85th Infantry Division relieved the 1st British Division until April 14 when the division advanced to Bologna. The 85th pushed through Lucca and Pistoia into the Po Valley as German resistance collapsed. The division's Operations Report states that on April 22, C Company, "motorized and traveled with the march command post in Regimental reserve" as the 337th fought for the Bomparto Bridge over the Panaro River. After successfully securing the bridge, C Company remained at the bridge while other units immediately crossed the Panaro and headed for the Po Bridge at Camposanto.[4] During the advance to the Po River, Private Henry Kroll was wounded and died at 170 Station Hospital, Parretta, Italy.[2]

By April 24, the Division had crossed both the Panero and Po rivers, forcing the German surrender on May 7, 1945. General Dwight D. Eisenhower gave this victory message to the Allied troops in Europe: *The route you have traveled…is marked by the graves of former comrades. Each of the fallen died as a member of the team to which you belong, bound together by a common love of liberty.*[5] One of Henry's comrades, Private Alfred Bruns (page 85), from St. Rosa, Minnesota, served with Henry in the 337th Infantry Regiment, and died on October 24, 1944, in Italy.

On August 2, 1945, the Army Effects Bureau notified Amelia Kroll that additional effects were discovered belonging to her son: did she want two pictures, a prayer book and a notebook, all bloodstained and torn? Mrs. Kroll replied: *Please forward all my son's personal effects to me, including the two pictures, prayer book and notebook, no matter if they are damaged, for I want everything that has belonged to him. It will be hard to bear, but they will be a living memory of my Beloved Son Henry.*[2]

Private Henry Kroll, son of Albert and Amelia (Nicholsen) Kroll, was buried at Castelfiorentino, Italy, on April 25, 1945, and reinterred in Lund Congregation Cemetery, Gully, Minnesota, in 1949. Survivors included his parents and five siblings.[1]

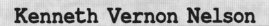

Kenneth Vernon Nelson

Sedan (Pope County)

Sixth Army, 25th Infantry "Tropic Lightning," Division, 27th Infantry Regiment, Private
MARCH 29, 1921–APRIL 27, 1945—Battle for Luzon, Philippines

Following graduation from Glenwood High School in 1939, Kenneth "Kenny" Nelson joined the Civilian Conservation Corps Camp in Ely, Minnesota for six months. Described as "a determined young man with a quiet disposition who was well liked by everyone," Kenny attended the William Hood Dunwoody vocational training school and worked for Austin Western in Minneapolis. A job offer at Consolidated Aircraft lured him to San Diego, California, for three years until he was drafted in August 1944. Kenny completed basic training at Camp Hood, Texas, and spent a 13-day furlough at Christmas with his family, which they described as one of the happiest they had spent together.[1]

Private Kenneth Nelson was assigned to the 25th Infantry Division, 27th Infantry Regiment, a renowned regiment with a unique history and name, the "Wolfhounds." Initially established in 1901 to end the Philippine Insurrection on the island of Mindanao, the 27th also served with the American Expeditionary Force sent to Siberia during the Russian Civil War in 1918. The tenacious fighting tactics of the regiment won the respect of the Bolsheviks, who named them the "Wolfhounds."

Stationed in Hawaii on December 7, 1941, the 27th Infantry Regiment fired at Japanese aircraft during the surprise attack on Pearl Harbor. After action in Guadalcanal and New Georgia, the 25th Division landed on Luzon on January 11, 1945, to regain the Philippines. As they drove through rice paddies across the central Luzon plain, the 25th battled the Japanese in Binalonan on January 17 and continued their advance to Umingan, Lupao and San Jose. On February 21, 1945, the "Tropic Lightning" Division attacked in the Caraballo Mountains along Highway 5, securing Digdig, Putlan and Kapintalan. By April 25, the 27th had a firm hold on Lone Tree hill at the juncture of Balete and Kapintalan Ridges and fought for Mt. Myoko. During the assault on Mt. Myoko and the battle for Belete Pass, Private Kenneth Nelson was killed in action.[2]

After securing Balete Pass on May 13, the division captured Santa Fe two weeks later and opened the door to the Cagayan Valley. As the war ground to an end, the division cleared the island of the remaining Japanese and moved to Japan on September 20 for occupation duty. While occupying Japan, the 27th Infantry initiated a unique relationship with the people.

During Christmas 1949, the 27th Infantry Regiment visited the Holy Family Home Orphanage, Osaka, Japan, to deliver gifts and hold a Christmas party for the children. The children captured their hearts, and the party launched a steady stream of food and essential supplies to the orphanage. The soldiers' love for the children built a bridge between two cultures, once bitter enemies. The 1955 film *Three Stripes in the Sun*, starring Aldo Ray told the story of their kindness. Since 1957, the "Wolfhounds" have also welcomed children from the orphanage to visit their base in Hawaii, "honoring the legacy that Master Sergeant Hugh O'Reilly started that has lasted over 50 years."[3, 4]

Private Kenneth Nelson, son of Reinarth and Emma (Klecacy) Nelson, is buried at Manila American Cemetery, Manila, Philippines. Survivors included his parents and a brother. His father was the postmaster in Sedan, Minnesota. Memorial services for Private Kenneth Nelson were held at Lane Field, San Diego, on May 27, 1945.[1]

The film and book *From Here to Eternity* by James Jones is based on "Wolfhound" regimental life. The 1953 film explores the lives of three soldiers, played by Montgomery Cliff, Frank Sinatra and Burt Lancaster, who are stationed in Hawaii before Pearl Harbor. The film's title comes from Rudyard Kipling's 1892 poem "Gentlemen-Rankers," about British soldiers who lost their way and were "damned from here to eternity." In 1998, director Terrance Malick produced *The Thin Red Line*, a movie based on another novel by James Jones set in World War II on Guadalcanal. It portrays soldiers of the 27th Infantry Regiment, 25th Infantry Division.[5]

Ira Leroy Bashore

Seventh Army, 103rd Infantry "Cactus" Division, 328th Engineer Combat Battalion, A Company, Private First Class

FEBRUARY 11, 1908–APRIL 27, 1945—Advance from the Danube River to the Austrian Border, Germany

After enlisting in the army on December 4, 1942, Ira Bashore joined the 328th Engineer Combat Battalion, a unit of the 103rd Infantry Division. Highly regarded by their fellow soldiers, the *Cactus Caravan* described their combat engineers as: *nice guys to have on your side. They clear the path for their own forces, put stumbling blocks in the path of the enemy. They're a rugged battalion with the brains, brawn and equipment to do any job construction or demolition that may be necessary—and in a hurry, too. They're always ready to join in the firefight, too.* Engineering battalions also supported front line units with road and bridge repair, clearing obstacles like concertina wire, and sweeping minefields.[1]

Founded in 1942, the 103rd Infantry Division landed in Marseilles, France, on October 20, 1944, a few months after the Allies had invaded Europe on D-Day, June 6, 1944. The "Cactus" Division left the port of Marseille and advanced north through the Vosges Mountains, eventually crossing the Lauter River into Germany on December 15, 1944. The Germans launched the Battle of the Bulge the next day in the Ardennes Forest in Belgium, France and Luxembourg. The 103rd moved back across the border to Alsace-Lorraine to confront German Operation Nordwind, the last Nazi offensive. By mid-January, the Germans were losing ground and the 103rd moved to defend along the Sauer River. On March 15, 1945, the division crossed the Moder and Zintzel Rivers, taking Mühlhausen. Once again they crossed the Lauter River and continued their steady advance to Germany. As the enemy backpedaled home, the 103rd crossed the Danube River on April 26, and on April 27, Private First Class Ira Bashore died of a gunshot wound near Bad-Worishofen, Germany.[2, 3]

On the day he died, his division entered Landsberg and liberated Kaufering subcamp, part of the infamous Dachau Concentration Camp. There, prisoners had been forced to build a factory that Nazi officials hoped would construct the Messerschmitt ME-262 Luftwaffe jet fighter. The soldiers encountered a grueling sight as described in *The Story of the 103rd Infantry Division*: *At one camp alone 300 bodies lay on the barren, filthy ground while 600 living "zombies"—weak from five and six years of starvation, shuffled aimlessly. Inside many of the huts which lie half-dug into the ground—about 5 feet high and 24 feet long—lay prisoners who could not walk or move, those who*

would not live. Military doctors prescribed a diet, and military officers scoured the countryside for supplies, 1,000 loaves of bread, 1,000 quarts of milk, 750 pounds of fresh meat a day, plus all the Wehrmacht stocks in the vicinity, in an almost futile attempt to save the lives of these 50- and 60-pound remnants of human beings.[4]

Arriving at Dachau, Major Richard Winters voiced the emotions of his fellow soldiers, "Now I know why I am here."[5]

The 103rd Infantry Division is recognized as a liberating unit and the colors of the unit hang on permanent display in the United States Holocaust Museum in Washington, D.C.[1, 2, 3]

A 1927 graduate of McGrath High School, Private First Class Ira Bashore was the son of Daniel and Opal (Jay) Bashore. Survivors included his mother and five siblings. His sister Florence stated: *Ira took over as head of the household when our father died. He was a good brother. The family did not find out that Ira had died until after the war ended. I was told that Ira was killed on April 27th by strafing from a plane, while building bridges.*[6]

On May 27, 1945, a joint memorial service was held at Calvary Presbyterian Church in McGrath for Private First Class Ira Bashore and his good friend, Private First Class Robert Horne (page 132), who died a month earlier at Speyer, Germany. At the request of their mothers, the men were buried side by side in Fort Snelling National Cemetery.[7]

Just before the Texas/Oklahoma border, north of Gainesville on I-35, a nine-foot sculpture of an infantryman honors the 103rd Infantry Division, the brave men of the "Cactus" Division. Named "A Call to Duty," 5 larger markers fan out behind the sculpture, listing the names of more than 800 members of the 103rd Infantry Division who lost their lives in World War II, including Private First Class Ira Bashore from McGrath and Private Helmer Eichten (page 99) from Wanda, Minnesota.[2]

Othmar Peter Braun

Regal (Kandiyohi County)

U.S. Navy, USS Luce DD-552, Seaman First Class
NOVEMBER 13, 191–MAY 4, 1945—Battle for Okinawa, Okinawa

Virgil Braun, then 11 years old, still remembers the car that drove to their farm and delivered the telegram to his parents informing them that their son, Seaman First Class Othmar Braun, was missing in action: *I deeply regret to inform you that your son Othmar Peter Braun is missing following action in the service of his country. Your great anxiety is appreciated, and you will be furnished details when received.*[1]

The fifth of nine children, Othmar enlisted in the navy on May 25, 1944. His brother Virgil and 17-year-old brother Mike remained home to do the farmwork. After his training at the Great Lakes Naval Base, he was assigned to the USS *Luce*, a 2,050-ton destroyer, which was his only ship. In a letter written in February 1945 to his brother Al, Othmar reported that he had participated in the invasions of the Leyte Gulf and Luzon in the Philippines, and: *had a few air attacks but wasn't much.*[1, 5]

In his book *The Second World War,* John Keegan wrote that American forces landed on Okinawa in April 1945 without Japanese resistance. By then the Japanese had changed their strategy to allow American forces to land on Okinawa while they prepared a line of defense inland. They also planned kamikaze attacks on U.S. Navy ships in an attempt to strand the landing force.[1]

The USS *Luce* was on picket duty 30 miles west of Okinawa, when 2 kamikaze planes broke off from the attack on the USS *Morrison*, several miles away, and attacked the *Luce* on May 4, 1945. Captain Waterhouse told the *Associated Press* that it was possible to see the dogfight of planes above the USS *Morrison* from the deck of the USS *Luce* around 0800. The captain of the *Luce* managed to swerve the boat to avoid the first plane, but the second hit the *Luce* astern. The Action Report for May 4 states: *0810–The explosion of the bomb carried by this plane caused power to be lost for a short time on all radars, and caused power failure as noted on ordnance. This necessitated training all guns manually. Immediately after the crash of the first plane, a second plane was reported about 5000 yards, low on the water, heading for the ship from the port quarter. All guns commenced training in manual toward this plane, but only the port 20 mm guns were brought to bear before the plane crashed into the after part of the ship at 0811. Damage resulted which knocked out the port engine and tore away large sections of the starboard shell plating. Immediately before this hit, power was restored to radars and guns, and appeared to function normally in forward port of ship. We were flooding aft from starboard side and rudder, which was jarred hard right apparently held ship on an even keel. 0814–Commenced taking heavy list to starboard. Gave order "Stand by to abandon ship," followed almost immediately by "Abandon Ship" when it was observed that the stern was going under water as list was increasing rapidly. The word did not reach all below deck stations due to ruptured communications.*

Within four minutes, the *Luce* sank at 0815 with 149 killed and missing, and 40 wounded. The Japanese kamikazes also sank the *Morrison*; together, the *Luce* and the *Morrison* were the 312th and 313th U.S. ships lost in the war with Japan.[3]

Captain J.W. Waterhouse, Othmar's commanding office, wrote a letter to his parents dated July 1945, notifying them of his death following the sinking of the *Luce*: *Your son's regular battle station was on a 40 mm gun. Othmar's calm and efficient work under the strain of enemy action on previous occasions contributed greatly to making that gun a thoroughly dependable unit of the ship's company. We know this was the case on the morning the ship was sunk.*[4]

A memorial service for Othmar Braun was held at St. Margaret's Catholic Church in Lake Henry, Minnesota, in July 1945. Othmar is memorialized on the Courts of the Missing, National Memorial Cemetery of the Pacific, Honolulu, Hawaii, and in St. Margaret's Cemetery, Lake Henry, Minnesota. His name also lives on at the Othmar Braun American Legion Post 612 in Lake Henry, Minnesota, organized in April 1947. Urban Spannier, a founder of Post 612, stated that the post proudly honors Othmar's memory.[1, 5] Left to mourn his death were his parents, John and Susan (Heinen) Braun, and seven brothers and sisters.[6]

Gerald T. Reinart

U.S. Army Air Forces, 13th Air Force, 42nd Medium Bomb Group, 69th Bomb Squadron, Staff Sergeant

MARCH 6, 1921–MAY 6, 1945—Air Crash, Palawan, Philippines

In 1931, Gerald Reinart and his family moved from Avoca, Minnesota, to Barry, a small agricultural community located on the railroad. He grew up on the family farm just south of town and joined the Army Air Corps on September 11, 1942. At Sheppard Field, near Wichita Falls, Texas, Gerald completed technical service training for the Northrup B-25, named the Mitchell after General William Mitchell, the "Father of the U.S. Air Force." He also earned certification as a flight engineer, a position with vast knowledge of the aircraft's engines, guns and control systems. In an emergency, the flight engineer assisted the pilot in manning the controls. Staff Sergeant Reinart, a good marksman, also served as a gunnery instructor at Greenville, South Carolina, before moving to Hawaii to join his permanent crew.[1, 2]

From Hawaii, the B-25 crews moved to New Guinea and then to the Dutch East Indies where they joined the 69th Bomb Squadron, 42nd Bomb Group, nicknamed "The Crusaders." They patrolled the coasts of New Guinea, Celebes (Sulawesi) and Halmahera, bombing enemy ships, airfields, supply lines and ground troops. Beginning in March 1943, the 42nd Bomb Group operated from bases in the Solomon Islands where they flew new B-25s to attack airfields and other Japanese installations. When Sergeant Reinart and the bomber group moved to the Philippines in March 1945, they targeted shipping and land installations along the China coast, French Indochina (later named Vietnam) and Borneo.[3, 4]

By December 1944, the B-25s switched from medium-level bombing to low-level bombing and strafing. Air Force operations found out that no matter how heavily or frequently Japanese airfields were bombed from a high level, their aircraft continued to harass the Allies. When the "Crusaders" dropped to minimum altitude, the Japanese attacks ceased. The formations skimmed their targets so low that a Woodcutters Club was formed—the pilots brought back samples of the Hamaher, Celebes and Ceram forests as well as coconuts, which clung to the underside of their B-25.[3, 4]

In the dark early morning hours of May 6, 1945, 14 B-25 planes from the 42nd Bomb Group (6 planes from the 69th Squadron, including Staff Sergeant Gerald Reinart; 6 planes from the 75th Squadron; and 2 from the 100th Squadron) were scheduled to take off from Palawan airfield in

the Philippines, to provide air support for ground forces in Tarakan, North Borneo. Staff Sergeant Gerald Reinart served as flight engineer on 2nd Lieutenant Robert William's crew, along with four other airmen. As his B-25, the second in line, took off without the runway lights turned on, one wheel on the plane slipped off the runway. After clearing the ground, the plane hit a parked truck along the side of the runway and crashed. Out of the six-man crew, only two survived. Staff Sergeant Gerald Reinart died in the crash.[5] He is buried at Manila American Cemetery, Fort Bonifacio, Manila, Philippines.[1]

Howard Clinton White

Squaw Lake (Itasca County)

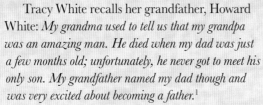

77th Infantry "Statue of Liberty" Division, 307th Infantry Regiment, 2nd Battalion, E Company, 1st Sergeant

MARCH 29, 1910–MAY 20, 1945—Battle of Okinawa, Okinawa

Tracy White recalls her grandfather, Howard White: *My grandma used to tell us that my grandpa was an amazing man. He died when my dad was just a few months old; unfortunately, he never got to meet his only son. My grandfather named my dad though and was very excited about becoming a father.*[1]

By April 1945, Germany hung on the verge of collapse, but Japan continued to fight American advances across the Pacific. In order to end the war, the Allies needed to capture Okinawa, an island 400 miles south of Japan in the Ryukyu Islands. The airfields and harbors on Okinawa were essential for an invasion of Japan, which seemed inevitable at the time.

The 77th Infantry Division, nicknamed the "Statue of Liberty" Division as it hailed from New York, along with the 1st and 6th Marine Divisions, were ordered to take Okinawa. 1st Sergeant Howard C. White, assigned to E Company, 307th Infantry Regiment, belonged to one of three regiments in the division. After fighting through Guam and Leyte, the 77th Infantry Division landed on Ie Shima, a small island off Okinawa, and within five days, they secured the island on April 21, 1945.[2, 3, 4, 5] Two days later, Ernie Pyle, famed war correspondent who traveled with the 77th Division, was slain by a Japanese sniper. 1st Sergeant Howard White assisted with the burial and helped erect a wooden monument to the beloved Pulitzer Prize winner.[6]

The authors of *Okinawa: The Last Battle* describe the attack on Ishimmi ridge in detail. On May 17, 1st Lieutenant Theodore Bell ordered 1st Sergeant Howard White and E Company to launch a surprise night attack on Ishimmi Ridge, west of the town of Ishimmi, in order to break the Shuri Line of defense. The company reached Ishimmi Ridge just before dawn and began the difficult task of digging into coral and rock formation. The Japanese fired from all directions, knocking out most of E Company's heavy guns and all but one radio. During the night, a rescue force tried to reach E Company, but the Japanese ambushed the force and the survivors turned back. Bombarded during the night by artillery, mortars and "buzz bombs," the soldiers on Ishimmi Ridge stopped several attempts at infiltration.

As dawn broke, reinforcements attempted a rescue, but only a handful made it. Finally, reinforcements from the 305th finally arrived late that night. The men had secured Ishimmi Ridge against all odds.[2, 3, 4, 5]

As E Company continued their advance on Shuri, Commander 1st Lieutenant Theodore Bell witnessed 1st Sergeant Howard White as he was killed on a ridge by a shell fired from a tank.[7] 1st Sergeant White was awarded the Silver Star: *For gallantry in action on Okinawa, Ryukyus Islands, on 20 May 1945. After taking a heavily fortified Japanese position, Sergeant White's company was cut off from supplies for two days and repeatedly subjected to savage enemy counterattacks. Casualties reduced the company strength to 31 men. In this valiant stand, which proved to be a deciding factor in the cracking of the Shuri defense line, Sergeant White displayed undaunted courage and superb leadership in the face of enemy fire. Casualties had reduced the noncommissioned officer strength to two in addition to Sergeant White, and the company commander and one platoon leader were the only officers remaining in action. Sergeant White assumed command of the depleted squads, kept them organized and encouraged the remaining men to hold their ground. While the enemy laid down a heavy mortar barrage in preparation for his seventh counterattack, Sergeant White left his position in order to observe and relay adjustments of fire to the company commander for transmission to our mortars. From his exposed observation point he effected such accurate fire direction that the counterattack was broken up. Sergeant White was killed while directing this fire. His gallantry, determination and aggressive leadership in the face of heavy enemy counterattacks were major factors in enabling his company commander to rally and reorganize the decimated company. The high morale of the group was the direct result of the inspiring example set by Sergeant White.*[8]

In March 2013, 1st Lieutenant Theodore Bell returned to Okinawa to revisit the ridge where he led his 200-man company on the assault on Ishimmi Ridge. Just 22 men survived. Here the Japanese erected a Peace Park with long black stone walls etched with the name of every person, American or Japanese, killed in battle. Bell lingered in the American section, finding the name of the men in his company who were killed, especially 1st Sergeant Howard White, who served with him throughout the war.[7, 9]

Howard White, son of Leonard and Eva (Willford) White, was buried at Lakeview Cemetery, Big Fork, Minnesota. Survivors included his parents, his wife, a six-month-old son, Gene Howard, whom he never met, and eight siblings. Grace White Haley posted on the World War II Registry: *He wrote and said he helped put the flag up.* A seasoned infantryman since September 19, 1940, White was among the 239 men who died with the 77th on Ie Shima.[11]

Darvin Fred Lange

Wanda (Redwood County)

25th Infantry "Tropic Lightning" Division, 35th Infantry Regiment, B Company, Private First Class
FEBRUARY 24, 1926–MAY 21, 1945—Battle for Luzon, Philippines

On December 25, 1944, two months after his draft into the service, Darvin Lange wrote home from Camp Hood: *Dear Mother, Dad, Sister and Brothers: Well, I am going to spend Christmas evening in the barracks. First thing I got your package today just for Christmas and you never know how much or how it feels to get a package like that right on Christmas. It makes the tears come when one gets a package from home, and think how I would like to be home. I shall never forget that nice package. Sure wish I could have sent you all something for Christmas but one can't get much around here.*[1]

Private First Class Darvin Lange joined the 25th Infantry Division, a young division just over two months old and stationed at Schofield Barrack on Oahu, Hawaii, when the Japanese bombed Pearl Harbor on December 7, 1941. After the attack, the division defended Oahu from invasion until November 25, 1942, when they landed on Guadalcanal. Their quick action and superior performance earned the 25th the nickname "Tropic Lightning."

After battling through the Solomons Campaign, the 25th moved to New Caledonia on February 8, 1944, to prepare for the invasion of the Philippines. Landing on Luzon on January 11, 1945, they drove across the central plain of Luzon, where they secured the cities of Umingan, Lupao and San Jose on their way to the Caraballo Mountains. Along Highway 5, the division fought from hill to hill taking Digdig, Putlan and Kapintalan in an attempt to secure the key Balete Pass.

Private First Class Darvin Lange arrived on the Philippines April 14, shortly before the Allies secured the town of Kapintalan on April 21, and went into action May 4 on Luzon. The fierce battle for Balete Pass, the only connection between central Luzon and the Cagayan Valley, continued until May 13, 1945. After securing the pass, the 25th advanced to Santa Fe with Private First Class Darvin Lange and the 35th Regiment straddling the highway.[2, 3] In a letter to Darvin's parents, Chaplain Sanford Shafland explained what happened on May 20, 1945: *Darvin died of injuries, which he had received at the explosion of a Japanese cave near Balete Pass. This explosion was a terrific one and claimed the lives of several other American soldiers. Your son was injured by flying rocks, from which injuries he later died. He was well liked by those who knew him, and his absence is a distinct loss to his company. His comrades and superior officers alike tell me that he conducted himself according to the highest standards of our soldiers in battle and that he quit himself like the man that he was.*[4]

Private First Class Lange died the following day at the 63rd Port Surgical Hospital, five miles north of Digdig, Luzon.[5] The 35th Regiment reached Santa Fe five days later and on July 4, 1945, the Luzon campaign ended. Plans called for the 25th Division to lead the invasion of Japan; however, dropping the atomic bombs on Hiroshima and Nagasaki forced Japan's surrender on August 15, 1945.[2, 3]

At a Memorial Day service, Darlene Lange Haug spoke about her brother: *Darvin, 18 years old was drafted and left October 17, 1944 for Camp Hood, Texas, for basic training. Eight months and one furlough later, he was dead. Those days each week the newspapers carried "wounded in action, missing in action, and killed in action" columns, along with families' names and addresses. Mom wrote many letters, trying to find anyone who knew Darvin or anything about his death. It was learned Darvin and three other men were ordered to go ahead and check for land mines—there was an explosion. Those were the days of no email, cell phones, or grief support groups. It was so hard on my parents. A couple years later the government sent his body home. The casket came to Lamberton on the train accompanied by a military escort. Having his body back home opened old wounds and brought back many questions. Those years it was custom to have the body in the home. I remember being in the living room near the casket and thinking, "Is it really Darvin's body in there? But, there was his dog tag and serial number. I was 12 years old.*[5]

Survivors included his parents, Walter and Erna (Buetow) Lange, and four siblings. He was initially buried in Santa Barbara Cemetery, Luzon, Philippines, and reinterred in 1948 in Waterbury Lutheran Cemetery, Lamberton, Minnesota.[6]

Kenneth Roy Davis

U.S. Navy Hospital Corps, 6th Marine "The Striking Sixth" Division, 6th Medical Battalion,
E Medical Company, Hospital Corpsman, Hospital Apprentice First Class
DECEMBER 7, 1925–JUNE 4, 1945—Battle of Okinawa, Okinawa

Kenneth Davis enlisted in the navy in November, 1943, a month before his eighteenth birthday and signed up for the medical corps. As historian Mark Flowers points out, most people don't realize that some navy corpsmen are assigned to the marines, who do not have their own medical branch. After training at a hospital corps school, Davis was assigned to the U.S. Marine Corps and attended Field Medical Service School in Camp Pendleton, California, for advanced training in emergency battlefield medical treatment, evacuation and sanitation. Corpsmen were also trained to use an M-1 carbine for combat, and often ended up as active participants in a battle, when they too were under attack.[1]

In World War II, hospital corpsmen hit the beach with marines in every battle in the Pacific. From April 1 to June 21, the 6th Division secured Yontan Airfield and captured Ishikawa Isthmus, the town of Nago and the Motobu Peninsula. After securing most of northern Okinawa, the men headed south to the Shuri Line along the southern coastline where they seized Sugar Loaf Hill, followed by the capital city of Naha.

On June 4, Hospital Corpsman Kenneth Davis accompanied two regiments of the 6th Marine Division as they attacked the Oroku Peninsula on Okinawa, home to Japan's navy base and Okinawa air base. Determined to fight to the last man, 5,000 Japanese made a final stand on the peninsula on a rainy, muddy day. Impassable inland roads and heavily mined rice paddies and hills eliminated the use of tanks for rifle company support. On June 4, during the advance on the Oroku Peninsula, 19-year-old Hospital Apprentice First Class Kenneth Davis died, nine days before the Allies captured the harbor and Naha airfield.[2, 3]

The battle on Okinawa ended June 21, 1945, and took a heavy toll on both sides. On land, the Americans lost 7,373 men killed and 32,056 wounded. At sea, the Americans lost 5,000 killed and 4,600 wounded. Japanese casualties included 107,000 killed and 7,400 men taken prisoner. A total of 1,149 hospital corpsmen, including 1,046 enlisted corpsmen, were killed in action during World War II, the majority while serving with U.S. Marine Corps units.[4] As the corpsmen accompanied the marines into battle, they were shot as often as the troops to whom they gave aid. Scott McGaugh

calls the medics "Battlefield Angels": *A battlefield angel is the corpsman or medic willing to risk his or her life to save another, sometimes under enemy fire. When battlefield conditions dictate that troops take cover, that's usually when a corpsman or medic is called on to become exposed to mortars and shrapnel in order to save lives. More than one soldier has looked up at a corpsman or medic and called him "my angel." … They do their duty for the sake of helping others, never in quest of the spotlight.*[5, 6]

Hospital Apprentice First Class Kenneth Davis was survived by his parents and four siblings. He is buried in National Memorial Cemetery of the Pacific, Honolulu, Hawaii, and his name is hand-etched on stone at Memorial Park, Mizpah, Minnesota. Kenneth attended grade school in Mizpah and high school in Northome. During high school, he worked during the summer for the Minnesota Ontario Paper Company in Northome.[7]

Jerome Louis Gorres

Wanda (Redwood County)

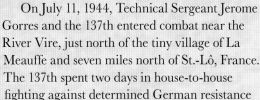

Third Army, 35th Infantry "Santa Fe" Division, 137th Infantry Regiment, 2nd Battalion, G Company, Technical Sergeant

AUGUST 11, 1921–JUNE 13, 1945—Occupation Zone West of the Rhine River, Germany

On July 11, 1944, Technical Sergeant Jerome Gorres and the 137th entered combat near the River Vire, just north of the tiny village of La Meauffe and seven miles north of St.-Lô, France. The 137th spent two days in house-to-house fighting against determined German resistance before successfully entering St.-Lô ahead of other Allied units. Following the race across France, the 35th Division participated in the operations against Metz, France—the "Lorraine Gateway" into Germany.[1, 2]

As the 35th Division fought its way through the Maginot Line defenses ten miles south of Metz, Technical Sergeant Jerome Gorres was awarded the Silver Star Medal for gallantry in action on November 2, 1944: *Sergeant Gorres, a platoon guide with the 137th Infantry Regiment assumed command of all available men in his platoon after a squad leader and second in command became casualties. In the absence of the platoon leader, he reorganized his unit in the face of heavy enemy fire and led them forward about 15 yards, until pinned down by direct fire from an enemy machine gun emplacement to the front. Rather than risk the lives of his men, Sergeant Gorres charged the enemy position alone, firing his rifle from the hip. He counted for two of the three enemy crewmembers, jumped into the emplacement and killed the third German with his bayonet. He then led his troops into the village the enemy had been defending, established security positions, then organized and supervised a hand-carrying detail to replenish the rations, ammunition and water supply of the troops in the village.[3, 4]*

Following the defeat of the Germans during the Battle of the Bulge in January 1945, the 137th Infantry spearheaded the way for the rest of the division across the Roer River at Korrenzig, Germany, on February 23, 1945. Ordered to control the Rhine River bridges between Wesel and Duisburg, Technical Sergeant Gorres and his G Company, supported by tanks and artillery, fought hard for a well-defended outpost. Their success forced the Germans to retreat, and by March 26, the 35th Division crossed the Rhine.

Germany surrendered on May 8, 1945, and on June 1, 1945, the 137th Infantry Regiment joined the Allied army of occupation. They took control of a zone west of the Rhine River, including the towns of St. Goar, Zell, Cochem and Simmern. Technical Sergeant Jerome Gorres and the 2nd Battalion, held in reserve at Simmern, were responsible for 9 security missions covering over 1,000 miles, a nearly impossible task.[1, 2]

After surviving battles across France and Germany, Technical Sergeant Gorres lost his life in an accident while on a patrol mission. On June 13, Technical Sergeant Gorres and a seven-man patrol discovered a route of approach to Lintfort, Germany, during the last days of isolated pockets of German resistance. During the night, the patrol decided to enter the city, but within 100 yards of Lintfort, they met enemy fire and returned to their company. On the way back, Technical Sergeant Jerome Gorres and one other soldier died on Highway 329 near Halsenbach, Germany, when their jeep overturned.[5] Jerome's family learned the news from relatives of a soldier from Revere, Minnesota. The newspaper reported: *From a letter received by Redwood County relatives of Sergeant Henry Hoffrogge, Revere, who had entered the service with the former in September 1944, and had been with him through the German campaign, they learned that Gorres and another soldier had met death in Germany when a truck tipped over.*

Jerome Gorres entered the service August 22, 1942. Survivors included his parents and six siblings. A family full of talented musicians, Jerome and his siblings worked in the family hotel and restaurant business. He was buried in St. Mathias Cemetery, Wanda, Minnesota.[6, 7]

Gordon Orlean Nelson

Strandquist (Marshall County)

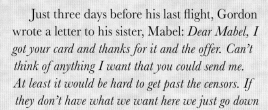

U.S. Army Air Forces, 20th Air Force, 19th Very Heavy Bomb Group, 93rd Bomb Squadron, Staff Sergeant

JUNE 14, 1923–JUNE 22, 1945—Bombing Mission over Tamashima, Japan

Just three days before his last flight, Gordon wrote a letter to his sister, Mabel: *Dear Mabel, I got your card and thanks for it and the offer. Can't think of anything I want that you could send me. At least it would be hard to get past the censors. If they don't have what we want here we just go down to some Seabee camp and they'll usually sell it to us. If you want to waste some ration points you could send me some cheese spread and a couple of small boxes of crackers. Sounds silly, but its pretty good with a bottle of beer. Last night we went out and burned down the town of Kagoshima. That was our 16th mission and a very pretty sight it was. I don't particularly like these night missions but they're a lot more colorful than day raids. They were throwing up tracers at us, and it looked like a misplaced 4th of July celebration. Rumors (which are about all we hear) have it that crews will be going home with 30 missions now. Even that is quite a way off but at least we're over the halfway mark if it's true. We could be home by mid-August if we kept up our present pace. I just hope they don't make us stay here as instructors for a couple of months, after we finish our tour. Well, no news is good news so this probably sent you into raptures of joy. Write soon. As ever, Gordon*[1]

Gordon Nelson graduated from Strandquist High School in 1941, and entered the service on December 10, 1942, in San Diego, California. Following graduation from radio and gunnery school, Gordon was assigned to the 20th Air Force, a strategic bombing command formed by General Henry "Hap" Arnold and headquartered in the United States.[2] Before the war, General Arnold led a design team that set the specifications for the B-29 Superfortress and decided to use his B-29s in the China-Burma-Indian theater and the Pacific, not in Europe.[3]

On April 1, 1944, the 19th Bomb Group began training for combat on the B-29 Superfortress. In December, Staff Sergeant Gordon Nelson and the 19th Bomb Group moved to Guam, an island in the Marianas, for duty with the 20th Air Force. Beginning with the Japanese airfield on Rota, Marianas Islands, in February 1944, the 19th raided other enemy airfields used to launch kamikaze attacks during the battle for Okinawa. The group also bombed industrial targets throughout the major cities of Japan, including Tokyo.[4]

On a clear day, June 22, 1945, Staff Sergeant Gordon Nelson, gunner for a B-29 nicknamed *Maximum Effort No. 3* left with a crew of 11 for his final mission. Pilot William Miller's bomber, loaded with 12 Browning machine guns, headed to Tamashima, Japan, for a general purpose bombing. Eyewitnesses in Group S-2, reported the following: *Captain Miller's plane was at the assembly point when enemy fighters came through the formation and attacked his plane. No. 1 engine was feathered and No. 3 and No. 4 engines were smoking. The plane then went into a slow spin, but straightened out again. The plane started straight down, the right wing broke off, and then the plane exploded. Four or seven parachutes were seen to open. The aircraft crashed into the sea. Five white spots and one yellow spot were observed near the wreckage.*[5]

After bombing the Mitsubishi Aircraft Factory, the B-29 crashed over Okayama, a major transportation hub on the Seto Inland Sea. The last two raids by the 20th Air Force forced the end of the war. On August 6, the *Enola Gay*, piloted by Colonel Paul Tibbets, Jr., dropped the first atomic bomb on Hiroshima, and three days later *Bockscar*, flown by Major Charles Sweeney, dropped another bomb over Nagasaki. Six days later the Japanese surrendered.[4]

Sergeant Gordon Nelson is memorialized on the Tablets of the Missing, Honolulu, Hawaii, and at Zion Cemetery, Marshall County, Minnesota. He received the Air Medal with Oak Leaf Cluster and the Purple Heart. Survivors included his parents and eight siblings.[1]

Allen Duane Nelson

Comstock (Clay County)

U.S. Navy Patrol Bomb Squadron (VPB)-118 "The Old Crows," Crew 11,
Aviation Machinist's Mate Second Class

NOVEMBER 3, 1922–JULY 22, 1945—Search Patrol Near the Mouth of the Yangtze River, China

Allen D. Nelson is Lost in Action

Allen D. Nelson, aviation machinist's mate second class, and son of Mr. and Mrs. Oliver B. Nelson, Comstock, has been lost in action, according to word received by his parents from the navy department. He previously had been reported missing since July 23.

Nelson was a gunner on a plane, which was doing patrol duty off the China coast. When the plane circled an enemy ship to investigate it, the vessel opened fire. The plane was hit, began to lose altitude, and finally crashed. Seven crewmembers escaped but Nelson and six other men were lost when the plane broke in half and sank in less than a minute. Allen Nelson was born November 3, 1923, and graduated from Comstock High School in June 1939. He was a member of the Swedish Lutheran Church. He joined the service in January 1942, and went overseas in the spring of 1944. Besides his parents is a brother, Donald B., eight years old, at home.[1]

After Nazi Germany surrendered on May 8, 1945, Japan was the remaining Axis power still on the battlefield. When the navy needed a long-range land-based aircraft for patrols against enemy shipping and submarines, they purchased 739 PB4Y-2 Privateers, long-range patrol bombers with increased capacity for arms and distance. Patrol bomber squadron VPB-118 "The Old Crows" was the first squadron to fly the Privateer, and trained on the plane in August 1944 at Crows Landing, California, before the rest of the world knew it existed. "The Old Crows" played a crucial role in the Allied victory by raiding Japan's harbors and sending tons of supplies plundered by Japan into the sea, further diminishing Japan's ability to wage war.[2, 3, 6]

Aviation Machinist's Mate Second Class Allen D. Nelson, 22 years old and a mechanic/port waist turret, trained on the Privateer and belonged to Crew 11 of VPB-118, piloted by Lieutenant Leland "Mac" McCutcheon. On July 21, 1945, Lieutenant McCutcheon, lead plane commander of Crew 11 and a group of planes, were flying patrol over a specific section of ocean off the coast of China to observe any enemy activity. Author James Pettit wrote about what happened: *Crew 11 was shot down by an ambush of concealed heavy AA guns on a ferry/gunboat that they intercepted near Shanghai.*

When McCutcheon approached the boat to inspect it, the boat opened up with a devastating hail of AA fire. Ensign Bucklew was incapacitated or killed immediately. A fire engulfed Lieutenant McCutcheon's lower body. Despite the excruciation that he must have been subject to, he succeeded in executing a flaps-up ditch into the ocean. The plane broke up on impact but some of the crew, though injured, was able to get into life rafts. The survivors were then in danger of attack from the ferry/gunboat, which was approaching rapidly. McCutcheon's wingman, "Horse" Thompson (Crew 17), courageously chased off the boat after making two or three strafing runs at this heavily armed boat. After about two hours, a PB2Y-2 Coronado recovered the survivors. Six crew were killed in action and three were seriously injured. Four had less serious injuries and returned to the squadron after recovering. Allen Nelson was one of those who perished.[2, 4]

Nelson's Individual Deceased Personnel File reported: *Three searches of the area where this aircraft was reported to have crashed have revealed no trace of any of the crew or any wreckage of the aircraft.*[5]

Aviation Machinist's Mate Second Class Allen Nelson, son of Oliver B. and Martha (Ness) Nelson, is memorialized at Fort William McKinley, Manila, Philippines, and Clara Cemetery, Comstock, Minnesota.[1]

Herman Arthur Thelander

Kinbrae (Nobles County)

U.S. Naval Reserve, Flight 19 Squadron, Seaman First Class

1926?-DECEMBER 5, 1945—Flight 19, Bermuda Triangle

In December of 1945, World War II had been over for nearly four months, but a large number of navy and marine personnel still awaited discharge at Fort Lauderdale Naval Air Station. According to the Naval Air Station Fort Lauderdale, December 5 was a typical south Florida winter day with variable winds and clear skies. On that day, 14 navy and marine airmen on Flight 19 Squadron reported to the operations center for a routine navigation exercise across the Gulf of Florida. No one would know that their operation would end in what the navy would later refer to as one of the "strangest unsolved mysteries of the sea." Lieutenant Charles C. Taylor, a six-year navy veteran, commanded Flight 19, a squadron of five torpedo bombers. Three crewman flew in plane FT-3, including Seaman First Class Herman Thelander, from Kinbrae, Minnesota.

The five pilots and their crews reported to the flight line at 1:30 p.m. for a preflight check on the TBM Avenger Torpedo Bombers, one of the largest and most powerful single-engine propeller planes ever built. At 2:00 p.m., Lieutenant Taylor's plane and four other planes were airborne and in formation, heading for the wreck of a ship just south of Bimini in the Bahamas. After several practice torpedo runs at the concrete hulk, Flight 19 began the day's mission—a routine navigation training flight east for 160 miles, north for 40 miles, and then back to their base, a triangular course into the Bermuda or "Devil's Triangle."[1, 2, 3]

Just before 4:00 p.m., the tower operators at Fort Lauderdale Naval Air Station received a frantic message from Lieutenant Taylor: *"Calling tower, this is an emergency. We seem to be off course. We cannot see land...repeat... we cannot see land." "What is your position?"* The tower radioed back: *"We are not sure of our position,"* radioed Lieutenant Taylor. *"We can't be sure just where we are. We seem to be lost."* The tower operators were stunned that five planes with experienced crews were lost in fair to good flight conditions. They radioed back, "Assume bearing due west." Taylor answered, *"We don't know which way is west. Everything is wrong...strange. We can't be sure of any direction. Even the ocean doesn't look as it should!"*

At 4:25, the flight leader suddenly turned the command over to Captain Stivers, who reported: *"We are not sure where we are. We think we must be 225 miles northeast of base. It looks like we are entering white water. We're completely lost."* Then silence.[1]

After losing contact with the squadron, Lieutenant Harry Cone took off in a PBM-5 Mariner, a plane bigger than a B-17 Flying Fortress, to search for Flight 19. Her crew of 13 was well experienced in search and rescue operations. Less than half an hour later the Mariner's radio operator radioed the base that they were nearing the last assumed position of the five lost Avengers but could see nothing. The Mariner sent in one more position report and then Lieutenant Harry Cone and his crew of 12 were never heard from again. The SS *Gaines Mills*, a ship in the general area where Lieutenant Cone disappeared, witnessed an explosion with 100-foot flames about that time, and reported an oil slick, but no fragments of that plane were found.[2]

Despite an intensive 5-day search that covered 280,000 square miles, including the Everglades and the Gulf of Mexico, all 6 planes and 27 men disappeared forever.[1, 2, 3]

Dennis Zierke remembers his cousin: *I was only six years old when Buddy (as named by the family), went missing in the Bermuda Triangle on December 5, 1945. He was planning to come home for Christmas leave. He was called Buddy because his Grandpa Zierke was named Herman. Buddy was born September 3, 1926, and his sister, Fern, in 1931. They lived on a farm about one mile from Kinbrae. His father always farmed with horses. When they got their first tractor, Buddy was the one to drive it. His dad still preferred the horses.*[4]

Seaman First Class Herman Thelander enlisted on September 26, 1944. Survivors included his parents and a sister, Fern.[5]

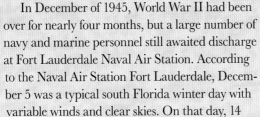

Other Wartime Casualties from Little Minnesota

Not all wartime casualties happen in battle. Training accidents, illnesses and air crashes all take their toll. The following men from tiny Minnesota towns died while serving their country overseas. We've included as much information as we have about them, but it was not enough to produce a full-fledged account.

Name	Town	Service Branch	Notes
Radioman Second Class Halge Hojem Smestad, Jr. May 19, 1919–December 7, 1941	Dovray Murray County	U.S. Navy	While serving aboard the USS *Arizona*, Radioman Second Class, Halge Smestad died during the bombing of Pearl Harbor. Halge is memorialized at Our Savior's Cemetery, Dovray, Minnesota, and the Honolulu Memorial and USS *Arizona* Memorial, Honolulu, Hawaii.
Private John A. Wojciak January 23, 1918–June 9, 1942	Hillman Morrison County	U.S. Army, 32nd Coast Artillery Corps, C Battery	Private Wojciak died during a training exercise at Camp Wallace Texas. The Wojciak-Talberg American Legion Post 602 in Hillman is named for John Wojciak and William Talberg. He is buried in St. Elizabeth's Cemetery, Brennyville, Minnesota.
Private Wilford Strom	Henriette, Pine County	U.S. Army	While serving his country, Private Wilford Strom died due to injuries sustained away from the battlefield. He is buried in Henriette Cemetery, Henriette, Minnesota.
Seaman First Class Harry James Ambroz	Heidelberg La Sueur County	U.S. Naval Reserve	Seaman First Class Harry Ambroz died in an accident at Dutch Harbor, Alaska. Harry Ambroz is buried St. Scholastic Cemetery, Heidelberg, Minnesota.
First Lieutenant Clarence Housman June 24, 1919–July 26, 1943	Delhi Redwood County	U.S. Army Air Corps, 84th Bomb Group, 302nd Bomb Squadron	First Lieutenant Housman disappeared on a routine training flight, was found on April 22, 1944, and buried in Echo, Minnesota.
Ensign Anthony Joseph Merck, Jr. January 29, 1925–July 28, 1943	Humboldt Kittson County	U.S. Navy Air Wing	A bombardier, Ensign Merck died in a midair collision near Jacksonville, Florida. Anthony Merck is buried in Greenwood Cemetery, Hallock, Minnesota.
Aviation Ordnanceman Third Class Eino August Miettinen February 10, 1922–November 4, 1943	Squaw Lake Itasca County	U.S. Navy	While posted to the crew of USS *Copahee*, an escort carrier and working on a landing strip, a bomb from TBF Avenger aircraft exploded on a landing strip, killing 13 ground crew including Aviation Ordnanceman Third Class Eino Miettinen. He is buried at Oneota Cemetery, Duluth, Minnesota.
Staff Sergeant Donald A. Krogman February 26, 1925–April 8, 1944	Dundee Nobles County	U.S. Army Air Forces, 9th Air Force, 394th Bomb Group, 585th Bomb Squadron	Staff Sergeant Krogman died when his B-26 Marauder crashed due to engine failure shortly after leaving Dunmow Airbase, Essex, England. He is buried in St. Mary's Cemetery, Dundee, Minnesota.
Private First Class Clarence E. Jourdet 1915–June 6, 1944	Gully/Gonvick Polk County	U.S. Army, 58th Armored Field Artillery Battalion	Private First Class Clarence Jourdet was killed in action during the D-Day landing, Normandy, France. He is buried at Normandy American Cemetery and Memorial, France.
Technician Fifth Grade Orval Henry Christianson September 17, 1918–August 1, 1944	Vining Otter Tail County	U.S. Army	Technician Fifth Grade Orval Christianson died following a tonsillectomy at an army hospital at Camp Howze, Texas. He is buried in Vining Lutheran Cemetery, Vining, Minnesota.
Technician Fifth Grade Edward Sylvester Stoering January 13, 1915–September 18, 1944	Richville Otter Tail County	U.S. Army, 206th Coast Artillery, Anti-Aircraft Battalion	Technician Fifth Grade Edward Stoering died when his C-47 transport plane crashed on the ridge of Mt. McKinley, Alaska. Edward Stoering is memorialized on the Tablets of the Missing, Honolulu, Hawaii, and at St. John's Lutheran Cemetery, Richville, Minnesota.
Machinist's Mate Third Class Warren Grover Moore June 27, 1921–November 4, 1944	Effie Itasca County	U.S. Navy	Machinist's Mate Third Class Warren Moore died on the TWA Flight 8 crash near Hanford, California. Warren Moore is buried in Big Fork Cemetery, Big Fork, Minnesota.
First Lieutenant Duane Alfred Dahlquist September 25, 1921–August 19, 1944	Hadley Murray County	U.S. Marine Corps Reserve, 4th Marine Base Defense Aircraft, Marine Aircraft Group, 22nd Squadron	First Lieutenant Duane Dahlquist died during a crash landing of his Corsair at Stickell Field, Eniwetok Island, Marshall Islands. First Lieutenant Dahlquist is buried in Slayton Cemetery, Slayton, Minnesota.

(continued on next page)

Other Wartime Casualties from Little Minnesota (continued)

Name	Town	Service Branch	Notes
Ensign William Murray August 5, 1921–November 8, 1944	Donaldson Kittson County	U.S. Naval Reserve, Navy Lightning Squadron (V-12)	While on a training flight, Ensign Murray's plane crashed into the sea near North Bend, Oregon. He is buried at Stephen Cemetery, Stephen, Minnesota.
Private Clarence W. Hassler August 10, 1908–November 17, 1944	Myrtle Freeborn County	U.S. Army, 91st Infantry Division, 361st Infantry Regiment, 1st Battalion, D Company	Private Clarence Hassler died from hepatitis at the 55th Station Hospital in Scarperia, Italy. He is buried at Hillcrest Memorial Park, Albert Lea, Minnesota.
Private Hilbert George Haugan April 27, 1910–January 1, 1945	Gully Polk County	U.S. Army	Private Haugan died of non-battle injuries at Base E Field Hospital, Papua, New Guinea. Hilbert served in the army two years and nine months in the Quartermaster Corps. He is buried in Fort Snelling Cemetery, Minneapolis, Minnesota.
Flight Officer Donovan Joseph Hogan October 22, 1906–January 6, 1945	Kerrick Pine County	U.S. Army Air Forces, 556th Base Unit	While serving in Reno, Nevada, Flight Officer Donovan Hogan died in an air accident on Lahontan Emergency Air Strip, Carson City, Nevada. Donovan is buried in St. Michael's Cemetery, Kerrick, Minnesota.
Ensign Sigurd Harold Myhr Lindseth August 28, 1923–January 19, 1945	Borup Norman County	U.S. Naval Reserve	While aboard the USS *Manileno*, Ensign Sigurd Lindseth died in an accident when the hawser broke loose and knocked him overboard. Sigurd had married his fiancée, Caryl, on October 2, 1944, just eleven days before he left for Guam. He is buried at Trysil-Bethesda Cemetery, Holmes City, Minnesota.
Ensign Orville Thorson November 6, 1920–February 18, 1945	Henriette Pine County	U.S. Naval Reserve, Naval Air Corps, Squadron 95	Ensign Thorson died in an air accident at Naval Air Station, Wildwood, New Jersey. He is buried in Henriette Cemetery, Henriette, Minnesota
Sergeant Earl Leo Gross January 19, 1925–June 15, 1945	Lastrup Morrison County	U.S. Army Air Forces, 4th Air Force, 317th Wing, 423rd Base Unit	While serving as a radio operator stationed at Walla Walla Airfield, Washington, Sergeant Gross died in a B-24 air crash. He is buried in St. John's Cemetery, Lastrup, Minnesota.
Aviation Ordnanceman Third Class Homer Bertel Hanson June 6, 1925–June 22, 1945	Delhi Redwood County	U.S. Navy, Patrol Squadron, VPB-117 "Blue Raiders"	Aviation Ordnanceman Third Class Homer Bertel died in a plane crash shortly after takeoff from McGuire Field, Mindora, Philippines.
Aviation Machinist's Mate Third Class Bruce Christian Cleveland Johnson May 19, 1923–July 31,1945	Boy River Cass County	United States Navy Patrol Squadron, VPB-200	Aviation Machinist's Mate Third Class Bruce Johnson died in an air accident near Oahu, Hawaii. He is buried in Zachary Taylor National Cemetery, Louisville, Kentucky.
Private Edward Herman Dahl September 5, 1916–October 21, 1945	Farwell Pope County	U.S. Army Air Forces, 11th Air Force, 54th Troop Carrier Squadron	An engineer on a transport plane, Private Dahl died in an air crash near Elmendorf Field, Alaska, Anchorage, Alaska. He is buried in Fort Richardson National Cemetery, Anchorage, Alaska.

Military Unit Sizes, Ranks and Command Hierarchies

Unit Name	Military Group/ Unit Composition	Rough Number of Personnel	Usually Commanded By
Army	2 or more Corps	100,000 to 150,000 (or more)	General or Field Marshal
Corps	2 or more Divisions	25,000 to 50,000	General or Lieutenant General
Division	3 or more Brigades or Regiments depending on the country.	10,000 to 15,000	Lieutenant General or Major General
Brigade	3 or more Battalions	1500 to 3500	Major General, Brigadier General, or Colonel
Regiment	2 or more Battalions	1000 to 2000	Colonel
Battalion	3 or more Companies	400 to 1000	Lieutenant Colonel
Company	2 or more Platoons	100 to 250	Captain or Major
Platoon or Troop	2 or more Squads	16 to 50	1st Lieutenant
Squad	2 or more Sections	8 to 24	Sergeant
Section or Fire Team		4 to 12	Sergeant or Corporal

Data and table adapted with permission of World War 2 Facts, www.worldwar2facts.org

A General Summary of Ranks for Enlisted Men in World War II

Pay Grade (lower is better)	Army	Navy	Marines	U.S. Army Air Forces/Army Air Corps
1	Master Sergeant/ First Sergeant	Chief Petty Officer	Sergeant Major/1st Sergeant/ Master Gunnery Sergeant/ Master Technical Sergeant	Master Sergeant/ First Sergeant
2	Technical Sergeant/Staff Sergeant	Petty Officer, First Class	Gunnery Sergeant/ Technical Sergeant	Staff Sergeant
3	Technician Third Grade	Petty Officer, Second Class	Staff Sergeant/ Platoon Sergeant	—
4	Sergeant/Technician Fourth Grade	Petty Officer, Third Class	Sergeant	Sergeant
5	Corporal/Technician Fifth Grade	Seaman First Class/Fireman First Class	Corporal	Corporal
6	Private First Class	Seaman Second Class/Fireman Second Class	Private First Class	Private First Class
7	Private	Apprentice Seaman	Private	Private

Deciphering World War II-era Military Unit Sizes and Ranks

For those who haven't been in the Armed Forces, military hierarchies and rank structures can be a bit intimidating. In particular, it can be hard to know the difference between a brigade and a company, or to know just by how much a Petty Officer First Class outranks a Fireman Second Class. That's why we've compiled the two tables to the left. The first gives you the basics of how military land units were organized, and how large they were. The second chart gives a rough rundown of the rank structure for enlisted men and women across the U.S. Army, Navy, Marines and Army Air Forces/Army Air Corps.

In addition to a base rank, soldiers had a wide variety of different specialties and titles—from cook and pilot to quartermaster and radioman. Given how many specializations there were—a World War II-era poster shows dozens in the army alone—covering them succinctly isn't possible. Nonetheless, if you know the basics of the tables, you can usually get a handle on where someone fell in terms of rank.

Officers, Warrant Officers, NCOs, and Enlisted Men

Another complication for those delving into military history is knowing the nuances of military hierarchy, especially the difference between commissioned and non-commissioned officers, warrant officers and enlisted men. Brief summaries of each are below.

Commissioned Officers were officers who outranked all enlisted men and non-commissioned officers. They obtained a "commission" from the President of the United States, and their job was to serve as leaders. The higher their rank, the more people they led. In World War II, the only ways to obtain a commission was either by being selected to attend each branch's specific Officer Candidate School, or by graduating from a military academy (West Point, the Naval Academy, etc.).

Warrant officers were specialists with a higher rank/pay grade than any enlisted men, but below that of commissioned officers.

Non-commissioned officers (NCOs) were enlisted men who rose in the ranks high enough to command those of lesser ranks.

Enlisted men volunteered for service or were drafted; they were commanded by non-commissioned officers.

Sources

Emery, John

1. Emery, John Marvin. Karig, Walter and Welbourn Kelley. *Battle Report*. Individual Deceased Personnel File. Washington, D.C.: Department of the Army, 4 November 1949.

2. "By the Numbers: Pearl Harbor." New Orleans. National World War II Museum. www.nationalww2museum.org/assets/pdfs/pearl-harbor-fact-sheet-1.pdf

3. Gore, Leada. "Pearl Harbor: 74th Anniversary: 7 Facts about Dec. 7, 1941, a date which will live in infamy." Alabama Media Group, 7 December 2015. www.al.com/news/index.ssf/2015/12/pearl_harbor_74th_anniversary.htm

4. Kent, Molly. *USS* Arizona's *Last Band: The History of U.S. Navy Band Number 22*. Silent Song, 1996.

5. "USS *Arizona* Memorial." National Park Service. www.pearlharborhistoricsites.org/pearl-harbor/arizona-memorial

6. Mauk, Cathy. "Fifty Years Haven't Erased Pain of War for Local Family." *Fargo Forum*, B10, 8 December 1991.

Johnson, Aaron

1. Johnson, John. Phone interview with author, 14 December 2014.

2. Schmidt, Natalie. Letter to author, 9 January 2015.

3. Swanson, Nathan. "Story of Aaron Luverne Johnson." 4-H Project, 2001.

4. Johnson, Aaron Luverne. Letter to parents, 2 February 1941. From the files of John Johnson.

5. Maher, Captain Arthur L. "Narrative on USS *Houston* in Sunda Strait." Fold3 Historical Military Records, 5 December 1945. https://blog.fold3.com/find-personal-interviews-in-the-wwii-war-diaries, 13 October, 2014.

6. "USS *Houston*." HMAS *Perth*. Accessed via http://perthone.com

7. Hornfischer, James. *Ship of Ghosts*. New York: Random House, 2006.

8. Wikipedia contributors. "Battle of Makassar Strait." Wikipedia, The Free Encyclopedia, 1 December 2015. https://en.wikipedia.org

9. "Luverne Johnson Killed in Line of Duty in Asiatic Waters; In Navy 4 Years." *Murray County Herald*, 19 February 1942. Obituary used with permission, courtesy of *Murray County Herald*.

10. Charles, Dana. "USS *Houston* CA-30 Survivors Association and Next Generations." Email to author, 1 October 2012.

Tester, Rodney

1. Backus, Janice Tester. Email to author, 8 September 2014. Letter to author, 13 September 2014.

2. Aircraft Accident and Incident Reports 1940 thru 1948. National Archives and Records Service, World War II Records Division, 27 September 1958.

3. Ostlund, Dave. "Douglas B 18-A Bolo A/C No. 37-522." Kodiak Military History Museum. www.kadiak.org/crash/b-18a_crash_summary.html, 18 March 2009.

Snell, Harold

1. Kayser, Zach. "Walt Straka: The Last Man of A Company, 194th Tank Battalion. Minnesota Man Tells of Surviving Bataan Death March." *Brainerd Dispatch*, 10 November 2015.

2. Crosby, Jackie. "Bataan survivor gave kindness." *Metro Star Tribune*, 24 November 2013.

3. Snell, Private Harold A. Finding of Death of Missing Person. Individual Deceased Personnel File. Washington, D.C.: War Department, 27 May 1944.

4. Opolony, Jim. "Private Harold A. Snell." Find A Grave Memorial, 18 May 2009. www.findagrave.com

5. Lackie, George. "34th Tank Company History: Company A. 194th Tank Battalion." Japanese WWII POW Camp Fukuoka #17, February 2016. www.lindavdahl.com/FrontPage_Links/194thTank%20Battalion%20History.htm

6. O'Rourke, Mike. "Bataan Day at State Capitol." *Brainerd Dispatch*, 10 April 2002.

7. Quinlen, Clinton. "Straka, Walt. 194th GHQ Light Tank Battalion." A Company 194th Bataan Project. Proviso East High School Baatan Commemorative Research Project, 8 January 2016. bataanproject.com/

8. Erickson, Matt. "Sentimental Experience." *Brainerd Dispatch*, 10 April 2011.

9. The Battle of Bataan and the 194th Tank Battalion. Minnesota National Guard, 10 March 2015. www.minnesotanationalguard.org/bataan/The_Battle_of_Bataan_and_the_194th_Tank_Battalion.pdf

Rahier, Elwyn

1. "B-17E Chief Seattle," 10 August 2015. www.pacificwrecks.com

2. Spieth, Glen E. "Chief Seattle" from the Pacific Northwest. 1991. www.lanbob.com

3. Missing Air Crew Report #16345. Washington, D.C.: War Department, Headquarters Army Air Forces, 10 April 1946.

4. Rahier, Boyd. Email to author, 29 July 2014.

5. Compton, John T. "Chief Seattle and Crew." Peter Dunn's Australia @ War. Quote and photo used with permission. www.ozatwar.com/usaaf/chiefofseattle.htm

6. Poor, Joe. Email to author, 30 July 2014. Photos from collection of Joe Poor, 17 August 2014.

7. Poor, Richard. Email to author, 28 July 2014.

8. "Staff Sargeant Elwyn O. Rahier." Find A Grave Memorial, 8 August 2010. www.findagrave.com

Rose, Donald

1. Sambito, Major William J. *A History of Marine Fighter Squadron 232*. Washington, D.C.: History and Museums Division Headquarters, 1978. www.marines.mil/Portals/59/Publications/A%20History%20of%20Marine%20Fighter%20Attack%20Squadron%20232%20%20PCN%2019000308100_1.pdf

2. Flowers, Mark. "The First Marine Division. The Old Breed." WW2Gyrene—a Tribute to the World War II Marine. 2004. www.ww2gyrene.org

3. Hanson, David. "Marine Scout Bombing Squadron 232." A Tribute to the Cactus Air Force. http://www.daveswarbirds.com/cactus/2 January 2013

4. Report of Action of Marine Aircraft Group 23 for the period 31 August to 15 September 1942. Unit Diary. National Archives and Records Administration, 31 December 2012.

5. Hall of Valor Data Base. "Rose, Donald V." Military Times Hall of Valor. http://valor.militarytimes.com/

6. "He Made the Supreme Sacrifice." From the WW II files at Whalan Museum, Whalan, Minnesota. Courtesy of Donna Novotny.

7. Lynch, Richard A. Email to author, 28 January 2014.

8. Rose, Donald V. Report of Interment. Individual Deceased Personnel File. Washington, D.C.: War Department, 13 September 1942.

9. "Donald V. Rose." *Wykoff Enterprise*, 5 March 1948.

Kolstad, Omar

1. Chen, Peter. "Heavy Cruiser USS *Vincennes*." World War II Database. http:// ww2db.com/ship_spec.php?ship_id=302

2. "The Pacific War, 1942: The Battle of Savo Island-August 9, 1942." World War II in the Pacific. www.ww2pacific.com/

3. *Swift County Monitor-News*. Quote by Martin Schneller used with permission, courtesy of Reed Anfinson, Publisher.

4. Schneller, Milton. "Omar Julian Kolstad." Find A Grave Memorial, 9 January 2013. www.findagrave.com

5. "Services Held in Memory of Omar Kolstad." *Glenwood Herald*, 28 October 1943.

6. Kolstad, Omar Julian. Individual Deceased Personnel File. Washington, D.C.: Department of the Navy, 11 February 1949.

Haarstad, Ernest

1. Comstock Centennial Committee. *Comstock Centennial 1890–1990*. Gwinner, ND: J&M Printing, 1990.

2. Atkinson, Rick. *An Army at Dawn*. New York: Henry Holt & Company, 2002.

3. "Comstock Youth Reported Missing." *Moorhead Daily News*, 12 December 1942.

4. Kolbicz, Rainer. "USS *Tasker Bliss* AP-42" on www.uboat.net

5. "Hold Haarstad Memorial Rites." *Moorhead Daily News*, 29 January 1944.

6. Klemann, Ryan. Phone interview with author, 27 April 2015.

7. Olson, Shane. "Ernest Haarstad." Find A Grave Memorial, 6 August 2010. www.findagrave.com

Johnson, Clayton

1. "Former Clark Youth Reported Missing in Action; Was Pearl Harbor Attack Survivor." *The Evening Huronite*, 14 January 1943.

2. Brown, David. *Warship Losses of World War Two*. London: Arms and Armour, 1990.

3. Cressman, Robert J. "*Barton I* (DD-599)." Naval History and Heritage Command, 27 February 2006. https://www.history.navy.mil/search

4. McComb, David. "USS *Barton*." Destroyer History Foundation. destroyerhistory.org/destroyers/aboutus/

5. Wikipedia contributors. "USS *Barton* (DD-599)." Wikipedia, The Free Encyclopedia, 21 January 2016. https://en.wikipedia.org

6. Johnson, Clayton Ordin. Individual Deceased Personnel File. Washington, D.C.: War Department, 30 November 1943.

7. Pocock, Michael W. Email to author, 7 July 2014.

Clewitt, William

1. Birkitt, Philip. *Guadalcanal Legacy 50th Anniversary*, pp. 87–90. Nashville: Turner Publishing Company, 1992.

2. "Battle Biographies-American Division." Wartime Press. www.wartimepress.com

3. "American Infantry Division." Combat Chronicles. Reproduced from *The Army Almanac: A Book of Facts Concerning the Army of the United States*, pp. 510–592. Washington D.C.: U.S. Government Printing Office, 1950.

4. Baglien, Colonel Samuel. "Diary of Col. Samuel Baglien and Photos." Courtesy of Shirley J. Olgeirson, Lt. Col. (Ret.), 164th Infantry Association. TheyWereReady@hotmail.com

5. Olgeirson, Shirley J. Lt. Col. (Ret.). Email to author, 24 March 2015.

6. Baglien, Samuel. "Diary of Col. Samuel Baglien: An Account of the 164th Infantry Regiment." North Dakota National Guard. TheyWereReady@hotmail.com

7. Shoptaugh, Terry L. *They Were Ready: The 164th Infantry in the Pacific War, 1942–1945*, pp. 181–182. Valley City, ND: 164th Infantry Association of the United States, 2010.

8. Cluett, Venice. Phone interview with author, 10 July 2014.

9. Head, Fern. Phone interview with author, 9 July 2014.

Anderson, Robert

1. Risen, Cindy. Email to author, 6 July 2015.

2. Moe, Amy and Cindy Risen. Personal correspondence and photos pertaining to Armistice Day Blizzard.

3. Flowers, Mark. "The Sixth Marine Regiment on Guadalcanal." World War II Gyrene. www.ww2gyrene.org

4. Frank, Richard B. *Guadalcanal*. New York: Random House, 1990.

5. Jones, Lieutenant General William K., Editor. "A Brief History of the 6th Marines." Marine Corps Historical Division, 1987. www.marines.mil/

6. Soleta, Laura. "Robert Anderson Killed in Action." *Aitkin Independent Age*. "A" Obituaries, Aitkin County, Minnesota. The USGenWeb Project.

Curb, Cyril

1. Steinbeck, John. *Bombs Away: The Story of a Bomber Team*. New York: Viking Press, 1942.

2. Freeman, Roger. *Mighty Eighth War Diary*. New York: Jane's Publishing Incorporated, 1981.

3. Edmondson, Jolee. "The Mighty Eighth." 91st Bomb Group. www.91stbombgroup.com/

4. Perri, Nancy. "Dailies of the 323rd Squadron 1943. 91st Bomb Group." 91st Bomb Group. www.91stbombgroup.com

5. Curb, Cyril E. Individual Deceased Personnel File. Washington D.C.: War Department, 10 September 1982.

6. "Harold Victor Curb Obituary." Cease Family Funeral Home, 20 June 2012.

Baumgart, Herman

1. Anderson, Charles R. "Tunisia: The U.S. Army Campaigns of World War II," CMH Pub 72-12. U.S. Army Center of Military History. www.history.army.mil

2. Beckers, Yuri. "47th Regiment" and "North Africa: The Algeria-French Morocco Campaign." 9th Infantry Division. https://9thinfantrydivision.net/

3. Huxen, Keith. "The Battle at Kasserine Pass, North Africa February 19–25, 1944." The National World War II Museum. www.nationalww2museum.org/

4. Phillips, Henry Gerard. *Sedjenane: The Pay-Off Battle: Leading to the Capture of Bizerte, Tunisia, by the 9th U.S. Infantry Division, May 9, 1943*. Penn Valley, CA: Henry Gerard Phillips, 1993.

5. Sperry, John. *9th Infantry Division: Old Reliables*. Turner Publishing Company, 2000.

6. Chen, C. Peter. "Battle of El Guettar." World War II Database. www.ww2db.com

7. Atkinson, Rick. *The War in North Africa, 1942–1943*. New York: Henry Holt & Company, 2002.

8. Baumgart, Herman W. Report of Death. Individual Deceased Personnel File. Washington, D.C.: War Department, 4 April 1943.

9. Zepper, Rita. Letter to author, 3 March 2016.

Niemi, Mathews

1. Atkinson, Rick. *The War in North Africa, 1942–1943*. New York: Henry Holt & Company, 2002.

2. 9th Infantry Division. "Battle of Tunisia." Booklet. https://9thinfantrydivision.net

3. Chen, C. Peter. "Battle of El Guettar 23 March 1943–7 April 1944." World War II Database. www.ww2db.com

4. 9th Infantry Division. Hold Fast. "North Africa: The Algeria-French-Morocco Campaign." Booklet. https://9thinfantrydivision.net

5. Huxen, Keith. "The Battle at Kasserine Pass, North Africa February 19–25, 1944." National World War II Museum. www.nationalww2museum.org

6. Phillips, Henry Gerard. *Sedjenane: The Pay-Off Battle: Leading to the Capture of Bizerte, Tunisia, by the 9th U.S. Infantry Division, May 9, 1943*. Penn Valley, CA: Henry Gerard Phillips, 1993.

7. Niemi, Mathews J. Report of Death. Individual Deceased Personnel File. Washington, D.C.: War Department, 24 May 1943.

8. Niemi, Errol. Emails to author, 17 July 2014 and 1 February 2015.

9. "Marvin Niemi." Find A Grave Memorial, 17 July 2012. www.findagrave.com

Suomi, Einar

1. Dhennin, Jerry. Email to author, 28 July 2015.

2. "Can Do—History of the Group." 305th Bombardment Group (Heavy) Official Website. www.305thbombgroup.com

3. Freeman, Roger A. *Mighty Eighth War Diary*. New York: Jane's Publishing Incorporated, 1981.

4. "General Curtis Emerson LeMay." U.S. Air Force official site. www.af.mil

5. Morrison, Wilbur H. *The Incredible 305th: The "Can Do" Bombers of World War II*. New York: Duell, Sloan and Pearce, 1962.

6. Missing Air Crew Report, Serial #0-791342. Washington, D.C.: War Department, Headquarters Army Air Forces, 1 May 1943.

Bettin, Frank

1. Dorn, Bettin Hildegarde. Letter to author, 10 July 2015.

2. Mitchell, Robert J. *The Capture of Attu: A World War II Battle as Told by the Five Men who Fought There*. Lincoln: University of Nebraska Press, 2000.

3. "Battle of Attu." 2009. History.com Staff. www.history.com

4. Kostka, Del. "Banzai Attack on Attu! US Army Combat Engineers in the Aleutian Islands Campaign." www.militaryhistoryonline.com, 2011.

5. Wikipedia contributors. "Aleutian Islands Campaign." Wikipedia, The Free Encyclopedia, 26 December 2015. https://en.wikipedia.org

6. U.S. War Department. *The Capture of Attu as Told by the Men Who Fought There.* Washington, D.C.: Infantry Journal Press, 1944.

7. Bettin, Frank. Report of Death. Individual Deceased Personnel File. Washington, D.C.: War Department, 21 June 1943.

8. "Reburial Rites Held Monday For Urbank Man." *Parkers Prairie Independent*, 7 October 1948.

Borgeson, Victor

1. Borgeson, Dale Victor. Email to author, 29 November 2014. Letter and photo used with permission.

2. Brenner, Dean. "The Flag Raisers: A History of Herman-Norcross Men and Women during World War II," 1991.

3. "Goes to Watery Grave with Ill-Fated Ship." *Grant County Herald*, 4 November 1943.

4. "Kula Reporter Tells of Battle." USS *Helena*. www.usshelena.org, 8 February 2010.

5. Borgeson, Victor. Data on Remains Not Yet Recovered. Individual Deceased Personnel File. Washington, D.C.: War Department, 10 August 1945.

6. "Reckner, Amy Borgeson," 30 May 2013. www.findagrave.com

Gooselaw, Jerome Jr.

1. Cameron, Robert. Phone interview with author, 2 July 2014.

2. Lindvall, August. "St. Vincent Memories: Indian Woman, 98 Years Old Still Lives in Log Home, Her Minnesota Abode for More than Eighty Years." St. Vincent Memories, December 2006. www.56755.blogspot.com

3. Lofgren, Stephen J. "Northern Solomons: The U.S. Army Campaigns of World War II," 3 October 2003. U.S. Army Center of Military History. www.history.army.mil

4. Schwaller, Shannon. "The Harsh Realities of Warfare," 14 February 2011. The Official Home Page of the United States Army. www.army.mil

5. Hammel, Eric. *Munda Trail*. New York: Orion Books, 1989.

6. Gooselaw, Jerome. Individual Deceased Personnel File. Washington, D.C.: War Department, 4 August 1943.

7. "Jerome Gooselaw Reported Killed in Pacific Theatre of War." *Kittson County Enterprise*, 4 August 1943.

8. "Jerome Gooselaw." Find A Grave Memorial, 11 May 2007. www.findagrave.com

Jorgensen, Glen

1. "Arco Young Man Dies in Battle." *Tyler Journal-Herald*, 19 August 1943.

2. Schwaller, Shannon. "The Harsh Realities of Warfare," 14 February 2011. The Official Home Page of the United States Army. www.army.mil

3. U.S. Army Operations Report. "43rd Infantry Division: 103rd Infantry Regiment, 169th Infantry Regiment and 172nd Infantry Regiment," 1943–1944. U.S. Army Maneuver Center of Excellence. www.benning.army.mil

4. Jorgensen, Glen L. Report of Death. Individual Deceased Personnel File. Washington, D.C.: 19 August 1943.

Holen, Arnold

1. Anderson, Donnie. Grandpa Holen's Long Lost Son, Arnold. 21 November 2001.

2. Anderson, Lorna. Letter and correspondence to author, 15 January 2015 and 12 April, 2017.

3. Buer, Jeane. Letter to author, 25 November 2014.

4. "The Historical Narrative of the Ninety-third Bombardment Group (Heavy)" USAF record, August 1943. Courtesy of USAF Historical Division Archives Research and the 93rd Bomb Group. www.93bg.com

5. "Bombing Raid on Ploeşti, 1943," 2008. www.eyewitnesstohistory.com

6. Missing Air Crew Report. Washington, D.C.: War Department, Headquarters Army Air Forces, 8 December 1943.

7. "The Entire History of the 93rd Bombardment Group." 93rd Bomb Group. www.93bg.com

8. U.S. Air Force Historical Study No. 103. "August 1, 1943: Operation Tidal Wave." Ploeşti Story. www.afhistory.af.mil

9. Duran, Phyllis Avendano and Joe. Email to author, 1 January 2012.

10. Morrison, Don. Email to author, 2 September 2011.

11. Olson, Shane. "Arnold M. Holen." Find A Grave Memorial, 7 August 2010. www.findagrave.com

Mikel, Lawrence

1. Sledge, E.B. *With the Old Breed at Peleliu and Okinawa*. New York: Presidio Press, 1981.

2. "The Bloody Battle of Tarawa, 1943," 2003. www.eyewitnesstohistory.com

3. Rud, Major Robert H. Marine After Action Report, Reports of Battalion Commanders, 22 December 1943. HyperWar: Tarawa—2nd Marine Division After Action Report.

4. Mikel, Lawrence N. Individual Deceased Personnel File. Washington, D.C.: Department of the Army, 14 October 1949.

5. Falk, Renee. Email to author, 5 May 2015.

6. "Cooper, Leon. "Return to Tarawa: Leon Cooper Story." You Tube, 13 March 2008. www.youtube.com

7. Hartmann, Paul. Email to author, 5 May 2015.

8. Hildebrand, Jim. Email to author, 19 September 2011.

9. Hildebrand, Jim. Marines and Corpsmen: Tarawa & Guadalcanal. www.tarawa1943.com

10. Morrison, Jennifer. Email to author, 7 March 2015.

11. Walters Family Lost Son in Action." *The Wells Mirror*, 10 February 1944.

Vaughan, Welver

1. "All Children in Family to Join Service." *The Wells Mirror*. Courtesy of the Wells Depot Museum.

2. Michelson, Madeline Vaughan. Phone interview with author, 26 March 2015.

3. Antill, Peter, Operation Galvanic (1): The Battle for Tarawa November 1943, 22 January 2002. www.historyofwar.org/articles/battles_tarawa.html

4. "Battle of Tarawa," 2009. www.history.com

5. Ryan, Major Michael P. Marine After Action Report, Reports of Battalion Commanders, 22 December 1943. HyperWar: Tarawa—2nd Marine Division After Action Report. https://www.ibiblio.org/hyperwar/USMC/rep/Tarawa/2dMarDiv-AR.html#BnRpts

6. "Walters Family Lost Son in Action." *The Wells Mirror*, 10 February 1944.

7. Hildebrand, Jim. Email to author, 19 September 2011.

8. Vaughan, Welver. Individual Deceased Personnel File. Washington, D.C.: Department of the Army, 31 October 1949.

Terho, Harold

1. "Former IJC Student Killed in Italy." *The Itasca Iron News*, 10 May 1945.

2. Terho, Patsy. "Harold Terho," 6 September 2010.

3. "HQ 321st BG War Diary: 2 December 1943," pg. 17. Zachary Taylor National Cemetery Memorial. www.cem.va.gov/cems/nchp/zacharytaylor.asp

4. Rickard, J. "321st Bombardment Group: 1942–43," 7 October 2013. Military History Encyclopedia on the Web. www.historyofwar.org

5. Terho, Staff Sergeant Harold V. Missing Air Crew Report. Individual Deceased Personnel File. Washington, D.C.: War Department, Headquarters Army Air Forces, 5 December 1943.

Chernich, Peter

1. Costello, Ailie Chernich. Letter to author, 1 May 2015. Interview with author, 9 September 2015.

2. "26th General Hospital: Unit History." WW2 US Medical Research Centre. https://www.med-dept.com/unit-histories/26th-general-hospital/

3. American Merchant Marine at War. "U.S. Merchant Marine in World War II." www.usmm.org

4. Chernich, Peter. Data on Remains Not Yet Recovered. Individual Deceased Personnel File. Washington, D.C.: War Department, 7 April 1949.

5. Infield, Glenn B. *Disaster at Bari*. New York: Macmillan Co., 1971.

6. "Merchant Seaman from Cromwell is Missing in Action." *Carlton County Vidette*, 6 January 1944.

7. Niderost, Eric. "World War II: German Raid on Bari." *World War II Magazine*, 12 December 2006.

8. Reminick, Gerald. *Nightmare in Bari*. Palo Alto: Glencannon Press, 2001.

9. Satterwhite, Mary. Phone interview with author, 24 April 2015.

10. Walli, Shirley. Phone interview with author, 13 June 2015.

Zeiner, Leighton

1. "Zeiner Memorial Services Held at Dundee Sunday." *Worthington Daily Globe*, 19 January 1944.

2. "351st Bomb Group." American Air Museum in Britain, 7 February 2015. www.americanairmuseum.com/unit/293

3. "History of the 351st Bombardment Group (Heavy)" U.S. Air Force mission records, 24 November 1942 to December 1943. Courtesy of Craig Mackey, Air Force Historical Research Agency.

4. "Lt. L.K. Zeiner Killed in England." *Worthington Daily Globe*, 10 January 1944.

5. "WAC Mother Loses Son to Enemy." *Drew Field Echoes*, 20 January 1944. University of Florida Digital Collections.

6. Zeiner, Leighton. Individual Deceased Personnel File. Washington, D.C.: War Department, 17 January 1944.

Santjer, Ben

1. Knowles, Sena J. Letter to author, 19 August 2014.

2. U.S. Army. *We the 48th*, 1945. World War Regimental Histories, Book 200. Bangor Community Digital Commons@bpl. http://digicom.bpl.lib.me.us/ww_reg_his/200

3. U.S. Army. *We the 48th*, 1945. World War Regimental Histories, Book 200. Bangor Community Digital Commons@bpl. http://digicom.bpl.lib.me.us/ww_reg_his/200

4. U.S. Army staff. The Battalions: History of the 1108 Combat Engineer Group.

5. Santjer, Ben. Report of Death. Individual Deceased Personnel File. Washington, D.C.: War Department, 18 February 1944.

6. "Santjer, Ben." Military Times Hall of Valor, 9 March 1944. http://valor.militarytimes.com

7. Olson, Shane. "Ben Santjer." Find A Grave Memorial, 20 September 2010. www.findagrave.com

8. "Gold Star Deaths, Calvin College." *Young Calvinist*, pg. 22. April 1944.

Meyer, Harold

1. Johnson, Jack K. "The 34th 'Red Bull' Infantry Division." Military Historical Society of Minnesota. www.mnmilitarymuseum.org

2. 34th Infantry Division Association. "135th Infantry Regiment." www.mnmilitarymuseum.org

3. Wallace, Robert. *The Italian Campaign: World War II Series*. Alexandria, VA: Time-Life Books, 1978.

4. Meyer, Harold M. Report of Death. Individual Deceased Personnel File. Washington, D.C.: War Department, 8 March 1944.

5. Trueman, C.N. "The Battle of Monte Cassino (Second Phase)." History Learning Site. www.historylearningsite.co.uk/world-war-two/war-in-the-mediterranean-sea/the-battle-of-monte-cassino-second-phase/

6. Weigel, Don. Email to author, 7 September 2014.

7. "Obituary Harold Meyer." Courtesy of Lac qui Parle County Historical Society, Madison, Minnesota.

8. Wikipedia contributors. "Battle of Monte Cassino." Wikipedia, The Free Encyclopedia, 12 January 2016. https://en.wikipedia.org

9. Trojahn, Ted. Phone interview with author, 23 January 2015.

Nicholas, Lloyd

1. Johnson, Elizabeth. Phone interview with author, 10 September 2014.

2. Shepherd, James. "Truk Atoll: February 16–17, 1944." USS *Enterprise* CV-6. www.cv6.org/1944/truk

3. Nicholas, Lloyd K. Casualty Report. Individual Deceased Personnel Report. Washington, D.C.: Department of the Navy, 8 February 1946.

4. "Presidential Citation Awarded to Elcor Airman." *Virginia Daily Enterprise*, 9 October 1944.

5. Elcor Reunion Committee. "Elcor's Honored War Dead." Phillipich, Leonard, et al. *Elba-Elcor Reunion 1897–1956: A Collection of Memories*. Gilbert, Minnesota, 1982.

6. Wikipedia contributors. "Chuuk Lagoon." Wikipedia, The Free Encyclopedia, 29 January 2016. https://en.wikipedia.org

7. Nicholas, William E. Letter to author, 30 July 2014.

8. Glavan, Gregory. Email to author, 20 March 2011.

Olson, Morris

1. Johnson, Merna Olson. Letter to Gerard O'Regan, 22 April 1988, courtesy of Carolyn O'Brien.

2. O'Brien, Carolyn. Emails to author, 2 June 2015 and 6 January 2016.

3. O'Regan, Gerard. "Skellig Michael." Wartime Aircraft Crashes in County Kerry 1939–1945. homepage.eircom.net/~wrgi/pb4y2.html

4. Sundin, Beth C. "Woman Travels to Ireland to Attend Memorial Service for Twin." *Grand Rapids Herald-Review*, 8 August 1990.

5. Burke, Dennis. Foreign Aircraft Landings: Ireland 1939–1945. www.csn.ui.ie/~dan/war/crashes.htm

6. "Kendall Lee Bowman." Find A Grave Memorial, 1 November 2013. www.findagrave.com

Probasco, Alvin

1. St. John, Phillip. *History of the Third Infantry Division*. Turner Publishing Company, 1994.

2. "The Anzio Landing 22–29 January" and "The Enemy Attacks" via U.S. Army Center of Military History. www.history.army.mil

3. "World War II History of the 3rd Marne Infantry Division." The Italian Campaign of World War II June 1944–May 1945. Custermen: Home of the 85th Division. www.custermen.com

4. Hickman, Kennedy. "Battle of Anzio," 20 March 2015. Military History—about.com.

5. Neumiller, Robert. "751st Tank Battalion." Email to author, 14 June 2012.

6. Zaske, Nancy Probasco. Letter to author, 7 September 2014.

7. Probasco, Alvin G. Report of Death. Individual Deceased Personnel File. Washington, D.C.: War Department, 14 April 1944.

8. Gilmore, Gayle. Email to author, 18 July 2014.

Harju, Robert

1. Maki, Olga. Interview with author, 18 June 2015.

2. Laurie, Clayton. "Anzio 1944," 21 January 2010. U.S. Army Center of Military History. www.history.army.mil

3. Dunigan, Sergeant James. "History of the 30th Infantry Regiment," 24 July 2011. 6th Corps Combat Engineers WWII. www.6thcorpscombatengineers.com

4. Harju, Robert. Individual Deceased Personnel File: Washington, D.C.: War Department, 17 August 1945.

5. Aubin, Gay Jokela. Interview with author, 18 June 2015.

6. Newhouse, Velma Pulju. Interview with author, 18 June 2015.

7. Berry, Christopher and Judy. "Esther Harju-Genealogy." www.genealogy.com

Kanne, Robert

1. Treadwell, Theodore R. *Splinter Fleet: The Wooden Subchasers of World War II.* Annapolis, MD: Naval Institute Press, 2000.

2. Matyas, Mark. "Information on WWII SCs." Patrol Craft Sailor Association. www.ww2pcsa.org

3. Kanne, Lois. Phone interview with author, 9 January 2015.

4. Kanne, Robert Dean. Report of Interment. Individual Deceased Personnel File. Washington, D.C.: War Department, 5 April 1944.

5. Treadwell, Theodore. "Subchaser Hulls Still Afloat: SC 718 *Hitra*," 1999. Splinter Fleet. www.splinterfleet.org

Engholm, Waldo

1. Atkinson, Rick. *The Day of Battle: The War in Sicily and Italy 1943–44.* New York: Henry Holt & Company, 2008.

2. Ward, Geoffrey C. and Ken Burns. *The War: An Intimate History, 1941–1945.* New York: Alfred A. Knopf, 2007.

3. Mauldin, Bill. "No Rear...Anzio was Unique." Military History Network. Excerpted from *The Taste of Courage: The War, 1939–1945.* Edited by Desmond Flower and James Reeves. New York: Harper & Row, 1960.

4. Pyle, Ernie. *Brave Men.* Lincoln: University of Nebraska Press, 2001.

5. "W.L. Engholm Killed in Action at Anzio, Italy." *Sleepy Eye Dispatch,* 20 April 1944.

6. Haegelin, Colonel. Quartermaster Report. 3rd Infantry Division War Room Journal, 16 March 1944. Dwight D. Eisenhower Presidential Library and Museum, Abilene, Kansas.

7. Engholm, Waldo. Report of Death. Individual Deceased Personnel File. Washington, D.C.: War Department, 19 April 1944.

8. Engholm, Mava. Phone interview with author, 27 April 2015.

9. Letter from Ernest Heitmanek to H.A. Engblom, 25 August, 1944. From the files of Mava Engholm, 8 May 2015.

10. Lendt, Leona. Letter to author, 25 March 2015.

11. Weiss, Dave. "Edwin 'Ed' Waldo Engholm." Find A Grave Memorial, 9 March 2010. www.findagrave.com

Goudy, Robert

1. "Lt. R.L. Goudy is Reported Killed." *Redwood Falls Gazette,* 13 June 1944.

2. "Anzio and Rome Campaigns: A Partial History 135th Infantry Regiment, 34th Infantry Division." 34th Infantry Division Association. www.34infdiv.org

3. "Regimental History: 34th Infantry Division Association, 135th Infantry, October 1944." Iowa Gold Star Military Museum. www.goldstarmuseum.iowa.gov

4. Goudy, Robert L. Report of Death. Individual Deceased Personnel File. Washington, D.C.: War Department, 17 June 1944.

Rowe, Rolland

1. Taggert, Donald G. *History of the Third Infantry Division in World War II.* Washington, D.C.: Infantry Journal Press, 1947.

2. Allen, William L. Anzio: *Edge of Disaster.* New York: E.P. Dutton, 1978.

3. Wikipedia contributors. "15th Infantry Regiment (United States)." Wikipedia, The Free Encyclopedia, 13 February 2016. https://en.wikipedia.org

4. Harding, Gregory Allen. "Third Infantry Division at the Battle of Anzio-Nettuno." M.A. thesis, U.S. Army Command and General Staff College, 1995. Doc ADA299430. www.dtic.mil

5. Hildrup, Robert. Email to author, 27 June 2012.

6. Hoskins, Shirley. Phone interview with author, 20 July 2014.

7. Rowe, Rolland R. Report of Burial. Individual Deceased Personnel File. Washington, D.C.: War Department, 2 June 1944.

8. "Rolland Rowe." Military Times Hall of Valor. http://valor.militarytimes.com

Sundstad, Herman

1. "Perley Officer Reported Killed in Burma Action." From the files of the Norman County Historical and Genealogical Society, Minnesota, 28 September 2013.

2. Jacobson, Deb. Email to author, 28 September 2013.

3. Passanisi, Robert. "Unit History." Merrill's Marauders: 5307 Composite Unit (Provisional), 29 June 2001. www.marauder.org/history.htm

4. Passanisi, Robert. Email to author with excerpt from *The Marauders* by Charlton Ogburn, Jr., 9 July 2013.

5. Bjorge, Gary. Merrill's Marauders: Combined Operation in Northern Burma in 1944. combat Studies Institute: U.S. Army Command and General Staff College, 1966. U.S. Army Center of Military History. www.usacac.army.mil

6. "Merrill's Marauders Hit Burma," 24 February 1944, www.history.com Staff. www.history.com

7. Hopkins, James. *Spearhead: A Complete History of Merrill's Marauder Rangers.* Baltimore: Galahad Press, 1999.

8. Carbine, Dianne Sundstad. Letter to author, 13 March 2015.

9. Hunter, Charles N. *Galahad*. San Antonio: Naylor Press, 1963.

10. Carbine, Dianne Sundstad. Phone interviews with author in March 2015.

11. Perley, Minnesota Centennial, 1883–1983. Perley, Minnesota, 1983.

12. Sundstad, Herman. Individual Deceased Personnel File. Washington, D.C.: War Department, 10 July 1944.

Kostrzewski, Walter

1. Bradley, Omar and Clay Blair. *A General's Life*. New York: Simon & Schuster, 1983.

2. Reed, Paul. "Omaha Beach." Paul Reed's Battlefields of WW2, 3 April 2014. battlefieldsww2.50megs.com

3. Baumgarten, Harold. *D-Day Survivor*. Gretna, LA: Pelican Publishing, 2006.

4. Lefebvre, Laurent. "116th Reg. 1st Bn. A Co—Group critique Notes–June 1944." 29th Infantry Division Historical Society. www.29infdiv.org

5. Bennett, G.H. *Destination Normandy: Three American Regiments on D-Day*. Mechanicsburg, PA: Stackpole Books, 2009.

6. Department of Defense. "Combat Interview of D-Day Survivors from the 116th Infantry Regiment." Record Group 407. The National Archives Catalog. www.milestonedocuments.com

7. "Nelson Park Lad Missing in Action." *Stephen Messenger*, pg. 1, 24 August 1944.

8. Kostrzewski, Rose. Letter to Army in Individual Deceased Personnel File for Walter Kostrzewski. Washington, D.C.: War Department, 16 September 1944.

9. Kostrzewski, Walter. Phone interview with author, 29 January 2017.

Onger, Ellsworth

1. Bando, Mark. Email to author, 24 November 2015.

2. Bando, Mark. "Lest We Forget." Trigger Time 101st Airborne WW2, August 2000. www.101airborneww2.com

3. Bando, Mark. *101st Airborne: The Screaming Eagles at Normandy*. Minneapolis: Zenith Press, 2011.

4. "The 501st Parachute Infantry Regiment." The 101st Airborne in World War II. www.ww2-airborne.us/units/501/501

5. Kline, Orville. "Onger, Ellsworth H." World War II Registry. www.wwiimemorial.com/Registry

6. Olson, Shane. "Gustaf Adolph Onger." Find A Grave Memorial, 1 April 2010. www.findagrave.com

7. Zdon, Al. *War Stories: Accounts of Minnesotans Who Defended Their Nation*. Moonlit Eagle Productions, 2002.

Wilsing, Arnold

1. "80th Airborne Anti-Aircraft Battalion." 505th Regimental Combat Team www.505rct.org

2. Houterman, Hans and Jeroen Koppes. 82nd Airborne Division After Action Report, 6 June 1944. World War II Unit Histories and Officers. www.unithistories.com

3. Masters, Charles J. *Glider Men of Neptune*. Carbondale: Southern Illinois University Press, 1995.

4. Ward, Geoffrey C. and Ken Burns. *The War: An Intimate History, 1941–1945*. New York: Alfred A. Knopf, 2007.

5. "World War II CG-4A Glider Exhibit." U.S. Army Center of Military History. www.history.army.mil

6. Nordyke, Phil. *The All Americans in World War II*. St. Paul: Zenith Press, 2006.

7. Nellis, Gary. Phone interview with author, 17 March 2017.

8. Nellis, Sandra. Phone interview with author, 8 July 2014.

9. "All American: The Story of the 82nd Airborne Division." G.I. Stories: *Stars and Stripes*, Paris, 1945. www.lonesentry.com

10. Kline, Joan. Phone interview with author, 17 March 2017.

Wendt, William

1. Pile, Roberta and David Schroeder. "Uncle Bill": Pilot Officer William D. Wendt RCAF. Ozark, MO: Dogwood Printing, 2014.

2. Fydenchuk, W. Peter. *Immigrants of War: American Volunteers with the Royal Air Force and Royal Canadian Air Force During World War II*. WPF Publications, 2013.

3. "Escapes from German Prison Camp in Italy." *Pope County Tribune*, 6 January 1944.

4. Gilmour, W.C.H. "Circumstantial Report of Casualty Involving Mustang ### FZ. 141 and J.38957 P.O.W. W.D. Wendt—No. 19 Squadron." Royal Air Force, Canada. 7 June 1944.

5. "Mystery of Pilot's Death is Revealed." *Pope County Tribune*, 13 September 1945.

6. "William Wendt is Killed in Action." *Glenwood Herald*, 5 July 1945. Used with permission of *Pope County Tribune*.

7. "Sgt. Wm. Wendt Prisoner, Writes Letter." *Glenwood Herald*, 18 November 1943.

Emery, Carl

1. Mauk, Cathy. "Fifty Years Haven't Erased Pain of War for Local Family" *Fargo Forum*, B10, 8 December 1991.

2. Bobbitt, Chird. "A History of the 526 Tank Ordnance Company." www.bobbittville.com/526ordnance.htm

3. Mayo, Lida. *The Ordnance Department: On Beachhead and Battlefront.* Office of the Chief of Military History. Washington, D.C.: U.S. Army, 1968. www.history.army.mil

4. Wikipedia contributors. "Sullivan Brothers." Wikipedia, The Free Encyclopedia, 3 January 2016. https://en.wikipedia.org

Lusk, Eugene

1. Bennett, G.H. *Destination Normandy: Three American Regiments on D-Day.* Mechanicsburg, PA: Stackpole Books, 2009.

2. Curran, Pat, Administrator. Whitebeam Battlefield Research Forum. http://normandy. whitebeamimages.ie/forum

3. Devlin, Gerard M. "The 507th Parachute Infantry Regiment." The 507th Parachute Infantry Regiment, the 82nd Airborne World War II. www.ww2-airborne. us/units/507

4. Ross, Daniel. "Sergeant Bob Bearden, H Company, 507th Parachute Infantry Regiment, Invaded Behind the Lines on D-Day." Civilian Intelligence Military Group, 15 September 2009. https://civilianintelligencegroup.com

5. Ridgway, General Major Matthew. "US Airborne in Cotentin Peninsula. Action Report June 6, 1944: 507th Infantry Regiment." D-Day Etat des Lieux. www.ww2- airborne.usdivision/82

6. Lusk, Eugene. Report of Burial. Individual Deceased Personnel File. Washington, D.C.: War Department, 24 June 1944.

7. Public Broadcasting Service. D-Day: Down to Earth: Return of the 507th. Documentary, 2004.

Oja, August

1. Alexander, Colonel Joseph. "World War II: 50 Years Ago: Saipan's Bloody Legacy," June 1944. Marine Corps Association and Foundation. www.mca-marines.org

2. Historical Branch, G-3 Division, HQMC. "The Seizure of Saipan," 23 January 1969. USMC History Division.

3. Oja, August. Individual Deceased Personnel File. Washington, D.C.: Department of the Army, 1 May 1946.

Bush, Fernly

1. "Pfc. Fernly Bush of Myrtle Killed in Action," *The Evening Tribune*, pg. 4, Albert Lea, Minnesota, 29 July 1944.

2. Lefebrve, Laurent. "29th Division World War II Documents. 175th After Action Report –June 1944." 29th Infantry Division Historical Society. www.29infantrydivision.org

3. "175th Infantry." 29th Division Association, 2001. www.29thdivisionassociation.org

4. Cosmas, Graham and Albert Cowdrey. "Medical Service in the European Theater of Operations." Washington, D.C.: Center for Military History, 1992. www.history.army. mil/html/books/010/10-23/CMH_Pub_10-23-1.pdf

5. Bush, Fernly E. Report of Burial. Individual Deceased Personnel File. Washington, D.C.: War Department, 19 June 1944.

6. Ziemann, Linda. "Fernly E. Bush, Pvt. 1924–1944." *Mason City Globe-Gazette*, July 30, 1944. Chickasaw Obituaries. The IAGenWeb Project.

7. Bellerichard, Bush Barbara. Phone interview with author, 27 May 2015.

Forsberg, Robert

1. Forsberg, Robert. Letter to his mother, 21 April 1944.

2. Forsberg, Gerald, son of Adolph Forsberg. Phone interviews with author, 18 June 2014 and 8 February 2015.

3. Alexander, Colonel Joseph. "World War II: 50 Years Ago: Saipan's Bloody Legacy," June 1944. Marine Corps Association and Foundation. www.ca-marines.org

4. Rasmussen, Frederick. "Culotta as Navy Corpsman Survived Nine Pacific Landings." *The Baltimore Sun*, 14 June 2009.

5. Santelli, James. "A Brief History of the 8th Marines." Washington, D.C.: History and Museums Division, Headquarters Marine Division, 1976. Marine Corps University. www.marines.mil

6. Forsberg, Robert. Individual Deceased Personnel File. Washington, D.C.: Department of the Navy, 29 April 1949.

7. Kelley, John. Letter to Agnes Forsberg Wilson, 15 May 1945.

8. "Harold John Forsberg." Find A Grave Memorial, 14 August 2011. www.findagrave.com

9. Dickelman, Teresa Ross. Phone interview with author, 19 June 2014.

10. Forsberg, Susan. Email to author, 22 February 2015.

11. Family history editing courtesy of Jacqueline Forsberg Phipps, daughter of Adolph Forsberg, August 2015.

12. Family history courtesy of Dee Millard, daughter of Elizabeth Forsberg Millard, August 2015.

Indihar, Rudolph

1. Elcor Reunion Committee. "Elcor's Honored War Dead." Phillipich, Leonard, et al. *Elba-Elcor Reunion 1897–1956: A Collection of Memories.* Gilbert, Minnesota, 1982.

2. "Elcor: A Gentle, Good Neighborhood Now More Than 50 Years Gone." *Mesabi Daily News*, 18 March 2008.

3. Beckers, Yuri. "The Battle for Normandy." 9th Infantry Division. https://9thinfantrydivision.net

4. Urick, Anthony. Letter to author, 10 April 2015.

5. Pyle, Ernie. 'A Captured Hun was Camera-Shy' in "Hitler's Nemesis:

The 9th Infantry Division." G.I. Stories: *Stars and Stripes*, Paris, 1944. www.lonesentry.com

Lound, Ray

1. U.S. Army. "The Story of the Powder River/ Let'er Buck, 91st Infantry Division: August 1917–January 1945." History of the 91st "Powder River" Infantry Division. 10 September 2012. www.custermen.com/ItalyWW2/Units/Division91

2. Robbins, Robert. *The 91st Infantry Division in World War II*. Washington, D.C.: Infantry Journal Press, 1947.

3. Cavalli, Karen Lound. Email to author, 6 December 2014.

4. "Killed in Action on Italian Front." *Askov American*, 3 August 1944.

5. Norbeck, Margaret Lound. Phone interview with author, 9 December 1914.

6. Lound, Ray. Report of Death. Individual Deceased Personnel File. Washington, D.C.: War Department, 11 August 1944.

Shefveland, Stanton

1. "Memorial Rites Were Held for Perley Soldier: Services for Pfc. Stanton Shefveland Held at Bethania Church Sunday." From the files of the Norman County Historical and Genealogy Society, Ada, Minnesota. Email to author from Deb Jacobson, 31 August 2013.

2. Perley, Minnesota Centennial, 1883–1983. Perley, Minnesota, 1983.

3. Price, Thomas E. "A Brief History of the U.S. Army 6th Infantry Division." 1996. National Association of the 6th Infantry Association. www.6thinfantry.com

4. Division Public Relations Section. *The Sixth Infantry Division in World War II, 1939–1945*. Nashville: Battery Press, 1983.

5. Shefveland, Stanton. Report of Death. Individual Deceased Personnel File. Washington, D.C.: War Department, 7 August 1944.

6. Rue, Ilane. Letter to author, 27 March 2015.

Iverson, Edwin

1. Pearson, Evon. Letter to author, 25 January 2015. Phone interviews with author, 9 December 2014, 20 January 2015.

2. Goldberg, Harold J. "Saipan (15 June–9 July 1944)." Public Broadcasting Service. www.pbs.org/thewar/detail_5219

3. New York State Military Museum and Veterans Research Center. "105th Infantry Regiment World War Two," 10 October 2012. https://dmna.ny.gov/historic/reghist/wii/infantry

4. O'Brien, Francis A. *Battling for Saipan: The True Story of an American Hero-Lt. Col. William J. O'Brien*. New York: Ballantine Publishing, 2003.

5. O'Brien, Francis A. "Battle of Saipan." May 1997. www.historynet.com/battle-of-saipan

6. Iverson, Edwin Joel. Individual Deceased Personnel File. Washington, D.C.: War Department, 9 August 1944.

7. Belsky, Darlene. Email to author, 19 September 2014.

8. "Re-Interment Services for Edwin Iverson." *Aitkin Independent Age*, 1 July 1948.

Holmstrom, Herman

1. Beckers, Yuri. "47th Infantry Regiment: The Raiders." 9th Infantry Division. https://9thinfantrydivision.net

2. Bearden, Bob. *To D-Day and Back*. St. Paul: Zenith Press, 2007.

3. Holmstrom, Herman. Report of Death. Individual Deceased Personnel File. Washington, D.C.: War Department, 8 August 1944.

4. The Normandy Campaign: Report of Operations, 12 July 1944. Dwight D. Eisenhower Presidential Library and Museum, Abilene, Kansas, 15 December 2015.

5. "Strandquist Man Re-interred Saturday." *Stephen Messenger*, pg. 8, 16 September 1948.

6. Wetterland, Cindy. Email to author, 14 June 2015.

Iverson, Lloyd

1. Briski, Judy Iverson. Email to author, 29 July 2015.

2. Skogerboe, Judy. Phone interview with author, 29 March 2017.

3. "Memorial Services Are Sunday Afternoon for Sgt. Lloyd H. Iverson." *Thief River Falls Times*, 1944.

4. "2nd Lieutenant James Merrill Redin." Find A Grave Memorial, 22 October 2010. www.findagrave.com

5. Headquarters: Ninety Fifth Bombardment Group (H). Office of the Operations Officer, 12 July 1944. Fold3.com https://www.fold3.com/document/29404249

6. Missing Air Force Report. Washington, D.C.: War Department, Headquarters Army Air Forces, 15 March 1946.

7. Iverson, Lloyd. Individual Deceased Personnel File. Washington, D.C.: War Department, 10 September 1982.

Winjum, Harold

1. Kaiser, Don. Email to author, 12 January 2012.

2. Kaiser, Don. "Tactical Diary: 489th Bombardment Squadron in Corsica," pg. 207, 12 July 1944. www.warwingsart.com

3. U.S. Army. "War Diary, 1st Emergency Rescue Squadron," 13 July 1944. Camden, New Jersey, 61st Station Hospital, United States Army. www.dvrbs.com/camden/CooperHospital-61stStationHospital.htm

4. Mitchell, Captain John. Letter to Major William D. Sanders, 23 November 1945. From the files of Don Kaiser.

5. Winjum, Harold. Individual Deceased Personnel File. Washington, D.C.: War Department, Headquarters Army Air Forces, 10 September 1982.

6. Evanstad, Marlyn. Letter to author, 20 November 2014.

7. "Former Roseau Lad Missing in Action." *Roseau Times-Region*, 8 August 1945.

8. Blume, Burton. "War Diary of the 340th Bombardment Group, July 12 1944 Addendum." 2013. 57th Bomb Wing Association. http://57thbombwing.com

9. Varner, Sandra Winjum. Phone interview with author, 9 September 2014.

10. Winjum, Orel Raymond. Ancestry and Descendants of Ida Christina Knutson, October 2, 1881 to April 10, 1919, and Ole J. Winjum, September 18, 1876 to November 29, 1932. California, 1975.

Hoffrogge, Herman

1. Pederson, Jim. Letter to author, 9 September 2014.

2. U.S. Army Center of Military History. "American Forces in Action, St. Lo: 7 July to 19 July 1944." Historical Division, War Department, 21 August 1946. www.history.army.mil

3. Headquarters 137th Infantry After Action Reports, Battle History 137th Infantry, July 1944. 35th Infantry Division Memory. https://35thinfantrydivision-memory.com

4. Stephenson, O'Connell, Butler, Jackson and Smith. "Combat History of the 137th Infantry Regiment," 1946. 134th Infantry Regiment Website. www.coulthart.com/134/137

5. Hoffrogge, Herman. Report of Death. Individual Deceased Personnel File. Washington, D.C.: War Department, 10 August 1944.

6. Carlson, Leon. Email to author, 10 September 2014.

7. "Herman Hoffrogge of Revere Killed on Normandy Battlefront." *Redwood Falls Gazette*, 10 August 1944.

Bliven, Paul

1. Bliven, Robert. Email to author, 18 November 2014.

2. Burns, Daniel M. "121st Infantry: The 'Gray Bonnet' Regiment," *The Gray Bonnet: Combat History of the 121st Infantry Regiment 1810–1945*, 1946. The Eighth Infantry Division Archives. www.8thinfdiv.com

3. Hammond, William. "Normandy: The U.S. Army Campaigns of World War II." U.S. Army Center of Military History. www.history.army.mil

4. Kagan, Neil and Stephen G. Hyslop. "Eyewitness to World War II." Washington, D.C.: *National Geographic*, 2012.

5. Barrett, Roseanne. Phone interview with author, 3 December 2004.

6. Bliven, Paul. Report of Death. Individual Deceased Personnel File. Washington, D.C.: War Department, 17 August 1944.

7. "Lt. Paul Bliven Killed in Action." *Willmar Daily Tribune*, 5 August 1944.

8. "Lt. Paul Bliven." *Willmar Daily Tribune*, 22 August 1944.

Hegna, Verlyn

1. Nielsen, Wandah. Phone interview with author, 5 February 2014.

2. Beckers, Yuri. "Northern France-Belgium." 9th Infantry Division, 24 January 2016. https://9thinfantrydivision.net

3. Hogan, David W. "Northern France." Washington, D.C.: Department of the Army Historical Division, 1947. www.history.army.mil, 26 February 2016.

4. Ruppenthal, Major Roland G. "Utah Beach to Cherbourg." Washington, D.C.: Department of the Army Historical Division, 1947. www.history.army.mil

5. Hegna, Verlyn. Individual Deceased Personnel File. Washington, D.C.: War Department, 10 August 1944.

6. Yonce, Grover and Charles Rose, Harold Turley and Edward Roberts. "Request for rear duty, due to length of time in combat." 60th Infantry Regiment Research and Preservation, Archives: 2008, 25 June 2008. 60th Infantry Regiment. www.60thinfantry.com/postarchive.php?ayear=2008

Anderson, Leon

1. Anderson, Erling. Letter to author, 3 December 2011.

2. Anderson, Erling. Phone interview by author, 2 June 2013.

3. Creighton, Jenna. "In Memory of U.S. Army 1st Lieutenant Leon Gilmore Anderson," May 2002. Fallen Son and Daughter Profiles. https://vetaffairs.sd.gov/sdwwiimemorial/SubPages/profiles/Display.asp?P=48

4. "Memorial for Leon Anderson." *Granite Falls Tribune*, 5 October 1944.

5. Atkinson, Rick. "Operation COBRA and the Breakout at Normandy," 22 July 2010. The Official Home Page of the United States Army. www.army.mil

6. Granier, Major Thomas. "Analysis of Operation Cobra and the Falaise Gap Maneuvers in World War II," April 1985. Air Command and Staff College, Maxwell Air Force Base, Alabama. www.dtic.mil/dtic/tr/fulltext/u2/a156116.pdf

7. Weaver, Michael. *Guard Wars: The 28th Infantry Division in World War II*. Bloomington: Indiana University Press, 2010.

8. Anderson, Leon G. Report of Death. Individual Deceased Personnel File. Washington, D.C.: War Department, 24 August 1944.

9. Distad, Rodney. Phone interview with author, 7 January 2015.

Berger, Jack

1. Ambrose, Stephen. *Band of Brothers*. New York: Simon & Schuster, 2001.

2. Curry, Dave. "Normandy: Brothers-in-Arms." 83rd Division, 331st Infantry. https://83rdinfdivdocs.org/units/331st-ir

3. Pearson, Fred. "A Brief History of the 453rd A.A.A. (S.W.) Battalion." 83rd Infantry Division Documents. https://83rdinfdivdocs.org/units/453rd-aaa-aw-bn

4. 453rd Anti-Aircraft Artillery Battalion After Action Report, August, 7 September 1944. 83rd Infantry Division Documents. https://83rdinfdivdocs.org/units/453rd-aaa-aw-bn

5. Berger, Jack. Individual Deceased Personnel File. Washington, D.C.: War Department, 21 September 1944.

6. "Kerrick Memorial Services." *Askov American*, 31 August 1944.

7. Gunderson, Julie. Phone interview with author, 28 May 2015.

Petersen, Gerhard

1. Jacobson, Debra. Email to author, 29 August 2013.

2. "Gerhard Burton Petersen." Find A Grave Memorial, 7 August 2010. www.findagrave.com

3. Savelkoul, Ben. "Joel Dykstra: 743rd Tank Battalion D-Day Invasion," 26 July 2002. Ben Savelkoul.nl, www.bensavelkoul.nl/Joel_Dykstra.htm

4. "743rd Tank Battalion S3 Journal History: 1 Oct. to 31 Oct. 1944," 2009. World War II Operational Documents. Ike Skelton Combined Arms Research Library Digital Library. http://cgsc.cdmhost.com

5. Nordyke, Phil. *American Heroes of World War II: Normandy June 6, 1944.* Charleston, SC: Historic Ventures, 2014.

6. Petersen, Gerhard B. The Distinguished Service Cross. Home of Heroes. www.homeofheroes.com

7. Yeide, Harry. *Steel Victory*, pg. 53. New York: Random House, 2003.

8. Hagen, Ray. "Tractors to Tanks Part VI—The Norman County Boys—C Company 743rd Tank Battalion," 8 April 2015. From the Cornfields to the Hedgerows. https://cornfieldstohedgerows.wordpress.com

Nelson, LaVern

1. Nelson, Muriel Verna. Letter to author, 10 March 2015.

2. Richardson, June. Phone interview with author, 13 March 2015. Interview with Muriel Nelson sent to author, 2 April 2015. Letter to author, 4 May 2015.

3. Carlson, Ed. *We Honor Our Fallen Comrades-In-Arms.* Jackson, MN: Livewire Printing, 1989.

4. *From Normandy to the Elbe.* 30th Infantry Division, July 1945. 30th Infantry Division. www.oldhickory30th.com

5. "Breakthrough by the 120th Infantry on 25 July 1944." 30th Infantry Division. www.30thinfantry.org

6. Nelson, LaVern W. Report of Death. Individual Deceased Personnel File. Washington, D.C.: War Department, 4 September 1944.

Hoff, Vernon

1. Hoff, Scott. Letter to author, December 2014.

2. "Memorial Services for Perley Soldier on November 19." From the files of Norman County Historical and Genealogy Society, Ada, Minnesota. Email to author from Deb Jacobson, 31 August 2013.

3. Hoff, Vernon. Letter to his mother, Anna Hoff, 22 July 1944. From the personal files of Scott Hoff.

4. 737th Tank Battalion After Action Report, 1 September 1944. www.coulthart.com/134/aa-737-tb/737-t-bn-1944-8%201%20thru%208%2031.pdf

5. Fussell, Paul. *The Boys' Crusade: The American Infantry in Northwestern Europe, 1944–45.* New York: Modern Library, 2005.

6. Reardon, Mark. *Victory at Mortain*, pg. 208. Lawrence: University Press of Kansas, 2002.

7. Hoff, Vernon J. Report of Death. Individual Deceased Personnel File. Washington, D.C.: War Department, 6 November 1944.

8. *Perley, Minnesota, Centennial, 1883–1983: July 8–9–10.* Perley, MN: 1983.

Graba, James

1. Childers, Jim. "1st Lieutenant James Graba." Find A Grave Memorial, 6 August 2010. www.findagrave.com

2. Conser, Sergeant LR James Graba. Report of Aircraft Accident #42-97182. Individual Deceased Personnel File. Washington, D.C.: War Department, U.S. Army Air Forces, 11 September 1944.

Johnson, Leroy

1. Johnson, Leroy E. Missing Air Crew Report. Individual Deceased Personnel File. Washington, D.C.: War Department, Adjutant General's Office, 30 August 1944.

2. Amos, Robert F., et al, 2nd Bomb Group Historians. *Defenders of Liberty, 2nd Bombardment Group Wing: 1918–1993.* Nashville: Turner Publishing Company, 1996. Second Bombardment Association. www.2ndbombgroup.org

3. Richards, Charles W. *The Second Was First.* Bend, OR: Maverick Productions, 1999. (References "Missing Air Crew Report A/C #42-31885—20th Squadron")

4. Dickinson, Loy. "Air Battle Over the White Carpathian Mountains: Moravia, Czech Republic, 29 August 1944—60 Years Later." Second Bombardment Association. www.2ndbombgroup.org

5. Nordsiden, Dannie. Email to author, 28 March 2015.

6. McVey, Charles. Letter to Daisy Johnson, 3 August 1945. From the files of Sandra Coulter.

7. Susil, Roman. Email to author, 16 April 2015.

8. Gafney, Maura. "Letter to Joseph Owsianik, 20th Squadron POW," August 2001. Second Bombardment Association. www.2ndbombgroup.org

9. U.S. National Cemetery Interment Control Forms, 1928–1962. "Leroy E. Johnson." www.ancestry.com

Hogetvedt, Joseph

1. Donigan, Major Henry. "Peleliu: The Forgotten Battle," September 1994. Marine Corps Association and Foundation. https://www.mca-marines.org/leatherneck/peleliu-forgotten-battle

2. Niderost, Eric. "Unnecessary Hell: The Battle of Peleliu." Warfare History Network, 10 August 2016. http://warfarehistorynetwork.com

3. Sledge, E.B. *With the Old Breed at Okinawa and Peleliu*. Novato, CA: Presidio Press, 1980.

4. Ward, Geoffrey C. and Ken Burns. *The War: An Intimate History, 1941–1945*. New York: Alfred Knopf, 2007.

5. Hogetvedt, Private Joseph R. Individual Deceased Personnel File. Washington, D.C.: War Department, 18 July 1947.

6. Hogetvedt, Leo. Letter to author, 15 October 2014.

Pearson, Vernon

1. Bomber Command Museum of Canada. "The Americans in the RCAF." www.bombercommandmuseum.ca/americansrcaf.html

2. "Pearson, Vernon Lawrence." Commonwealth War Graves Commission. www.cwgc.org/find-war-dead.aspx

3. McDonald, A.R. and F.R. Walker. Proceeding of Court of Inquiry or Investigation. Canadian Royal Air Force. Ottawa, Ontario: Department of National Defense, 14 November 1944.

4. Halliday, Hugh. "Lost!—Dakota KG592," 22 March 2005. Royal Air Force Commands. www.rafcommands.com/archives/12702.php

5. Welting, Henk. "Still Lost!—Dakota KG592," 24 March 2005. Royal Air Force Commands. www.rafcommands.com/archives/12702.php

Veralrud, LeRoy

1. Elcor Reunion Committee. "Elcor's Honored War Dead." Phillipich, Leonard, et al. *Elba-Elcor Reunion 1897–1956: A Collection of Memories*. Gilbert, Minnesota, 1982.

2. "Preparation for and crossing of the Moselle River: 1–15 September 1944." 80th Infantry Division. www.80thdivision.com

3. Adkins, Andy. Digital Archives Company K Morning Reports, 2 September 1944. 80th Infantry Division. www.80thdivision.com

4. Veralrud, LeRoy T. Individual Deceased Personnel File. Washington, D.C.: War Department, 4 September 1944.

5. "Elcor: A Gentle, Good Neighborhood Now More Than 50 Years Gone." *Mesabi Daily News*, 18 March 2008.

6. Glavan, Gregory. Email to author, 20 March 2011.

Maxa, Gordon

1. Anderson, Jean. Emails to author, 19 December 2012 and 5 January 2013. Letter from Betty Maxa to Doris Anderson courtesy of Jean Anderson.

2. 384th Bomb Group Missing Air Crew Report #9414, 3 October 1944. http://384thbombgroup.com/_content/MACRs/MACR9414.pdf

3. Maxa, Gordon R. Individual Deceased Personnel File. Washington, D.C.: War Department, 13 July 1945.

4. Maxa, Vernon. "Gordon Maxa." Email to author, 12 September 2013. Phone interview with author, 6 September 2013.

Sersha, John

1. Lohry, Richard. Phone interview with author, 16 August 2016.

2. Hanna, Bill. "Pvt. Sersha's remains to be buried 72 years after his death in WWII." *Mesabi Daily News*, 26 May 2016.

3. Masters, Charles J. *Glider Men of Neptune*. Carbondale: Southern Illinois University Press, 1995.

4. Ward, Geoffrey C. and Ken Burns. *The War: An Intimate History, 1941–1945*. New York: Alfred A. Knopf, 2007.

5. "World War II CG-4A Glider Exhibit." U.S. Army Center of Military History. www.history.army.mil

6. Warren, Dr. John C. "Airborne Operations In World War II, European Theater," pp. 101–149, 1956. USAF Historical Studies (97), USAF Historical Division, Research Studies Institute. www.dtic.mil/dtic/tr/fulltext/u2/a438105.pdf

7. Robins, Elsa. "Remains of World War II Vet Declared MIA Possibly Identified." KBJR News. www.northlandsnewscenter.com/news/iron-range/241894781.html, 24 January 2014.

8. Von Erp, Astrid and Laura Phillips. "Sersha, John P." Fields of Honor Database. www.fieldsofhonor-database.com

Kurth, Walter

1. Kirtz, Lorie Kurth. Email to author, 22 October 2014.

2. "Sgt. Walter Kurth Killed in Italy." From the personal files of Lorie Kurth Kirtz, 22 October 2014.

3. Allied Force Headquarters. "A Partial History 135th Infantry Regiment," 16 March 2004. 34th Infantry Division Association. www.34thinfdiv.org

4. Kurth, Walter. Individual Deceased Personnel File. Washington, D.C.: War Department, 18 October 1944.

5. "Sgt. Walter Kurth is Decorated Posthumously." From the personal files of Lorie Kurth Kirtz, 22 October 2014.

Talberg, William

1. Pyle, Ernie. *Brave Men*. Lincoln: University of Nebraska Press, 2001.

2. Hoover, Lieutenant Colonel Lawrence. "History of 345th Engineer General Service Regiment." 1946. VI Corps of Combat Engineers. www.6thcorpscombatengineers.com

3. "Hillman Legion Dedicates Post Sunday, Sept. 20." From the files of Donald H. Talberg, 4 August 2014.

4. Talberg, Donald H. Letter to author, 30 July 2014.

Mittag, Harland

1. "Another Freeborn County Boy Killed in Action." *The Evening Tribune*, pg. 1, 9 October 1944.

2. "History 133rd Infantry, 34th Infantry Division." 34th Infantry Division. www.34thinfantry.com

3. Mittag, Private First Class Harland. Individual Deceased Personnel File. Washington, D.C.: War Department, 23 October 1944.

Longhenry, Albert

1. "Pfc. Albert Longhenry Killed in Action in France on October 11." From the files of the Lac qui Parle County Historical Society, Madison, Minnesota.

2. Munsell, Warren P. *The Story of a Regiment: A History of the 179th Regimental Combat Team*, 1946. World War Regimental Histories, Book 34. Bangor Community Digital Commons@bpl. http://digicom.bpl.lib.me.us/ww_reg_his/34

3. Bonn, Keith E. *When the Odds Were Even*. Novato, CA: Presidio Press, 1994.

4. Longhenry, Albert. Individual Deceased Personnel File. Washington, D.C.: War Department, 14 November 1944.

5. Cordova, Amos. Email to author, 25 March 2015, 45th Infantry Action Report, U.S. Army War Journal.

6. Siret, Jean-Marie. Email to author, 18 February 2015.

Doyle, Donald

1. McFarland, Stephen L. *Conquering the Night: Army Air Forces Night Fighters at War*, 1998. Washington, D.C.: Air Force History and Museums Program, National Archives. https://archive.org/stream/ ConqueringtheNightArmyAirForcesNight- FightersatWar

2. Thompson, Warren. *P-61 Black Widow Units of World War 2*. Oxford, England: Osprey Publishing, 1998.

3. Chen, L. Peter. "P-61 Black Widow." World War II Database. www.ww2db.com

4. Missing Air Crew Report #9539. Individual Deceased Personnel File. Washington, D.C.: War Department, Headquarters Army Air Forces, 14 October 1944.

Bollum, Donald

1. Ketchum, Michael D. "Battle for the Foret de Parroy. 25 September–21 October, 1944," 2015. The WW2 Letters of Private Melvin W. Johnson. www.privateletters. net/featured_foretdeparroy.html

2. Staff Group C. "Foret de Parroy: Offensive Deliberate Attack, 79th Infantry Division, 25 September–24 October 1944," May 1984. Ike Skelton Combined Arms Research Library Digital Library. http://cgsc.contentdm.oclc.org

3. "The Cross of Lorraine Division: The Story of the 79th." G.I. Stories: *Stars and Stripes*, Paris, 1944. www.lonesentry.com index.html

4. Bollum, Donald. Letter to Jeannette Bollum, 6 October 1944.

5. Bollum, Steve. Letters and phone interview with author, 8 January 2015.

6. Deutchman, Bernard Captain. Letter to Jeanette Bollum, 7 April 1945.

7. Bollum, Donald. Report of Burial. Individual Deceased Personnel File. Washington, D.C.: War Department, 29 October 1944.

8. "Donald Bollum Gives His Life For Country." *Pope County Tribune*, 2 November 1944.

9. Turnquist, Gladys. History of Farwell, Minnesota: 1986.

Burger, Earl

1. Burger, Gary. Email to author, 22 November 2010.

2. Knight, Fred. "LST Diary/Fred Knight Memoir: 17 and 18 June 1944." More Than Words Can Express, 24 February 2010. https://ww2letters.wordpress.com/ lst-277

3. Chen, Peter C. "Philippines Campaign, Phase 1, the Leyte Campaign: 22 October– 21 December 1944." World War II Database. www.ww2db.com

4. MacArthur, Douglas. *Reminiscences*. New York: McGraw-Hill, 1964.

5. Burger, Earl. Report of Casualty. Individual Deceased Personnel File. Washington, D.C.: Department of the Army, 7 December 1944.

6. Houston, Myrtle Burger. Phone interview with author, 9 February 2015.

7. Burger, Cindy. Email to author, 3 February 2015.

8. McKeig, Cecelia. "Helen Coleman Hofmeister." Find A Grave Memorial, 1 October 2013. www.findagrave.com

Kuznia, Ferdinand

1. Kuznia, Ferdinand. Letter to family, 8 November 1941. From the personal archives of Ferdinand Stanley Kuznia.

2. Bowen, William. "The *Arisan Maru* Tragedy." U.S.-Japan Dialogue on POWs. www.us-japandialogueonpows.org/Bowen.htm

3. Ross, Jay D. and Judith E. Nichols. *Banners at Sunset: An Anthology of WWII Stories from Veterans of the Big Stone Country/Big Stone Lake Area*, 2012.

4. "Ferdinand Kuznia Thought Lost at Sea." *Stephen Messenger*, 21 June 1945.

5. Kuznia, Ferdinand. Data on Remains Not Yet Recovered or Identified. Individual Deceased Personnel File. Washington, D.C.: War Department, 5 September 1947.

6. "Florian to Honor Ferdinand Kuznia." *Stephen Messenger*, 18 October 1945.

Bruns, Alfred

1. Pyle, Ernie. *Brave Men*. Lincoln: University of Nebraska Press, 2001.

2. Heiser, John. "Custer Division: The 85th Infantry Division in World War II," 26 January 2012. 85th Infantry Division. http://user.pa.net/~cjheiser

3. Jones, Don. "Unit History: Report of Operations, 14 October–20 October 1944." National Archives. The 337th Infantry in Italy in WW II. www.337thinfantry.net/unit.php

4. Bruns, Alfred P. Individual Deceased Personnel File. Washington, D.C.: War Department, 12 November 1944.

5. Butkowski, Ralph. Email to author, 7 May 2015.

Gordon, Malcolm

1. Callan, A.T. "U.S.S. *Kalinin Bay* (CVE-68) Aircraft Action Report, Number 113." United States Naval Reserve, 25 October 1944. www.navsource.org/archives/03/068.htm

2. Cox, Robert J. Email to author, 7 April 2012.

3. Cox, Robert J. *The Battle Off Samar: Taffy III at Leyte Gulf*. Wakefield, MI: Agogeebic Press, 2010.

4. Fader, Michael. "CVE-68 USS *Kalinin Bay*," 1 January 2007. www.wings-aviation.ch

5. "USS *Kalinin Bay* (CVE 68)." uboat.net. http://uboat.net/allies/warships/ship/2442.html

6. Gordon, Malcolm. Report of Casualty. Individual Deceased Personnel File. Washington, D.C.: Bureau of Naval Personnel, 5 December 1945.

7. Hornfischer, James. *The Last Stand of the Tin Can Sailors*. New York: Random House, 2004.

8. Sweetman, Jack, Editor. *Great American Naval Battles*. Annapolis, MD: Naval Institute Press, 1998.

9. Gordon, Tim. Phone interview with author, 25 June 2014.

Reardon, John

1. "Johnson Flyer is Reported Missing in Action Over Germany Since Nov. 2." *Graceville Enterprise*, 21 November 1944.

2. "Johnson Flyer Dies of Wounds." *Graceville Enterprise*, 9 January 1945.

3. Maslen, Vic. "615th Bombardment Squadron (H) 401st Bombardment Group (H) Squadron History." November 1944 Missions. 401st Bomb Group Association. http://401bg.org

4. Reardon, John J. Narrative of Investigation. Individual Deceased Personnel File. Washington, D.C.: War Department, Adjutant General's Office, 19 August 1948.

5. Swinnen, Andy. "John Joseph Reardon: Remember Our Heroes," 2012. Remember Our Heroes. www.remember-our-heroes.n/us_reardon.htm

Horton, Carl

1. American Battle Monuments Commission. "World War II Honor Roll: Joseph R. Shapley." Camden War Dead. www.DVRBS.com

2. "The Philadelphia Transit Strike of 1944." Civil Rights in a Northern City: Philadelphia. Temple University Library. http://northerncity.library.temple.edu/exhibits/show/civil-rights-in-a-northern-cit/collections/philadelphia-transit-strike-of.

3. Winkler, Allan M. "The Philadelphia Transit Strike of 1944." *The Journal of American History*, 59:1, pp. 73–89, 1972.

4. Wolfinger, James. *Philadelphia Divided: Race and Politics in the City of Brotherly Love*. University of North Carolina Press, 2011.

5. Wikipedia contributors. "Philadelphia Transit Strike of 1944." Wikipedia, The Free Encyclopedia, 8 January 2016. https://en.wikipedia.org

6. Mick, Allan H. "102nd thru Germany: WWII Unit History 102nd Infantry Division." Public Relations Office, July 1945. 5 December 2015. www.lonesentry.com

7. Horton, Carl. Report of Death. Individual Deceased Personnel File. Washington, D.C.: War Department, 23 December 1944.

8. Moore, Don. "Sgt. Fred Strass remembers 'Gardelegen Massacre' at close of war." 406th Infantry Regiment War Tales, 8 June 2011. https://donmooreswartales.com

Peterson, Otto

1. Weaver, Michael. *Guard Wars: The 28th Division in World War II*. Bloomington: Indiana University Press, 2010.

2. Kitchen, Lieutenant Colonel James W. "Vivid Memory of World War II." liberationparis1944.blogspotcom

3. Astor, Gerald. *The Greatest War: The Battle of the Bulge to Hiroshima, Volume 3*. Warner Books Edition, 1999.

4. Kemp, Harry. *The Regiment: Let the Citizens Bear Arms*. Austin: Nortex Press, 1990.

5. McKeig, Cecelia. *History of Boy River: 1889–1998*, pg. 114.

6. Peterson, Otto W. Individual Deceased Personnel File. Washington, D.C.: War Department, 6 April 1945.

7. Peterson, Steven. Email to author, 14 September.

Roner, Rudolph

1. Lindstrom, Harriet. Email to author, 6 January 2015.

2. "80th Infantry Division." U.S. Army Center of Military History. http://www.history.army.mil/documents/ETO-OB/80ID-ETO.htm

3. "History of the 80th." 80th Infantry Division. www.80thdivision.com/80thHistory.com

4. "Forward 80th: The Story of the 80th Infantry Division." G.I. Stories: *Stars and Stripes*, Paris, 1945. www.lonesentry.com

5. Gabel, Dr. Christopher R. The Lorraine Campaign: An Overview, September–December 1944.combat Studies Institute, February 1985. usacac.army.mil/cac2/cgsc/carl/download/csipubs/gabel3.pdf

6. Murrell, Robert T. *318th Infantry Regiment History*. Lewistown, PA: CreateSpace Independent Publishing Platform, 6 November 2015.

7. Bier, Lieutenant John. "318th/3Bn Seille and Nied River Crossings: 8 November 1944–4 December 1944," 22 June 1945. 80th Infantry Division. www.80thdivision.com/ WebArchives/MiscReports.htm

8. Roner, Rudolph T. Individual Deceased Personnel File. Washington, D.C.: War Department, 28 November 1944.

9. Janssen, Jennifer Anderson. History of Strandquist, Minnesota: 1904–2004.

10. "Strandquist Soldier Killed in France." *Argyle Banner*, pg. 1, 30 November 1944.

King, Ernest

1. Witschen, Gertrude. Phone interview with author, 2 August 2014.

2. Blaney, Captain Kermit B. "The Operations of Company L, 21st Infantry." U.S. Maneuver Center of Excellence Libraries—Fort Benning, 1949–1950. www.benning.army.mil

3. King, Clara. Letter to War Department, 8 October 1945. From the Individual Deceased Personnel File of Ernest King.

4. King, Ernest R. Report of Death. Individual Deceased Personnel File. Washington, D.C.: War Department, 16 December 1944.

5. "SSgt. Ernest King, Seaforth, is Killed in Action on Leyte." *Redwood Falls Gazette*, 21 December 1944.

6. Crump, Jean. "Ernest R. King: Redwood County Minnesota Obituary Directory." RootsWeb at www.ancestry.com

Lee, Roy

1. Bruner, D.W. "Able in Combat: Company A, 399th Infantry Regiment, 100th Division." George C. Marshall Foundation. marshallfoundation.org/100th-infantry/wp-content/uploads/sites/27/2014/06/Able_in_Combat_Co.A_399th.pdf

2. Gurley, Frank. "399th in Action: With the 100th Infantry Division," 1945. George C. Marshall Foundation. marshallfoundation.org/100th-infantry/399th-infantryregiment/

3. The War Years. 1 November 1944–30 April 1945." George C. Marshall Foundation. http://marshallfoundation.org/100th-infantry/wp-content/uploads/sites/27/2014/06/DruryPart1.pdf

4. Lee, Roy M. Individual Deceased Personnel File. Washington, D.C.: War Department, 27 November 1944.

5. Zimmerman, DiAnn. Email to author, 26 December 2015.

Gooselaw, Arthur

1. Bouvette, Rose. Arthur E. Gooselaw, Individual Deceased Personnel File. Washington, D.C.: War Department, 11 December 1944.

2. Olson, Shane. "Arthur Eugene Gooselaw." Find A Grave Memorial, 11 May 2007. www.findagrave.com

3. "Bravest of the Brave: The Story of the 95th Infantry Division." G.I. Stories: *Stars and Stripes*, Paris, 1945. www.lonesentry.com

4. Cole, Hugh M. "The Lorraine Campaign: The November Battle for Metz." Washington, D.C.: 1997. U.S. Army Center of Military History. www.history.army.mil/ html/books/007/7-6-1/CMH_Pub_7-6-1.pdf

5. "95th Infantry Division, Iron Men of Metz." The Patriot Files. www.patriotfiles.com/index.php?name=Sections&req=viewarticle&artid

6. Lindvall, August. "St. Vincent Memories: Indian Woman, 98 Years Old Still Lives in Log Home, Her Minnesota Abode for More than Eighty Years." St. Vincent Memories Blogspot, December 2006. 56755.blogspot.com/2006/12/profile-angelica- zasta-gooselaw.html

Hanson, Oscar

1. Hanson, Jim. Letter to author, 8 October 2014. Phone interview with author, 24 November 2015.

2. Ferrell, Gary. "Merseburg Mission #95, Missing Crew Report #10841," 34th Bomb Group Mission Diary. Valor to Victory 34th Bomb Group. http://valortovictory.tripod.com/1944-11.htm

3. Hanson, Captain Oscar T. Individual Deceased Personnel File. Washington, D.C.: War Department, 10 September 1982.

4. Hanson, Dawn. Phone interview with author, 17 August 2015. Letter to author, 29 August 2015.

5. Janssen, EvaLee. Letter to author, 17 September 2014.

Brady, Robert

1. Joseph Driscoll quote from "Bravest of the Brave: The Story of the 95th Infantry Division." G.I. Stories: *Stars and Stripes*, Paris, 1945. www.lonesentry.com

2. Fuermann, George M. and F. Edward Cranz, Editors. "95th Infantry Division History 1918–1946." www.archive.org

3. Kinslow, Albert V. CPT. "Operations of the 1st Battalion, 379th Infantry, 95th Infantry Division. Saarlautern, Germany, 2–6 December 1944. (Rhineland Campaign)" U.S. Army Maneuver Center of Excellence. www.benning.army.mil

4. Brady, Robert H. Individual Deceased Personnel File. Washington, D.C.: War Department, 10 December 1944.

5. Brady, Carl H. Obituary. *Duluth Star Tribune*, 19 September 2007.

6. Elcor Reunion Committee. "Elcor's Honored War Dead." Phillipich, Leonard, et al. *Elba-Elcor Reunion 1897–1956: A Collection of Memories*. Gilbert, Minnesota, 1982.

Hackbarth, Arthur

1. Dunn, Carol. Hackbarth Genealogy. philandcarol.com/cjgene/hackbarthmain.htm

2. Sebby, Daniel. "Let's Go! Northern California's 184th Infantry Regiment (2d California) During World War II." California Military Department. www.militarymuseum.org.184th.html.

3. "History of the 7th Infantry Division." 7th Infantry Division Association. www.7ida.us

4. Love, Edmund. *The Hourglass: A History of the 7th Infantry Division in World War II*. Washington, D.C.: Infantry Journal Press, 1950.

5. Brook, Scott. "Company G's History." *Chico Enterprise Record*, 11 November 2007.

6. Hackbarth, Arthur. Individual Deceased Personnel File. Washington, D.C.: War Department, 12 February 1945.

7. "Arthur Hackbarth Wounded at Leyte, Died December 10." *Independent Review*, 15 January 1945. Accessed via the hutchinsonleader.com at www.crowrivermedia.com

McNew, Larry

1. McNew, Dodie. Phone interview with author, 10 September 2014.

2. Kocher, Leo. "The 511th Parachute Infantry Regiment Unit History." The 11th Airborne World War II. www.ww2-airborne.us/units/511/511.html

3. Flanagan, Major Edward M. *The Angels: A History of the 11th Airborne Division 1943–1946*. Washington, D.C.: Infantry Journal Press, 1943. https://archive.org/details/TheAngels11thAirborneDiv

4. McNew, Larry. Letters to his mother, Isabell McNew. From the files of Bonnie Matheson.

5. McNew, Larry A. Individual Deceased Personnel File. Washington, D.C.: War Department, Adjutant General's Office, 26 January 1945.

6. Wikipedia contributors. "Rod Serling." Wikipedia, The Free Encyclopedia, 24 January 2016. https://en.wikipedia.org

7. Matheson, Bonnie McNew. Phone interview with author, 12 December 2014.

Swanson, Kenneth

1. Comstock Centennial Committee. *Comstock Centennial 1890–1990*. Gwinner, ND: J&M Printing, 1990.

2. Pennartz, Sam. "Sargeant Kenneth W. Swanson." Find A Grave Memorial, 6 August 2010. www.findagrave.com

3. Swinhart, Earl. "Boeing B-29 Superfortress." The Aviation History Online Museum. 2014. www.aviation-history.com

4. U.S. Army Air Forces. *The Story of the 73rd: The Unofficial History of the 73rd Bomb Wing*. World War Regimental Histories, Book 154. Bangor Public Library. digicom.bpl.lib.me.us

5. Hammel, Eric. *Air War Pacific Chronology: Americas War Against Japan in East Asia and the Pacific 1941–1945*. Pacifica, CA: Pacifica Press, 1988.

6. Burkett, Captain Prentiss. *The Unofficial History of the 499th Bomb Group (VH)*. Temple City, CA: Historical Aviation Album, 1981.

7. Dana, Caleb. "Caleb's Diary: 11/1944–9/1945, The Story of the 73rd's Missions." Old New Orleans. www.old-new-orleans.com/Mission_Diary.html

8. Missing Air Crew Report #10654. Alabama: Department of the Air Force, Maxwell Air Force Base, 19 December 1945.

Eichten, Helmer

1. Eichten, Doug. Email to author, 20 July 2015.

2. "103rd Infantry Division." U.S. Army Center of Military History. www.history.army.mil

3. Shelby, Marlys. Helmer Mathias Eichten "Turk." Story emailed to author, 18 October 2016.

4. Wayne, Larry. Email to author, 17 May 2015.

5. Eichten, Helmer. Bronze Star for Heroism. General Order #46, 30 January 1945.

6. Branton, Harold M. *103rd Infantry Division: The Trail of the Cactus*. Paducah, KY: Turner Publishing Company, 1993. www.103rdcactus.com

7. U.S. Army. *103rd Infantry Division Cactus Caravan*. Atlanta: Albert Love Enterprises, 1944. 103rd Cactus Division. www.103rdcactus.com

8. United States Army 411th Infantry. *From Bruyeres to Brenner: The Combat Story of the Fighting 411th*, 1939–1945. Don Bennett's War. www.don.genemcguire.com

9. Eichten, Private Helmer. Report of Death. Individual Deceased Personnel File. Washington, D.C.: War Department, Adjutant General's Office, 20 January 1945.

10. Helmer Eichten Killed in France." *Redwood Falls Gazette*, 23 January 1945.

11. Eichten, Gary. Email to author, 26 March 2015.

12. Eichten, Pauline. Email to author, 16 May 2015.

Typhoon Cobra: Armbrust, Hakenson, Kaufman, Lundgren

1. Drury, Bob and Tom Clavin. *Halsey's Typhoon*. New York: Grove Press, 2007.

2. Wikipedia contributors. "Typhoon Cobra 1944." Wikipedia, The Free Encyclopedia, 22 December 2015. https://en.wikipedia.org

3. "Lost in Pacific Typhoon." *Grant County Herald*, 8 March 1945.

4. Armbrust, Almon. Report of Casualty. Individual Deceased Personnel File. Washington, D.C.: War Department, 10 February 1945.

5. Brenner, Dean. "The Flag Raisers: A History of Herman-Norcross Men and Women during World War II," 1991.

6. Hakenson, Warren. Report of Casualty. Individual Deceased Personnel File. Washington, D.C.: War Department, 10 February 1945.

7. Lundgren, Lloyd. Report of Casualty. Individual Deceased Personnel File. Washington, D.C.: War Department, 13 February 1945.

8. Kaufman, Harold. Letter to Alice Struck, 4 December 1944. From the personal files of Paul and Pam Struck.

9. Kaufman, Harold. Report of Casualty. Individual Deceased Personnel File. Washington, D.C.: War Department, 10 February 1945.

10. Kaufman, Irvin. Phone interview with author, 9 February 2015.

11. "Obituary Mrs. Theresa Kaufman." *Madison Press*, pg. 9, 20 April 1955.

12. Wikipedia contributors. "The Caine Mutiny." Wikipedia, The Free Encyclopedia, 25 January 2016. https://en.wikipedia.org

13. Struck, Paul. Phone interview with author, 9 January 2015.

Malmrose, Victor

1. "Gladys Wendland Ramm Obituary." *Ortonville Independent*, 23 August 2003.

2. "Victor A. Malmrose." Find A Grave Memorial, 4 March 2000. www.findagrave.com

3. Malmrose, Victor A. Individual Deceased Personnel File. Washington, D.C.: War Department, 19 January 1945.

4. Seitz, 1st Lieutenant Clinton. "The 495th: As Crowfoot Saw the War." 12 Armored Division Museum. www.12tharmoredmuseum.com

5. Wendland, Dennis. Email to author, 12 November 2015.

Bruns, Norbert

1. Bruns, Norbert. Report of Death. Individual Deceased Personnel Report. Washington, D.C.: War Department, 14 February 1945.

2. Adkins, Andrew. "Company Morning Report Company K, 317th Infantry Regiment, 26 December 1944." 80th Infantry Division. www.80thdivision.com

3. Adkins, Andrew. *You Can't Get Much Closer Than This: Combat with Company H, 317th Infantry Regiment, 80th Division*, Chapter 9. Havertown, PA: CaseMate Publisher, 2005. www.80thdivision.com

4. Adkins, Andrew. "History of the 80th Infantry Division." 80th Division Digital Archives Project. www.80thdivision.com

5. Atkinson, Rick. *The Guns at Last Light: The War in Western Europe, 1944–1945*. Thorndike Press, Henry Holt & Company, 2013.

6. Dominique, Dean James. "The Attack Will Go On: The 317th Infantry Regiment in World War II, A Thesis." Louisiana State University, 2003. digitalcommons.lsu. edu

7. Headquarters 317th Infantry After Action Report (S-3), 1 January 1945. 80th Infantry Division. www.80thdivision.com

8. "Bruns, Corporal Norbert," Silver Star Citation, 8 March 1945. Military Times Hall of Valor. http://valor.militarytimes.com

9. Butkowski, Ralph. Email to author, 7 May 2015.

Dolan, Vincent

1. Gallagher, Wes. "French Children Saved in Heroic Yank Rescue." *Oregonian*, 19 October 1944. 134th Infantry Regiment Website. www.coulthart.com/134/index. htm

2. "The Baby Patrol." *Time*, 30 October 1944. 134th Infantry Regiment Website. www.coulthart.com/134/index.htm

3. After Action Reports, January 1945. 134th Infantry Regiment Website. www.coulthart.com/134/index.htm

4. Russo, Roberta. "Dolan, Vincent J. 37541143 Condolence Report." Accessed via email to author, 5 April 2012.

5. Connolly, Clara Dolan. "Dolan History." November 1978.

6. Dolan, Vincent J. Individual Deceased Personnel File. Washington, D.C.: War Department, 5 January 1945.

7. "Double Rites for Vets at Danvers Monday." *Swift County Monitor-News*, 21 January 1949.

8. Tisdell, Joseph. Phone interview with author, 7 April 2015.

Gustafson, Bertil

1. Anderson, Hal. Interview with author, 25 August 2015.

2. "Memorial Rites for Pvt. B.Q. Gustafson Held Sunday in Viking." *Thief River Falls Times*, pg. 4, 15 February 1945.

3. Weber, William E. "517th Parachute Regimental Combat Team: A Short History from Airborne Quarterly," 1998. www.517prct.org

4. "517th Parachute Infantry Regiment." United States Airborne World War II. http://www.ww2-airborne.us/units/517/517.html

5. U.S. Armed Forces. *517th Parachute Infantry: Book VII, 13th Airborne Division 1943–1946 History,* 1949. www.517prct.org

6. Landreth, Mark. "Chronology of the 517th PIR with emphasis on 2nd Battalion and E Company," March 2009. 517th Parachute Infantry Regiment. www.517prct.org

7. Graves, R.D. "Christmas Greetings. 517th Parachute Infantry Combat Team: Christmas in France 1944." 517th Parachute Regimental Combat Team. www.517prct.org

8. Barrett, Bob. "Pvt. Bertil Gustafson." Email to Jill Johnson, 18 August 2012.

9. Gustafson, Bertil Q. Report of Death. Individual Deceased Personnel File. Washington, D.C.: War Department, 25 January 1945.

10. Tostrup, John. Phone interview with author, 7 March 2015.

Meling, Truman

1. Meling, Donald. Christiansen, Kenneth and Bradley Christiansen, Editors. "Jake and Clela Meling: A Family Story," 2003. www.yumpu.com

2. "The 327th Glider Infantry Regiment Unit History." The 101st Airborne World War II. http://www.ww2-airborne.us/units/327/327.html

3. Harper, Colonel Joseph. 327th Glider Infantry After Action Report, December 1944, 12 March 1945. Dwight D. Eisenhower Presidential Library and Museum, Abilene, Kansas.

4. O'Halloran, Captain John T. "The Operations of the 1st Platoon, Company B, 401st Glider Infantry in the battle of Bastogne, Belgium, 25 December 1944." Maneuver Center of Excellence. United States Army—Fort Benning. http://www.benning.army.mil/library/content/Virtual/Donovanpapers/wwii/

5. Meling, Truman. Individual Deceased Personnel File. Washington, D.C.: War Department, 29 January 1945.

Brummer, Andrew

1. Knudson, Isabella. "Andrew R. Brummer." World War II Awards. http://en.ww2awards.com/person/36641

2. Russo, Roberta. "Brummer, Andrew, R37164839 KIA DOW Report." Email to author, 5 April 2012.

3. Brummer, Andrew. Report of Death. Individual Deceased Personnel File. Washington, D.C.: War Department, 12 July 1945.

4. "Killed in Action in Belgium January 7." *Little Falls Daily Transcript*, 19 July 1945.

5. Kruishaar, Frits. "Private Andrew Richard 'Andy' Brummer." Find A Grave Memorial, 6 August 2010. www.findagrave.com

6. Miltonberger, Major General Butler B. and Major James A. Huston. "The Ardennes Bulge." 134th Infantry Regiment Website. www.coulthart.com/134/index.htm

7. Linquata, Michael. "35th Division Monument-Lutremange, Belgium." 134th Infantry Regiment Website. www.coulthart.com/134/index.htm

Boe, George

1. "Memorial Service for Pfc. George Alton Boe," in World War II file, Kandiyohi County Historical Society, Willmar, Minnesota.

2. Boe, Bob. Phone interview with author, 30 July 2014.

3. Gurley, Frank, Editor. "399th In Action with the 100th Infantry Division." George C. Marshall Foundation. http://marshallfoundation.org/100th-infantry/399thinfantry-regiment/

4. "Who We Are: 100th Infantry Division." George C. Marshall Foundation. http://marshallfoundation.org/100th-infantry/399th-infantry-regiment/

5. Lindstrand, Jon. "Boe, George." Memorial to Fallen-USMHC-United States Military Historical Collection. http://www.usmhc.org/Fallen/Boe_George_Alton.pdf

6. "Silver Star Citation for George A. Boe." Military Times Hall of Valor. http://valor.militarytimes.com

7. Boe, George A. Individual Deceased Personnel File. Washington, D.C.: War Department, 21 February 1945.

Skaar, Wallace

1. Miller, Keith. "Military: The 329th Regiment." History News Network. www.historynewsnetwork.org/article/395

2. Childers, Jim. "Letter to Glen from Wallie." Email to author, 15 July 2014.

3. Childers, Jim. "Private Wallace Adolph Skaar." Find A Grave Memorial, 19 April 2010. www.findagrave.com

4. "United States Army Infantry Regiment 329th, 2nd Battalion." *Combat Digest, 2nd Battalion, 329 Infantry*, pg. 59, 1945.

5. Headquarters 329th Infantry After Action Reports, 9 January 1945. 83rd Infantry Division. http://www.83rdinfantrydivision.info/#329

6. U.S. Army and Goguen, Raymond J. *329 "Buckshot" Infantry Regiment: A History*, 1945. World War Regimental Histories, Book 26. Bangor Community Digital Commons@bpl. http://digicom.bpl.lib.me.us/ww_reg_his/26/

Colson, Wallace

1. Helgason, Gudmundur. "U-1055. German U-Boats of World War II." Accessed via uboat.net at http://uboat.net/boats/u1055.htm

2. Niestle, Axel. "German U-Boat Losses During World War II." United States Naval Institute, 1998. Accessed via uboat.net at http://uboat.net/fates/losses/

3. Gong, Yingxi. "Biography Jonas Lie." The Caldwell Gallery. http://www.caldwellgallery.com/bios/lie-biography.html

4. Colson, Wallace Dean. Individual Deceased Personnel File. Washington, D.C.: Office of the Quartermaster General, 1 September 1949.

5. Ships Hit by U-Boats, *Jonas Lie*: American Steam merchant. uboat.net. http://uboat.net/allies/merchants/3414.html

6. Olson, Shane. "Wallace Dean Colson." Find A Grave Memorial, 19 December 2011. www.findagrave.org

7. "SS *Jonas Lie*." The Wreck Site. http://www.wrecksite.eu/wreck.aspx?10421

Cummings, Russell

1. Naval Institute Archives. "SeaBees Name and Insignia Officially Recognized." Naval History Blog, 29 February 2012. https://www.navalhistory.org/2012/02/29/seabees-name-and-insignia-officially-authorized

2. "Seabee History: Formation of the Seabees and World War II." Naval History and Heritage Command, 16 August 2015. https://www.history.navy.mil/research/ library/online-reading-room/title-list-alphabetically/s/seabee-history0/world-warii. html

3. "Seabee History." Seabee Museum and Memorial Park. www.seabeesmuseum.com

4. Hughes, Lieutenant Russell F., Editor. *The Island X-quire: CBMU 540*. "History and Log, CBMU 540" and "Company C" roster. New York: John White, Jr., Lt.com., 1945

5. Cummings, Russell. Individual Deceased Personnel File. Washington, D.C.: War Department, 12 January 1945.

6. "Cummings is Killed in West Indies." *Cass Lake Times*, 18 January 1945.

7. Bratell, Truman. "Gordon Langlie." Find A Grave Memorial, 14 October 2013. www.findagrave.com

Kolberg, Arthur

1. "Kolberg Memorial Service." From the World War II Files, Roseau County Historical Society, Roseau, Minnesota, 16 May 2014.

2. Price, Thomas E. "A Brief History of the U.S Army 6th Infantry Division," 15 April 2011. National Association of the 6th Infantry Association. www.6thinfantry.com

3. Division Public Relations Section. *The 6th Infantry Division in World War II, 1939–1945*. Nashville: Battery Press, 1983.

4. Kolberg, Arthur. Individual Deceased Personnel File. Washington, D.C.: War Department, Adjutant General's Office, 15 February 1945.

Beckman, Sylvester

1. "S.M. Beckman of Tintah Killed in Luzon Battle." From the files of Phyllis Beckman.

2. Beckman, Phyllis. Phone interview with author, 16 June 2014.

3. "43rd Infantry Division." U.S. Army Center of Military History. http://www.history.army.mil/html/forcestruc/cbtchron/cc/043id.htm

4. Barker, Harold R. "History of the 43rd Division Artillery World War II 1941–1945." 152nd Field Artillery Association. http://www.152fieldartilleryassociation.org/Documents.html

5. Beckman, Sylvester. Individual Deceased Personnel File. Washington, D.C.: War Department, 17 February 1945.

6. "Three Grant County Men Reported Missing or Dead." *Grant County Herald*, 15 February 1945.

Hanson, Howard

1. "Howard Hanson Killed in Action." *Adams Review*, 22 February 1945. Obituary permission courtesy of *Review Monitor*, Adams, Minnesota.

2. Ballard, Ted. "Rhineland." U.S. Army Center of Military History. www.history. army.mil

3. Cole, Hugh M. "Ardennes: The Battle of the Bulge." U.S. Army Center of Military History. www.history.army.mil

4. National 4th Infantry Division Association. "Division History," 2015. www.4thinfantry.org

5. Astor, Gerald. "Battle of Hürtgen Forest." *World War II Magazine*, 2004. http://www.historynet.com/battle-of-hurtgen-forest.htm

6. Hanson, Howard. Individual Deceased Personnel File. Washington, D.C.: War Department, 8 February 1945.

Ranum, Glenn

1. Ranum, Elodee Mae. Email to author, 26 July 2011.

2. "Pfc. Glenn Ranum, 21, Gives Life on Luzon Island January 27." *Warren Sheaf*, 28 February 1945.

3. Olson, Shane. "Glenn A. Ranum." Find A Grave Memorial, 6 June 2008. www.findagrave.com

4. "A Brief History of the 25th Infantry Division." 25th Infantry Division Association Website. www.25thida.org

5. Denfeld, Duane. "161st Infantry Regiment, Washington National Guard," 1 February 2012. http://www.historylink.org/File/10021

6. Johnson, June Hodik. Phone interview with author, 8 March 2015 and 25 March 2015.

7. Ranum, Glenn A. Report of Interment. Individual Deceased Personnel File. Washington, D.C.: War Department, 16 February 1948.

8. Ranum, Lowell. Phone interview with author, 7 March 2015.

Wright, Wilbur

1. "Services to Be Held Sunday for Wilbur C. Wright." *Worthington Daily Globe*, 1 March 1945.

2. Lord, William G. *History of the 508th Parachute Infantry.* Washington, D.C.: Infantry Journal Press, 1948.

3. "All American: The Story of the 82nd Airborne Division." G.I. Stories: *Stars and Stripes*, Paris, 1945. www.lonesentry.com

4. 82nd Airborne During World War II. "Campaigns: Ardennes-Alsasce." http:// www.ww2-airborne.us/division/campaigns/belgium.html

5. Geertsema, Margaret. Letters and photos from her personal files to author, 11 August 2014.

6. Wright, Wilbur. Letter to Mabel Wright, 20 January 1945.

Engblom, Edward

1. Wepplo, John. Letters to author, 19 March 2015. Email to author, 23 March 2015.

2. Perry, Everett M. "USS *Canopus* AS-9." evperry.com

3. Perry, Everett M. Email to author, 10 April 2014.

4. Edward Engblom. "USS *Canopus* (AS-9)." On Eternal Patrol. http://www.oneternalpatrol.com/uss-canopus-as-9.htm

5. Engblom, Edward. Report of Casualty. Individual Deceased Personnel File. Washington, D.C.: War Department, 22 June 1945.

Loucks, Emmett

1. "SSgt. Emmett T. Loucks." *The Itasca Iron News*, January 1945, in Itasca County Historical Society "Obituary" file, Grand Rapids, Minnesota.

2. "134th Infantry Regiment: Combat History of World War II." 134th Infantry Regiment Website. http://www.coulthart.com/134/

3. Loucks, Emmett T. Individual Deceased Personnel File. Washington, D.C.: War Department, Adjutant General's Office, 12 March 1945.

4. Loucks, Colin and James Loucks. "County land trade would be a disgrace to veterans." Courtesy of *Grand Rapids Herald-Review*, 2 June 2012.

5. Loucks, Kathleen. Phone interview, 7 November 2013.

Swenson, Donald

1. Whiting, Jerry. Emails to author, 17 August 2013 and 3 October 2013.

2. Whiting, Jerry. "History of the 485th Bomb Group." 485th Bomb Group Association. www.485thbg.org

3. Whiting, Jerry. "Wydler Crew-831st Squadron Replacement Crew." 485th Bomb Group Association. www.485thbg.org

4. "Lieutenant Swenson." From the files of the Norman County Historical and Genealogy Society, Ada, Minnesota. Email to author from Deb Jacobson, 31 August 2013.

5. Fredrikson, Ardis. Phone interview with author, 11 November 2014. Letter to author, 20 November 2015.

Olson, Archie

1. Nord, Kay. Email to author, 30 August 2014.

2. Sloan, Bill. "Corregidor: The Last Battle in the Fall of the Philippines," 23 April 2012. http://www.historynet.com/corregidor-the-last-battle-in-the-fall-of-thephilippines. htm

3. Mansell, Roger. "Fukuoka #3 POW Camp." Center for Research: Allied POWs Under the Japanese, 11 February 2016. www.mansell.com

4. Humphries, 2nd Lieutenant Inf. Robert E. "Prisoner of War Camp No. 3 (Fukuoka)" Investigation Report in the case of prisoner of war camp investigations. Center for Research: Allied POWs Under the Japanese. www.mansell.com

5. Archie L. Olson—Prisoner of War Record. Mooseroots. http://wwii-pows.mooseroots.com/l/139087/Archie-L-Olson

6. Markowitz, Herbert. "Memorandum for the Officer in Charge." Center for Research: Allied POWs Under the Japanese. www.mansell.com

7. Olson, Archie L. Report of Death. Individual Deceased Personnel File. Washington, D.C.: War Department, 4 February 1946.

8. Olson, Shane. "Archie L. Olson." *Red Lake Falls Gazette*, 21 March 1946. Accessed via Find A Grave Memorial at www.findagrave.com

Knight, James

1. Evensen, Janice Knight. Email to author, 10 September 2014.

2. "James T. Knight," *The Itasca Iron News*, January 1945, in Itasca County Historical Society "Obituary" file, Grand Rapids, Minnesota.

3. Dodds, Wayne S. "History: At War–Northern Italy." Official Website of the 57th Fighter Group. www.57thfightergroup.org

4. Knight, 2nd Lieutenant James T. "Aircraft Accident and Incident Reports 1941–1948." World War II Records Division, General Services Administration, 21 February 1945.

Ness, Rubin

1. Vangness, Dave. "Rubin L. Ness." Find A Grave Memorial, 4 March 2000. www.findagrave.com

2. Smith, Robert Ross. *Triumph in the Philippines*, 1963. Washington, D.C.: U.S. Army Center of Military History. www.history.army.mil

3. The 130th Infantry Division Historical Committee. *The Golden Cross: A History of the 33rd Infantry Division in World War II.* Washington, D.C.: Infantry Journal Press, 1948. https://archive.org/details/TheGoldenCross

4. Derks, Tracy. "Battling Toward Baguio." *World War II Magazine*, 2002. 33rd Infantry Division Association. www.33rdinfantrydivision.org

5. 33rd Infantry Division. Sixth U.S. Army Report of the Luzon Campaign: 9 January 1945–30 June 1945. www.33rdinfantrydivision.org

6. Erickson, Gladys Ness. Letter to author, 17 September 2014.

7. "Luzon 1944–1945." U.S. Army Center of Military History. www.history.army.mil

8. Ness, Rubin L. Individual Deceased Personnel File. Washington, D.C.: War Department, 21 May 1945.

9. "Memorial Services Sunday at Holt for Rubin Ness." *Thief River Falls Times*, pg. 14, 19 April 1945.

Lundgren, Myril

1. Pauling, Mary Jo. Phone interviews with author, 23 February 2015 and 7 April 2015.

2. U.S. Army Artillery Board. "Report on Study of Field Artillery Operations." Xenophon Group International, 20 November 1945. http://www.xenophon-mil.org/milhist/usarmy/boardreports/artilleryboard61.htm

3. Reamey, H.K. "CSI Battlebook: Roer River Crossing." Combat Studies Institute, May 1984. Defense Technical Information Center. http://www.dtic.mil/dtic/tr/ fulltext/u2/a163873.pdf

4. Lundgren, Myril. Individual Deceased Personnel File. Washington, D.C.: War Department, 15 March 1945.

5. Rossow, Joyce. Phone interview with author.

6. Carlson, Ed. *We Honor Our Fallen Comrades-In-Arms*. Jackson, MN: Livewire Printing, 1989.

Bixby, Glen

1. Bixby, Glen. Letter to his family, 30 August 1944. From the files of Sandy Duerre.

2. Nalty, Bernard C. and Danny Crawford. *The United States Marines on Iwo Jima: The Battle and the Flag Raising*. U.S. Marines Electronic Library, 5 June 2014. http://www.marines.mil/News/Publications/ELECTRONIC-LIBRARY/

3. Military History Encyclopedia on the Web. "Operation Detachment: The Battle for Iwo Jima February–March 1945." http://www.historyofwar.org/articles/battles_iwojima.html

4. Ward, Geoffrey C. and Ken Burns. *The War: An Intimate History 1941–1945*. New York: Alfred A. Knopf, 2007.

5. Bixby, Glen. USMC Casualty Report. Individual Deceased Personnel File. Washington, D.C.: War Department, 8 March 1945.

6. Duerre, Steven. Email to author, 11 November 2014.

7. "Glen Bixby Killed in Action." *Fergus Falls Daily Journal*, 20 March 1945.

Ringstad, Palmer

1. Berg, Richard. Email to author, 31 May 2013.

2. Aykroyd, Captain Albert. "CCA 10th Armored Division from Trier to Landau," 1 May 1948. Armor School Student Papers. U.S. Maneuver Center of Excellence—Fort Benning. http://www.benning.army.mil/library/content/Virtual/Armorpapers/AykroydAlbert%20W.%20CPT.pdf

3. Morris, Major General H.H., Jr. "Terrify and Destroy: The Story of the 10th Armored Division." G.I. Stories: *Stars and Stripes*, Paris, 1945. www.lonesentry.com

4. "Reburial Service Held at Gully for Fatality for War." *Crookston Daily Times*, 7 October 1948.

5. Ringstad, Palmer. Individual Deceased Personnel File. Washington, D.C.: War Department, 11 March 1945.

Parker, John

1. Maher, Joan. Phone interviews with author, 16 July 2014 and 14 October 2015.

2. "Kerrick Boy Dies in Grim Struggle for Pacific Isle." From the files of Christine Carlson.

3. Antill, P. "The Battle for Iwo Jima," 6 April 2001. http://www.historyofwar.org/articles/battles_iwojima.html

4. Nalty, Bernard C. and Danny Crawford. *The United States Marines on Iwo Jima: The Battle and the Flag Raising*. U.S. Marines Electronic Library, 5 June 2014. http://www.marines.mil/News/Publications/ELECTRONIC-LIBRARY/

5. Parker, John W. USMC Casualty Report. Individual Deceased Personnel File. Washington, D.C.: War Department, 27 March 1945.

Hunkins, Henry

1. Price, Thomas E. "A Brief History of the 6th Infantry Division." 6th Infantry: The Sightseeing Sixth Infantry Division, 15 April 2011. www.6thinfantry.com

2. Andrade, Dale. "Luzon." World War II Campaign Brochures, CMH Pub 72-78. Washington, D.C.: U.S. Army Center of Military History. www.history.army. mil

3. Division Public Relations Section, 6th Infantry Division. Washington, D.C.: Infantry Journal Press, 1947. http://www.6thinfantry.com/category/documents/

4. Gowin, James. Letter to author, 20 July 2014.

5. Hunkins, Henry. Individual Deceased Personnel Report. Washington, D.C.: War Department, 6 April 1945.

6. Kastelle, Russell. Phone interview, 26 September 2016.

7. Telegram courtesy of James Gowin.

Lehner, Clarence

1. Wilson, Jessica. Email to author, 3 August 2014.

2. Blakely, Major H.W. "Famous Fourth: The Story of the Fourth Division." G.I. Stories: *Stars and Stripes*, Paris, 1945. www.lonesentry.com

3. Lehner, Clarence. Report of Death. Individual Deceased Personnel File. Washington, D.C.: War Department, 13 April 1945.

4. Babcock, Robert. "This Week in WWII: March 3–March 31, 1945," 30 March 2015. War Stories. Athens, GA: Deeds Publishing.

Stoll, Milton

1. Price, Thomas. "A Brief History of the U.S. Army 6th Infantry Division." National Association 6th Infantry Division, 1996. www.6thinfantry.com

2. Division Public Relations Section. *The 6th Infantry Division*. Washington, D.C.: Infantry Journal Press, 1947. http://www.6thinfantry.com/category/documents/

3. Division Public Relations Section. *The Sixth Infantry Division in World War II, 1939–1945*. Nashville: Battery Press, 1983. http://www.6thinfantry.com/category/documents/

4. Stoll, Milton. Individual Deceased Personnel File. Washington, D.C.: War Department, 24 April 1945.

5. "Died in Philippines." *Litchfield Independent Review*, 10 May 1945.

6. Stoll, Larry and Lois. Letter to author, 15 August 2015.

Leitner, Frank

1. Leitner, Leo. Email to author, 23 February 2015.

2. Bedessem, Edward N. Central Europe: 22 March–11 May 1945. U.S. Army Center of Military History. www.history.army.mil

3. Liddell, Major Robert J. "Rhine River Crossing Conducted by the Third US Army and the Fifth Infantry Division: Offensive, Deliberate Assault, River Crossing, 22–24 March 1945." *CSI Battlebook*. Fort Leavenworth, KS: Combat Studies Institute, 22 June 1984. www.dtic.mil

4. Chen, Peter. "Crossing the Rhine. 22 March 1945–1 April 1945." World War II Database. http://ww2db.com/battle_spec.php?battle_id=134

5. Black, Colonel Paul. Letter to Mrs. Johanna Leitner, 7 April 1945.

6. Leitner, Frank. Individual Deceased Personnel File. Washington, D.C.: War Department, 9 April 1945.

7. Biederman, Mary. Email to author, 26 February 2015.

8. Schwan, Joanne. Phone interview with author, 6 September 2014.

Stevenson, Cecil

1. Stevenson, Cecil. Letter to his sister, Madge Elliot, 18 October 1944.

2. Elliot, Larry L. Phone interview with author, 18 August 2014. Letter to author, 28 August 2014.

3. "12th Armored Division." U.S. Army Center of Military History. www.history. army.mil

4. Eaglefeld, Dr. Max S. 82nd Armored Med Bn. Co. C. 12th AD. "Personal recollections and oral history video." www.12tharmoredmuseum.com

5. Nugent, John M. "56th Armored Infantry Battalion–12th Armored Division Memories." 12th Armored Division Museum, 1994. www.12tharmoredmuseum.com

6. "Speed is the Password: The Story of the 12th Armored Division." G.I. Stories: *Stars and Stripes*, Paris, 1945. www.lonesentry.com

7. Stern, Pfc. Bernard. "92nd Cavalry Reconnaissance Squadron: 12th Armored Division, Troop C." 12th Armored Division Museum. www.12tharmoredmuseum.com

8. Stevenson, Cecil R. Report of Burial. Individual Deceased Personnel File. Washington, D.C.: War Department, 9 April 1945.

Horne, Robert

1. "12th Armored Division." U.S. Army Center of Military History. www.history. army.mil

2. "Speed is the Password: The Story of the 12th Armored Division." G.I. Stories: *Stars and Stripes*, Paris, 1945. www.lonesentry.com

3. Nugent, John M. "Excerpts from the Diary of Elmer Bright: 56th Armored Infantry Battalion-12th Armored Division Memories." 12th Armored Division Museum, 1994. www.12tharmoredmuseum.com

4. Horne, Robert E. Report of Burial. Individual Deceased Personnel File. Washington, D.C.: War Department, 7 April 1945.

5. "Two Well Known McGrath Boys Make Supreme Sacrifice." *Aitkin Independent Age*, 1945. From the files of the Aitkin County Historical Society, Aitkin, Minnesota.

Kittelson, Elmer

1. Daly, Hugh C. *42nd "Rainbow" Infantry Division: A Combat History of World War II*. Baton Rouge, LA: Army & Navy Publishing, 1946. Bangor Community Digital Commons@bpl. http://digicom.bpl.lib.me.us/ww_reg_his/64/

2. "Memorial Services Held for Sgt. Elmer Kittelson." *Stephen Messenger*, pg. 8, 10 May 1945.

3. Jacobson, Corienne. Letter to author, 23 July 2014.

4. Kittelson, Elmer. Report of Burial. Individual Deceased Personnel File. Washington, D.C.: War Department, 12 April 1945.

5. "WWII: Liberation of Dachau Concentration Camp." Rainbow Veterans Memorial Foundation. http://www.rainbowvets.org/wwii#dachau

Anderson, Sigwald

1. "Beltrami Man Killed in Action." *Fertile Journal*, 17 May 1945.

2. Price, Thomas E. "A Brief History of the U.S. Army 6th Infantry Division," 1996. National Association 6th Infantry Division. www.6thinfantry.com

3. Division Public Relations Section. *The 6th Infantry Division in World War II, 1939–1945*. Washington, D.C.: Infantry Journal Press, 1947. http://www.6thinfantry.com/category/documents/

4. Palmer, Lieutenant Colonel Bruce, Jr. "Award of Bronze Star Medal." General Order #24, Headquarters 6th Infantry Division, 21 July 1944.

5. Broden, Phylis. Letter to author, 11 September 2014.

Peterson, Vernon

1. Peterson, Vernon. Letter to Lloyd Paulson, 10 March 1944. From the personal files of Karen Paulson Syverson.

2. "30th Infantry Regiment, Lineage and Honors." U.S. Army Center of Military History. www.history.army.mil

3. Dunigan, Sergeant James. "History of the U.S. 30th Infantry Regiment." VI Corps Combat Engineers WWII, 24 July 2011.

4. Peterson, Vernon R. Report of Investigation Area Search. Individual Deceased Personnel File. Washington, D.C.: War Department, 21 February 1946.

5. "Reburial Service for Staff Sergeant Vernon R. Peterson." *West Central Tribune*, 10 February 1949.

6. Uscola, Linda. Email translation from German to English, 24 March 2013.

Tongen, Jerald

1. Lofgren, Stephen F. "Southern Philippines: The U.S. Army Campaigns of World War II," CMH Pub 72-40. U.S. Army Center of Military History. www.history.army.mil

2. Mayo, Lida. "The Philippines: The Southern Islands," Chapter XXII. *The Ordnance Department: On Beachhead and Battlefront*. Washington, D.C.: U.S. Army, Center of Military History, 1991. www.history.army.mil

3. Pike, John. "40th Infantry Division (Mechanized)." 2000. GlobalSecurity.org

4. Colton, John. Letter to Jim Tongen, 23 April 1945, from the files of the Veterans Service Center, Granite Falls, Minnesota. Letter to Jim Tongen courtesy of Brenda Brusven.

5. "Body of Hazel Run Soldier to be Returned Soon." *Granite Falls Tribune*, 12 August 1948.

6. "Sgt. Jerald Tongen Remains Reinterred." *Granite Falls Tribune*, 9 September 1948.

Daufney, Glynn

1. Ripley, Rodney. Email to author, 1 July 2015.

2. Missing Air Crew Report #13877, 10 April 1945. www.fold3.com

3. Daufney, Glynn. Finding of Death of Missing Person. Individual Deceased Personnel File. Washington, D.C.: War Department, 20 February 1948.

4. Van Erp, Astrid. "Glynn A. Daufney." Foundation Adopters American War Graves. Field of Honor Database. www.fieldsofhonordatabase.com

5. Backus, Jan. Email to author, 8 September 2014.

Storch, Lawrence

1. "Lawrence Storch Listed Missing in Action in Germany since April 13." *Redwood Falls Gazette*, 15 May 1945.

2. Headquarters 83rd Infantry Division, 331st Infantry Regiment After Action Report, April 1945. 83rd Infantry Division Documents. www.83rdinvdivdocs.com

3. Headquarters 83rd Infantry Division, 83rd Division Radio News, 13 April 1945. 83rd Infantry Division Documents. www.83rdinvdivdocs.com

4. Straus, Jack M. *We Saw It Through: History of the Three Thirty First (331st) Combat Team – Today Tomorrow Forever [World War II]*. Munich, Germany: F. Bruckmann, 1945. www.83rdinvdivdocs.com

5. Storch, Lawrence. Report of Death. Individual Deceased Personnel File. Washington, D.C.: War Department, 7 June 1945.

6. Coulter, Darold and Sharon. Phone interview with author, 26 May 2015.

Stevenson, John

1. "John Stevenson Killed in Pacific in Marine Group." *Redwood Falls Gazette*, 10 May 1945.

2. Appleman, Roy, James Burns, Russell Gugeler and John Stevens. "Okinawa: The Last Battle." Washington, D.C.: U.S. Government Printing Office, 1948. U.S. Army Center of Military History. www.history.army.mil

3. Ambrose, Stephen. *The Good Fight*. New York: Simon & Schuster, 2001.

4. Santelli, James S. *A Brief History of the 4th Marines*. Washington, D.C.: Historical Division, Marine Headquarters, U.S. Marine Corps, 1970. www.marines.mil

5. Stevenson, John Gray. USMC Casualty Report. Individual Deceased Personnel File. Washington, D.C.: War Department, 7 May 1945.

Thompson, Clifford

1. Zweibel, Lieutenant Colonel David. "The 777th Tank Battalion-the Fighting 69th Infantry Division." The Fighting 69th Infantry Division Website. http://www.69th-infantrydivision.com/histories/777.html

2. Ziemke, Earl F. "Eclipse: The Ruhr Pocket," Chapter XIV. *The U.S. Army in the Occupation of Germany, 1944–1946*. Washington, D.C.: U.S. Army Center of Military History, 1990. www.history.army.mil

3. United States Holocaust Museum. "The 69th Infantry Division." Holocaust Encyclopedia, 29 January 2016. https://www.ushmm.org/wlc/en/article.php?ModuleId=10006167

4. U.S. Army. "Pictorial History of the 69th Infantry Division, 15 May 1943 to 15 May 1945." The Fighting 69th Infantry Division Website. Accessed via Lipsius, Major Joseph, Webmaster. Email to author, 10 May 2013. http://www.69thinfantry- division.com

5. "American War Cemetery Margraten." Fields of Honor Database. http://www.fieldsofhonor-database.com/index.php/en/margraten-2

6. Thompson, Clifford. Individual Deceased Personnel File. Washington, D.C.: War Department, 18 June 1945.

Kroll, Henry

1. "Kroll Memorial Services Planned in June; Was Killed in Italy." *The Thirteen Towns*, 11 May 1945.

2. Kroll, Henry. Army Effects Bureau. Individual Deceased Personnel File. Washington D.C.: War Department, 26 April 1945.

3. Jones, Don. The 337th Infantry Regiment in Italy World War II. Accessed via email to author, 24 April 2012.

4. National Archives. "Operation Reports: April 1945, Headquarters 337th Infantry," 28 May 1945. The 337th Infantry Regiment in Italy World War II. http://www.337thinfantry.net/

Nelson, Kenneth

1. "Kenneth Nelson Makes Supreme Sacrifice." *Glenwood Herald*, 14 June 1945.

2. "25th Infantry Division Chronicle WW2." 25th Infantry Division Association. U.S. Army Center of Military History. www.history.army.mil

3. Alberts, Sargeant Mike. "Wolfhounds make a difference in lives of Japanese orphans," 1 August 2008. The Official Home Page of the United States Army. https://www.army.mil/article/11405/wolfhounds-make-a-difference-in-lives-of-japaneseorphans

4. Ives, Sargeant Ian. "Continuing a 50 year legacy; Soldiers welcome orphans from Japan into their homes," 23 July 2015. The Official Home Page of the United States Army. https://www.army.mil/article/152781/Continuing_a_50_year_legacy__Soldiers_welcome_orphans_from_Japan_into_their_homes

5. Wikipedia contributors. "27th Infantry Regiment (United States)." Wikipedia, The Free Encyclopedia, 25 January 2016. https://en.wikipedia.org

Bashore, Ira

1. U.S. Army. "103rd Infantry Division Cactus Caravan." Atlanta: Albert Love Enterprises, 1944. www.103rdcactus.com

2. Kestner, Laura. "A Memorial to the 103rd Infantry Division." Texas Places and Faces. www.texasplacesandfaces.com

3. "103rd Infantry Division in World War II." U.S. Army Center of Military History. www.history.army.mil

4. Mueller, Ralph and Jerry Turk. *Report After Action: The Story of the 103rd Infantry Division*. Nashville: Battery Press, 1987. www.103rdcactus.com

5. Ambrose, Stephen. *The Good Fight*. New York: Simon & Schuster, 2001.

6. Bashore, Florence. Phone interview with author, 5 July 2013.

7. Bashore, Ira L. Report of Burial. Individual Deceased Personnel File. Washington, D.C.: War Department, 11 September 1945.

8. Frank, Barbara. "The Town of McGrath, Minnesota: Homecoming Through the Years 1929–1941." The USGenWeb Project. http://www.rootsweb.ancestry.com/~mnaitkin/mcgrath.htm

Braun, Othmar

1. Jacobson, Michael. "Lost at Sea." *Paynesville Press*, 25 May 2005.

2. Keegan, John. *The Second World War*. New York: Penguin Putnam, 2005.

3. "Action Report on Ryukyus Operation, 24 March – 4 May 1945." Battle of May 4, 1945. http://cs.iupui.edu/~ateal/Ingraham/May4/May4.html, 31 December 2015.

4. Braun, Othmar. Casualty Report. Individual Deceased Personnel File. Washington D.C.: War Department, 21 July 1945.

5. Braun, Peter. "Othmar Peter Braun." Find A Grave Memorial, 6 August 2010. www.findagrave.com

6. "Othmar Braun Dies in Action." *Melrose Beacon*, 19 July 1945.

Reinart, Gerald

1. "Staff Sgt. Gerald T. Reinart Killed in Action on Palawan in Philippines May 6," *Graceville Enterprise*, 1945. Obituary file, Big Stone County Historical Society, Ortonville, Minnesota.

2. Ross, Jay and Judith Nichols. "Banners At Sunset: An Anthology of WWII Stories from Veterans of the Big Stone County/Big Stone Lake Area," 26 November 2012.

3. "42nd Bombardment Group." Army Air Corps Library and Museum. http://www.armyaircorpsmuseum.org/42nd_Bombardment_Group.cfm

4. Maurer, Maurer. *Air Force Combat Units of World War II*. Washington, D.C.: Office of Air Force History, 1961, 1983. Accessed via https://media.defense.gov/2010/Sep/21/2001330256/-1/-1/0/AFD-100921-044.pdf

5. Headquarters 42nd Bombardment Group (M). Standard Mission Report 42-19. Washington, D.C.: War Department, 7 May 1945. U.S. Air Force Research Studies Institute.

White, Howard

1. White, Tracy. Email to author, 18 June 2015.

2. "Battle of Okinawa." http://www.globalsecurity.org/military/ facility/okinawa-battle.htm

3. Myers, Max. *Ours to Hold It High: History of 77th Division in WW2*. Washington, D.C.: Washington Infantry Press, 1947. https://books.google.com/

4. Appleman, Roy, James Burns, Russell Gugeler and John Stevens. "Okinawa: The Last Battle," 2000. U.S. Army Center of Military History. www.history.army.mil

5. Tsukiyama, Ted. "Battle of Okinawa." The Hawaii Nisei Project, 2006. www.nisei. hawaii.edu

6. "Serg. White Aided in Burial of Ernie Pyle in Okinawa." *Glasgow Courier*, 20 August 1945.

7. Valdovinos, Agustin. Phone call to author, 27 August 2013.

8. Witsel, Major General Edward. Silver Star Citation First Sergeant Howard C. White. Washington, D.C.: War Department, 26 September 1945.

9. Wilkinson, Jeff. "Columbia WWII vet revisits 3 terrible days on a ridge in Japan," 9 March 2013. The State. http://www.thestate.com/news/local/military/article14423468.html

10. Haley, Grace. "Howard White: World War II Registry." World War II Memorial. www.wwiimemorial.com

11. "Howard White Killed on Okinawa." *Itasca Progress*, 12 July 1945.

12. Fleck, Linda White. Email to author, 5 December 2015.

Lange, Darvin

1. Lange, Darvin. Letter to family, 25 December 1944. From the personal files of Darlene Lange Haug.

2. "A Brief History of the 25th Infantry Division." 25th Infantry Division Association. www.25thida.org

3. "Luzon: The 1st Battalion Drive Astride Highway #5 15–27 May 1945." 35th Infantry Regiment Association. www.cacti35th.org

4. Shafland, Sanford. Letter to Erna Lange, 24 July 1945. From the personal files of Darlene Lange Haug.

5. Hauge, Darlene Lange. "Memorial Speech."

6. Lange, Private Darvin. Individual Deceased Personnel File. Washington, D.C.: War Department, 14 June 1945.

Davis, Kenneth

1. Flowers, Mark. "The FMF Hospital Corpsman." World War II Gyrene, 2004. www.facebook.com/ww2gyrene/?ref=py_c

2. Stockman, James R. *The Sixth Marine Division*. Washington, D.C.: U.S. Marine Corps, Historical Division Headquarters, 1946. The Sixth Marine Division. Accessed via Internet Archive at https://archive.org/details/sixthmarinedivis00stoc

3. Davis, Kenneth. Report of Casualty. Individual Deceased Personnel File. Washington, D.C.: War Department, 21 June 1945.

4. U.S. Navy Bureau of Medicine and Surgery. "The History of the Medical Department of the United States Navy in World War II: A Compilation of the Killed, Wounded and Decorated Personnel, Volume 2." U.S. Navy Bureau of Medicine and Surgery Office of Medical History Collection, 1953. Accessed via Internet Archive at https://archive.org/details/HistoryOfNavyMedicalDeptInWW2Vol.2

5. Thompson, Mark. "Bless the Battlefield Angels," 14 June 2011. http://nation.time.com/2011/06/14/bless-the-battlefield-angels/

6. Hospital Corpsman (HM). Navy Recruiting Command. http://www.cool.navy.mil/usn/LaDR/hm_e1_e9.pdf

7. "Kenneth Roy Davis Killed in Action." *Northome Record* and *Mizpah Message*, 6 July 1945.

Gorres, Jerome

1. 137th Infantry Regiment After Action Report, June 1945. 134th Infantry Regiment Website, 1 July 1945. www.coulthart.com/134/index.htm

2. The World War II Re-enactment Society and G Company, 137th Infantry Regiment. "G Company Headquarters: History of the Santa Fe Division." www.137thinfantry.us

3. Russo, Roberta. "World War II Awards to the Members of the 35th Division," 2 November 1944. 134th Infantry Regiment Website. www.coulthart.com/134/ index. htm

4. "Jerome Gorres Wins Silver Star." *Redwood Falls Gazette*, 13 March 1945.

5. Gorres, Jerome. Report of Death. Individual Deceased Personnel File. Washington, D.C.: War Department, 31 July 1945.

6. "Former Wanda Man Was With Patrol in Germany." *Redwood Falls Gazette*, 5 July 1945.

7. "Truck Accident Kills Former Wanda Soldier." *Redwood Falls Gazette*, June 1945. From the files of La Vonne Portner.

8. Portner, LaVonne. Letter to author, 10 February 2015.

Nelson, Gordon

1. "Gordon Nelson." *Stephen Messenger*, pg. 8, 2 August 1945.

2. Nelson, Gordon. Letter to Mabel Tomhave, 18 June 1945, courtesy of Nancy Tomhave. Phone interview with author, 13 July 2015.

3. Hearn, Chester G. *Air Force: An Illustrated History*. Minneapolis: Zenith Press, 2008.

4. "19th Bombardment Group." Army Air Corps Library and Museum. www.armyaircorpsmuseum.org

5. Nelson, Gordon O. Missing Air Crew Report. Individual Deceased Personnel File. Washington, D.C.: War Department, 10 September 1982.

Nelson, Allen

1. "Allen D. Nelson is Lost in Action." *Moorhead Daily News*, 17 September 1945.

2. Peterson, Richard. "VPB-118 Crews: Crew 11 McCutcheon." U.S. Navy VPB-118—The Old Crows. Accessed via email to author, 25 September 2013. www.vpb-118.com

3. Roberts, Michael D. *Dictionary of American Naval Squadrons, Volume 2*. Naval Historical Center, Department of the Navy, 2000. www.history.navy.mil

4. Pettit, James. *VPB 118: The History of Navy Bombing Squadron 118 "The Old Crows."* Tucson: Fisher Books, 1992.

5. Nelson, Allen Duane. Report of Casualty. Individual Deceased Personnel File. Washington, D.C.: Bureau of Naval Personnel, 1 November 1945.

6. Aviation History and Research in DCNO (Air). "Bombing Squadron 118." *Naval Aviation News*, July 1949. Accessed via www.vpnavy.com

7. Comstock Centennial Committee. *Comstock Centennial 1890–1990*. Gwinner, ND: J&M Printing, 1990.

8. White, Darrel Allen. Email to author, 10 October 2014.

Thelander, Herman

1. "The Mystery of Flight 19." Naval Air Station Fort Lauderdale Museum, 3 August 2010. www.nasflmuseum.com

2. "NAS Jacksonville Board of Investigation into 5 missing TBM Airplanes and one PBM Airplane, Flight 19," 7 December 1945. Transcribed by Harry Allston for the HyperWar Foundation. Accessed via www.ibiblio.org

3. Winer, Richard. *The Devil's Triangle*. New York: Bantam Books, 1974.

4. Zierke, Dennis. Email to author, 19 February 2015.

5. "Kinbrae Sailor Among Missing on Overseas Flight." *Worthington Daily Globe*, 7 December 1945.

Photo Credits

Emery, John

1. Photo of John Emery courtesy of Jarrett Emery Halvorson

2. Photo of USS *Arizona* underway courtesy of Michael W. Pocock, www.maritimequest.com

3. Photo USS *Arizona* ablaze courtesy of U.S. National Archives

Johnson, Aaron

1. Photo of Aaron Johnson and Button Plate courtesy of Natalie Schmidt

2. Photo of USS *Houston* courtesy of Michael W. Pocock, www.maritimequest.com

Tester, Rodney

1. Photo of Rodney Tester courtesy of Janice Tester Backus

2. Douglas B-18A courtesy of Joe Stevens, Kodiak Island Military History

Snell, Harold

1. Both photos courtesy of Jim Opolony

Rahier, Elwyn

1. Photos of Elwyn Rahier courtesy of Joe Poor

2. Photo of Effie Veterans Memorial courtesy of Matthew David

Rose, Donald

1. Donald Rose photo courtesy of Donna Novotny, Director Whalan Museum

2. Photo of Marine Corps F4F Wildcat Fighter at Henderson Field, February 1943 U.S. National Archives

Kolstad, Omar

1. Photo courtesy of Omar Kolstad of Merlin Peterson, Pope County Historical Society

2. Map courtesy of U.S. Navy, *All Hands Magazine*, pg. 46, November 1980

3. Photo of USS *Vincennes* courtesy of U.S. Navy

Haarstad, Ernest

1. Family photos and letter courtesy of Ryan Klemann

2. Photo of USS *Tasker Bliss* courtesy of Ranier Kolbicz (www.uboat.net) and U.S. Navy

Johnson, Clayton

1. "Man the Guns" courtesy of U.S. National Archives

2. Photo of ship courtesy of Michael W. Pocock, www.maritimequest.com

3. Map courtesy of U.S. Navy, Office of Naval Intelligence

Clewitt, William

1. Photo and passages from "Diary of Col. Samuel Baglien" courtesy of Shirley J. Olgeirson, Lt. Col. (ret), 164th Infantry Association

Anderson, Robert

1. Photos of Robert Anderson courtesy of Cindy Risen and Amy Moe

Curb, Cyril

1. Photo of Cryil Curb courtesy of Lori Fraley

2. Photo of Mizpah II courtesy of 91st Bomb Group, www.91stbombgroup.com

3. Photo of 323rd Bomb Squadron, 91st Bomb Group, courtesy of 91st Bomb Group, www.91stbombgroup.com

Baumgart, Herman

1. Photos of Herman Baumgart courtesy of Rita Baumgart Zepper

2. Photo of a German tank destroyed by artillery at El Guettar from National Archives

3. Crewmen with an anti-tank gun near Sidi Bou Zod, 14 February 1943, U.S. Army Signal Corps

Niemi, Mathews

1. Photos courtesy of Yuri Beckers, 9th Infantry Division Website. Source: NARA "9th Infantry Division Patrol" and "Infantry Men on the Move"

Suomi, Einar

1. Photo of Einar Suomi and his cousin Henry Dhennin courtesy of Jerry Dhennin

2. Photo of B-17, 366th Bomb Squadron, courtesy of Department of Defense

Bettin, Frank

1. Photos of Frank Bettin courtesy of Hildegarde Bettin Dorn

2. Photo of American troops hauling supplies on Attu 1943 courtesy of Department of Defense

Borgeson, Victor

1. Photo courtesy of Dale Victor Borgeson

2. Photo of USS *Helena* courtesy of U.S. Naval Historical Center

Gooselaw, Jerome

1. Photo of Jerome Gooselaw courtesy of Deborah Gooselaw Kopylov and *Kittson County Enterprise*

2. Photo of 172nd Infantry Regiment wading across a creek on the Munda Trail, New Georgia, July 1943, courtesy of U.S. Army

3. Photo of Landing Operations on Rendova Island, Solomon Islands, 30 June 1943, courtesy of U.S. National Archives

Jorgensen, Glen

1. Photo courtesy of Laurie Lewis, *Tyler Tribute*

2. LCIs unloading at Rendova courtesy of U.S. Army

3. Map of Solomon Islands courtesy of U.S. Central Intelligence Agency

Holen, Arnold

1. Photo of Arnold Holen and Jack Reed courtesy of Joe Duran

2. Photo of B-24 bombing Ploieşti courtesy of Carl Savich

Mikel, Lawrence

1. Photos of Lawrence Mikel courtesy of Donald and Paul Hartmann

2. Photo of a marine firing on a Japanese pillbox on Tarawa courtesy of U.S. Navy

3. Photo of marines storming Tarawa, November 1943, courtesy of U.S. National Archives

Vaughan, Welver

1. Newspaper photo of Welver Vaughan courtesy of the Wells Depot Museum

2. Marines and sailors traveling on board a troop transport receive their initial briefing on the landing plan for Betio, photo courtesy of Department of Defense

3. Marines seek cover among the dead and wounded behind the sea wall on Red Beach 3, Tarawa, photo courtesy of U.S. Marine Corps

Terho, Harold

1. Photos of Harold Terho courtesy of Patsy Terho

Chernich, Peter

1. Photos of Peter Chernich courtesy of Ailie Chernich Costello

Zeiner, Leighton

1. Photo permission of Ryan McGaughey, *Worthington Daily Globe*, Worthington, Minnesota

2. Photo of B-17 courtesy of U.S. Air Force Historical Research Agency

3. Photo of Kinbrae by Deane Johnson

Santjer, Ben

1. Photo of Ben Santjer courtesy of Sena Santjer Knowles

2. U.S. Army Corps of Engineers poster courtesy of U.S. National Archives

Meyer, Harold

1. Photo of Harold Meyer courtesy of Lac qui Parle History Center, Madison, Minnesota

2. Photo of American soldiers fighting near Monte Cassino courtesy of U.S. Army

Nicholas, Lloyd

1. Photo of Lloyd Nicholas with goggles courtesy of William E. Nicholas

2. Photo of Lloyd Nicholas in pilot's cap courtesy of Iron Range Historical Society

3. Unaltered image of "Fujikawa Maru – Ship's Gun, Chuuk 2009" by Flickr user Stephen Masters. Licensed via a Creative Commons 2.0 License (https://creativecommons. org/licenses/by/2.0/). Original available at https://www.flickr.com/photos/gratiartis/4768851731/

Olson, Morris

1. Photo of Morris Olson courtesy of Carolyn O'Brien

2. Photo of PB4Y-1 Liberator courtesy of U.S. National Archives

3. Photo of Skellig Michael via Shutterstock

Probasco, Alvin

1. Photos and letter courtesy of Nancy Probasco Zaske

2. Photo of tank courtesy of Robert Neumiller, 751st Tank Battalion

Harju, Robert

1. Photos of Robert Harju courtesy of Gay Aubin

2. Map via American Forces in Action Series: Anzio, courtesy of U.S. War Department

Kanne, Robert

1. Photo of Robert Kanne courtesy of Lois Kanne

2. Photo of subchaser courtesy of Theodore Treadwell

3. Subchaser poster courtesy of the U.S. Navy

Engholm, Waldo

1. Photos of Waldo Engholm courtesy of Mava Engholm

Goudy, Robert

1. Photo of Robert Goudy courtesy of University of Minnesota, Forestry Club, The 1937 Gopher Peavey, http://hdl.handle.net/11299/170565

2. "US Army troops landing at Anzio in Operation Shingle—on 22 January 1944," from Fifth Army Antiaircraft artillery—Salerno to Florence, courtesy of U.S. Army and www.lonesentry.com

Rowe, Rolland

1. Photo of Rolland Rowe courtesy of Margaret Sehnert

2. Troops of U.S. 3rd Division entering Valmontone, Italy, circa May 1944, courtesy of U.S. Army Center of Military History

Sundstad, Herman
1. Photos of Herman Sundstad courtesy of Mary Beth Sundstad and Dianne Sundstad Carbine

Kostrzewski, Walter
1. Photo of D-Day Rescuing a Survivor, U.S. National Archives, courtesy of Jess Zimmerman, History by Zim

2. "Into the Jaws of Death" courtesy of U.S. Coast Guard Chief Petty Officer Robert F. Sargent

3. Photos of Walter Kostrzewski courtesy of Gary Kostrzewski and Patricia Braaten

Onger, Ellsworth
1. Photo of Ellsworth Onger courtesy of Corienne Jacobson

2. Photo of General Eisenhower giving the order of the day "Full victory—nothing else" to paratroopers in England, just before they board their airplanes for D-Day, 6 June 1944, courtesy of U.S. Army

3. Photo of Douglas C-47 Skytrain, courtesy of U.S. Air Force

Wilsing, Arnold
1. Photos of Arnold Wilsing courtesy of Joan Kline and Gary Nellis

2. Photo of glider courtesy of James D. West, www.indianamilitary.org

Wendt, William
1. Photos and quotes courtesy of Dave Schroeder

Emery, Carl
1. All photos courtesy of Connie Halvorson Walsh and Jarrett Halverson

Lusk, Eugene
1. Airborne paratroopers jump from a C-47 in a training exercise, courtesy of U.S. National Archives

Oja, August
1. Photo of marines hit by Japanese sniper on Saipan's Red Beach, 15 June 1944, courtesy of U.S. Marine Corps

2. Map of Saipan courtesy of U.S. Army Center of Military History, CMH Pub 72-29

3. U.S. reinforcements wade ashore from LSTs off Saipan, 15 June 1944, courtesy of U.S. National Archives

4. Tamarack War Memorial photo by Deane Johnson

Bush, Fernly
1. Photo courtesy of Linda Ziemann

2. St.-Lô. Courtesy of Conseil Régional de Basse-Normandie/U.S. National Archives

Forsberg, Robert
1. Photos of Robert Forsberg and letter courtesy of Gerald Forsberg, son of Adolph Forsberg

2. "Wounded Marines are helped by corpsman" courtesy of U.S. Marine Corps via U.S. National Archives

Indihar, Rudolph
1. Photo of Rudolph Indihar and text from *Elcor's Honored War Dead* courtesy of Iron Range Historical Society

2. 9th Infantry Division men take cover near the seawall on Utah Beach, June 1944, courtesy of U.S. Navy

Lound, Ray
1. Photos of Ray Lound courtesy of Margaret Norbeck

Shefveland, Stanton
1. Photo of Stanton Shefveland courtesy of Ilane Shefveland Rue

2. Map of eastern New Guinea, New Britain, New Island and neighboring islands with locations of importance in World War II 1944, courtesy of U.S. Army via "The War in the Pacific," U.S. Army in World War II

3. Photo of 163rd Infantry Regiment debarking from Higgins boats during invasion of Wadke Island, New Guinea, Lt. Kent Rooks, 18 May 1944, courtesy of U.S. National Archives

4. Photo of troops during the New Guinea campaign courtesy of Department of the Army

Iverson, Edwin
1. Photos of Edwin Iverson courtesy of Evon Pearson

2. Photo of army soldiers disembarking from LSTs across coral reef to shores of Saipan, June/July 1944, courtesy of U.S. National Archives

3. Army recruiting poster courtesy of Jes Wilhelm Schlaikjer, U.S. War Department

Holmstrom, Herman
1. Photo of Herman Holstrom courtesy of Carol Holmstrom Thompson

2. Photo of 9th Infantry Division men near St. Sauveur le Vicomte, 21 June 1944, courtesy of Yuri Beckers, 9th Infantry Division Website

3. "Map of Bocage Country, 2 July 1944" courtesy of the U.S. Army Center of Military History via www.army.mil/cmh-pg/brochures/normandy/p33.jpg

Iverson, Lloyd
1. Photo of Lloyd Iverson and James Redin Flight Crew courtesy of the 95th Bomb Group and Josh Tharaldson

2. Photo of Goodridge Veterans Memorial courtesy of Goodridge Centennial, 2015

3. Photo of Judy Iverson courtesy of *Thief River Falls Times* and Judy Briski

Winjum, Harold

1. Photos of Harold Winjum courtesy of Marlyn Evenstad

2. Photo of Corsica map courtesy of Don Kaiser, www.warwingsart.com

Hoffrogge, Herman

1. Photo of Hoffrogge brothers courtesy of Jim Pederson

Bliven, Paul

1. Photos of Paul Bliven courtesy of Robert Bliven

Hegna, Verlyn

1. Photo of Verlyn Hegna courtesy of Renae and Joey Woods

Anderson, Leon

1. Photo of Leon Anderson courtesy of *The Brookings Register*

2. American Legion Post photo by Deane Johnson

Berger, Jack

1. Photo of Jack Berger courtesy of Helen Krajewski and Christine Carlson

2. Jackie Berger Memorial Park photo courtesy of Deb Stadin

Petersen, Gerhard

1. Photos of Gerhard Petersen courtesy of Deb Jacobson

2. Photo of 743rd Tank courtesy of Ben Savelkoul

Nelson, LaVern

1. Photos of LaVern Nelson courtesy of Muriel Nelson

Hoff, Vernon

1. Photo of Vernon Hoff and letter courtesy of Scott Hoff

Graba, James

1. Photos courtesy of 390th Memorial Museum Foundation

Johnson, Leroy

1. Photo of crew courtesy of Roman Susil and Jan Mahr

2. Photos of Leroy Johnson courtesy of Dannie Nordsiden

Hogetvedt, Joseph

1. Photo of Joseph Hogetvedt courtesy of Leo Hogetvedt

2. Photo of LVTs landing on Peleliu, 15 September 1944, courtesy of U.S. Navy

Pearson, Vernon

1. Photo of Vernon Pearson courtesy of British Royal Air Force Service Records. Accessed via http://collectionscanada.ca/obj/001056/f2/p/sww-28398-pearsonvernon_lawrence-j87426.pdf

Veralrud, LeRoy

1. Photo of LeRoy Veralrud courtesy of the Iron Range Historical Society

2. Tank ferry photo and men relaxing courtesy of Andy Adkins

Maxa, Gordon

1. Photos of Gordon Maxa courtesy of Mark Bliss, Gordon's nephew

2. Photo of B-17 Flying Fortress courtesy of Fred Preller and the 384thBombGroup.com

Sersha, John

1. Photos of John Sersha courtesy of Dick Lohry

Kurth, Walter

1. Photo courtesy of Lorie Kurth Kirtz

Talberg, William

1. Photo of William Talberg courtesy of *Morrison County Record*

2. Photo of engineers building bridge in Italy, from *The Liberation Trilogy* by Rick Atkinson

3. Photo of the American Legion by Deane Johnson

Mittag, Harland

1. Photos of Harland Mittag courtesy of Barbara Allen Moe

Longhenry, Albert

1. Photo of Albert Longhenry from the files of Lac qui Parle County Historical Society, courtesy of Barb Redpenning

2. Photo of 45th Infantry Division landing Sainte-Maxime, France, 15 August 1944, courtesy of U.S. National Archives, U.S. Army Center of Military History, from "Southern France: The U.S. Army Campaigns of World War II"

Doyle, Donald

1. Photos of Donald Doyle courtesy of Eric Montgomery and John W. Anderson; photo of Donald (on the right) and friend with captured German helmets

2. Photo of P-61 Black Widow, U.S. Air Force

Bollum, Donald

1. Photos and letters courtesy of Steve Bollum

2. Photo of 79th Infantry Division in France, July 1944, courtesy of U.S. Army Signal Corps

Burger, Earl

1. Photo of Earl Burger courtesy of Myrtle Burger Houston

2. Photo of USS *LST 277*, U.S. Navy, courtesy of Frank R. Crow and Rebecca Crow

Kuznia, Ferdinand

1. Photo courtesy of Ferdinand S. Kuznia

Bruns, Alfred

1. Photo of Alfred Bruns as a toddler and postcard courtesy of Ralph Butkowski

2. Photo of 337th Infantry Regiment in Italy, "Soldiers push jeep bogged down in mud," courtesy of U.S. National Archives and Don Jones, 337th Infantry Regiment historian, U.S. Army Signal Corps photo

Gordon, Malcolm

1. Photo courtesy of Tim Gordon

2. "Two U.S. Navy Grumman TBF-1 Avenger torpedo bombers in flight, circa 1942," courtesy of U.S. Navy, Naval Air Station Jacksonville

3. Photo of USS *Kalinin Bay*, Navy Archives, courtesy of U.S. Navy

Reardon, John

1. Photos of John Reardon courtesy of Andy Swinnen, http://www.remember-our-heroes.nl

Horton, Carl

1. Under the direction of an American soldier, German civilians from Gardelegen carry wooden crosses to the site where they were ordered to bury the bodies of concentration camp prisoners killed by the SS in a barn just outside the town, courtesy of U.S. Army Signal Corps

2. Photo of the 102nd Infantry Division in Germany from the booklet "With the 102nd Infantry Division in Germany" by Allen Mick, courtesy of U.S. Army Signal Corps

Peterson, Otto

1. Photo of Otto Peterson and journal courtesy of Steven Peterson

2. Photo of American Troops of the 28th Infantry Division march down the Avenue des Champs-Élysées, Paris in the 'Victory' Parade, courtesy of U.S. Army Signal Corps and U.S. National Archives

Roner, Rudolph

1. Photo of Rudolph Roner (left) and his cousin Norman Johnson (right) courtesy of Bernice Johnson

2. Photo of Rudolph Roner and Ken Roner courtesy of Harriet Lindstrom

3. Photo of Roner Store courtesy of Connie Fedick

4. Photo of Company I, 318th Infantry Regiment, November 1944, from the photo collection of Chris Harris, www.80thdivision.com

King, Ernest

1. Photo of Ernest King courtesy of Leon King

2. Map of Invasion of Leyte, courtesy of the U.S. Army Center of Military History, via "Leyte: The U.S. Army Campaigns of World War II," CMH Pub 72-27

3. Photo "LCM carrying troops up the Mindano River to Fort Pikit" from Chapter XXII, "The Philippines, the Southern Islands," in *The Ordnance Department: On Beachhead and Battlefront*, courtesy of the U.S. Army Center of Military History

Lee, Roy

1. Photos and permission courtesy of DiAnn Zimmerman

Gooselaw, Arthur

1. Photos of Arthur Gooselaw courtesy of Deborah Gooselaw Kopylov and *Kittson County Enterprise*

Hanson, Oscar

1. All photos courtesy of Jim Hanson

Brady, Robert

1. Photo of Robert Brady and Elcor, circa 1916, courtesy of the Iron Range Historical Society

2. Photo of men entering Metz 17 November 1944, courtesy of the U.S. Army Center of Military History, via "The Lorraine Campaign: The U.S. Army Campaigns of

3. World War II," www.history.army.mil/html/books/007/7-6-1/CMH_Pub_7-6-1.pdf

Hackbarth, Arthur

1. Photo of Arthur Hackbarth and poem courtesy of Carol J. Dunn

2. Map of Invasion of Leyte, courtesy of U.S. Army Center of Military History, via "Leyte: The U.S. Army Campaigns of World War II," CMH Pub 72-27

McNew, Larry

1. Photo of Larry McNew courtesy of Bonnie McNew Matheson

Swanson, Kenneth

1. Photo B-17 flying near Mt. Fuji courtesy of U.S. Air Force

2. Photo signs on Isley Field courtesy of M.S. Hennessy

Eichten, Helmer

1. Photos of Helmer Eichten and family courtesy of Pauline Eichten

Typhoon Cobra: Armbrust, Hakenson, Kaufman, Lundgren

1. Photo of Almon Armbrust courtesy of Duluth Public Library

2. Photos of Lloyd Lundgren and Warren Hakenson courtesy of *Grant County Herald* and Patty Benson, Grant County Historical Society

3. Photo of USS *Spence* courtesy of U.S. Navy, photo 5305-43

4. Photo of Harold Kaufman courtesy of Paul and Pam Struck

Malmrose, Victor

1. Photo of Victor and Gladys Malmrose courtesy of Charles and Bill Ramm

2. Photo of bugler courtesy of 12 Armored Division Museum, from The 495th: As Crowfoot Saw the War by First Lieutenant Clinton E. Seitz

Bruns, Norbert

1. Photos of Norbert Bruns courtesy of Ralph Butkowski

Dolan, Vincent

1. Photo of Vincent Dolan courtesy of Joseph Tisdell

Gustafson, Bertil

1. Both photos courtesy of Gary Anderson and John Tostrup

Meling, Truman

1. Photo courtesy of Ken Christensen

2. Photo of Company B, 327th Glider Infantry Regiment courtesy of Haywood S. Anderson

3. Photo of Waco glider CG-4A courtesy of USAAF National Museum of the U.S. Air Force

Brummer, Andrew

1. Photo of Andrew Brummer courtesy of Kathy Peterson

2. Photo of 134th Infantry Regiment carrying wounded at Lutrebois courtesy of 134th Infantry Regiment, Roberta Russo

Boe, George

1. Photo of George Boe courtesy of Jon Lindstrand

2. Photo of 399th Infantry Regiment near Saarbourg, France, courtesy of U.S. Army Signal Corps

3. Photo of medic helping injured soldier, France, 1944, courtesy of U.S. National Archives

Skaar, Wallace

1. Photo of Wallace Skaar courtesy of Violet Downer

2. Photo of Wallace Skaar Memorial Park courtesy of Jim Childers (edited)

Colson, Wallace

1. Photos of Wallace Colson courtesy of Kay Powell, a relative on www.ancestry.com

2. Photo of a U-boat torpedoing a merchant ship, courtesy of IWM Collections, IWM Photo No. MISC 51237

3. Photo of poster courtesy of U.S. National Archives

Cummings, Russell

1. Photo courtesy of *The Island X-quire: CBMU 540*. Lieutenant Russell F. Hughes, CEC, USNR, Editor. Lieutenant Commander John J. White, CEC, USNR, Publisher. New York: F. Hubner & Co., 1946.

2. "Build Your Navy," Muchley, Robert, courtesy of Library of Congress Work Projects Administration Poster Collection, LC-USZC2-924

Kolberg, Arthur

1. Photo of Arthur Kolberg from files of the Roseau County Historical Society

2. "6th ID Assaults Beachhead, Luzon, Philippines" National Archive photo, courtesy of Thomas E. Price, National Association of the 6th Infantry Association

3. Photo of Veterans Memorial, Lake Bronson, courtesy of Shane Olson, on www.findagrave.com

Beckman, Sylvester

1. Photo of Sylvester Beckman and poem courtesy of Phyllis Beckman

Hanson, Howard

1. Photo courtesy of Jim Kiefer

Ranum, Glenn

1. Photos of Glenn Ranum courtesy of June Johnson

Wright, Wilbur

1. Photos and letters courtesy of Margaret Geertsema

Engblom, Edward

1. Photo and telegrams courtesy of John Wepplo

Loucks, Emmett

1. Photo courtesy of *Grand Rapids Herald Review* and Itasca County Historical Society

Swenson, Donald

1. Photos of Donald Swenson courtesy of Jerry Whiting, 485th Bomb Group

Olson, Archie

1. Photo of Archie Olson courtesy of Joy Paulson

2. Map courtesy of Wes Injerd, Center for Research, Allied POWs Under the Japanese

3. Photo of surrender of American troops at Corregidor, Philippine Islands, May 1942, courtesy of U.S. National Archives, 1942. 208-AA-80B-1, National Archives Identifier 535553

Knight, James

1. Photo of James Knight courtesy of Janice Knight Evensen

2. Photo of P-40F Warhawk courtesy of the 57th Bomb Wing Association

3. Photo of Republic P-47 N Thunderbolt courtesy of the U.S. Air Force

Ness, Rubin

1. Photo of Rubin Ness and graveyard note courtesy of Gladys Ness Erickson

Lundgren, Myril

1. Photos of Myril Lundgren and Jackson County selective servicemen courtesy of Mary Jo Pauling

Bixby, Glen

1. Photo of Glen Bixby courtesy of *Fergus Falls Daily Journal*

2. Photo of a Water Buffalo, loaded with marines, bound for Tinian Island, July 1944, courtesy of U.S. Coast Guard via U.S. National Archives

Ringstad, Palmer

1. Photos of Palmer Ringstad courtesy of Joy Paulson and Arnold Ringstad

Parker, John

1. Photo of John Parker courtesy of Joan Maher

2. Photo of 5th Marine Division on Iwo Jima, 19 February 1945, courtesy of U.S. National Archives

Hunkins, Henry

1. Photo of Henry Hunkins courtesy of Roseanne Nolan

2. Telegram courtesy of James Gowin

Lehner, Clarence

1. Photo of Clarence Lehner and squirrel story courtesy of Jessica Wilson

2. Courtesy of the National Archives

Stoll, Milton

1. Permission courtesy of Carol Dunn.

2. Courtesy of the Minnesota Military Museum at Fort Ripley.

3. Permission courtesy of the *Hutchinson Leader*.

Leitner, Frank

1. Photo of Frank Leitner, gravestone and letters courtesy of Leo Leitner

Stevenson, Cecil

1. Photos and letter courtesy of Larry Elliot

Horne, Robert

1. Courtesy of *Aitkin Independent Age*, Kevin Anderson, Publisher and Adam Hoogenakker, editor

2. Photograph crossing the Rhine River under enemy fire, March 1945, courtesy of U.S. National Archives

Kittelson, Elmer

1. Photos of Elmer Kittelson and letters courtesy of Corienne Jacobson

2. Photo of Dachau Memorial Tablet by Wikipedia user "John," released into public domain

Anderson, Sigwald

1. Photos of Sigwald Anderson and trench art courtesy of Phyllis Broden

2. Photo of airplane trench art courtesy of Sandy Mosher

Peterson, Vernon

1. Photo of Vernon Peterson courtesy of Karen Paulson Syverson

2. Photo of U.S. troops marching into Germany through the Siegfried Line 1945, courtesy of National Archives

Tongen, Jerald

1. Photos of Jerald Tongen courtesy of Jennifer Tongen

2. Photo of American Legion sign by Deane Johnson

Daufney, Glynn

1. All photos courtesy of Rodney Ripley

Storch, Lawrence

1. Courtesy of U.S. Army Center of Military History, from *The Last Offensive*, www.history.army.mil/html/books/007/7-9-1/index.html

2. Map courtesy of Gary Smith, 83rd Infantry Association

Stevenson, John

1. Photo of John Stevenson courtesy of *Redwood Falls Gazette*

Thompson, Clifford

1. Photo of Clifford Thompson courtesy of Lac qui Parle County Historical Society, Madison, Minnesota

2. Photo of Company A, 777th Tank Battalion, courtesy of Michael McKibbon, 69th Infantry Division Next Generation Group, www.69th-infantry-division.com

Kroll, Henry

1. Photo of Henry Kroll courtesy of Ed Lavelle, *The Thirteen Towns*, Fosston, Minnesota

2. Photo of confirmation class courtesy of Pastor Dawn Hanson, Lund Lutheran Church, Gully, Minnesota

Nelson, Kenneth

1. Photo of Kenneth Nelson courtesy of Merlin Peterson, Pope County Historical Society

2. "Troops on Hill 604 fire on Japanese positions" photo courtesy of U.S. Army Center of Military History via National Archives, cover of Luzon, 1944–1959, www.history.army.mil/brochures/luzon/72-28.htm

Bashore, Ira

1. Photos of sign for 328th Combat Engineer Battalion and combat engineers building a bridge courtesy of Marion Chard, 6th Corps Combat Engineers of WW II

Braun, Othmar

1. Photo of Othmar Braun courtesy of *Paynesville Press* and editor Michael Jacobson

2. Photo USS *Luce* (DD-522) Photographed in 1944, while wearing Camouflage Measure 32, Design 18D, courtesy of the collections of the Naval Historical Center

Reinart, Gerald

1. Photo of Gerald Reinart in uniform courtesy of Joe and Arlene Reinart

2. Other photos courtesy of Mark Behrens

White, Howard

1. Photos of Howard White courtesy of Tracy White and Linda White Fleck

Lange, Darvin

1. Photos and letters courtesy of Darlene Lange Haug

Davis, Kenneth

1. Photo of medic treating a wounded marine on Iwo Jima courtesy of Department of Defense (still image from USMC combat camera film)

2. Photo of 6th Marine Division arriving on Okinawa, 1 April 1945, National Park Service, courtesy of U.S. National Archives

Gorres, Jerome

1. Photo of Jerome Gorres with cap courtesy of *Redwood Falls Gazette*

2. Photo of Jerome Gorres in suit courtesy of LaVonne Portner

3. Photo of Velle-sur-Moselle courtesy of Roberta Russo, 134th Infantry Regiment Website

Nelson, Gordon

1. Photo of Gordon Nelson courtesy of Nancy Tomhave

2. Photo of Gordon Nelson and his father, Ole Nelson, courtesy of Marilyn Nugent

3. Photo of B-29 U.S. Air Force courtesy of the National Museum of the U.S. Air Force

Nelson, Allen

1. Photos courtesy of Darrel Allen White and Richard Peterson

2. Photo of Consolidated PB4Y-2 Privateer NH 92485, courtesy of the U.S. Navy, Naval History and Heritage Command

Thelander, Herman

1. Photo courtesy of Dennis Zierke

2. Photo of TBM Avengers (7745138) courtesy of Naval Air Station Fort Lauderdale and Minerva Bloom

Index of Soldiers Lost from Little Minnesota

(continued on next page)

Index of Soldiers Lost from Little Minnesota (continued)

About the Authors

Jill and Deane Johnson share a love for small towns and state parks. Jill, a retired physical therapist who grew up in small towns, wrote *Little Minnesota: 100 Towns Around 100* and Deane, a retired physician, photographed each village. A year later, Deane wrote *The Best of Itasca* celebrating Minnesota's oldest state park. The couple created Beagle Books, an independent bookstore in Park Rapids, where their beagle, Kallie, held center court. They live in Park Rapids and enjoy music and the outdoor life.